"The man
who fights
for his
ideals
is the man
who
is alive."

CERVANTES
author of
DON QUIXOTE

June
21, 1981

Patricia and Michael
Rakavina

A GRAMMAR OF DREAMS

A GRAMMAR OF DREAMS

DAVID FOULKES

BASIC BOOKS, INC., PUBLISHERS

NEW YORK

The author gratefully acknowledges permission to reprint excerpts from the following:

The Interpretation of Dreams, by Sigmund Freud, pp. 169-173, translated from the German and edited by James Strachey, published in the United States by Basic Books, Inc., Publishers, New York, by arrangement with George Allen & Unwin Ltd. and the Hogarth Press, Ltd. London.

"The Current Status of Laboratory Dream Research," by David Foulkes and Gerald W. Vogel, M.D., pp. 7-23, which appeared in *Psychiatric Annals*, vol. 4, no. 7 (1974).

Library of Congress Cataloging in Publication Data

Foulkes, William David, 1935-
    A grammar of dreams.

    Bibliography: p. 429
    Includes indexes.
    1. Dreams. I. Title.
BF1078.F62   154.6'3   77-75243
ISBN: 0-465-02695-8

To Jerry Vogel

Contents

PART III

EMPIRICAL FOUNDATIONS FOR A CONTEMPORARY MODEL OF DREAMING: OBSERVATIONS FROM COGNATE SYMBOLIC DISCIPLINES

PART IV

SSLS: A MODEL OF DREAMING AND A METHOD OF DREAM ANALYSIS

PART V

APPLICATIONS/IMPLICATIONS OF THE MODEL

APPENDICES

Acknowledgments

Few books could owe as much to a particular place as does this one. Although hardly a single line of the current text dates back to the year I spent at the Center for Advanced Study in the Behavioral Sciences (1974-75), the book as a whole clearly is my "Center book." Intellectual life at the Center's campus in Stanford, California, was an incredibly heady experience for an otherwise relatively isolated scholar from the snow-swept plains of southeast Wyoming. I feel an immense debt of gratitude to the Center's administration and staff and to my fellow Fellows, which I hope this book will in some measure suggest, if not repay.

Although it surely would be unfair to attempt to decompose the glorious Center gestalt into separate elements, I would be remiss if I did not spend a line or two in giving special thanks to volleyballing friends and Dutch-Goose companions for any number of incubatory interludes. Marge Cruise took competent command of the "safe" project I had brought with me to the Center (in case no more creative line of thought developed), permitting me the luxury of developing the ideas contained in this book. Joan Warmbrunn was incredibly patient in typing not only scribbled texts, but also various charts and diagrams and what must have seemed like an infinite number of subscripts. I also am grateful to Ian Hacking, Michael Dempster, Gillian and David Sankoff, Tony Tanner, and Pam Gullard for their interest in my work, and to Pat Suppes and Hermine Warren for the opportunity of discussing with them the related work in which they were engaged at Stanford. My year at the Center was supported by a Career Development Award from the National Institute of Child Health and Human Development (5 K04 HD 46343).

At the University of Wyoming, Nancy Kerr and Dean Delis have purged my initial writing in the areas of cognitive psychology, transformational-generative grammar, and psycholinguistics of many (but, they're sure, not all) of its more egregious errors. Greg Jurkovic has made helpful comments on parts of the manuscript. Stephen Butler and Pat Maykuth have done me the honor of trying to put enough of Scoring System for Latent Structure (SSLS) into their heads to convince me it is more than an autistic fantasy, and have forced me to be sufficiently explicit to have made SSLS a disease which is at least partly communicable. They are coauthors with me of appendix B, on scoring reliability.

It is a pleasure also to acknowledge the continuing support my work has received from Terry Pivik and Gerald Vogel. Jerry is the dedicatee of this book because he has been, for more than a decade now, my mentor in psychoanalytic theory and my model in matters of scientific reasoning, judgment, and conduct. He is not, of course, guilty for the errors or oversimplifications contained herein, although he may well be directly responsible for whatever merits the book may possess.

Thanks also are due to Judy Green for a diligently, but cheerfully, performed variety of proofreading and checking tasks, to Brenda Hanson and Joyce Brekken for typing rough drafts, and to Alice Arnett and Jean Petrik for their typing of the final manuscript.

The "instigating stimulus" for this book was Bernie Webb's response to a position paper I gave in 1973 to the Association for the Psychophysiological Study of Sleep. I had urged that dream psychology return to Freud's model of dream interpretation/explanation via free association. Bernie, who delights in keeping the "soft-heads" of our field honest, said something to the effect that this would confirm dream psychology's status as an "art form"; science could not lie in that direction. This volume is my attempt to refute Bernie's attack by making free-association dream psychology more "scientific," which is probably the outcome he had in mind all along.

November 1976
Laramie, Wyoming

Additional thanks are due to the Georgia Mental Health Institute, Dr. Donald G. Miles, Superintendent, and to the Emory University School of Medicine, Department of Psychiatry, Dr. Bernard Holland, Chairman, for providing a most supportive environment in which final revisions of this manuscript and the detailed work of its preparation for publication have been accomplished. Amy Prather's assistance with final copy and with proofreading also is gratefully acknowledged.

September 1977
Atlanta, Georgia

A Guide to Reading

This Book

The author of a book presenting a grammatical analysis of a phenomenon accepts, for that phenomenon, the proposition that its understanding depends upon apprehension of its inner structure. Constituents must be identified, and a framework then must be presented in which these constituents are sensibly and systematically interrelated. It seems only fair that the author accept the same proposition, and follow the same procedures, in dealing with her or his readers. I want now, therefore, to acquaint you, the reader, with the "inner structure" of the narrative which follows.

The chapters of part I are written at a quite elementary level, and introduce the major ideas which are worked out in later chapters: that dreaming is a species of complex human thought (rather than, for example, a "perceptual" phenomenon); that its creation must, therefore, be modeled in like fashion as that of other cognitive or symbolic experiences, and that its theory must be informed by theorizing and experimentation in other areas of cognitive study; that the other cognitive phenomenon most akin to dreaming is language, and that models of linguistic competence and performance are highly relevant to conceptualization in dream psychology; that a cognitive-linguistic approach to dreaming is compatible with, indeed most strikingly encodes, the best insights of Freud's model of dream formation and of his method of dream interpretation; and that such an approach, in fact, may highlight the intimate interrelation of motivational constructs, the ostensible focus of Freud's dream theory, and mental representations and operations, the central topics of cognitive psychology, in a way which not only enriches classical dream theory with contemporary cognitive concepts but also helps to broaden the scope of cognitive psychology so that it can encompass motivationally rich phenomena such as dreaming, which have, for too long, lain outside its classically defined purview.

The succeeding two parts of the book consider, in much greater detail, the empirical resources currently available for a cognitive-linguistic synthesis of dreams. Part II considers those resources which have developed in dream psychology itself, part III those resources which have been generated by students of waking symbolic behavior.

Chapter 4 of part II reviews Freud's contributions to dream psychology through an extended analysis of *The Interpretation of Dreams*. In my reading of him, Freud is a cognitivist: what is valuable in his theory is conceivable in mentalistic terms and can be based on mentalistic method, while those portions of his theory not so conceived or based are neither integral to his own account of dreaming nor useful in defensibly reformulating that account today. Prior knowledge of Freud's book is not presupposed in reading chapter 4 (but it is, of course, highly recommended on a variety of other grounds), yet the interpretation of Freud to be found there is organized in a sufficiently novel way to recommend it to experienced readers as well.

By now, almost everyone has heard of "REMs" and of the psychophysiological approach to dreaming which their discovery has fostered. Many extensive reviews of this literature have appeared, most of them dwelling on physiological aspects of REM sleep and merely issuing promissory notes so far as real contributions to our understanding of dream experience are concerned. The review here is brief, but directed precisely to the latter point.

The five chapters of part III review recent developments in those cognate symbolic disciplines which seem to me to be most relevant to the task of formulating an empirically defensible, cognitively and linguistically based, but psychodynamically compatible, contemporary account of dreaming. Attention is given, in turn, to: psychoanalytic ego psychology; structuralism, particularly Piaget; linguistics, particularly Chomsky, and psycholinguistics; experimental cognitive psychology; and Soviet psychology and neuropsychology. Because I am a specialist in none of these areas, these chapters may seem both elementary and highly selective to the reader who is such a specialist. They should, by the same token, be reasonably accessible to those who share my lack of specialization. My aim in these chapters has not been to present a comprehensive survey of each area's accomplishments, but rather to bring together, in a single place, what seem to me to be those insights of fellow students of the human mind with maximal relevance for the serious student of dreaming. This student may, if my own experience in exploring these materials is any indication, heretofore only have had a vague awareness of their existence, nature, or import.

In part IV, a model of dreaming is presented which seems to me to comprehend both the best of classical Freudian theory and method and the most pertinent of observations made by contemporary students of the waking mind. The model clearly is not imagined to be Truth, but it is, I think, an important demonstration of possibilities of empirically based systemization in dream psychology. Because the model is presented largely through description of a series of novel empirical methods for the analysis of dreams, a different kind of reading is required for the chapters (11–15) of this section. Overview might well precede perusal. The reader may be well advised to read the chapters through as a block in a relatively superficial way, in order to see where the methods lead, before returning to a more intimate consideration of what those methods are.

Briefly, the plan of this difficult, but critically important, section is as follows. Chapter 11 presents an introduction to a method of content-analyzing dream and free-associative texts (with further details of method relegated to appendix A and reliability data to appendix B). Chapter 12 illustrates the content analysis by means of a complete scoring of a well-known dream and its associations. Chapter 13 shows some ways in which the separate scores of the content analysis can reliably and systematically be interrelated to produce putative underlying structures for the texts in question. Chapter 14 introduces a kind of mathematical analysis—digraph theory—which can be brought to bear on such structures, and chapter 15 attempts to indicate how digraph analysis permits precise identification of "mechanisms" of dream formation, following Freud's free-association model of dream explanation, and hence empirical investigations of the best single model we have of how and why we dream our dreams.

There undoubtedly will be a temptation for the reader of less rigorous tastes to skip the detail of these chapters or to accept or reject their content by faith alone. That, I believe, would be a mistake. *The essential point of this book is to show that evidentially based, reliable methods can be devised for the interpretation of dreams by means of an analysis of free associations and that these same methods permit reliable modeling of how it is that we come to dream the dreams we do.* The reader who skims lightly over part IV will be in a poor position either to apprehend this possibility or to evaluate its particular realization here.

Part V contains two brief chapters, written in much the same style as the introductory chapters of part I, which attempt to indicate some of the potential implications of the method for, and possible applications of the method to, clinical and experimental dream psychology. The aim here is not to be exhaustive so much as suggestive. It is hoped that the reader's mind will fan out from the few uses I have mentioned to many more which are either unmentioned or unthought of by the author, and that those readers who also are researchers will do me the ultimate favor of trying some of them out.

"in their games, dreams or wild imaginings . . . individuals never create absolutely, but merely choose certain combinations from an ideal repertoire that it should be possible to define."

Claude Lévi-Strauss,
Tristes Tropiques

PART I

CONCEPTUAL

FOUNDATIONS FOR

A CONTEMPORARY

MODEL OF

DREAMING

CHAPTER 1

Dreaming and Thinking

Dreams are thoughts. Dreaming is thinking. These two principles are at once so elementary that they have been the implicit foundation of almost every modern theory of dreaming and so difficult that they never have been assimilated fully by any such theory. What are the obstacles to accepting these principles? And, what would the implications for dream psychology be were they accepted in their entirety?

Problems for a Cognitive View of Dreams

One major obstacle to a full-fledged acceptance of dreaming as thinking is our reluctance to accept responsibility for our dreams. Among many lay people and students of psychology this reluctance often takes the form of a belief in the supernatural (e.g., religious, telepathic) determination of dream content. For those who think of themselves as scientists, however, there always has been a degree of commitment to the working hypothesis that dreams, like all other mental phenomena, must be explained in terms of the natural minds of the persons who experience them. But scientists are people, and dreamers, too, and their commitment to this working hypothesis often has been hedged with private reservations.

Paradoxically, the grounds for doubting our personal involvement in the creation of our dreams are of two diametrically opposed sorts: (1) that dreams are too crazy and illogical to have been thought of by us and (2) that dreams are too intricately organized ever to have been thought up by our sleepily inefficient minds. Freudian dream psychology (see chapter 4) has done much to dispel doubts of the first sort; we now realize that dreams rarely are as illogical as they first seem. Behind the madness, there is a definite method.

The second objection, however, is less easily turned aside. Dostoevsky remarks, regarding certain "morbid" dreams, that they

> often have a singular actuality, vividness and extraordinary semblance of reality. At times monstrous images are created, but the setting and the whole picture are so truthlike and filled with details so delicate, so unexpected, but so artistically consistent, that the dreamer, were he an artist like Pushkin or Turgenev even, could never have invented them in the waking state. [1866, p. 50]

This is a reflection of reservations many of us make regarding the scientific explanation of our dreams. How can it be that, with no deliberation at all, we effortlessly create with a sleeping mind delicate scenarios of a sort which forever elude the best intentions, the most elaborate preparations, and the most diligent efforts of our waking mind? It must be some kind of miracle. Surely *we* cannot be responsible for such creations.

And yet, unless we are to take the "miracle" hypothesis literally, unless, that is, we are going to accept some supernatural explanation of dreams, we *must* be assigned sole responsibility even for the most "delicate" of our dream scenarios. It can be no other way. We appropriately may stand in awe of the generativity of the sleeping mind which creates such dreams. But we must go beyond awe to understanding, the awe only indicating the boundaries within which successful explanation is likely to be achieved. Dreams can't be "nothing but" phenomena. And, if they are miracles, they are everyday ones, and we must recognize that our sense of the miraculous arises not so much from supernatural causes as from our—psychology's—persistent underestimation of the natural powers of the mind. If we are to take the working hypotheses of scientific psychology seriously, we must acknowledge the full creative potential of our sleeping minds and attempt to explain that potential in terms of sufficiently complex models of the ordinarily "miraculous" workings of mind in general. The only alternatives are the behaviorists' studied ignorance of dream complexity or the supernaturalists' hedge. Neither does credit to the potential of our own minds as dream theorists.

Another obstacle to the conceptualization of dreaming as thinking is the "sensory," or visual-pictorial, nature of the dream. Although we can, to varying degrees, "think in pictures" in waking life, the pictures generally aren't that impressive and seem subsidiary to a predominantly verbal mode of mental representation. Asleep, however, the pictures are sufficiently perceptlike generally to lead us to believe, until the moment of our awakening, that we actually are seeing real events. In these circumstances it is easy to imagine that dreaming is primarily a "perceptual" problem, rather than an issue in the psychology of "thinking."

This tendency has been powerfully reinforced for contemporary dream researchers by the discoveries that: (1) vivid, visual dreams are "indexed" by the occurrence of *rapid eye movements* (REMs) during sleep (Aserinsky and Kleitman, 1953); and (2) the rapid eye movements of sleep are preceded, at least in some species, by spikelike electrical discharges ascending the visual system from the *p*ons to the lateral *g*eniculate body to the *o*ccipital cortex (PGO spikes; Bizzi and Brooks, 1963). In the context of these two findings, it has been natural to think of dreaming more as a perceptual than as a "higher mental" phenomenon.

But this position rests on faulty understandings both of "normal" perception and of dreams. With respect to ordinary waking perception, it no longer seems plausible to imagine that perceptions can be explained by stimulus inputs passing through receptor mechanisms or that they are faint or distant "copies" of the original inputs. The current tendency is to see *all* perception as a constructive mental act (see chapters 7 and 9). Thus, to align dreams with perceptions is not to separate them out from those human activities requiring central, cognitive explanations.

Furthermore, it is difficult to see how stressing the perceptual presentational aspect of dreams obviates explaining them in central, cognitive terms. Even were ordinary perceptions to be explained by external stimuli which affect sensory-perceptual systems in rather direct and unmediated ways (i.e., we see trees because trees are there), how then could we explain the seemingly elaborate activity of these systems during periods of sleep, when external stimulus inputs are actively occluded (e.g., Rechtschaffen and Foulkes, 1965)? Clearly one would have to propose some nonsensory, i.e., higher cognitive, mechanism to capture and guide the activity of these sensory-perceptual systems. That is, if we are explaining tree-percepts in terms of physically present tree-objects, then the occurrence, in the absence of such objects, of either a dream-tree or a thought-tree would present an identically difficult situation. In neither case could the mental representation be derived from a sensory input. In both cases it would have to be centrally elaborated. Both cases, then, would fall squarely within the domain of cognitive psychology.

In this sense, the current fascination of dream psychophysiologists with eye movements and PGO spikes is analogous to the fascination the linguist might experience in her or his discovery of some of the central and peripheral mechanisms of articulation. The excitement would be genuine. But the linguist would not imagine that her or his phonological discoveries constituted the basis of an ultimate explanation of language. They would be understood as dealing with a particular surface realization of the cognitive systems underlying language. In like fashion, dream psychology needs to recognize more clearly than it has in recent years that the "pictorial" nature of "pictured thoughts" during sleep is a matter of surface realization which may have only limited explanatory value in reference to the content and organization of these thoughts.

To pursue the linguistic analogy a bit farther (cf. chapters 2 and 8), it need not follow from surface-level differences in representation that picture-thoughts have different underlying structural representations than word-thoughts, or thought in general. As we know from the dream case, picture-thoughts can be used at least equally well as word-thoughts to form complex narrative sequences. As we also know from the dream case, pictorial elements can be deployed with at least equal generative creativity as the elements of conventional language: we dream, as well as say, structures which, for the most part, we never have personally experienced before in just that way. From these perspectives, dreaming must be seen as something more than anomolous perceiving. It is a human conceptual achievement of the first magnitude, and one of the core problems of cognitive psychology. Dreaming needs once again, as it was by Freud (1900), to be recognized as a problem so central to the study of mind that its resolution can help to reveal the fundamental structures of human thought. It needs, that is, to be elevated to coordinate status with speech, which, thanks to Noam Chomsky (1957, 1965), now generally is acknowledged also to reveal these same structures.

If the experimentalist sometimes has segregated dreams from cognition by conceptualizing them as "mere" perceptions, the clinician frequently has achieved the same separation, but by a different means: by classifying dreams as symptoms. Where dreams are mentioned at all in introductory psychology textbooks, for instance, it is common to find them in chapters on personality and psychopathology. It is as if the dream narrative is felt more to be like a facial tic, or a depressed feeling, than like whatever it is these books discuss when their topic is "thinking" or "higher mental processes." This treatment and the ideology it reflects are, I think, further obstacles to the proper alignment of dreams within cognitive psychology.

Dreams clearly can be of value in diagnosing the motives and conflicts of the dreamer. But in this respect they are hardly unique. Any spontaneous narrative of the person has considerable diagnostic value. It is curious to note that if this narrative is a poem, it is approached with reverence as an elevated symbolic achievement, whereas if it is a dream, it is more likely to be patronized as a symptomatic excess. Dreams have had a most difficult time escaping the historical accident that they entered scientific psychology via the clinic.

But it was not, of course, purely an accident. A difference between dreams and other thoughts, as Freud long ago revealed, is that the need for motivational constructs is more apparent theoretically in sleep because the motivational base of dream thoughts is less apparent phenomenally. Most waking thoughts are simple motives; no separate motivational constructs need be elaborated for explanatory purposes. We think precisely what we want to think. Because dream thoughts reflect several simultaneously active, perhaps conflicting, motives, their motivational base is not manifest, but requires a careful unraveling. But this difference should not obscure the fact that *all* symbolic activity, *all* representational experience, needs to be traced back to a motivational base. A complete account of language, for example, must incorporate not only a description of how we organize thoughts into word-symbols and word-symbols into sounds but also an explanation of why we want to say anything at all, and why we want, now, to say this particular set of meanings-in-sound. A common failing of much "cognitive" and "linguistic" psychology today is that it does not address motivational issues of this sort (cf. Neisser, 1967, ch. 11). One of the advantages of the wholehearted incorporation of dream psychology within cognitive psychology would be the posing of thought-motive problems in unmistakably stark terms which cognitivists no longer could afford to ignore. And, it is important to reiterate, it is not that dreams are unique in their motivational-symbolic interrelatedness. It is only that they display, in a relatively flamboyant way, a motive-thought problem which is a major concern of all cognitive psychology.

There is some reason to believe that the resolution of this problem may have cognitive implications for personality psychology as fundamental as its motivational implications for cognitive psychology. The experimentalist who might want dreaming only to be "perception" finds that perception itself is a higher symbolic process. In like manner, the clinician who wants to consider dreaming only as a revelation of a set of motives or conflicts may find, on analysis, that motives and conflicts themselves must be conceptualized as higher symbolic processes (Leeper and Madison, 1959). Any serious attempt at integrating the seemingly diverse worlds of motivational and cognitive psychology is bound to reveal that the worlds aren't, in fact, so different after all. They exist within the same skin and mind, and they interrelate to the extent that they must share a common language. It is, again, one of the great advantages of the systematic study of dreams that it highlights this necessary connectedness of conation and cognition. For motivational psychology, the immediate gain may be the reformulation of motives as symbolic, representational structures rather than as an inchoate set of "urges," "instincts," "wants," or "feels" whose relationship to the rest of mind no one ever quite has been able to figure out (cf. chapter 3).

The most contemporary form in which introductory textbooks treat dreams, and the most contemporary obstacle to the recognition of dreaming as thinking, is the categorization of dreams as *altered states of consciousness* (ASCs; Tart, 1969). It is not quite clear what positive meaning this characterization has for the explanation of dreams, for no comprehensive explanation has evolved for ASCs. Negatively, however, the characterization seems to imply that: (1) explanations of ordinary experience will not generalize to dreams—dreams are exotic phenomena; and (2) more specifically, dreams lack the linear, verbal organization of ordinary reality-structuring, and hence cannot be explained, or even described very well, in verbal terms.

Descriptively, of course, dreaming is, in relation to much waking thought, an altered state of consciousness. And it is undeniably true that some of the drug-induced visions or satorilike states of greatest interest to many students of "altered states" are difficult to describe or comprehend verbally. But it is not self-evident that the programming of dream experience, i.e., its deeper structure, is more like that of satori, say, than of telling a friend what's on your mind.

As I understand it, the essence of satori is to transcend a verbal structuring of reality and its attendant subject-object dichotomization and sense of individual existence (Luk, 1960a, 1960b, 1962). Ekai is said to have used *koans* to undo his "students' word-drunkenness" (Reps, 1934, p. 85). Heller, following Schopenhauer, speaks of "language with its nouns and verbs and particularizing adjectives" as "the idiom of *principium individuationis*" (1974, p. 33). Lilly (1972a) describes the abandonment of words, sentences, syntax, and grammar as a consequence (mechanism?) of the approach to satori. Of satori itself, Ekai said, "You cannot describe it, you cannot picture it" (Reps, 1934, p. 109). This is an account of a genuine human experience, one with which any mature psychology must grapple. But it does not sound much like a dream—at least, like a REM-sleep dream.

The typical REM dream has a linear narrative structure, much like the structure of a verbal narrative: first this, then this, then this; with the various "this's" having some sensible thematic connection with one another. The representation of a particular person or setting or relationship or conflict generally oversees the narrative as a constraint which keeps it linear in just this way. The typical REM dream contains verbalizable relationships (A hit B; C followed D), and evidences subject-object dichotomies (A hit me; I followed D).

As to how well we can describe our dreams in words, I find the following account by Rechtschaffen to be congruent with my own experience, and utterly persuasive:

> When laboratory subjects are awakened from the rapid eye movement (REM) stage of sleep, they generally have little difficulty in giving fairly long, detailed reports of dreams, with transcripts sometimes running to several typed pages. Indeed, it is often easier to get detailed, articulate reports of ASCs than detailed reports of normal waking consciousness. When I catch my friends off guard and ask them what had been going through their minds, they generally acknowledge that something had been going on more or less continuously, but the description most often consists of a few relatively noncommunicative, stumbling phrases . . . .
> [1975, p. 143]

It seems fairly clear, then, that in these respects the achievements of dreaming are: "ordinary" rather than "exotic"; linear rather than nonlinear; propositional and dichotomous rather than ineffably, primitively unifying; and well capable of being expressed in words. Perhaps, as Rechtschaffen suggests, REM dreams are even more prototypic of linear, narrative-style thinking than much of our ordinary waking thought. At any rate, it seems more profitable at present to focus on the many strong structural parallels between dreams and "ordinary," linguistically guided, serially organized thinking than to dwell on the few phenomenological features dreams may share with that odd variety of poorly understood and highly specialized mental states most appropriately designated as altered states of consciousness. Indeed, the epochal contribution of dreaming's greatest student, Freud, might be summarized in the following way: he showed us, at a deep structural level, just how ordinary dreams are. Once we transcend the peculiarities of pictographic representation and a "dream-work" grammar, we see, from his research, how assimilable dreams are to our understanding of waking thought and speech (see chapter 4).

Implications of a Cognitive View of Dreams

Readers with at least a generation's familiarity with dream psychology will recall that Calvin Hall (1953*a*, *b*, *c*) many years ago argued for "the proposition that dreaming is a cognitive process" (1953*a*, p. 273). Hall saw the images of dreams as "the embodiment of thoughts. They are the medium by which a psychological process, cognition, is transformed into a form that can be perceived" (ibid., p. 274). In this sense, the images of dreams perform, according to Hall, a function comparable to that served by words and gestures in wakefulness; they are the elements of a language in which thoughts can be expressed. Dreaming is realized thinking, then, and its perceptual constituents can be made to reveal, as surely as the words of wakefulness, the content of the underlying thoughts seeking expression.

Thus the position being advocated in this chapter—that dreaming is thinking and that scientifically it must be conceptualized in parallel with other high-level cognitive processes—is hardly new. Or is it? Exactly what position was Hall taking in 1953, and how does the present position differ from it?

Hall states that his "cognitive" theory is designed "to bring dream theory within the context of ego psychology . . ." (1953*a*, p. 273). That is, Hall's "cognitivism" was framed largely within the context of psychoanalytic ego psychology (Hartmann, 1939) and against the background of an id-dominated classical psychoanalysis (Freud, 1900). Hall wanted to say of dreams: they are ego-functions. The ego is active continuously in sleep, not merely in passive response to occasionally mounting id tensions, and it mediates conflicts with an eye to its own interests and goals rather than simply following the path of least resistance charted by other conflicting forces.

Thus, Hall's cognitive position ultimately became less a mentalist model of the dreaming process than a new set of criteria for psychoanalytic dream interpretation. It gave an ego-expanded view of the kinds of dreamer motives and thoughts one could read out of dream content. It was and is, in its fullest exposition, *The Meaning of Dreams* (1953*c*), a tremendously liberating statement for those who want the insights of classical psychoanalytic dream interpretation without its quasi-biological dogma.

And yet Hall's position did not place him within the boundaries of any group of academically based or experimentally inclined cognitive psychologists. His dichotomies of conceptual versus perceptual, thought versus expression must have struck whatever cognitive psychologists were about in the early

1950s as excessively and naively dualistic. Anyway, it was clear that Hall's statements weren't meant as serious proposals about the thinking process, only as rationalizations for a new psychoanalytic interpretive scheme, and there weren't that many cognitive psychologists around in those days to worry about it much, one way or the other. Thus, despite Hall's enormous impact on American dream psychology, it is safe to say that his cognitive position has had little impact on the psychology of higher mental functioning more generally.

In twenty-odd years, the contextual climate of dream psychology has changed drastically. The intra-psychoanalytic battles over the relative roles of id and ego have largely terminated, with a public victory, at least, for the forces of a stubbornly autonomous ego. Hall fought the good battle, and his side won. But the victory has turned out to be a somewhat hollow one, since the logical next step—a precise characterization of how a mind, liberated from instinctual bondage, does its dreaming—never was taken. Attention quickly was diverted from such mentalistic issues altogether, as the implications of psychophysiological discoveries about the REM state were pursued (e.g., Foulkes, 1966). "The biology of dreaming" (Hartmann, 1967) became dream psychology's consuming interest (see chapter 5).

Meanwhile, and, at the time, little-noticed by dream psychologists, serious and systematic efforts were being launched toward understanding the workings of the waking mind. Cognitive psychology became a coherent field, with distinctive methods, models, and results (e.g., Neisser, 1967). Chomsky's model of linguistic competence (1957, 1965) radically transformed our understanding of mind and effectively demolished the impoverished models with which psychology previously had tried to encompass linguistic phenomena (Chomsky, 1959). Within psychology itself, there arose a new field known as psycholinguistics (e.g., Slobin, 1971; Greene, 1972), which, again, developed its own unique methods, models, and findings. Mind, in short, once again became a respectable and productive topic of study for workers in psychology and related disciplines.

Thus a cognitive psychology of dreams in the mid-1970s faces quite a different set of tasks, and has an entirely new set of opportunities, than those feasible when Hall developed his cognitive theory of dreams in the 1950s. It no longer is necessary to belabor the point that dreaming is cognition. It now is necessary, and feasible, given recent developments in cognate fields of mind-study (see part III), to develop mentalist models of how mind creates dreams. Two decades of psychophysiological research have made it clear that this is not a job dream biology can or will do for us (see chapter 5). It is a task dream *psychology* must perform. No longer can we plead a lack of support from other cognitive studies; the tools are now there, if we choose to use them.

The present volume is intended as an initial effort in this direction. Without losing grasp of the insights of classical psychoanalytic dream theory—in fact, building upon them wherever possible (see chapter 4), I will be asking how these insights can be incorporated into a contemporary model of human cognition and how they can, in turn, enrich the understandings of mind which have arisen in recent years in the cognate fields of cognitive psychology, transformational-generative grammar, psycholinguistics, and other disciplined approaches to the waking mind. The ultimate goal, toward which any current effort can only haltingly point, is the restoration of dreaming to a central role among the concerns of cognitive psychology and the elevation of cognitive psychology and other distinctively symbolic human disciplines to a critical supporting position in the elaboration of models of dreaming.

It no longer suffices to say that dreaming is an ego-process or a form of cognition. We need now to understand *what kind* of ego-process and *what form* of cognition, and to this task we must bring some understanding not only of what the mind does when it is dreaming but also of what it is doing when it is not dreaming. Models of dreaming cannot stand apart from models of mind in general. Freud (1900) understood this; in fact, he wanted to elaborate a model of mind in general on the basis of dream observations. But dreams alone, however valuable they proved to be in Freud's hands, are a somewhat narrow base on which to characterize mind. Freud had the justifiable excuse that there was little other mind data available for his use. Even when Hall wrote (1953a, b, c), this still was true. It no longer is, and dream theory no longer can pretend that it is. If dreaming really is thinking, then questions about the processes and structure of dreaming must be asked, and answered, in the larger context of a consideration of thinking in general.

CHAPTER 2

Dreaming and Language

Prominent among the glib generalities which permeate the field of dream psychology is the notion that dreaming has its own unique language. This generalization contains, I think, a large measure of truth. But its implications never have been worked out in a highly systematic way.

Erich Fromm, for instance, once wrote a book on dreams entitled *The Forgotten Language* (1951). It is not a bad book, as books on dreaming go, and I have used it profitably in courses I teach on sleep and dreams. But it certainly evades the major implications of its title. At one point, Fromm speaks of the symbolism of the dream as constituting "a language with its own grammar and syntax, as it were" (p. 7). It is in Fromm's "as it were" that he reveals he intends "language" more in a metaphorical than in a literal sense. Nowhere in his book does he systematically characterize the grammar and syntax of dreaming. The linguistic analogy ultimately is revealed to be little more than a catchy figure of speech.

Likewise, we all are familiar with various dream "dictionaries" which purport to give us the correct verbal/emotional referents of various pictorial dream symbols. Even where the more reasonable and nonarbitrary procedure of free association (cf. chapter 4) is employed for "translating" such symbols, however, there is a tendency for dream interpreters to treat these symbols only as isolated semantic elements in the personality structure of the dreamer rather than as syntactic and semantic elements in the grammatical structure of a dream language.

These many failures to implement a linguistic model of dreams raise the question of whether such a project is, by its very nature, doomed. Perhaps the relationship between dreaming and language never can be anything more than passing metaphor. I happen to believe otherwise, and would like here to set down briefly my reasons for this belief. I hope to show that dreaming is, by any reasonable linguistic criterion, a form of natural language, and that this fact carries in its wake significant implications for the explanation and interpretation of dreams.

It is in the discussion of marginal cases that the criteria for language become most explicit. Are cackling chickens, foraging bees, or panel-pushing chimpanzees language users? What, really, if anything, is distinctive about human speech? Palmer opines that:

> . . . it is grammar that makes language so essentially a human characteristic. For though other creatures can make meaningful sounds, the link between sound and meaning is for them of a far more primitive kind than it is for man, and the link for man is grammar. Man is not merely *homo loquens;* he is *homo grammaticus.* [1971, p. 8]

What is this grammar which is alleged to be the essence of human language? It is, by one recent understanding (Chomsky, 1957), an economical set of rules for assigning valid structural descriptions to the components of expressive structures and for defining the ways in which such components may be combined to form that infinite set of expressive structures, and only that set, judged to be the entire corpus of the language under study. Can a grammar, in this sense, be said to characterize dreaming? I believe that it can.

It first needs to be established that dreams are structured, rather than randomly arranged, events, and that recurrent constituents of this dream structure can be reliably identified. Ordinary phenomenological data are sufficient to establish these points. It already has been noted (chapter 1) that dreams, much like verbal narratives and much unlike certain "poorly" structured altered states of consciousness, have a clear linear organization. Dream images generally are sequenced in such a manner as to lend thematic coherence to their progression. The dream is a drama, and, as such, has a tightly woven inner structure. Moreover, it is possible that the structure of all such dramatic expression is necessarily linguistically mediated. While elementary propositions can be formed nonlinguistically, indeed, are implicit in sensorimotor organization, it may be only with the development of linguistic competence that propositions can be hierarchically and serially organized in structures as complicated as thematic narratives.

Dream images, considered singly, also have structure. It is my belief that the inner structure of the image, like that of the sentence, is propositional. That is, despite the fact that the sentence forces successive expression while the image permits simultaneous expression, the contents expressed by the two structures may be formally equivalent. (It is my further belief that images have a verbal-propositional structure precisely because they are generated by mental systems which employ verbal codes; the evidence for this hypothesis will be discussed in chapter 9.) Where the verbal sentence expresses the idea that A hit B, the image pictures A hitting B. Where the verbal sentence expresses the more static relationship that A is associated with B, the image pictures A by B. Images code relationships, either dynamic/moving/interactive ones, or passive/static/associative ones, between discrete characters, objects, or events. In images, then, one may separate out as constituents terms of relationship ("verbs") and terms related ("nouns"). Each image is a pictorial sentence in which such verbs and nouns are combined according to rules much like those applying to verbal sentences.

It is for these reasons that dream images are relatively easy to translate into words (Rechtschaffen, 1975). Words are the form in which dream images originated, and verbal/propositional structures mold the way in which images are expressed. A *New Yorker* cartoon a number of years ago showed a patient lying on a couch with an indescribable phantasmagory of a dream filling a balloon over his head, and the psychiatrist saying something like "And now, just tell me your dream." The humor derives from the impossibility of the patient's ever complying with that request. The interesting thing to me about the cartoon, however, was how unrepresentative it was of the dream-telling situation in general. At certain points during the non-REM sleep-onset period (Vogel, Foulkes, and Trosman, 1966; Vogel, Barrowclough, and Giesler, 1972), and in certain schizophrenic REM dreams (Dement, 1955), there can be a breakdown in the linear ordering of dream images and/or in the propositional structure of single images. Events follow one another in chaotic fashion, or single images portray isolated objects simply hanging in space. But these degenerative organizational phenomena are so extraordinarily uncharacteristic of REM sleep that they clearly must be regarded as defective cases. The rule, both between and within images, is that dream expressions are linearly, propositionally structured and that constituent elements of these structures can be reliably identified and assigned meaningful structural labels.

The idea of grammar as a system of rules for combining grammatical constituents arises, in the verbal case, from the demonstration that a native speaker of English, say, is capable of generating an infinite number of grammatical sentences. Almost every sentence the speaker utters, moreover, will be novel; it neither will have been heard nor have been uttered before by this particular speaker. If we are to account for the behavior of this speaker in terms of her or his own experience, then, we must imagine that she or he has learned a set of rules for combining labelled grammatical constituents rather than a potentially infinite set of discrete sentence-generating habits. The essence of verbal grammar is *system*, and the concept of system is necessitated by the human improbability that an infinitely diverse set of verbal expressions could be generated any other way.

With dreams, I think, we have a precisely parallel situation. The creativeness, or generativity, of dream expression strikes us as well exceeding that even of speech. Under atypical circumstances, dreams may be repetitive or use stereotyped visual idioms, but the general rule is that we surprise ourselves with what we dream. Each dream contains images which we literally did not conceive that we could conceive. The creativeness of our dream imagery is infinite. *But, this infinite creativity of dream imagery is, in principle, no more miraculous than the demonstrated infinite creativity of verbal expression. It clearly is impossible to understand if we think of the dreamer as a bundle of discrete verbal and visual habit tendencies manipulated by a discrete set of environmental reinforcement contingencies. But when we attribute a system of combinatorial rules, or "grammatical competence," to the dreamer, human dream "utterance" becomes as comprehensible as human verbal utterance.*

Thus we are driven, as ineluctably as in the speech case, to imagine that there must be a systematic grammar guiding surface dream expression. The surface realizations can be reasonably explained only on this hypothesis. Only this hypothesis of dream generation is sufficiently economical in its assumptions to have any presumptive ecological/evolutionary validity.

The major implication of this hypothesis for dream psychology is that the primary task of this discipline now becomes the characterization of the grammar of dreams. This, in turn, implies needs for heightened sensitivity to syntactic rather than semantic issues and heightened awareness of the structural, as opposed to the "dynamic," properties of dreams. Both in interpretation and in explanation, students of dreams have for too long put themselves in the position of translators who have dictionaries but no elementary grammars. They hear the key words and, from them, pick up on some of the major concerns of the speaker. But they haven't done a very good job in learning the speaker's native tongue (or the structure of her or his thinking). That takes more than vocabulary lists or symbol dictionaries; it requires penetration of the inner structure of the foreign language being audited. In dream psychology today we need to grasp the inner structure, i.e., the grammar, of the peculiar foreign language of our own nighttime experience.

The only classical dream theorist with any real understanding of this requirement was Freud, and in this respect, Freud's theory of dreaming is the most contemporary in orientation of all the many dream theories now extant. In the introduction to chapter VI of *The Interpretation of Dreams* (1900), Freud develops a linguistic analogy. Dream content is, he says, like "a pictographic script, the characters of which [in dream *interpretation*] have to be transposed individually into the language of the dream-thoughts" (p. 277). In dream *formation*, on the other hand, dream-thoughts are put *into* this pictographic language, "whose characters and syntactic laws it is our business to discover by comparing the original and the translation" (ibid.). Free association is the technique for providing the original script with which the dream pictures are to be compared. As described in the body of his lengthy and brilliant sixth chapter, Freud's dream-work mechanisms (condensation, displacement, pictorial representability, and secondary revision) are attempts to characterize the grammatical rules governing the translation of a finite set of underlying, personally significant propositions into the infinitely various forms of dream imagery. They are, in short, transformational and combinational rules of a dream grammar. Precisely because of its highly contemporary cognitive-linguistic orientation, Freud's theory will be considered in much greater detail below (chapter 4).

It will prove interesting, moreover, to compare Freud's dream grammar with more recent verbal grammars (e.g., Chomsky, 1957, 1965). Although Freud devoted little systematic attention to language per se and although Chomsky has, to my knowledge, devoted none to dreams, there are so many parallels both in the original subject matters and in the two theorists' treatment of them, that numerous possibilities must exist for cross-fertilization (cf. Edelson, 1972).

Both dreams and speech have long been studied in disciplines separate from the mainstream of general human psychology. Both phenomena have been major explanatory problems for the ruling simplicities of academic psychology. Both dreams and speech involve the "externalization" of thought in terms of a sensory modality, and, perhaps because of this requirement of exteriorization, both have been regarded as particularly good levers with which to study thought structures ordinarily invisible and inaudible to introspective probes. Both dreams and speech pose, in the clearest form possible, Chomsky's problem of generativity: how can humans generate, from a finite base of discrete experience, an infinite set of realizable surface expressions?

Both Freud and Chomsky have answered this question by proposing two levels (latent/manifest content; deep/surface structure), the deeper of which is characterized by a relatively elementary set of rules of formation. Both theorists propose that the output of these basal structures then is subjected to an orderly series of transformations (dream-work processes, transformational rules) on its path to surface expression, and both theorists convincingly demonstrate that their two-level, transformational model efficiently and systematically accounts for a great diversity of surface expressions. The parallels between speech and dreams, or Chomsky and Freud, do not, of course, ultimately turn out to be quite so simple or direct, but they certainly are compelling enough to justify a reevaluation of Freud's dream grammar in terms of recent models of verbal grammar (see chapters 4, 6, and 8).

CHAPTER 3

A Propositional Unconscious

Among the very real problems historically impeding the integration of the study of dreams with that of other higher mental processes ("cognition," "language," etc.) has been the peculiarly uncognitive way in which dream theory has tended to conceptualize its motivational constructs. Unfortunately, this difficulty has been greatest for just that dream theory—Freud's—which otherwise is most cognitive in its assumptions. Freud's motivational theory presents one with a vast array of quasi-physical, quasi-biological concepts: psychic eneigy, libido, instinct, impulse, cathexis and countercathexis, and so on. How can concepts of this ilk be mapped into any space of mental representations? Specifically, how could a construct like "impulse" be portrayed as affecting a construct like "image"? It seems that the two constructs do not share enough of a conceptual locus ever to be able to get together, much less enough of a common language to be on speaking terms with one another. And yet one could hardly bring dreams into cognitive psychology while leaving motives, particularly unconscious or irrational ones, behind.

As will be elaborated later (chapter 6), recent developments within psychoanalysis itself have opened the way toward a reasonable resolution of this problem. Analytic theorists have begun to separate out those formal and psychological features of Freud's motivational constructs justified by data and the logic of scientific explanation from those reductionistic features which Freud added gratuitously, on the mistaken assumption that physical or biological content would increase their scientific stature. Thus we may retain unconscious motivation, but not psychic energy and its multitudinous vicissitudes.

As also will be elaborated below (chapter 4), Freud's specious biologizing is *not* an integral part of his dream theory. In fact, the theory probably makes more sense without it than with it. Thus it now seems possible to cast the motivational richness of psychoanalysis, which other cognitive disciplines so badly need, into terms which are at once both psychoanalytically respectable and compatible with the other concepts of more recently developing cognitive disciplines.

Specifically, I will propose (chapter 11) that motive structures, whether or not they are accessible to conscious awareness (i.e., whether "conscious" or "unconscious"), are representational or ideational in quality and linguistic and propositional in form. The infant's attachment to its mother, for instance, is imagined to be coded in the form: *I* (ego = subject) *want* (motive = verb) *her* (object, both in the psychoanalytic and grammatical senses).

This model does not imagine that all propositions or representations are motives, but it does specify that all motives are representational. It does not imply either that all motives are "rational" or that all motives are capable of being verbally formulated by their subject. It merely proposes that motive structures are psychologically coded in a form roughly coordinate with that of other associative structures of human thought.

Leeper and Madison developed the logic of this position a number of years ago in a neglected but still cogent treatise on personality. While their model tends to call perceptual what might better be labeled conceptual, it clearly recognizes the representational nature of emotional and motivational processes:

We may say that perceptual processes are like motion pictures. That is, they are processes that have some detail and fullness as representations of objective realities. Some of these motion pictures are merely in black and white. These might be compared to the perceptual processes that have no motivational character. But other motion pictures are in color. We might compare these latter movies to emotional processes. The fact that color (or motivational significance) is present in these perceptual processes does not mean that they are any less detailed, any less "perceptual" than those neutral perceptual processes usually employed in perceptual experiments. They do not have any less detail or less ideational content about them than the motivationally neutral perceptions; the difference is only that something has been added. [1959, p. 215]

Thus motives and emotions are maps of the world which represent ego's relationship to other significant features of those maps: *"you–make–me-feel-angry"*; *"you–make–me-feel-lusty"*; and so on. Were I to find fault with the Leeper-Madison analogy it would be on the ground that motives should be distinguished from other representations not so much on criteria of *dynamic* modification (shading or coloring) as on the basis of the "perceptual" *structure* itself. Some of the relationships we mentally represent are inherently motivating (e.g., you–make–me-feel-angry); others are not (e.g., tables–are–furniture). The former structures I call *interactive structures* (or, simply, motives); the latter I call *associative structures*.

As Leeper and Madison foresaw, their modeling of motives in representational terms would receive tremendous impetus from the continuing development of self-regulating machines. The concepts of motive and emotion legitimately originate in the context of the need to describe the instrumental and expressive *selectivity* of behavior: why, for instance, does the patient act toward, or feel about, father figures or women viewed bending over from behind in precisely this way (Freud, 1918)? In those self-regulating devices known as computers, we understand the selectivity of their treatment of environmental inputs in terms of how they have been programmed. And we know that the programs and metaprograms (Lilly, 1972*a, b*) which guide computer operations must be formulated in a language coordinate with that of its linguistically coded inputs and outputs. Given the overwhelming dominance of inputs and outputs coded in natural language over human experience, it is an almost inescapable conclusion that our programs–our motives–also must be so coded.

Furthermore, from a sociological perspective, language is society's major instrument for the organization of personal experience. In learning a language, we are learning how to identify and organize realities both without and within. For effective social living, the organizations and programs achieved by members of a given society should be roughly coordinate with one another. Once again, it seems almost inevitable that our major personal and interpersonal motives be programmed linguistically, in the natural language to which we are socialized.

This has been the belief both of those who reject and of those who accept the personal costs of social life. Language is the means by which we become alienated from our own experience, or the means through which we tame our primitive impulses and become civilized. Lacan (1966) (see chapter 6) has spoken of language as being fictitious, in the sense that it necessarily distorts experiences in the process of organizing and controlling them. Mediators try to recapture a primitive, preverbal awareness by putting regnant verbal structures "out of mind." Huxley, on the other hand, feels that "the consistency of human behavior, such as it is, is due entirely to the fact that men have formulated their desires, and subsequently rationalized them, in terms of words" (quoted by Slobin, 1971, p. 97). And Benedetti (1975) speaks of the need to transform "psychobiological tensions" into rationalized structures (words, images), in which they can be understood, objectified, and organized (cf. Rossi, 1972). Thus mental representations perform a valuable and totally necessary integrative function in tension regulation. Insofar as tensions "drive" behavior, they do so only through the mediation of mental representations, particularly verbal ones.

From a variety of *theoretical* perspectives, then, it seems reasonable to conceive the motives or programs guiding the selectivity of human behavior and experience in a verbal/propositional form. For dream theory, this view has immediate advantages. Freud, for example, imagines that unconscious instinctive wishes are the ultimate generators of dream images (see chapter 4). But, so long as the unconscious is viewed as a repository of biological entities, its integration with thought or image justifiably will appear to contemporary cognitivists as exceedingly difficult. However, where "the unconscious" simply designates a set of verbally formulated propositional structures of which the person is unaware, but which must be postulated to encompass the person's behavioral and experiential repertoire, then there should be little difficulty in having unconscious motives affect verbal or imaginal outputs. And the alleged rationalizing advantages for the individual of verbalizing deep motivational processes may be paralleled in similar advantages for the scientific understanding of deep motivational processes. Suppes and Warren (1975), for instance, have greatly clarified the conceptualization of defense mechanisms by imagining them as transformations worked upon primitive, motivationally significant propositions (see chapter 6).

The main theoretical *objection* to casting motives in a conceptual form probably would be that of the classical psychoanalyst: unconscious motives have been deprived of their depth and of their fundamental illogic. But, as Sartre (1956) has pointed out, any notion of an absolute unconscious, totally beyond the grasp of the knowledge structures of the ego, is itself illogical. If unconscious structures are to fulfill the functions they do in Freud's own theory, they cannot be as "deep" and inaccessible to rational structuring as Freud sometimes seems to want them to be. If the ego is to be able to defend itself against unconscious motives, for instance, it must "remain *continuously* cognizant" (Fingarette, 1969, p. 89) of them. But it cannot cognize them if they are not in a form susceptible to mental representation.

Fingarette goes on to observe that:

> As a matter of clinical fact, ... unconscious fantasies are found to be organized to a good extent according to the (rational) secondary process. ... Freud *over*stressed the fact that the element split off from the Ego takes on a markedly "primitive" character, and he fails adequately to stress the great extent to which the element split off still retains fundamental characteristics of the Ego. ... [1969, p. 92-93]

The conceptual model of motives being proposed here, then, goes a good distance toward rectifying the theoretical and clinical-empirical defects which have appeared in earlier, ultra-deep models of unconscious motivation. Those models themselves, on the other hand, turn out to be neither theoretically nor empirically justifiable.

Operationally, of course, there also are compelling reasons for treating motives as verbal-conceptual, rather than biophysical, structures. "The unconscious" is, in the dream case, at least, only an inference from two sets of verbal outputs—dream reports and free associations. Unconscious dream generators have been proposed legitimately only as hypothetical summaries and/or organizers of this verbal material. There seems to be no valid reason why such hypothetical unconscious constructs should be formulated in terms radically different from those of the data they seek to explain—it is not as if anyone ever has seen or directly measured Freud's physicalist concepts, or as if they could pretend to be more "real" than mentalist ones. All that Freud's biological unconscious has achieved for dream psychology has been an unnecessary complication of its explanatory aims. A propositional unconscious, on the other hand, frees Freud's valid and tremendously significant demonstration of the importance of unconscious motives from an outmoded concept of a quasi-biological system in which such motives "reside" and renders it possible to place such motives in the symbolic context in which they always have belonged. The propositional unconscious also, of course, places unconscious motives in a form in which they can be shared fruitfully with other disciplines devoted to the study of mind.

With a propositional unconscious, moreover, the aims of Freud's own dream psychology at once become very contemporary. Freud wanted to determine the deep propositional structures which underlie dream utterance and to characterize the transformational processes applied to these structures on their path to surface realization. In more modern terms, we might ask:

what is the semantic content of that portion of long-term storage ordinarily inaccessible to conscious analysis but active during REM sleep? What semantic and syntactic processes constrain these contents such that we must infer them from, rather than see them in, the verbal and pictographic outputs of REM dreams? These are questions not only faithful to Freud's intent but also compatible with the interests and competencies of contemporary disciplines studying human symbolic behavior. And this is precisely how it should be if dreams, and the classical contributions of Freudian dream psychology, are to become integral parts of today's psychology of higher mental processes.

PART II

EMPIRICAL

FOUNDATIONS FOR

A CONTEMPORARY

MODEL OF

DREAMING:

OBSERVATIONS FROM

DREAM PSYCHOLOGY

CHAPTER 4

Freud's Dream Theory

Introduction

First published at the turn of this century, Sigmund Freud's *The Interpretation of Dreams* (1900) remains dream psychology's single most important work. In perhaps no other area of scientific psychology has so old a source had such immense staying power. The longevity of this book is not attributable to a dearth of subsequent research—as will be demonstrated in the following chapter, the past twenty years have seen an enormous expansion of the experimental literature on dreams. Nor is its longevity a result of a failure of other theorists to come forth with theories of their own—there have been many theories of dreams since Freud. Freud's genius is best attested to by the fact, on the one hand, that subsequent empirical research rarely has been conducted without some direct influence of his views, and, on the other hand, that dream theory since 1900 has been, by and large, but a series of variations on Freud's early themes. Dream research has not always confirmed Freud, nor has dream theory invariably supported him, yet neither researcher nor theorist ever has been able to ignore him. He is the absolute starting point of any serious study of dreams today not merely because he was the first person to study dreams in a comprehensive and scientific way, but also because he remains the most gifted scholar ever to turn that kind of scientific attention to dream phenomena.

Indeed, the influence of *The Interpretation of Dreams* goes far beyond dream psychology. Freud's contribution was a major event in the intellectual history of Western civilization, one whose reverberations still are being felt in art, literature, politics, history, and social theory. Ostensibly dealing with the limited question of dreams and their meaning, Freud's actual goal was much broader than that: the promulgation of a unified view of mind and of a whole new theory of human nature. The theory was implicit in Freud's earlier writings, but what is important about its statement in *The Interpretation of Dreams* is that it here becomes the basis for a *general* human psychology, not merely one for neurotic patients. The scope and depth of this theory— "psychoanalysis"—is such that no other single declaration in the history of psychology has approached its impact. As Loevinger recently noted, "No other therapeutic ideology or explanation of human behavior has enough intellectual content to attract comparable study" (1969, p. 1389).

Dream phenomena may seem a strange base from which to project such a far-reaching intellectual enterprise. But Freud saw in dreams an opportunity which earlier theorists had missed: the chance to observe what the human mind does—what it is like—when it is operating on its own, freed from perceptual inputs and the imperatives of the social order outside. By systematically comparing this mind with the more familiar one of waking experience, Freud saw that he not only could assimilate dream phenomena to waking psychology but that he also could, at the same time, immensely expand the scope of waking psychology. The end result would be a more comprehensive view than had been achieved by earlier students of mind, who tended to view dreams only as stray curiosities. Freud's revaluation of dreams aligned him with prescientific thought, which was in the habit of taking dreams very seriously. Freud saw that you could have dreams, *and science too*. The marriage of these two passions in Freud's mind has been one of the most fruitful unions in our brief history as thinking beasts.

Freud's system developed, and long was nurtured, outside the boundaries of traditional psychology. It is symptomatic of the state of twentieth-century academic psychology, which at almost every choice-point in its maze-like history has taken the shorter path or smaller view, that only in recent years has it begun to appreciate the audacity of Freud's enterprise. For years, just like many of the nineteenth-century scholars justifiably chided in Freud's review of earlier dream literature, academic psychology considered dreams as minor curiosities to be "covered" in a paragraph or two in chapters on personality disorders. Reading Freud's title, rather than his material, it imagined that Freud's essential contribution was a therapeutic method, dream interpretation, to be employed with neurotic patients. But the Freud of *The Interpretation of Dreams* is no mere clinician looking for better diagnostic devices or therapeutic maneuvers. He is, above all else, a scientist looking for an explanation of how we think when we are asleep, and, through that portal, for an explanation of mind more generally.

This is the first and most basic point to be understood about *The Interpretation of Dreams*: it is a study of mind, a contribution to what today is called cognitive psychology. But, unlike much of contemporary cognitive psychology, it recognizes that you can't have thoughts without motives, and that you can't have a theory of mind until you show how thought and motive meld into experience and behavior.

The word "interpretation" in Freud's title, then, is, somewhat misleading, perhaps deliberately provocative (Ellenberger, 1970, p. 452). Freud did, in the second chapter of *The Interpretation of Dreams*, provide a method for interpreting dreams, but, as befits a scientific monograph, the method is only a prelude to the body of the research, whose results ultimately issue in a model—in this case a model of mind, both asleep and awake (Freud, 1900, ch. VII).

In our search for foundations of a contemporary cognitive approach to dreams (chapter 1), then, we first must turn to the scientist who most clearly embraced this perspective and try to determine what his approach was and how viable it still is. Although Freud continued to write about dreams throughout his lengthy career, he at no other place so clearly approached dreams as a scientific, and a cognitive, problem as in *The Interpretation of Dreams*, so our account will, for the most part, be limited to this relatively early contribution.

Freud's Literature Review: The State of Nineteenth-Century Dream Research

As suggested above, the structure of *The Interpretation of Dreams* is that of a scientific monograph. Such works traditionally begin with a review of the literature. Although Freud apparently was not very enthusiastic about meeting this requirement—his review chapter was the last part of his monograph to be completed—*The Interpretation of Dreams* does open with a scholarly survey of nineteenth-century scientific thought on dreams. Our interest in this material is not so much in what it is as in what Freud makes of it, for, in effect, Freud's review carefully sets the stage for his own contributions.

One of the most striking things about Freud's review is how quickly it contradicts the intention seemingly implied by the title of his book. He gives scant attention to prescientific theories of dream interpretation, i.e., to the practical use of dreams for divining the character or future of the dreamer.* Rather, Freud's primary interest is in basic scientific contributions to dream psychology, of which there were surprisingly many. Freud focuses not on those authorities who would tell us how to use our dreams for some purpose extrinsic to sleep, but on those scientists who were concerned with the questions of what dreams are like (*description*) and why they are the way they are (*explanation*). The very structure of Freud's review of earlier contributions, then, indicates the direction to be taken in the rest of his book: his concern is with the mind asleep; what does it typically do, and why? In this sense, Freud clearly meant to do much more than simply introduce a new method for "the interpretation of dreams."

We may summarize the data surveyed by Freud under the descriptive and explanatory headings suggested above.

Descriptive

What are dreams like? Unless earlier observers are to be considered totally untrustworthy, Freud's review suggests that dreams must be a mass of contradictions. Dreams seem capable both of leading us into a totally different world of fantasy and of continuing the main threads of our waking lives. They seem to use both recent and distant impressions of waking memory. The impressions they select can be either trivial (leading us sometimes to lament that, while all the interesting aspects of our waking life are ignored in dreams, the dream focuses on totally insubstantial happenings of daily life) or significant (at other times, we seem unable to shake off in sleep a problem which has been a serious concern to our waking mind). The quality of our thought during sleep can be laughably absurd or illogical, but cases also are presented in which dreams solve problems refractory to waking analysis or restore early memories hitherto inaccessible to waking recollection.

In the face of such contradictory ideas, supported in all cases by actual dream illustrations, it is tempting simply to give up the search for any unified comprehension of dreams. Why not just talk of different types of dreams, each one with its own set of unique qualities or rules? It is the preferred method of science, however, not to give up so easily on orderly and unified explanations of nature. Is there, perhaps, beneath this superficial array of disorderly facts, an underlying structure which is more coherent? Linguists have demon-

---

*It is instructive to contrast his approach with that of Erich Fromm, in chapter 5 of the latter's *The Forgotten Language* [1951]; Fromm *does* review the history of dream interpretation, and there is very little overlap between his review and that of Freud.

strated such structures for the incredible diversity of waking utterance (see chapter 8); is there not perhaps a comparable set of basic structures for sleeping "utterance" (chapter 2)? Freud thought that there was, and it was his approach to delve beneath the surface contradictions of the dream literature, looking for a more unified explanation of them at a subsurface level.

As clues to how this underlying unity might be conceived, Freud noted some generally agreed-upon characteristics at the surface. First, dreams are thoughts-in-pictures; their "language" is a visual-perceptual one. Nowhere can this property of sleeping thought be so clearly observed as in the transition from wakefulness to sleep; there thoughts are, almost literally "before one's eyes," transformed to images. One of Freud's followers, Silberer, later was to report a number of examples of this ("autosymbolic") phenomenon. Thinking, as he fell asleep, that he must tidy up the rough edges of a written composition, for instance, Silberer then found himself imagining that he was planing a piece of wood (Rapaport, 1951).

Second, dreams are "ego-alien"; that is, they seem to happen to us, rather than being recognized as something we ourselves do. This phenomenological *fact* has, of course, led many peoples to accept alienist *interpretations* of dreams: dreams *do* come from the gods, the dead, or other people. Freud, on the other hand, considered this same fact as one requiring explanation within the general position that dreams are, like waking thoughts, the products of our own minds.

Third, dreams are hallucinatory. There is, in Freud's terminology, a failure of reality testing. Until the moment at which we awaken, we believe that what we are imagining really is happening. In this sense, dreams seem more like *doing* something than like *thinking* about it. Our thoughts in sleep gather about them the hallucinated participation of the self in what is being imaged. It is not that, until we awakened, we thought about being in downtown Denver; it was as if we were there. This phenomenological fact has given rise to interpretations, both primitive and contemporary, that we can, in some sense, leave our bodies during sleep. To Freud, however, it was but another fact to be explained in terms of the vagaries of our own body-bound thought apparatus.

Fourth, dreams are dramatized. They have plots, characters, and settings, and beginnings, middles, and ends. They seem analogous to plays or movies which pass before the mind's eye in sleep. The organizational achievement represented by this fact argues against theories which treat dreams as idle sparks thrown off by machinery whose wiring has gone awry. Nothing so highly structured, we imagine, could be the product of random processes. This same achievement also argues against those physiologists of Freud's day and our own who conceive of dreams as some low-grade form of thinking, and it refutes behaviorists who must see dreams as involving only "a simple form of thought" (Murray, 1965, p. 85). Rather, as Freud recognizes, dreams must be "constructed by a highly complicated activity of the mind" (1900, p. 122).

Fifth, the dream portrays different moral standards than those characteristic of wakefulness, at least of the overt behavior seen in the waking state. In dreams, without anxiety or guilt, we arrange to have family members murdered or otherwise violated, and we yield readily to temptations strongly resisted by the waking mind.

Sixth, the associative processes of the state of sleep seem more fluid than those of wakefulness. Logic no longer orders associations, and connections are made between thought elements unrelated by the waking mind. "They are linked by associations of a kind that is scorned by our normal thinking and relegated to the use of jokes. In particular, we find associations based on homonyms and verbal similarities treated as equal in value to the rest" (Freud, 1900, p. 596). It is as if the mind's operations during the entire sleep period are characterized by the conditions characteristic of the kind of silliness or giddiness into which we occasionally fall in the waking state. Everything "loosens up." Associations often are made, for instance, on the basis of similarities of sound rather than those of meaning. Ralph Berger (1963) gives a nice experimental example in which the name Gillian, spoken to a dreamer during sleep, produced the dream response "a person from Chile," i.e., a Chilean.

Explanatory

These, then, are some of the facts of dream experiencing. How are they to be explained? In the literature examined by Freud, two types of explanations predominated: (1) dreams are the activity of a waking mind functioning under the altered conditions of sleep; (2) dreams are the activity of a partially awakened mind. The major problem with both explanations is what they fail to explain. What differences in conditions make the thought-products of sleep be so different from those of wakefulness? What parts of the partially aroused mind are awake, and what parts not, so that we may deduce the peculiar properties of dreams? Too little was then (and is yet) known about the properties of either sleep or partial awakening for these psychophysiological states to be of any genuine explanatory value. These theories resolve the mysteries of dreams by conjuring up the mysteries of sleep—the "explanatory" process turns out to be a tying one's self down to another's bootstraps.

The theory to which Freud himself inclined had been advanced, though it was not well fleshed-out, by several earlier authorities. Dreams are not the result of the same mind working under different conditions than, or at less than the full strength of, wakefulness. Rather, they are the outcome of a mental organization which is qualitatively different from that of the mind awake. This explanation, at least, has the advantage of making of dreams something more than a "nothing but" phenomenon. It focuses attention on the need to carefully describe, and then to contrast, the structure of waking mentation and that of dreams. It is this imperative to which the remainder of *The Interpretation of Dreams* is responsive.

The novelty of Freud's position, however, lay in his insistence that no general characterization of the conditions of the dreaming state ever could suffice to explain specific dream contents. Freud believed dreams to be valid mental acts. Their explanation, therefore, also must be sought in their mental context, i.e., by way of related mental acts of the particular persons dreaming these dreams.

The general logic of Freud's explanation of dreams, then, might be represented by a syllogistic schema of this form:

(a) These are the mental contents (thoughts, feelings, motives, impulses, memories) active during sleep;
(b) These are the peculiar processes by which the mental contents are transformed and attain conscious representation during sleep;
(c) This, therefore, is the dream, the logical outcome of these contents, as "worked over" by these transformational processes.

The crux of the explanation clearly is at level (b), the elucidation of *how* the mind works in sleep. And it is that elucidation, rather than any problems in practical dream interpretation, to which Freud addresses himself in the book he might better have titled *The Explanation of Dreams.*

Freud's Method: Free Association

Freud's introductory chapter opens with the claim that:

> I shall bring forward proof that there is a psychological technique which makes it possible to interpret dreams, and that, if that procedure is employed, every dream reveals itself as a psychical structure which has a meaning and which can be inserted at an assignable point in the mental activities of waking life. [1900, p. 1]

The end-product of a dream interpretation, as Freud sees it, is a rulefully achieved insertion of that dream in the larger stream of waking experiences of the dreamer, such that the dream no longer seems puzzling, or "out-of-place," when viewed from a perspective of waking life. The beginning of interpretation, on the other hand, is our puzzlement about a mental activity which seems not to make sense, which seems not to fit in with what we think, initially, we know of the dreamer awake (Levy, 1963). Dream interpretation is the ruleful process by which this second waking context—in which the dream fits—replaces the first—where our immediate response to the dream is only bewilderment: "I can't imagine why I'd dream something like *that*."

Or, to put all this in the context suggested above, in which "explanation" is equated with Freud's typical use of the term "interpretation," the problem is to explain how a mind, which initially (from our ordinary [waking] understanding of mental processes) seems unlikely to have generated such an experience as a dream, is capable of having done so. And, also as suggested earlier, Freud's great contribution to the solution of this riddle is that he saw not only that the dream needs to be bent toward a waking model of mind, but also that the ordinary waking model of mind needs to be bent toward the dream. In the process of showing us how to interpret dreams, Freud greatly expands our conception of the operations of the waking mind.

At the time Freud wrote *The Interpretation of Dreams*, there were three prevalent attitudes toward dream interpretation: (1) dreams do not have any meaning—they cannot be scientifically interpreted; (2) dreams can be interpreted in a synthetic or intuitive way, in which one whole story may be substituted for the dream narrative; and (3) dreams can be interpreted in an analytic, operational way, by the substitution of some other element for any element appearing in the dream. The first attitude characterized the scientists of Freud's day, of whom he reflected in another context, "*les savants ne sont pas curieux*." The latter two positions, on the other hand, were sustained more by a popular will to believe in dreams than by any scientific evidence. The second position was unscientific in form: no rules were, or could be, specified by which individual dreams were to be interpreted. The third position was operational—"horses" or "rainbows" could be given rulefully designated equivalents from a "dream dictionary"—but arbitrary—how could one know how to fill such a dictionary with symbolic equivalents, and how could one be sure that the equivalents were valid as applied to individual cases?

In form, Freud chose to follow the more operational third position, but with a significant modification to purge it of its arbitrariness. *The dictionary we need to decode dreams, he observed, is not to be found on our bookshelf, but in the mind of the dreamer.* The symbolic equivalences needed to explain the person's dream are equivalences which exist, first and foremost, in the very same mind which generated that dream. The methodological novelty of Freud's work, then, lay in its reliance on the dreamer, rather than upon various "authorities," to supply the mental context in which the dream could be understood.

Our mode of access to the dreamer's personal dictionary is *free association.* Free association's value as an interpretive technique was not Freud's discovery but that of Freud's earlier collaborator, Joseph Breuer—or, rather, of one of Breuer's patients, Anna O. (Breuer and Freud, 1895). Freud was impressed with how this procedure made it possible for the therapist to interpret hysterical symptoms. They too, like dreams, initially seemed incomprehensible; but, using free association, it was possible to show that they were symptomatic of conflicts in the patient's life. Dreams often were included in the patient's associations to her symptoms, so it was perhaps a natural step to assume that they too were part of a network of thoughts related to significant concerns in the dreamer's life, and that they, too, could be interpreted by free association. However obvious it now may seem that free association be extended to dream interpretation, in retrospect, it was Freud alone, in the closing years of the nineteenth century, who saw these possibilities and who brilliantly traced out their implications.

Free association is a state in which we let our thoughts wander where they seem to want to, rather than attempting to retain logical, conscious control. In free association, we are to try to stay those inner voices which seem to say "no, that's not nice," "no, that's crazy," or "no, that's not relevant." Attention must be paid to *all* the thoughts which flash across conscious awareness; and there should be as complete and unselective as possible a reporting of these facts to the interpreter (who might, of course, be one and the same person as the dreamer). We begin with some portion of the dream as a stimulus, and watch to see what happens next. It is an experiment, in which a conscious, deliberate self sets the stimulus, and then retires to observe what an involuntary self will make of it.

The logic of using free association to determine the conceptual equivalences represented in dreaming is quite simple. Free association recreates, as closely as any waking exercise could, the looseness of associative functioning assumed to characterize the state of sleep. Freud's general model justifying the use of free association is presented as figure 4-1. Freud's assumption was that, even if free association did not literally reactivate the specific pathways active in dream formation, it was, in effect, driving shafts into the same deep mine which eventually would merge with an already existing set of subterranean passageways. In dream interpretation (i.e., explanation by free

FIGURE 4-1

The Justification for Free Association

In dreaming, there is a looser, more relaxed, less judgmental associative process than
in wakefulness:

A. *Dreaming*

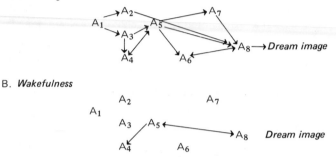

B. *Wakefulness*

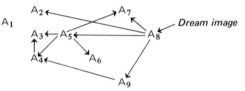

Thus, in wakefulness, the dream image makes no sense—it has no strong associative
connections with anything else in the dreamer's mind. Free association recreates, at
least in part, the fluidity of association assumed to characterize the state of sleep.

C. *Free Association*

association; figure 4-1, C) we are, essentially, tracing in a backward direction
some of the same associative pathways assumed to have been active in dream
formation (figure 4-1, A).

One clear implication of Freud's logic and his method is that dreams
cannot be explained without supporting free-associative data. That is, where
the dream has not been associated to by its creator, it is impossible to recreate the network of associative meanings from which it developed. This
fact has an important effect on the composition of *The Interpretation of
Dreams*: to illustrate his method, Freud could not use the many dreams previously reported in the scientific or popular dream literature. He needed the
sort of data only he was likely ever to have collected: dream reports *plus* free
associations to those reports. This meant he had, essentially, two choices: (1)
to use his own dreams or (2) to use those of his patients. Freud imagined the
objections of his readers that patients' dreams would be special cases, and,
besides, *The Interpretation of Dreams* was intended as a contribution to
general psychology. Thus, Freud was left in the situation that he must use his
own dreams to illustrate his new method of dream explanation.

This situation, in turn, posed a new problem. Freud wanted to illustrate his method with great detail and clarity. Yet he also was understandably reluctant to reveal too much of the particular contents of his own mind to his readers. The compromise which Freud effected between these claims—partial self-revelation, with only a partial application of his method actually illustrated—if understandable, was unfortunate. *The Interpretation of Dreams* does not, in fact, illustrate Freud's full and final approach to dream explanation, in which associations are traced back to childhood sexual situations and in which the dream is placed in a narrative consisting of the dreamer's entire life-history (Sherwood, 1969). For this sort of analysis, one needs to turn to Freud's few written accounts of his patients' case-histories, particularly, perhaps, to his "Wolf-Man" paper (Freud, 1918).[1]

In the context of Freud's purpose in writing *The Interpretation of Dreams*, the suppression of some of his associations and of a comprehensive life-history is especially unfortunate, because it makes his explanations appear to be much more speculative or intuitive than they actually were. With the wealth of biographical material which has become available in recent years (e.g., Freud, 1954; Grinstein, 1968), it is possible to fill in some of the gaps in Freud's own account. Yet, as we shall see, Freud's book remains flawed by its failure to illustrate what kind of explanation he ultimately considers satisfactory and why, on the basis of dream data, this must be so. In *The Interpretation of Dreams*, Freud, for want of delving more deeply into his own associations, presents what he himself would consider incomplete explanations of dreams as if they were complete ones.

Freud's Results: Wish-Fulfillment

A Specimen Analysis

To illustrate the possibilities, if not the full results, of his method, Freud presented and analyzed his own dream of "Irma's Injection" (Freud, 1900, ch. II). This dream, the so-called "dream specimen of psychoanalysis" (Erik-

---

[1] In a letter to Jung (written in 1911), Freud acknowledges these defects. In an earlier letter, Jung had characterized Freud's interpretations in *The Interpretation of Dreams* as superficial because they failed to demonstrate "the personally painful element in your own dreams" (McGuire, 1974, p. 392). Freud, in return (*ibid.*, p. 395), promises that *The Interpretation of Dreams* will not be reissued but will be replaced by a more comprehensive exposition of his views. In fact, of course, this substitution never was made.

FIGURE 4-2

Freud's Analysis of "Irma's Injection": An Outline

Verbal Outline

The dream: An "incomprehensible" sequence in which Freud's unsuccessfully treated patient Irma is shown to be suffering from organic symptoms, not psychogenic in origin, but attributable to an inappropriate injection from a dirty syringe administered by Freud's friend, "Otto."

Associations: A fanning out from a one-page dream text to ten pages of associations, touching on any number of events initially seeming to be unconnected with Irma's case: e.g., Freud's wife's birthday; a governess with false teeth; a friend of Irma's; an earlier illness of Freud's eldest daughter; Freud's research with cocaine and its unfortunate sequelae; a patient who died subsequent to an injection given by Freud; Freud's elder brother; a novel by Fritz Reuter; Freud's rheumatism; a patient with dysentery; a gift of liqueur from Otto; Freud's friend Fliess and his sexual theories; an old lady with phlebitis; etc.

Synthesis: *Wishes:* primarily, self-justification, specifically revenge against physicians who doubt the efficacy of Freud's treatments or theories; secondarily, "concern about my own and other people's health" (Freud, 1900, p. 120).

Schematic Outline

Dream elements

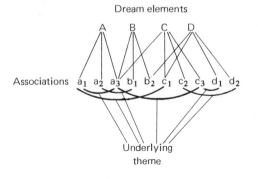

Analysis:
    Identification of the associative material and its interconnections

Synthesis:
    Reduction of the associative material to its most general common links (one or more elements serving as organizational foci within the associative network)

son, 1954), is so well known, and has been commented upon so lavishly in the dream literature (e.g., Erikson, 1954; Hadfield, 1954, ch. 7; Schur, 1966; Grinstein, 1968, ch. 1), that a full account of Freud's interpretation will not be given here.[2] Moreover, it is the form, rather than the substance, of Freud's analysis which now must attract our attention. To this end, an abbreviated verbal and schematic outline of Freud's interpretation is given in figure 4-2.

[2] Freud's own interpretation of another of his dreams—"Botanical Monograph"—is presented on pp. 51–54. For several reasons discussed in chapter 12, I have selected this dream as the specimen for the model of dream analysis presented in the fourth section of this volume. "Botanical Monograph" illustrates as well as "Irma" any of the points to be made here.

It will be clear that the initial result of the application of free association is an embarrassment of riches: far from having no meaning, the dream seems to be linked to so many waking situations that it is not clear that explanation can lie in this direction. Beginning with a moderately complex dream, we soon arrive at an incredibly complex amount of associative material. And, as the amount of this material increases, the number of its common properties necessarily decreases. It seems that free association has explained nothing, that it only has raised the initial explanatory problem to a still higher and more complex one. Now we must consider not only Irma's health and Freud's responsibility therefor, but also a whole host of other situations and relationships seemingly far removed from the events of the dream.

But the second result indicates that the extensive associative material produced is not discrete, but sufficiently interconnected to raise the possibility of its reduction in terms of a few common themes and recurring interests, which fit the dream as well. If free association initially broadens the scope of our view of relevant explanatory material, it then goes on to demonstrate that it is precisely this expanded view which permits a more orderly reductive synthesis of both the dream and its associative material. From this broader base, we now may project toward a few points subsuming the entire material. These points (wishes, motives, conflicts, etc.) are the organizing foci linking free associations to one another and to the dream.[3] It is in their synthesis that a dream *interpretation* (but not an explanation) is completed. To Freud, these synthesizing points invariably are wishes, and to many observers, this is the major finding of the "Irma" analysis.

Was this, in fact, Freud's great discovery in his analysis of the "Irma" dream? Clearly his fantasy, recorded in a letter to Fliess in 1900 (cited in Freud, 1900, p. 121*n*.), that someday a marble tablet might be placed on the site of the "Irma" dream, indicating that here "the Secret of Dreams was Revealed to Dr. Sigm. Freud," tells us that "Irma" was some sort of turning point in Freud's understanding of dreams.

[3] As we shall see, one recurrent source of ambiguity in Freud's model has to do with whether it is the dreamer's associations or the interpreter's activity which lead to this synthesis of the dream and associative material. At times, Freud writes as though the dreamer's comments themselves lead us directly to the organizing foci: "the dreamer's associations begin by *diverging* widely from the manifest elements, so that a great number of subjects and ranges of ideas are touched on, after which, a second series of associations quickly *converge* from these on to the dream-thoughts that are being looked for" (Freud, 1923*b*, p. 110). Or, alternatively, the interrelatedness of the associations is imagined to strongly indicate the essential dream synthesis: "where this meshwork is particularly close . . . the dream-wish grows up, like a mushroom out of its mycelium" (Freud, 1900, p. 525). However, there are reasons to doubt that the case is ever quite this simple: ultimately, the interpreter's role is a more active one than merely recognizing the synthesis provided by the dreamer-associator—it is, in fact, constructing such a synthesis on the basis of her or his own theory (see *The Contents of the Sleeping Mind*, pp. 54–59).

There are reasons to doubt the wish-fulfillment interpretation of the significance to Freud of the "Irma" dream. Grinstein points out that Freud already had identified a wish-fulfilling function for dreams. He concludes that

> what seems to be the most significant insight that Freud gained from this dream was that by systematically following the associations to the various dream elements, it was possible to see the existence of impulses and emotions that were not readily apparent in the manifest content and in this way to understand the meaning of the dream as a whole. [1968, p. 46]

Likewise, Schur also considers the successful working out of a general explanatory model, rather than any particular entry therein, to have been the significance of "Irma":

> *What Freud may have been attempting for the first time with the Irma dream was the systematic application of free association to every single element of the manifest dream, after which he connected these associations until a meaningful trend emerged.* [1966, p. 48]

There is reason to believe, then, that, in Freud's own mind, his great discovery about dreams was not any particular substantive result of his analysis of "Irma" but rather his implementation of a general explanatory framework for dreams which first elaborates free-associative material suggested by dream elements and then synthesizes this material with the dream in terms of a limited number of underlying "meaningful trends."

Whatever Freud's understanding of his discovery might have been, it is *my* assumption that *the explanatory framework given in the schematic outline of figure 4-2, rather than "wish-fulfillment," is Freud's most significant and enduring contribution to dream psychology.* Wish-fulfillment is, on this view, only a particular endpoint in a more general explanatory model selected by Freud. It is the model which permits the analysis of those operations of the sleeping mind Freud calls "dream-work" mechanisms. And it is the model which underlies the comprehensive dream psychology Freud develops in chapters V–VII of *The Interpretation of Dreams.*

From this perspective, "wish-fulfillment" turns out to be something of a red herring. The seeming arbitrariness with which Freud pushed his explanatory model to achieve that particular result often has been used as a basis for rejecting, or misconstruing, Freud's whole effort at explaining dreams. I want to insist here that the schematic outline of Freud's model be considered apart from any particular uses to which he may have put it. The outline may be acceptable, even if the wish-as-synthesizer hypothesis is not. Wish-fulfillment is a separate issue. The position being advanced here is that, quite apart from the adequacy or inadequacy of the wish-fulfillment hypothesis, *Freud's analysis of the "Irma" dream gives us a potentially reliable and useful general model for the explanation of dreams and for the characterization of the operations of the sleeping mind.*

In view of the diverse interpretations "Irma" itself has been given, it may be doubted that reliability can be a property of Freud's model. I think, however, that it can be shown that: (1) these differing interpretations are not entirely arbitrary but arise and are resolvable within a generally ruleful framework, and (2) however the framework has been used in the past, it *is* possible to specify rules for the analysis and synthesis of free-associative and dream material encompassed within this model such that dreams can be explained reliably and sleeping thought mechanisms can be identified reliably. The latter possibilities will be demonstrated in part IV.

That even the extant interpretations of "Irma" are not entirely arbitrary may be seen, first of all, in the fact that some consensus has been achieved on motives which are explanatory (e.g., Freud's wish that psychoanalytic treatment be effective and that psychoanalytic theory be confirmed) and on those which are not (no analyst, for example, has read "Irma" as being instigated by Freud's wish that his children be well-schooled). Second, where interpretations do vary, it often is on the basis of reconstructions of associative material suppressed by Freud. Had Freud not compromised his presentation of the "Irma" material, greater interpretive reliability might have been achieved. Finally, varying interpretations often represent different selections from the associative mass rather than contradictory uses of the same material. With rules enforcing more comprehensive consideration of the available data, many of the extant partial interpretations would be seen as possibly valid parts of a larger whole. In part IV, I also hope to demonstrate the possibility of writing such rules, i.e., of enjoining the interpreter to consider the entire dream/association protocol rather than merely those portions of it which appeal to her or him intuitively (or, projectively).

In principle, then, there is nothing inherently unreliable in the use and synthesis of free-association material in the explanation of dreams. Nor, it also should be noted, is there anything inherently unscientific in the form of Freud's dream explanations. Reference to two recent expositions of explanation in human psychology (Levy, 1963; Sherwood, 1969) reveals no significant discrepancy of Freud's dream-explanation model from their standards for satisfactory scientific explanations.

For Levy, for instance, interpretation begins with an incongruity, and it imparts to that incongruity a new frame of reference, in which the puzzle no longer puzzles. Clearly this is Freud's aim in the employment of free associations: they will generate an associative context in which the dream no longer stands alone as an absurd thought sequence but from which it "logically" flows. Moreover, Levy's analysis of two stages of the interpretive process—a "semantic" stage in which the inexplicable datum is translated to other terms and a "propositional" stage which synthesizes the newly translated material in generalizations and constructions that have empirically testable consequences—corresponds nicely with Freud's two-stage process of dream interpretation—the "translation" of dreams to free-associational elements and the location and characterization of organizing foci in the dream and association matrix which represent testable hypotheses about the character of the dreamer.

Both Levy and Sherwood point out that scientific interpretations cannot be judged "true" or "false" in the sense that statements about observables can be so judged. Nonetheless, both feel that derivation of such interpretations is an integral part of the scientific enterprise, and that there *are* criteria for judging their appropriateness, internal consistency, subsumptive power, and accuracy.

Sherwood distinguishes four types of explanations. One may explain a rat phobia, for example, in terms of its *origin* (childhood beatings by the father), its *genesis* (an account of the patient's intervening history in which that beating has, at critical times, become, for instance, the object of a recurring dream), its *function* (the suppression of hostility to the father), or its *significance* (rat = father's penis). A comprehensive explanation will touch both upon the history of the explicandum (origin, genesis) and upon its current functions and meanings.

It easily can be shown, I think, that Freud's dream-explanation model is, in this sense, a comprehensive explanatory framework. It is geared to determining *origins*—the distant associations (and their significances) ultimately assumed to be responsible for the dream. It is concerned with tracing the intervening associative network in which those origins have survived and through which they still exert their influence (*genesis*). And it insists that a complete interpretation will demonstrate the interrelations of the dream's associative and motivational contexts in terms of the motivational gratifications effected by the dream's associative elements (*function*) and that the explicandum, to be properly understood, must be translated into an alternate frame of reference (*significance*).

In an era in which technology (the gathering of facts for the prediction and control of human behavior) poses as science (these goals *plus* the requirement of explanation or understanding), it is perhaps not inappropriate to remind ourselves that dream "interpretations" play a valid role in the scientific study of dreams. Moreover, it seems that Freud's general explanatory framework for dreams is not inconsistent with explanation as it is practiced elsewhere in contemporary human psychology or in science more generally.

Wish-Fulfillment

It now is time to turn our attention to the aforementioned red fish, which has, for so long, posed as the great catch of the "Irma" expedition. Freud is alleged to have "discovered," via "Irma," that all dreams fulfill disguised, unacceptable wishes which are active during sleep and which, if not gratified in dreams, would disturb the state of sleep. First of all, it must be noted that this particular synthesis of the "Irma" material was not isolated by any explicit, ruleful procedure. This is not to say that dream syntheses need be intuitive (cf. part IV) but only that, in Freud's hands, they turn out to have that aspect. The lack of systematic rules underlying the wish-fulfillment discovery has made many of Freud's readers skeptical about it, and suspicious that, besides being intuitive, it also may be arbitrary. I number myself among these readers. I believe it to be an unresolved empirical question as to whether, in fact, reasonable rules ever can be written which, without logically prejudging the case, almost invariably lead to the empirical conclusion that it is "wishes" which "instigate"—i.e., ultimately are required to explain—particular dreams.

The wish-fulfillment hypothesis has other problems besides (but not unrelated to) its method of derivation. There are any number of ostensible empirical obstacles to the acceptance of the notion of wish-primacy in sleep (e.g., anxiety dreams, nightmares, self-punishment dreams). Freud recognized, and tried to explain, these seeming exceptions to wish-fulfillment. For reasons to be discussed later, I do not believe that he was successful in this effort, at least not in the terms he initially set for himself. Moreover, it also will be shown that Freud did not fully face up to an equally formidable set of formal and logical objections to his wish-fulfillment hypothesis. Let me now briefly and critically review Freud's evaluation of the evidence for and against his hypothesis, as that evidence is discussed, respectively, in chapters III and IV of *The Interpretation of Dreams.*

Freud adduces five classes of data in support of his wish-fulfillment hypothesis: (1) "dreams of convenience," in which an intrusive external or internal "physical" stimulus impinging on the dreamer is so transformed as to deny its noxious quality—the dream's response to a toothache, for example, may be that the tooth is painlessly removed from one's mouth; (2) anecdotal accounts from adult dreamers in which the dream expresses directly the fulfillment of a significant daytime "psychical" wish—Freud cites the case of a woman who, suspecting an unwanted pregnancy, dreamed that she had her menstrual period; (3) children's dreams, alleged to show in a rather less complicated way than adult dreams the generally wish-fulfilling nature of nocturnal fantasy—Freud's nephew, Hermann, after reluctantly being induced to surrender a basket of cherries to his Uncle Sigmund, dreamed that "Hermann eaten all the chewwies" (Freud, 1900, p. 131); (4) the folk-wisdom contained in proverbs—e.g., geese dream of maize; (5) the denotations and connotations of the word "dream" itself—we say "dream on . . ." to the "dreamer" who unabashedly expresses the content of her or his most basic wishes.

Dreams in which "physical" stimuli are transformed so as to deny their arousing property *are* impressive testimony to the force of at least one wish active during sleep—"*the wish to sleep*" (1900, p. 234). Experimental attempts to influence dreams (reviewed, e.g., in Foulkes, 1966) offer some support for Freud's idea that "the currently active sensation is woven into a dream *in order to rob it of reality*" (ibid.). Freud's generalization that the dream's treatment of aperiodic physical stimuli is a model for the dream's way of coping with all stimuli "currently active" during sleep—"psychical" as well as "physical"—is not unreasonable, but neither does it follow directly from the data on dreams of convenience. It is not clear that "psychical" wishes threaten sleep in the same way as do alarm clocks or toothaches, nor is it clear that, if they did, the fulfillment of the wish to preserve sleep necessarily entails the fulfillment of the "psychical" wish itself. With respect to the anecdotal accounts of adults' and children's dreams, it does not seem that very many of our own dreams have an obvious wish-fulfilling character, and systematic study of children's dreams (Foulkes and Shepherd, 1972*a*; Foulkes, Shepherd, and Scott, 1974; Foulkes, 1977) indicates that children's dreams seldom have that character, either. Furthermore, while the very simple character of children's dreams may, in some respects, be an evidential advantage, equal attention also must be paid to the "complications" which gather about the dream process with passing years. Popular conceptions of dreams built into myth and language surely are relevant and interesting forms of evidence, but they do not carry the conviction of dream observations themselves.

Nevertheless, by the start of chapter IV of *The Interpretation of Dreams*, Freud is ready to move toward the universal positive assertion that "the meaning of *every* dream is the fulfillment of a wish" (p. 134). Elsewhere (1900, p. 554), Freud seems to recognize the impossibility of confirming a universal positive, but clearly now he wants to hold that the wish-fulfillment hypothesis is generally true. But he immediately recognizes some of the difficulties facing this proposition. If dreams fulfill wishes, why don't more dreams have an obvious wish-fulfilling character? And how is one to account for the early evidence (Hallam and Weed, 1896), supported more recently by extensive observations by Calvin Hall (n.d.), that dreams tend more often to be unpleasant than pleasant? Doesn't that fact suggest that dreams express fears, rather than wishes? And what of dreams which are affectively neutral and which seem neither to fulfill nor to frustrate our hopes and wishes?

In addressing these issues, Freud insists that we must distinguish between the *manifest dream*—the dream experience or report itself—and the *latent dream*—the interpreted associative context of the dream as revealed by the analytic and synthetic stages of his dream-explanation model. Basically, Freud wants to show that wish-fulfillment always is present in the latent dream.

But there is a semantic confusion here, for the latent dream is not a dream at all but an interpretive construction. So what Freud really is saying is that it always is possible to achieve a dream explanation in terms of wish-fulfillment. That certainly is true, but it is not a discovery about dreams. It is more in the nature of a statement about (one) man's ingenuity in interpreting them. The question that needs to be asked about such ingenious unitary explanations is whether, from a scientific point of view, they are good ones, or the best ones available. As we have seen, there are criteria for evaluating explanations. Prominent among these criteria are the standards of internal consistency and parsimony. I think it is clear that Freud's attempts to wrap all dreams within the functional hypothesis of wish-fulfillment, while clever, often fail to be consistent or parsimonious. In dealing with ostensible negative evidence on wish-fulfillment, Freud misconstrues his task: it is not to show that unpleasant dreams, for example, *can* be interpreted in terms of wish-fulfillment; it is to show that wish-fulfillment offers the most consistent and parsimonious explanation of all such dreams. By confusing explanation with observation—e.g., the use of the observational term "dream" in his theoretical construct of "latent dream"—Freud manages to obscure this distinction. But what clearly is at issue is not the nature of the true dream, but that of the best explanation, and it is in those latter terms that wish-fulfillment must be evaluated.

The cleverness of Freud's interpretations of the ostensible negative evidence is a tribute to his ingenuity. But what is lacking is what is lacking for the wish-fulfillment hypothesis more generally—clearly stated rules *and* rules which do not hopelessly prejudge outcomes of rule-application.[4]

---

[4] As Gerald Vogel has pointed out to me, the arbitrariness of the derivation of the wish-fulfillment hypothesis now begins to become apparent. The derivation is arbitrary in the sense that wish-fulfillment is the only possible outcome of Freud's use of free

Working without such rules, any adept interpreter can explain all dreams within the framework of any unitary hypothesis. The data always can be made to fit the mold. Again, the critical question is whether, in the case of the wish-fulfillment hypothesis, this can be done by reference to a generally applicable, nonarbitrary, and economically stated set of rules. Freud does not show that this is so, nor has anyone else ever succeeded where he failed.

Furthermore, in Freud's illustrations of manifestly nonwishful dreams which are alleged to be latently wishful (i.e., *can* be interpreted as wish-fulfillments), he himself introduces new elements which challenge the primacy he heretofore has accorded wishes. We learn that, however necessary wishes may be, they are insufficient to explain dreams. Another factor is required. The unpleasant dream may be lacking in manifest wish-fulfillment because this second factor—wish-censorship—intervenes between the active wish and its final, conscious representation in the dream. Because wish-fulfillment is both desired *and* feared, the dream is a *compromise* between the wish and thoughts and motives set in motion by the anxiety the wish engenders. Thus, an appealingly simple one-factor (wish) hypothesis suddenly is metamorphosed into a two-factor one. The latter formulation certainly fits the data of self-punishment dreams, for instance, in a more adequate way than does the one-factor hypothesis.[5] But it is important to note just how large a shift this revision represents in terms of the original hypothesis. It moves us, for example, much closer to the waking case, in which

---

association, given the requirements of his reference system. Freud has assumed that: (a) the best, soundest sleep is mindless sleep; (b) dreams seem to arise in response to external sleep disturbers and to have the property of denying their arousal value; (c) since, however, most dreams cannot be traced to external sleep disturbers, they must be assumed to be hallucinatory, arousal-denying responses to *internal* sleep disturbers; (d) free association can reveal these disturbers, much as it reveals the disturbers of the waking thoughts of hysterical patients; (e) unconscious internal wishes of the sort known to disturb the thought of hysterics also could be considered presumptive sleep disturbers; (f) such wishes are, in fact, the only conceivable contents likely both to be active during sleep and to be sufficiently strong to threaten the continuance of the state of sleep; (g) free association to dream content, therefore, must be pursued until the point at which its data suggest an unconscious, unacceptable, and potentially sleep-disturbing wish. Thus, in Freud's hands, the only acceptable "latent dream," or interpretive construction, can be one which includes an unconscious wish disturbing sleep by its pressure for gratification.

[5] It also proves to be more consistent with the associative data generated by less obviously painful dreams. In the "Botanical Monograph" associations presented below (pp. 51–54), for instance, it is notable how each grandiose wish—of Freud's surgically attacking his father or of his completing his important dream book, for example—is quickly met by associations casting doubt or invoking recriminations on the dreamer. Likewise, the "Irma" dream of "self-justification" stimulated many associations which point equally clearly to self-humiliation (Hadfield, 1954, ch. 7). *In general, we might conclude that the evidence is clearer for the proposition that dreams refer to wishes than for the hypothesis that they express them.* There are countervailing forces actively opposing wishes in all but a few, very simple dreams.

we also have wishes, but where their progress to active expression is blocked by other thoughts or motives.

Freud manages to disguise the radical nature of this shift by calling his interpretations another kind of "dream," and by insisting that, in this more basic dream, wishes still are primary. The primacy of wishes in Freud's interpretations, however, is an outcome of arbitrary features of the reference system he imposes on free-associative data (see *n.* 4, pp. 45–46). And, of course, there is only one *dream* to be explained. If the dreamed dream is a compromise formation resulting from the interaction of the two forces Freud has identified, then his vaunting of the wish (it is *"creative,"* while censorship merely is *"defensive"* [1900, p. 146]) is not justified. The dreamed or reported dream must bear the creative stamp of *both* agencies. Thus, in the course of defending wish-fulfillment in the face of ostensible negative cases, Freud, in fact, elaborates a new hypothesis: *the dream is a symptom of conflicting or simultaneously acting mental elements active during sleep*. The wish has been dethroned as the reigning monarch of the dream world.

In formulating this new hypothesis, Freud is, in fact, doing nothing more than returning to the first and most basic empirical result of his free-association technique, a result since obscured by his insistence on a unitary reduction of the associative material. That result is that each dream element, rather than being meaningless, has a whole host of associative connections simultaneously giving it many meanings. Freud did a disservice to his own technique in stressing a certain kind of synthesis of the associative material before considering the immense significance of his results at the analytic stage of free association. In the latter context, Freud's major discovery is the finding that dreams appear nonsensical only because the peculiar conditions of sleep (an associative "looseness"; the relative lack of guiding logical or rational structures; and so on) permit greater simultaneity of action to discrepant or inconsistent thought elements. (This discovery runs parallel to the Pavlovian observation that in sleep, "the law of strength, according to which strong stimuli evoke strong, and weak stimuli evoke weak responses, no longer applies" [Luria, 1973, p. 273].) To say that the dream is a compromise formation among such elements is, essentially, to solve the riddle of dreams at a schematic level. Free association is the tool for bringing this general formula to bear on the particular puzzles of particular dreams, thanks to its potential for identifying both the elements in question and the transformational processes which operate upon them (see pp. 54–76).

In implicitly renouncing his one-factor hypothesis, Freud also has made a significant theoretical discovery, one whose import far overshadows that generally ascribed to the wish-fulfillment hypothesis. The discovery is that the better dream explanation is one which ascribes more complexity to the sleeping mind, one which remains more open to the creative role in dream formation of a variety of mental contents. It is, in fact, but a short jump from a two-factor hypothesis to a more general multi-factor hypothesis, and Freud soon takes that jump. One of Freud's patients dreamed of spending her vacation with her mother-in-law, an outcome which was quite at variance with her waking desires. Freud interprets this dream as fulfilling the patient's wish to disprove Freud's theory of wish-fulfillment. (As Salmon [1959, p. 282-83] points out, such wishes certainly are admissible, if independently derived, and are, in fact, to be expected during that phase of analysis in which resistance is at its height.) The more general point Freud makes about such dreams is that, in fulfilling one wish, sometimes another wish must be negated. Later on, with the elaboration of his structural model, these wish-wish conflicts will be cast in "agency" terms: in self-punishment dreams, the superego's wish may be gratified, while that of the id is negated (Freud, 1900, p. 476, *n.* 2). Thus, neither wish nor, presumably, censor is to be understood monolithically. The sleeping mind is a vast repository of many conflicting wishes and fears, and the dream emerges not solely from a wish but out of a complicated wish-reality matrix.

But, in terms of Freud's general dream-explanation model, the dream cannot emerge from an *infinite* number of psychic contents. The rules of the game still are that the conflicting or simultaneously active elements which are used to explain the dream must be identified from its free associations and from the constraints imposed on these associations by the interpreter's reference system. Freud's second hypothesis of dream function, then, is one which permits recourse to a multiplicity of determinative elements but which also circumscribes in a highly operational way the boundaries of this multiplicity.

Is Freud's "second hypothesis," as I have interpreted it, the one to which he really subscribes? That, ultimately, is neither an answerable nor an important question. The hypothesis is one to which his own analysis and data point. It also is an hypothesis which, in its disavowal of a penchant for a priori unitary explanation, can be operationalized in terms of a limited set of reasonable rules which operate on free associations to define underlying dream determinants (see part IV). These are sufficient reasons to prefer it to Freud's earlier emphasis on the necessary primacy of "wishes" in dream formation.

Nevertheless, I think Freud can be read in a manner consistent with my interpretation, and there is even more telling evidence for this analysis than has yet been mentioned. In his discussion of "secondary revision," for example (see pp. 68–73), Freud strongly implies that thought elements of a motivationally neutral sort also enter into dream formation, that it is not the entire manifest dream which reflects the determinative force of wishes, either simply *or* complexly conceived. Freud himself asks, *where*, in the manifest dream—the dream we have to explain—are wishes fulfilled? In *every* image, thought, affect, or sensation thereof? Freud tells us that a "peculiar sensory intensity" attaches to that part of the dream which is "the direct representation of the wish-fulfillment" (1900, p. 561; see also p. 330). (In fact, "The elements in the *neighbourhood* of the wish-fulfillment often . . . turn out to be derivatives of distressing thoughts that run contrary to the wish" [1900, p. 562].) If only some images in the dream fulfill wishes, then dreams clearly cannot be explained solely in terms of "creative" wishes. The remainder of the dream has been *created* through some other operations; these operations must be accorded equal explanatory status in any comprehensive account of dreams.

In fact, there is reason to believe that, in assuming the explanatory burden of subsuming unpleasant or manifestly counter-wish dreams under the rubric of wish-fulfillment, Freud has neglected the more difficult cases. In the dramatically counterintuitive cases Freud selected, it is not so difficult to identify wishes, or wishes-in-conflict, which might explain the dream. But there are other dreams, less dramatic, but more injurious to his position. Consider, for example, those dreams, not uncommon among children (e.g., Foulkes and Shepherd, 1972*a*), which are totally lacking in affective intensity of either the pleasant or unpleasant variety but which merely seem to reflect the mundane nature of current reality. These dreams are pictorialized versions of waking sorts of reflections to which we ordinarily would hesitate to apply the wish-fulfillment hypothesis. To explain them in terms of latent wishes is to explain something which needs no explanation, and, in the process, to discard the standard of parsimonious interpretation.[6] It is a clear advantage of what I have called Freud's second hypothesis that its greater openness to a variety of empirically achieved interpretive syntheses, i.e., its abandonment of the insistence on a simple a priori reduction of the dream material, makes it more generally compatible with the possibility that wishes might not have to be invoked at all in the explanation of dreams. *We usually*

---

[6] Silberer's autosymbolic phenomena (Freud, 1900, pp. 344–45), although more symbolic or less mundane in form, also may not require deeper, wishful interpretations. For instance, on the night immediately after making a rough draft of this section, I dreamed of walking along a stream toward its underground source. A large gnarled tree obscured the course. The waking thought corresponding to these images was the entirely realistic reflection that there are many knotty problems obscuring the underlying source of contents in the stream of consciousness.

do not require that all waking thought be interpretable in terms of underlying wishes. It seems desirable to reserve this same possibility, at least, for sleeping thought.

Where has Freud's argument taken us? Quite a distance from the conclusion of the "Irma" interpretation that *"a dream is the fulfillment of a wish"* (1900, p. 121). Freud's own formula now reads that the dream is *"a (disguised) fulfillment"* (1900, p. 160) of a wish, but we have seen that the new, parenthetical, entry is no mere modification, but a radical transformation, of the earlier statement. Wishes *are* active during sleep, and Freud has shown us that this is more true than we had perhaps realized. However, they are by no means the only contents so active, and any comprehensive explanation of dreams must give us an account of other contents, which generally modulate, and sometimes may completely overshadow, the raw wish doing what it knows best—pressing for gratification. Freud's account begins with a disarmingly simple promise, that there is a unitary explanation of dreams, but it ends with the realization that the mind asleep is as potentially varied and multifaceted in its composition as is the mind awake. And yet, thanks to the operations attendant to Freud's method of free association, this complexity poses no hopeless analytic task. There are ways, in principle reliable, to identify those contents which may lie behind each manifest dream.

Chapters III and IV of *The Interpretation of Dreams* contain Freud's arguments concerning dream function. The idea of discovering a unitary formula for dream function captivated Freud's mind, and, in its grips, his logic sometimes seems to falter. However, as already stated, I do not see the wish-fulfillment hypothesis as Freud's major contribution, nor its adequacy as the key to evaluating his more general explanatory model. Moreover, in the course of his "defense" of the wish-fulfillment hypothesis, Freud does, in fact, evolve a more adequate and less arbitrary hypothesis about the determinants of dream experience. In part IV of this book I hope to show that Freud's second hypothesis provides a viable base for a rigorously empirical approach to dream explanation.

In chapters V and VI of *The Interpretation of Dreams*, Freud turns his attention from *why* questions to *how* questions. Using the free-association technique as his method, he attempts to elucidate the associative mechanisms of sleeping thought, perhaps of mind in general. The polemical assault of chapters III and IV is mostly left behind, and we return to the main questions at hand: (a) what are the contents of the sleeping mind; (b) how are they transformed; (c) so that they result in the manifest dream? The result is a well-elaborated dream-process model. This model contains what I believe to be the main body of Freud's empirically generated "results." Before turning to these results, let us consider a second specimen dream, Freud's "Dream of the Botanical Monograph." "Botanical Monograph" stands in relation to Freud's dream-process model as "Irma" does in relation to the less valuable functional hypothesis of wish-fulfillment. Consequently, "Botanical Monograph" is the specimen of greater interest in the present account, and I now quote extensively from Freud's analysis of it.

Freud's Results: "Dream-Work"

A Specimen Dream[7]

DREAM OF THE BOTANICAL MONOGRAPH

I had written a monograph on a certain plant. The book lay before me and I was at the moment turning over a folded coloured plate. Bound up in each copy there was a dried specimen of the plant, as though it had been taken from a herbarium.

Analysis [Associations]

That morning I had seen a new book in the window of a bookshop, bearing the title *The Genus Cyclamen*—evidently a *monograph* on that plant.

Cyclamens, I reflected, were my wife's *favourite flowers* and I reproached myself for so rarely remembering to *bring* her *flowers*, which was what she liked. —The subject of *"bringing flowers"* recalled an anecdote which I had recently repeated to a circle of friends and which I had used as evidence in favour of my theory that forgetting is very often determined by an unconscious purpose and that it always enables one to deduce the secret intentions of the person who forgets. A young woman was accustomed to receiving a bouquet of flowers from her husband on her birthday. One year this token of his affection failed to appear, and she burst into tears. Her husband came in and had no idea why she was crying till she told him that to-day was her birthday. He clasped his hand to his head and exclaimed: "I'm so sorry, but I'd quite forgotten. I'll go out at once and fetch your *flowers*." But she was not to be consoled; for she recognized that her husband's forgetfulness was a proof that she no longer had the same place in his thoughts as she had for-

[7]From S. Freud, *The Interpretation of Dreams*. New York: Basic Books, Inc., 1956 (Original, 1900), pp. 169–73.

merly. —This lady, Frau L., had met my wife two days before I had the dream, had told her that she was feeling quite well and enquired after me. Some years ago she had come to me for treatment.

I now made a fresh start. Once, I recalled, I really *had* written something in the nature of a *monograph on a plant*, namely a dissertation on the *coca-plant* [Freud, 1884], which had drawn Karl Koller's attention to the anaesthetic properties of cocaine. I had myself indicated this application of the alkaloid in my published paper, but I had not been thorough enough to pursue the matter further. This reminded me that on the morning of the day after the dream—I had not found time to interpret it till the evening—I had thought about cocaine in a kind of day-dream. If ever I got glaucoma, I had thought, I should travel to Berlin and get myself operated on, incognito, in my friend's [Fliess's] house, by a surgeon recommended by him. The operating surgeon, who would have no idea of my identity, would boast once again of how easily such operations could be performed since the introduction of cocaine; and I should not give the slightest hint that I myself had had a share in the discovery. This phantasy had led on to reflections of how awkward it is, when all is said and done, for a physician to ask for medical treatment for himself from his professional colleagues. The Berlin eye-surgeon would not know me, and I should be able to pay his fees like anyone else. It was not until I had recalled this day-dream that I realized that the recollection of a specific event lay behind it. Shortly after Koller's discovery, my father had in fact been attacked by glaucoma; my friend Dr. Königstein, the ophthalmic surgeon, had operated on him; while Dr. Koller had been in charge of the cocaine anaesthesia and had commented on the fact that this case had brought together all of the three men who had had a share in the introduction of cocaine.

My thoughts then went on to the occasion when I had last been reminded of this business of the cocaine. It had been a few days earlier, when I had been looking at a copy of a *Festschrift* in which grateful pupils had celebrated the jubilee of their teacher and laboratory director. Among the laboratory's claims to distinction which were enumerated in this book I had seen a mention of the fact that Koller had made his discovery there of the anaesthetic properties of cocaine. I then suddenly perceived that my dream was connected with an event of the previous evening. I had walked home precisely with Dr. Königstein and had got into conversation with him about a matter which never fails to excite my feelings whenever it is raised. While I was talking to him in the entrance-hall, Professor *Gärtner* [Gardener] and his wife had joined us; and I could not help congratulating them both on their *blooming* looks.

But Professor Gärtner was one of the authors of the *Festschift* I have just mentioned, and may well have reminded me of it. Moreover, the Frau L., whose disappointment on her birthday I described earlier, was mentioned—though only, it is true, in another connection—in my conversation with Dr. Königstein.

I will make an attempt at interpreting the other determinants of the content of the dream as well. There was *a dried specimen of the plant* included in the monograph, as though it had been a *herbarium*. This led me to a memory from my secondary school. Our headmaster once called together the boys from the higher forms and handed over the school's herbarium to them to be looked through and cleaned. Some small worms—book-worms— had found their way into it. He does not seem to have had much confidence in my helpfulness, for he handed me only a few sheets. These, as I could still recall, included some Crucifers. I never had a specially intimate contact with botany. In my preliminary examination in botany I was also given a Crucifer to identify—and failed to do so. My prospects would not have been too bright, if I had not been helped out by my theoretical knowledge. I went on from the Cruciferae to the Compositae. It occurred to me that artichokes were Compositae, and indeed I might fairly have called them my *favourite flowers*. Being more generous than I am, my wife often brought me back these favourite flowers of mine from the market.

I saw the monograph which I had written *lying before me*. This again led me back to something. I had had a letter from my friend [Fliess] in Berlin the day before in which he had shown his power of visualization: "I am very much occupied with your dream-book. *I see it lying finished before me and I see myself turning over its pages.*" How much I envied him his gift as a seer! If only *I* could have seen it lying finished before me!

The folded coloured plate. While I was a medical student I was the constant victim of an impulse only to learn things out of *monographs*. In spite of my limited means, I succeeded in getting hold of a number of volumes of the proceedings of medical societies and was enthralled by their *coloured plates*. I was proud of my hankering for thoroughness. When I myself had begun to publish papers, I had been obliged to make my own drawings to illustrate them and I remembered that one of them had been so wretched that a friendly colleague had jeered at me over it. There followed, I could not quite make out how, a recollection from very early youth. It had once amused my father to hand over a book with *coloured plates* (an account of a journey through Persia) for me and my eldest sister to destroy. Not easy to justify from the educational point of view! I had been five years old at the time and my sister not yet three; and the picture of the two of us blissfully pulling the book to pieces (leaf by leaf, like an *artichoke*, I found myself saying) was almost the only plastic memory that I retained from that period of my life. Then, when I became a student, I had developed a passion for collecting and owning books, which was analogous to my liking for learning out of monographs: a *favourite hobby*. (The idea of *"favourite"* had already appeared in connection with cyclamens and artichokes.) I had become a *book-worm*. I had always, from the time I first began to think about my-self, referred this first passion of mine back to the childhood memory I have mentioned. Or rather, I had recognized that the childhood scene was a "screen memory" for my later bibliophile propensities.[1] And I had early discovered, of course, that passions often lead to sorrow. When I was seventeen I had run up a largish account at the bookseller's and had nothing to meet it with; and my father had scarcely taken it as an excuse that my inclinations might have chosen a worse outlet. The recol-lection of this experience from the later years of my youth at once brought back to my mind the conversation with my friend Dr. König-stein. For in the course of it we had discussed the same question of my being blamed for being too much absorbed in my *favourite hobbies*.

The Contents of the Sleeping Mind

The title of Freud's fifth chapter indicates that it deals with the material and sources of dreams. In terms of the syllogistic explanatory schema which I have suggested Freud is using, the concern is with the first term: "these are the mental contents active during sleep." The ostensible framework of Freud's analysis is a reexamination of the contradictory hypotheses offered by earlier authors (see Freud's Literature Review, pp. 29–33). The question is whether the free-associative technique permits any definitive resolution of issues such as the indifferent versus significant meaning, the recent versus distant time-reference, and the physical versus psychical nature, of dream in-stigators. Freud wants to show that it does, and in this effort he is largely successful.

Freud's first result is that "in every dream it is possible to find a point of contact with the experiences of the previous day" (1900, p. 165). The day in question is called the "dream-day," and the experience in question is called a "day-residue." For example, Freud notes that on the morning of the dream-day of "Botanical Monograph," he "had seen a *monograph* on the genus Cyclamen in the window of a book-shop" (ibid.). By itself, this instance seems

[1] Cf. my paper on screen memories [Freud, 1899].

to suggest that indifferent dream-day material may stimulate a dream. But the full analysis of "Botanical Monograph," as cited above, indicates that such indifferent residues are but connective elements in a larger network which spreads from the dream to more significant material. The notion that dreams may have insignificant instigators can only rest on an incomplete dream analysis which fails to pierce the work of dream censorship. The fully analyzed (associated to) dream always will be seen to have a connection with a significant experience in the dreamer's life: "Dreams are never concerned with trivialities" (1900, p. 182). Insignificant impressions may figure in the *genesis* of the dream, but they are never its *origin*.

The day-residue need not be an insignificant event of the dream-day. In "Irma," for example, the day-residue was Otto's implication, of great significance to Freud, that Irma is "better, but not quite well" (1900, p. 106). At times, then, censorship is not required or, at least, not successful in obscuring the dream's relation to the main events of the dreamer's life. The only unvarying condition Freud imposes on day-residues is that they be very recent impressions: "a day (or at the most a few days)" old (1900, p. 181). "From this we must conclude that the freshness of an impression gives it some kind of psychical value for purposes of dream-construction . . . ." (ibid.)

The question of the significance or insignificance of the dream's instigation soon becomes transformed, in Freud's account, to that of its "innocence" or lack thereof. Freud's analyses of dreams with seemingly trivial instigation invariably seem to disclose associative material of a sexual nature. In terms of the wish-fulfillment hypothesis, it is generally wishes of a sexual sort which Freud feels are active in dream formation. But he is not yet insisting that this must invariably be the case; he is only reporting a generally observed "result" of the application of his method, and, at least for the dream analyses he has reported, it is difficult to take exception to his characterization of that result.

How far back beyond the dream-day does the free-associative network extend? Some dreams manifestly contain childhood impressions, and even seem directly to gratify childish wishes. But such dreams are relatively rare. Using the free-association technique to supplement manifest dream analysis, Freud states that "experiences from childhood also play a part in dreams whose content would never have led one to suppose it" (1900, p. 191). "Botanical Monograph" is such a dream. Freud's analysis focuses particularly upon his childhood association of destroying the book with colored plates, but the cryptic "Cf. my paper on screen memories" association also leads back to a childhood scene, whose significance has been well assessed by Grinstein (1968, ch. 2). Freud "assures" us "that the ultimate meaning of the dream, which I have not disclosed, is intimately related to the subject of the [former] childhood scene" (1900, p. 191). More generally, he concludes that the more comprehensive the analysis of the dream, the more likely one is to discover childhood determinants. At the inductive or evidential level at which he now is proceeding, Freud seemingly is hesitant to conclude that all dreams derive from such determinants, but not too hesitant to suggest, by analogy to his model of hysterical symptom formation, that the "bottom-most" wish fulfilled in dreams invariably is a childish one. We begin to see, too, from Freud's analogy and from his examples, that a certain kind of childish wish is particularly likely to be assigned this bottom-most position: a sexual wish.

Freud effectively demolishes the hypothesis that external or somatic stimuli active during sleep can be significant elements in dream formation or dream explanation. The occurrence of such stimuli is neither frequent nor dependable enough to account for the fact of dreaming, nor does their nature as physical stimuli explain the diverse interpretations they receive in the dream. Why is the alarm-clock buzzer a church bell today while yesterday the same sound signaled the activation of an ejection mechanism in a speeding race car? Clearly it is the demands of the already ongoing narrative, rather than those of the external or somatic stimuli, which are dominant. The narrative shapes the stimulus, rather than vice versa. In fact, the demands of that narrative, and/or the aforementioned wish to protect sleep, most generally simply occlude such stimuli altogether (this evidence is discussed in the next chapter). And, when somatic or external stimuli do play a role in dream construction, i.e., when they can be used in dream explanation, Freud says that they are, like the indifferent residues of the dream-day, "some cheap material always ready to hand . . . in contrast to a precious material which itself prescribes the way in which it shall be employed" (1900, p. 237). In effect, they are "night-residues."

Freud's search for the contents "currently active" (1900, p. 228) in dream formation has left us, so far, with well-defined but relatively minor roles assigned to a number of leading candidates for the position of dream instigator. Most day-residues and the somatic and external stimuli occurring during sleep play only a subsidiary role in dream formation, i.e., they are not considered powerful explanatory concepts in relation to the manifest dream. Freud's remarks have implied some special role for sexual wishes, and for childhood determinants, but no unequivocal statement has yet emerged characterizing the contents whose activity is critical to dream formation or dream explanation. This reticence continues in the final section of chapter V, labeled simply "Typical Dreams." It seems we are in for a disappointing finale. We might rather have preferred to see a section entitled "The True Determinants of Dream Experience."

In fact, we do get at least some of what the latter title might promise. Freud does begin to acknowledge the factor which he finally holds responsible for the formation of dreams: repressed infantile or childhood sexual wishes. What we actually are given at the close of chapter V, then, is an introduction to those "typical" childhood sexual themes which live on in the adult mind and which, almost incidentally, now are being held responsible for certain species of typical dreams. What is important in Freud's account, but obscured by his title, is that "typical" dreams are not really at issue at all; what is most germane to the logic of Freud's argument is that the contents he introduces by reference to the so-called typical dreams are assumed to be those "bottom-most" wishes which ultimately explain any dream.

This logic must explain Freud's selection of "typical" dreams. Among Freud's examples are: embarrassing dreams of being naked (childhood exhibitionism); dreams, accompanied by grief, of the death of a loved one (childhood feelings of sibling rivalry; Oedipal ambivalence to the like-sexed parent); dreams of flying (childhood pleasure in movement, interpreted in a sexual manner); and examination dreams (tests of sexual maturity). Surely another compilation of equally "typical" dreams could have been supplied which would have led us much less surely, if at all, to Freud's high estimation of the role to be accorded early sexual wishes in dream formation and dream explanation.

Moreover, if the sampling bias is disturbing, this proves not to be the most troublesome aspect of his "discovery" of the centrality of childhood sexuality in dream instigation. We learn at the outset of Freud's discussion that infantile sexuality has not been discovered through dreamers' associations to even those "typical" dreams upon which he builds his own argument. What distinguishes the case of each of these typical dreams is that "the dreamer fails as a rule to produce the associations which would in other cases have led us to understand it" (1900, p. 241). Later we are told that "it is but rarely that the material with which the dreamer provides us in associations is sufficient to interpret the dream. It is only by collecting a considerable number of examples of such dreams that we can arrive at a better understanding of them" (1900, p. 275). As was also true of the discovery of wish-fulfillment, Freud's "discovery" of the nature of the wishes ultimately fulfilled by the dream, i.e., of the role of infantile sexuality in dream formation, turns out to be the result of Freud's reference system, rather than of a ruleful application of his method.

Clearly what has happened is something like this: Freud found that dream-elicited free associations often led back to childhood scenes. Yet these scenes, without further interpretation, did not seem to resolve the puzzle of the dreams which stimulated their recall. They were in the nature of *screen memories*, which, like many day-residues, are significant not in and of themselves, but only in light of the additional meanings they carry in disguised form. Thus, they too needed interpretation or translation to some other frame of reference. In this case, however, the translations were not, and, in principle, because of *primal repression*, could not be, supplied by the dreamer. That is, we are no longer dealing with the repression of derivatives of early repressed material but with the repression of that material itself. We are at root bottom. Hence, translations of puzzling childhood scenes must be supplied by the analyst's theory, rather than by the dreamer's associations.[8] In principle, I see nothing wrong with this procedure, if there are, within the analyst's theory, explicit and orderly rules to guide the translation process. The problem is that Freud neither supplies, nor seems to rigorously adhere to, any such set of rules in his dream explanations.

Methodologically, Freud's perception of the need to resort to a theoretically based set of association-translations may well be valid. That is, it seems unlikely that the dreamer's free associations, standing alone and quite uninterpreted, will invariably resolve her or his dreams. They will not often simply "speak for themselves." If this is the case, we have two alternatives: we can immediately and intuitively speak for them or we can slowly and patiently try to build up a set of reasonable rules for their translation to some possibly more useful explanatory frame of reference. Freud seems to have chosen the former alternative. However, I believe the latter alternative to be viable, to be more defensible scientifically, and yet to remain true to the spirit of Freud's discovery of dynamically unconscious influences on dream formation, i.e., to the observation that, as valuable as they are, the dreamer's free associations are not sufficient to explain her or his dream because the

---

[8]Alternatively, one might simply say that, quite apart from the specific hypothesis of repressed infantile sexuality, any psychological explanation in terms of a comprehensive life history always will reach back beyond a point to which the adult in question is privy. Purged of its specifically sexual features, Freud's argument is no more than one for a life-history perspective in the explanation of psychological phenomena. As Sherwood (1969) has argued, this is the distinctive formal property of psychoanalytic explanations. It also can be read as the major substantive contribution of psychoanalysis to psychology: the demonstration that each present situation is defined by the person not only in terms of its recognized, "objective" parameters but also in terms of many earlier situations to which it is automatically and subconsciously related by the mind.

Unfortunately for the argument of chapter V, neither the form nor substance of life-history explanations is well illustrated there. The now-familiar reasons are that Freud chooses not to give us his own life history and feels that those of his patients would introduce too many new issues relating to pathology. However, his later "Rat-Man" (Freud, 1909) and "Wolf-Man" (Freud, 1918; Gardiner, 1971) case histories fill this gap convincingly (see also Sherwood, 1969, who shows the scientific explanatory value of Freud's "psychoanalytic narrative" in the Rat-Man case).

dreamer is not aware, and cannot become aware, of the dream's "bottom-most" determinants.

Thus, summarizing Freud's careful survey of the contents "currently active" in the sleeping mind as revealed by his free-association technique, he has reached some important conclusions: (1) the near-universality of the presence of day-residue material in dream formation; (2) the universality of the principle that meaningful personal concerns, rather than randomly selected trivial impressions, guide the process of dream formation; (3) the minimal significance of sensory or somatic stimuli in dream formation; (4) the generally underestimated but highly significant role childhood impressions play in dream formation; and (5) the inability of the dreamer's own free associations, without their subjection to some process of theoretically generated translation, to completely identify the active contents of the sleeping mind. The last conclusion brings us to the brink of Freud's "Unconscious." At this point, however, we need not abandon the heretofore orderly and scientifically grounded explanatory system Freud has been evolving. I believe that there is nothing in principle to prevent us from both dealing with the realm Freud has brought us to and remaining within the general framework of scientific explanation. In part IV I hope to demonstrate that rules, based on a psychoanalytic understanding of motives and their development, can be written for the translation of free-association statements such that we no longer need be bound by the manifest content of the dreamer's associations in synthesizing her or his dream. These rules may bring us, in a lawful way, to Freud's insight that the best explanation of a dream may transcend the dreamer's own wisdom, may indeed be so "deep" that the dreamer herself/himself is reluctant to accept it (cf. Levy, 1963).

The Transformational Processes of the Sleeping Mind

Chapter V of *The Interpretation of Dreams* attempts to characterize the endpoints of free-association trains and the principles of their interrelatedness. It ends with an intuitive, and controversial, assertion: that behind the empirically determined endpoints, it is necessary to assume the existence of a set of theoretically defined endpoints consisting of infantile sexual wishes. Chapter VI contains the major substantive contribution of Freud's book: the characterization of how the sleeping mind may be hypothesized to transform the *empirically determined* endpoints of free association, now conceived as origins, into the manifest dream, now conceived as the endpoint. "Dream-work" is the generic term for these transformational processes.

Because of the shift back to empirical endpoints, we can accept Freud's characterization of the dream-work in chapter VI without commitment to any particular stance regarding theoretically defined endpoints of free-association chains. That is, because it deals with the more operationally defined analytic phase of the dream-interpretation model, the dream-work argument is largely independent of the wish-fulfillment and infantile-sexuality arguments of earlier chapters. Thus, we find in chapter VI that the analytically defined concept of "latent dream-thoughts," or more simply "dream-thoughts," replaces the synthetically defined concept of "the latent dream." Latent dream-thoughts are simply those thought elements "arrived at by means of our procedure [free association]" (Freud, 1900, p. 277). Dream-work consists of the processes by which these latent dream-thoughts are transformed into manifest dream content. As we shall see later (chapter 15), Freud's characterizations of these processes prove to be sufficiently precise even to permit their translation into structural-mathematical terms.

It is critical to my interpretation of Freud that these transformational processes be understood as cognitive ones. And I think it can be shown that, within the operational and analytic boundaries which he sets for himself in chapter VI, Freud does define dream-work as thought-thought relationships, rather than as relationships of thought with phenomena from some other realm (impulses, instincts, perceptions) or as relationships within another such realm (cf. chapter 3 herein). First, we may note Freud's refutation of the idea that the manifest dream is to be conceived as a perceptual process:

> ... the dream-content seems like a transcript of the dream-thoughts into another mode of expression ... expressed as it were in a pictographic script.... If we attempted to read these characters according to their *pictorial value* instead of according to their *symbolic relation*, we should clearly be led into error. Suppose I have a picture puzzle, a rebus, in front of me. It depicts a house with a boat on its roof, a single letter of the alphabet, the figure of a running man whose head has been conjured away, and so on. Now I might be misled into raising objections and declaring that the picture as a whole and its component parts are nonsensical. A boat has no business to be on the roof of a house, and a headless man cannot run.... But obviously we can only form a proper judgment of the rebus if we put aside criticisms such as these ... and if, instead, we try to replace each separate element by a syllable or word that can be represented by that element in some way or other.... A dream is a picture-puzzle of this sort and our predecessors in the field of dream-interpretation have made the mistake of treating the rebus as a *pictorial composition*.... [Freud, 1900, pp. 277–78, italics added]

The manifest dream, then, is a verbal thought-process cast in pictorial form, rather than a perceptual process per se. In sleep, consciousness, ordinarily "a sense organ for perceptions alone . . . [becomes] a sense organ for a portion of our thought-processes" (1900, p. 574).

What of the underlying dream-thoughts? Are they to be identified with interpretive constructs such as unconscious impulses, or are they simply the verbal thought-elements achieved through the free-association method? In chapter VI, the answer clearly is the latter. Speaking of "the essential dream-thoughts," Freud remarks that "these usually emerge as a complex of thoughts and memories of the most intricate possible structure, *with all the attributes of the trains of thought familiar to us in waking life*" (1900, pp. 311-12, italics added). These thoughts stand "in the most manifold *logical* relations to one another" (1900, p. 312, italics added). In fact, Freud devotes a whole section (C) of chapter VI to considering how the logical relationships assumed to exist among the underlying dream-thoughts can be translated into the more restrictive language of the manifest dream. "The dream-thoughts are entirely rational" (1900, p. 506). In conjuring up a hypothetical example, Freud imagines that dream-thoughts might be something like this: "Since this was so and so, such and such was bound to happen" (1900, p. 315). It is clear that Freud here is considering his points of origin as linguistic and propositional in form, rather than as members of some underlying domain of impulses which is devoid of logic (cf. also 1900, pp. 592-93).[9]

Finally, it is clear that Freud conceives the intermediate dream-work mechanisms themselves as verbal processes: "We may suppose that a good part of the intermediate work done during the formation of a dream . . . proceeds along the line of finding appropriate *verbal transformations* for the individual thoughts" (1900, p. 340, italics added). The dream-work's transformations are from one language to another language (ibid.), and the intervening steps are linguistic as well. Freud remarks that "there is no need to be astonished at the part played by words in dream formation. Words . . . are the nodal points of numerous ideas . . ." (ibid.). Thus dream-work has at its disposal jokes, quotations, songs, proverbs, and the various other forms of verbal wit and association (ibid., pp. 340, 345), including those verbal reversals (black–white, up–down) which prove to be so closely interconnected in experimental free-association tasks (Kent and Rosanoff, 1910; Freud, 1900, pp. 326-29). Even in the immediate search for an appropriate pictorial representation, "the dream-work does not shrink from the effort of recasting unadaptable thoughts into a new *verbal* [italics added] form—even into a less usual one—provided that that process facilitates representation . . ." (Freud, 1900, p. 344). Freud makes the important observation (cf. chapter 9 herein)

[9] In keeping with the more analytic and operational "conflict" model of chapter IV, Freud also notes that "each train of thought is almost invariably accompanied by its contradictory counterpart, linked with it by antithetical association" (1900, p. 312).

that "for the purpose of representation in dreams, the spelling of words is far less important than their sound" (1900, p. 406). That is, it is acoustic, rather than visual, representations of words which constitute the verbal medium of dream-work processes. *Dream-work is, in short, a set of inner-speech processes* (cf. also 1900, p. 574, where it is stated that dream-thoughts "attract consciousness" through qualities attaching to "linguistic symbols").

Now it may be objected that, since Freud's dream-process model is built upon the verbal data of the free-association technique, it hardly could be otherwise than that his characterization of dream processes would stress their verbal nature. In fact, it could be otherwise: the data generated by free association could be interpreted in terms of some other, extraverbal process. The point to be made is simply this: in chapter VI Freud is not performing such interpretations—he is taking the results of the free-association technique at face value. And since that choice has been made, it then does follow that Freud's conceptualization of dream-work will be as a set of verbal-transformation processes. Thus "dream-content seems like a transcript of the dream-thoughts into another mode of expression, whose characters and syntactic laws it is our business to discover by comparing the original and the translation" (Freud, 1900, p. 277).

Let us now consider the specific dream-work mechanisms proposed by Freud. "The first thing that becomes clear to anyone who compares the dream-content with the dream-thoughts is that a work of *condensation* on a large scale has been carried out. Dreams are brief, meagre and laconic in comparison with the range and wealth of the dream-thoughts" (1900, p. 279). Thus, in the specimen dream we have been considering, "'botanical' and 'monograph' found their way into the content of the dream because they possessed copious contacts with the majority of the dream-thoughts, because, that is to say, they constituted 'nodal points' upon which a great number of the dream-thoughts converged . . ." (ibid., p. 283). Another way of expressing the condensation concept is that "each of the elements of the dream's content turns out to have been 'overdetermined'—to have been represented in the dream-thoughts many times over" (ibid.).

A comparable process, not specifically labeled by Freud, is that "individual dream-thoughts are represented in the dream by several elements. . . . [Not only do] associative paths lead from one element of the dream to several dream-thoughts, . . . [they also lead] from one dream-thought to several elements of the dream"[10] (1900, p. 284).

[10]Note the close correspondence between Freud's terminology and that of mathematical structural analysis (cf. chapters 13–15, herein): "nodal *points*," "associative *paths*." It seems likely that Freud performed some sort of schematic reconstructions of dream-work processes such as those I will be proposing (chapter 15). Unfortunately, we

Freud's discussion then moves to several discrete classes of the condensation phenomenon: the nodal point is a *collective image* (i.e., it is identical
with one dream-thought element, which corresponds to a real person, object,
and so on, and comes to "stand for" many other such elements); the nodal
point is a *composite image* (i.e., it is identical with none of the original
dream-thought elements, but unites their features in the fashion of Galton's
[1883] composite photographs); the nodal point is a *compromise* among several dream-thought elements, but lacks a clear "family resemblance" to them.
In the last case, it is not certain, however, that we are dealing strictly with
condensation. Freud says that, in the formation of such "intermediate common entities," "attention is without hesitation *displaced* from what is actually intended on to some neighbouring association" (1900, p. 295, italics
added). On the basis of this reading, we might be justified in asserting that,
for Freud, condensation basically is a process of efficient representation of
many simultaneously active dream-thoughts and that when disguise, rather
than a merely abbreviated expression, is the result, displacement also is involved. And it also seems that, rather than representing discrete processes,
condensation and displacement shade into one another.

The result of the process of displacement is a different "centration" of
the manifest dream than that which is to be found in the dream-thoughts.
Thus, on Freud's own analysis of "Botanical Monograph":

> the central point of the dream-content was obviously the element
> "botanical"; whereas the dream-thoughts were concerned with the
> complications and conflicts arising between colleagues from their pro-
> fessional obligations, and further with the charge that I was in the habit
> of sacrificing too much for the sake of my hobbies. The element "botan-
> ical" had no place whatever in this core of the dream-thoughts, unless it
> was loosely connected with it by an antithesis—the fact that botany
> never had a place among my favourite studies. [1900, p. 305]

The process of displacement itself involves "a transvaluation of all
psychical values" (1900, p. 507).

---

learn that these reconstructions were suppressed: ". . . the easiest way of making those
[dream-work] processes clear and of defending their trustworthiness against criticism
would be to take some particular dream as a sample, go through its interpretation . . .
and then collect the dream-thoughts which I have discovered and go on to reconstruct
from them the process by which the dream was formed—in other words, to complete a
dream-analysis by a dream-synthesis. I have in fact carried out that task for my own instruction on several specimens; but I cannot reproduce them here, since I am forbidden
to do so for reasons connected with the nature of the psychical material involved. . . .
Such considerations interfered less in the *analysis* of dreams, since an analysis could be
incomplete and nevertheless retain its value, even though it penetrated only a small way
into the texture of the dream. But in the case of the *synthesis* of a dream I do not see
how it can be convincing unless it is complete" (1900, p. 310).

> There is never any doubt as to which of the elements of the dream-thoughts have the highest psychical value; we learn that by direct judgment. In the course of the formation of a dream these essential elements, charged, as they are, with intense interest, may be treated as though they were of small value, and their place may be taken in the dream by other elements, of whose small value in the dream-thoughts there can be no question. [1900, p. 306]

The concept of psychic value suggests motivational structures. Structures with high value can be identified, according to Freud, by the facts of their recurrence in the dream-thoughts and that "the different dream-thoughts will, as it were, *radiate out from them*" (1900, pp. 306–7, italics added). Yet displacement can occur in that the "dream can reject elements which are thus both highly stressed in themselves and reinforced from many directions, and can select for its content other elements which possess only the second of these attributes [i.e., are condensed]" (1900, p. 307). This analysis, then, seems to suggest that condensation involves an associative process of foreshortening, while displacement involves processes of motive-structure substitution. They work conjunctively in the sense that condensation may proceed along associative lines which permit such motive substitution but eschew associative lines which preclude it.

Freud speaks, then, of two conditions which "must be satisfied by those elements of the dream-thoughts which make their way into the dream" (1900, p. 308). The first of these conditions refers to the associative connections impinging upon a dream-thought: the dream-thought must be associatively overdetermined. The second of these conditions refers to the intrinsic motivational value of the dream-thought: it must not carry a psychic value likely to generate anxiety were it to achieve conscious representation. Thus if condensation is an expressive "push" toward conscious expression along lines determined by the largest number of associative connections, then displacement is the constraint upon this approach vector that unacceptable thought-contents be "disguised" by transferring their value to associative elements heretofore without significant intrinsic valuation.

The distinction between associative and motivational factors I have drawn in the summary above clearly is implied in this passage by Freud:

> Among the thoughts that analysis brings to light are many which are relatively remote from the kernel of the dream and which look like artificial interpolations made for some particular purpose. That purpose is easy to divine. It is precisely *they* that constitute a connection, often a forced and far-fetched one, between the dream-content and the dream-

thoughts; and if these elements were weeded out of the analysis the result would often be that the component parts of the dream-content would be left not only without overdetermination but without any satisfactory determination at all. [1900, p. 307].

From this passage, we may assume that not all elements in the free-associative network have intrinsic value: some, lying at an associative distance from the manifest dream, have true value—these can be called the "essential dream-thoughts" (1900, p. 311); others (originally called by Freud "collaterals"— [ibid.*n*]), lying between the former elements and the manifest dream, constitute the associative pathway which makes it possible for basic dream-thoughts to find distorted expression in the manifest dream—their value is extrinsic. In communication terms, they don't originate messages, they simply serve as links in a transmission channel (cf. also ibid.).

When we go beyond condensation and displacement, we find that Freud's characterization of dream-work becomes somewhat less clear. He himself states that "dream-displacement and dream-condensation are the two governing factors to whose activity we may in essence ascribe the form assumed by dreams" (1900, p. 308). Yet Freud then devotes much further discussion (ibid., ch. VI, section C *ff.*) to dream-work, and various authors have read out of this lengthy discussion a variety of "mechanisms" supplementing condensation and displacement. The situation is somewhat reminiscent of that in perceptual psychology, where any two lists of Gestalt psychology's "laws" of perceptual organization would agree on a few points but then diverge in their characterization of further laws while still seeming to be talking about the same phenomena. Thus the discussion which follows may not contain items from everyone's favorite list of dream-work mechanisms. It will attempt, however, to be faithful to Freud's overall description of the mental processes operative during dream-formation.

A third factor in dream formation, another constraint upon the selection of material in the manifest dream, is the degree to which a given element lends itself to pictorial representation (1900, pp. 343–44). The manifest form of the dream, normally, is pictorial. The dream-thoughts may be assumed generally not to be pictorial. "I neglect my wife" is a thought/worry/concern whose most basic form probably is not iconic. Cyclamen (or dried specimens thereof) is a concept either whose most basic form is iconic or which certainly lends itself easily to perceptual representation. The dictionary is unlikely to illustrate "neglect" pictorially, although it would be unremarkable for it to give an ostensive iconic definition of cyclamen—in essence: plants/flowers that look like this.

What is involved here is something akin to the concept of codability as developed in psycholinguistic research where, for example, certain hue perceptions must be translated to a verbal form (Brown and Lenneberg, 1954). One pattern of light energy is readily translated as "red," while another finds only an awkward approximation "sort of greenish-yellowish, but more green than yellow." In the dream case, there also is a codability dimension, working in the opposite direction (words to pictures), such that some concepts (e.g., concrete objects) have more facile, precise, and accessible pictorial equivalents than do others (e.g., logical relationships). Freud is saying that favorability attaches, other things equal, to translations of high iconic codability, and that, sometimes at least, abstract notions, such as the ones conveyed linguistically in conjunctions such as "if," "because," and so on simply must be omitted in the translation from concept to percept: "For the most part dreams disregard all these conjunctions, and it is only the substantive content of the dream-thoughts that they take over and manipulate" (1900, p. 312). Some relational concepts are, on the other hand, of sufficient importance that certain conventional transformations have been devised: e.g., "either/ or" = a vagueness of perceptual quality; "similarity" = perceptual fusion.

One important dream-work mechanism, according to some authors, is "symbolization." According to Freud, however, there is no separate symbolizing process:

> there is no necessity to assume that any peculiar symbolizing activity of the mind is operating in the dream-work . . . [rather] dreams make use of any symbolizations which are already present in unconscious thinking, because they fit in better with the requirements of dream-construction on account of their representability and also because as a rule they escape censorship [i.e., serve the goal of displacement]. [1900, p. 349]

Symbols, then, are best conceived as somewhat stereotyped products of the operation of processes with which we already are familiar (including condensation, not mentioned above); they introduce no new process to Freud's characterization of the sleeping mind. Freud allows that these pictorial products may both reveal (express) and conceal (disguise) their conceptual/ motivational referents.

This denial of a separate and unique symbolizing process to the sleeping mind has two important methodological implications. First, it undercuts the essentially arbitrary symbolic interpretations of earlier dream commentators (especially Scherner—1900, pp. 83–87) who propose a "productive" symbolization process during sleep of a capriciously illogical sort. Second, it indicates that the symbolism which does occur in sleep is assimilable to a verbal/ linguistic model of dream-work: "In the case of symbolic dream-interpretation [e.g., Scherner] the key to the symbolization is arbitrarily chosen by the interpreter; whereas in our cases of verbal disguise the keys are generally known *and laid down by firmly established linguistic usage*" (1900, pp. 341-42, italics added).

It is, in fact, knowledge of this linguistic mold in which symbolization is achieved which opens the possibility of decoding dreams "wholly or in part even independently of information from the dreamer" (1900, p. 342). Bearing in mind the unscientific excesses of Scherner's approach, Freud professes to an attitude of "critical caution" (1900, p. 353) in so resolving dream symbols. One begins with the dreamer's associations. Then one may proceed to fill in remaining gaps of the analysis with translations found to be generally applicable in other cases. However, this is an uncertain process, and the ultimate criterion for satisfactory gap-filling lies within the dream itself: *"the correct interpretation can only be arrived at on each occasion from the context"* (ibid., italics added). It is clear, I believe, that Freud wants symbol resolution to be a ruleful process, that he does not mean at this point to open the door to "wild" interpretations of the sort for which he holds Wilhelm Stekel responsible (1900, pp. 350-51). He goes on, in fact, to provide, a set of translation rules governing typical symbolic equivalencies (e.g., king = father).

Unfortunately, these ready-made rules came to obscure the primacy of the free-association technique in successive editions of *The Interpretation of Dreams*. (There was no separate section on generally applicable symbolic translations in the 1900 edition.) They often, but certainly not invariably, involved the reduction of nonsexual images to sexual concepts (stick = penis; but, cf.: king = father). They are often built upon verbal transformations evident in jokes, slang, puns, or acoustic similarities. Formally, however, Freud continued to recognize the priority of free-associative material in dream interpretation: "both in practice and in theory the first place continues to be held by the procedure which I began by describing [i.e., his ch. II] and which attributes a decisive significance to the comments made by the dreamer, while the translation of symbols . . . is also at our disposal as an auxiliary method" (1900, p. 360). The testimony of those who undertook training analyses with Freud (e.g., Stern, 1922) also is that Freud relied "almost exclusively on the free associations of the patient" (Stern, p. 56) for the interpretation of dreams. Freud himself (1925b, p. 128) characterized dream interpretation performed without associations as "unscientific."

Freud's account of dream symbols has been the subject of two major criticisms: its alleged obsession with sexual symbolism and its arbitrariness. As noted above, it is clear that not all dream images of either the typical or idiosyncratic sort are directly resolved by Freud into sexual concepts. He does want to maintain that the nonsexual concepts represented by dream images often fit into a larger context of sexual wish-fulfillment. But, at least in the relatively data-bound account of chapter VI, this is shown to be a plausible emphasis (the sexual instinct is more highly suppressed than any other in the course of human development; thus it is likely to be peculiarly active when we have a chance to "think our own thoughts"), but only an emphasis, not an insistence ("I cannot dismiss the obvious fact that there are numerous dreams which satisfy needs other than those which are erotic in the widest sense of the word: dreams of hunger and thirst, dreams of convenience, etc. [1900, p. 396]").

The charge of arbitrariness is less easily answered. In theory, it is the dream or free associative *context* which should define the symbolism of dream imagery (1900, p. 353). This is true whether one is considering a single dream or trying to derive empirically a general resolution of a commonly appearing dream image. The major problem with Freud's symbol analyses is that his readings of contextual appropriateness tend to be more intuitive than explicitly ruleful. That is, he does supply particular interpretations, and general translation rules, of the form $X = Y$, but there are no clear base rules as to how we achieve interpretations, or form translation rules, of these sorts. One entirely reasonable base rule *is* cited approvingly: if X occurs simultaneously with orgasm or nocturnal emission, consider it as a sexual symbol (1900, pp. 335, 402). But this is a rule relating a dream image to an (at least initially, until incorporation occurs) extra-dream event. The difficulty is that no equally reasonable rules are supplied for using the internal evidence of dream and free-association texts to resolve dream symbols. As plausible as many of Freud's symbol resolutions are, the process he used in achieving them needs to be defined more operationally. It is my belief that this can be done, and I hope to demonstrate (chapter 11) one particular set of rules, which I consider reasonable, for using dream and free-association texts as a basis for contextually defining dream symbols. With rules of this latter sort, there is no reason why symbol decoding following Freud's principle of contextual definition need be at all arbitrary in outcome or intuitive in procedure.

What Freud refers to as "the fourth of the factors which govern the formation of dreams" (1900, p. 405) has an uncertain status as a dream-work mechanism. At times (1900, pp. 313, 490, *n.* 1) it is not so considered, while, at others, it is implied that it is active during sleep (1900, p. 505) and that its demands are active throughout dream formation (1900, pp. 499, 576). This process, *secondary revision* (originally translated in English as *secondary elaboration*), refers to a constraint upon dream formation such that the manifest dream be, other things equal, as coherent and intelligible as possible.

The best examples of secondary revision are seen in comparisons of dreams apprehended, perhaps in an only semi-wakeful way, right after their

occurrence with later reports of the "same" dreams. Partly through intervening interpolations and additions, the original reports tend to become progressively more coherent narratives. It is clear that this process is not unique
to sleep, indeed that its major domain is wakefulness (e.g., Bartlett, 1932).
In this sense, secondary revision seemed to Freud to be a less theoretically
interesting feature of sleeping thought than the dream-work processes so
far enumerated.

Moreover, it is a process whose study is perhaps best pursued outside
the framework of Freud's dream-explanation model (figure 4-2, Schematic
Outline, p. 38). (Whether secondary revision can be derived from this
model is, in fact, the operational form of the question as to whether
secondary revision is a dream-work mechanism.) Freud notes that secondary
revisions may not be "derived from the dream-thoughts," that sometimes "no
material connected with them is to be found in the dream-thoughts" (1900,
p. 489). Even in the more typical case, where there are some connections
back to the dream thoughts, Freud feels that they are not sufficient to
explain the dream interpolation (ibid.). Fortunately, there is an appropriate
empirical paradigm for the study of secondary revision: Bartlett's (1932)
method of repeated reproduction applied to the manifest dream. Secondary
revision is not, therefore, recalcitrant to empirical study in general, only to
analysis in terms of a model built upon the examination of transformations
between latent dream-thoughts and manifest dream imagery. In this basic
sense, it clearly seems not to be a dream-work mechanism.

Why, then, does Freud evidence such ambivalence about the status to
be accorded secondary revision? The answer is, I think, that Freud is being
driven by two conflicting forces: the desire that his newly isolated dream-
work mechanisms be "peculiar to dream-life" (1900, p. 507) and the wish
that dream-work provide a comprehensive explanation of dreams. The former
impulse forces Freud to deny the following waking-type thought operations
to sleep: mathematical calculations; the framing of speech utterance according to logico-grammatical rules; the making of judgments; the drawing of conclusions (1900, pp. 313, 418-19, 445, 450). Dream products may *appear* to
be the outcome of such operations. *In fact*, such products consist of ready-
made fragments in the dream-thoughts which have been used by dream-work
mechanisms. They are not the result of waking-type thought transformations
performed during the state of sleep: "The dream-work is not simply more
careless, more irrational, more forgetful and more incomplete than waking
thought; it is completely different from it qualitatively . . ." (1900, p. 507).

Signs of Freud's ambivalence abound. Freud notes that, at one time, he
considered postulating a separate class of "phantasies during sleep" (1900,
p. 331), a class to be defined by the absence of condensation and displace-

ment, the two essential dream-work mechanisms. Yet he abandoned this concept, based on his judgment that such experience, on closer examination, "showed the same gaps and flaws in its structure as any other" (ibid.). Yet a footnote adds, "Whether rightly I am now [1930] uncertain," (ibid.).

Similarly, the characterization of secondary revision itself vacillates mightily. Early on, we are told, rather grudgingly, that "I will not deny that critical thought-activity which is not a mere repetition of material in the dream-thoughts *does* have a share in the formation of dreams" (1900, p. 313). However, this thought-activity does its work after the dream "has already, in a certain sense, been completed" (ibid.). And yet, Freud later instructs us that this two-stage process of dream construction (first the essential dream, then the secondary revision) "is scarcely probable. We must assume rather that from the very first the demands of this second factor constitute one of the conditions which the dream must satisfy and that this condition, like those laid down by condensation, the censorship imposed by resistance [displacement], and [pictorial] representability, operates simultaneously in a conducive and selective sense upon the mass of material present in the dream-thoughts" (1900, p. 499). The very next sentence, however, tells us that secondary revision is "the least cogent" of those conditions; still later we learn it only "operates to an irregular degree" (1900, p. 507).

Secondary revision designates thought operations "indistinguishable" from those of wakefulness (1900, p. 489). It

> is to be identified with the activity of our waking thought. Our waking (preconscious) thinking behaves toward any perceptual material with which it meets in just the same way in which the function we are considering behaves toward the content of dreams. It is the nature of our waking thought to establish order in material of that kind, to set up relations in it and to make it conform to our expectations of an intelligible whole. [1900, p. 499]

Yet Freud also tells us that secondary revision's role is, in effect, generally an uncreative one—it does not fabricate new logical structures; rather "it exerts its influence principally by its preferences and selections from the psychical material in the dream-thoughts that has already been formed" (1900, p. 491). That is, its prime mode of operation is to select among the dream-thoughts those elements or preconstructed waking fantasies which best suit the "demand" that the dream be "intelligible" (1900, p. 500). This last statement seems to contradict Freud's earlier conclusion that the material underlying secondary revisions may not be found in the dream-thoughts (1900, p. 489).

And so it goes. Freud seems not to be sure whether secondary revision is a somewhat sluggish, *post facto* filling in of dream gaps or an important rational constraint on dream construction from the very outset. A significant motive underlying this conflict seems reasonably clear. Freud is at pains to refute those authors who wish to assimilate dreams to an entirely waking (logical, critical, creative) model of mind (1900, pp. 501-3). He foresees, correctly (e.g., Fromm, 1951), that once waking-type thought operations are permitted to sleep, the will to believe noble things of the human mind will obscure the essentially asocial contents operative in sleep and, therefore, the necessity to postulate "illogical" mechanisms which distort and otherwise modify such contents. That is, the very integrity of Freud's major discoveries is at stake. At this point, any surrender, however small, to rationalism would ultimately serve to put the entire psychoanalytic enterprise in jeopardy.[11]

The motive at the other pole of Freud's conflict is equally obvious: as a careful and scrupulous scientist, he wants to do justice to the facts of dreaming. And, ultimately, it is clear that the facts of dreaming require us to assume that dream-work mechanisms alone do not form the dream, that waking-type thought operations are present, in even greater measure than Freud ever allows, from the onset of dream formation. Put less hypothetically, it is clear that such operations are absolutely required to explain the phenomena of dream experience. The great explanatory power of Freud's dream-work processes is *semantic*. These processes enable us to explain the referents of discrete dream images, to unravel the sources from which we believe their meaning derives. The great explanatory shortcoming of such processes is *syntactic*. They do not explain a central fact of dream experience: how such multidetermined images are put together in the form of coherent dramatic episodes, stories with sensible beginnings, middles, and ends.

Freud's dream-work model of sleeping thought, by itself, considers the serial organization of the dream as unimportant. In

carrying out the work of interpretation . . . we should disregard the apparent coherence between a dream's constituents as an unessential illusion, and . . . should trace back the origin of each of its elements on its own account. A dream is a conglomerate which, for purposes of investigation, must be broken up once more into fragments. [1900, p. 449]

---

[11] Freud could not foresee another outcome: the development of a psychoanalytic ego psychology (Hartmann, 1939) which might preserve the core of his insights while simultaneously permitting greater scope to rationally organized ego functions (see chapter 6).

Free association is, essentially, a technique of semantic resolution of discrete dream elements. It does not explain how these elements are put together. Hence, we must postulate "a psychical force . . . at work in dreams which creates this apparent connectedness, which, that is to say, submits the material produced by the dream-work to a 'secondary revision'" (ibid.). Freud's problem is this: free association, the empirical base of the dream-work mechanisms, treats the dream as a conglomerate. But the dream manifestly is not a conglomerate, but a unity. Thus some additional form of explanation, over and above dream-work, is required if we are to account not only for the particular images of the dream but also for the manner in which they are strung together. This is the evidential basis for Freud's ambivalent feelings about secondary revision.

Freud notes that "the productions of the dream-work . . . *are not made with the intention of being understood*" (1900, p. 341); thus, from a semantic point of view, the serial organization of the manifest dream is irrelevant. *We* must note that the manifest dream experience *is* created under the evident influence of *the intention of coherence of the dramatic narrative*; thus any comprehensive explanation of that experience must invoke waking-type principles of syntactic organization, principles very much like those required to explain the coherence of extended episodes of waking speech and thought (cf. chapter 2 and part III). Freud seems to be correct in his assertion that, in the creation of discrete images, waking intelligibility is not a determinative factor (1900, p. 324). Yet that same argument does not generalize well to the dream experience as a whole.

Freud's faithfulness to the facts of dream experience leads him at one point to acknowledge that

> any one thought, whose form of expression may happen to be fixed for other reasons, will operate in a determinative and selective manner on the possible forms of expression allotted to the other thoughts, and it may do so, perhaps, from the very start—as is the case in writing a poem. [1900, p. 340]

That analogy—dreaming is like writing a poem—seems to me exact. What is required in the explanation of either is no mere filling in of gaps between separately determined images, but an overall plan or "purpose" (Bleuler, 1911) overseeing the creation of a narrative unity.

To imagine the explanatory power of Freud's dream-work mechanisms without such an over-arching purpose, one might consider an example of schizophrenic thought:

I always liked geography. My last teacher in that subject was Professor August A. He was a man with black eyes. I also like black eyes. There are also blue and gray eyes and other sorts, too. I have heard it that snakes have green eyes. All people have eyes. There are some, too, who are blind. These blind people are led about by a boy.... [quoted by Bleuler, 1911, p. 17]

Each phrase here is linked with an adjacent one, but the overall effect is chaotic—geography to teacher to eyes to snakes to blindness to boys. Compare this account with Freud's "Irma" dream, in which the concern about Irma's health—is she well? am I treating her appropriately?—exerts a guiding influence over the whole dream narrative, just as it might have over an extended waking rumination on the same topic. Some of the terms of the discourse may be unfamiliar, but there is no doubt but that it is a discourse.

Is our analysis of Freud's dream-work now complete? Freud states, recollecting his discussions of condensation, displacement, and a concern for pictorial representability, that

the dream-work consists in nothing more than a combination of the three factors I have mentioned—and of a fourth [secondary revision] ... it carries out no other function than the translation of dream-thoughts in accordance with the four conditions to which it is subject.... [1900, p. 445]

It remains, however, to consider the fate of affect during sleep. We have been considering the transformations which ideational elements undergo as the dream is constructed. What about feelings? First we must note their role in Freud's model. Affect is *"attached to the dream-thoughts"* (1900, p. 507, italics added). That is, it is not some free-floating element from another, non-ideational domain. It serves in the role of a modifier of thought-elements, and is an integral part of the thought complex itself (cf. chapter 11). Nonetheless, affective modification of thought structures is conceptually distinguishable from the constituents of those structures proper, and Freud notes one important empirical difference between the fate of dream-thoughts and that of dream-thought affects: affects are less susceptible to displacement and substitution than is ideational material (1900, p. 460). It is for this reason that the interpretation of a dream might well begin with its affect, for it is likely to be "real," even if, in the dream, it most often is attached to an "unreal" ideational element. In the beginning (in the dream-thoughts), there is an affect appropriately matched with a concept or proposition. However, "these two separate entities may be merely *soldered* together and can thus be detached from each other" during dream-formation (1900, p. 462); the concept or proposition is less likely to emerge directly in the dream than is the feeling.

Actually, at least four different possibilities exist for affective charges "carried" (cf. Freud, 1900, p. 468) by trains of underlying dream-thoughts: (1) they are detached from their original referent and displaced to some other one in unmodified form (note that this "displacement," unlike ideational displacement, involves no change in the nature of the original element itself, but refers only to a shift in its point of reference; the active process here is the ideational one, but the effect is an affective recentration); (2) they are altogether suppressed (1900, p. 467); (3) they "at least remain in contact with the ideational material which has replaced that to which the affect was originally attached" (1900, p. 463); (4) they are turned into their opposite— love becomes hate (1900, p. 471).

The inhibition of affect Freud sees "*as the second consequence of the censorship of dreams, just as dream-distortion is its first consequence*" (1900, p. 468). Since this statement aligns affect-inhibition with "displacement," we may assume that the second fate above represents the same mechanism which was elaborated earlier for ideational elements. The technique also is one of revaluation—here from latent value (affect) to a manifest lack of value (no affect). We might, in fact, expand Freud's definition of ideational displacement to include the obliteration in the manifest dream of a motive structure present in the latent dream thoughts as well as the substitution of some other innocuous motive structure for the originating one. Total devaluation is revaluation, also.

The affect-inhibiting process, as Freud notes, is very well illustrated by "Botanical Monograph":

> The thoughts corresponding to it consisted of a passionately agitated plea on behalf of my liberty to act as I chose to act and to govern my life as seemed right to me and me alone [the conversation with Königstein?]. The dream that arose from them has an indifferent ring about it: "I had written a monograph; it lay before me; it contained coloured plates; dried plants accompanied each copy." This reminds one of the peace that has descended upon a battlefield strewn with corpses; no trace is left of the struggle which raged over it. [1900, p. 467]

The reversal alternative is the most interesting theoretically. Affective reversals are plausible considering both their linguistic interconnectedness ("hate" as a frequent response to the associative stimulus "love") and every-day observations of how "opposite" feelings often succeed one another or coexist at one and the same time. The question raised by this alternative is whether it remains an affective modification (a shift of charge on a given thought-element), or whether it does not shade into becoming a motivational-structural one (a shift in the thought-element constituents, themselves). Changing, in a given situation, from feeling happy to feeling sad is one thing, but Freud seems to be talking more about love-hate reversals, i.e., reversals of the structure of the situation itself. I, therefore, am inclined to see Freud's typical case of "affect-reversal" as a motivational shift, a displacement in the original sense, in which a new motive concept ("I hate X") carries the meaning of an old one ("I love X").

Our discussion of the fate of dream-thought affect has, thus far, dwelt upon the displacement mechanism. Affect presumably seldom exists in like profusion as ideas, which must, perforce, be condensed. However, it is inter-esting to note Freud's statement that "sources of affect which are capable of producing the same affect come together in generating it" (1900, p. 480, italics omitted).

This, then, is Freud's characterization of the transformational processes of the sleeping mind. How central a concept is dream-work in Freud's explanation of dreams? Freud states:

> At bottom, dreams are nothing other than a particular *form* of thinking, made possible by the conditions of the state of sleep. It is the *dream-work* which creates that form, and it alone is the essence of dreaming—the explanation of its peculiar nature. [1900, pp. 506–7, *n.* 2]

Thus, my earlier claim that Freud's dream-work mechanisms are described in a sufficiently exact way to permit their mathematical definition, if true, means that the heart of Freud's theory of dream explanation can be opera-tionalized. That, in turn, would represent a very significant advance for both dream psychology and psychoanalysis. In chapter 15, I will attempt to demonstrate how such operationalization can be achieved.

Yet, as heady as this prospect is, we need also to remind ourselves that, while dream-work may be the key to explaining the "peculiar" features of dreaming—the compromise images which bear no clear relation to our ordinary perceptual experience, the feelings which seem so inappropriately related to objects, etc.—it hardly explains all the significant characteristics of dream experience. *In particular, it proves unable to explain the thematic coherence of the dream.* And, if the bizarre, separately considered elements of the dream require explanations, so too does the fact that these elements are strung, almost miraculously, into a tight dramatic narrative. But that, seemingly, is another story (cf. chapter 8).

Freud's Model: A Topographic-Economic View of Mind

In chapter VII of *The Interpretation of Dreams*, Freud's final and most difficult chapter, he rewrites chapters IV to VI at a more abstract level. His concern is to elaborate a model of mind, its contents and processes, both asleep and awake. Particular bits of dream data now recede to the background, and the argument no longer proceeds by citation of copious examples, but more from empirical and theoretical generalizations. Freud ultimately arrives at two interrelated models: the "topographic" one, which distinguishes three mental systems—Conscious (Cs), Preconscious (Pcs), and Unconscious (Ucs)— in terms of their accessibility to conscious representation and their own inner patterns of organization, and the "economic" one, which characterizes the distribution of "psychic energy" among and within these systems. Essentially, the topographical model is a structural one, designed to explain the hierarchical organization and long-run continuity of behavior, while the economic model is a dynamic one, designed to account for the fluidity and variability of behavior (cf. Hilgard, 1962).

Briefly, my evaluation of these models is as follows. The topographical model generally is considered to have been superseded by Freud's better-known and more highly regarded "structural" model (Ego, Id, Super-Ego; Freud, 1923*a*). However, the topographical model strikes me as a reasonable derivation from the more empirical of Freud's analyses of the results of his free-association model of dream-explanation, as he presents these results in chapters V and VI. For that reason, it still is of unique value in the attempt to explain dream phenomena from a scientific point of view.[12]

The economic model, on the other hand, grows out of the more tendentious portions of Freud's arguments in chapters IV and V, and, as Freud now first reveals in chapter VII, ultimately stems from an attempt to impose a model generated in another domain upon dream data. Furthermore, neither the phraseology nor the substance of this model seem compatible with

---

[12]In this regard, it is interesting to note the almost total convergence of Freud's model, built over seven decades ago upon observations of the mind unencumbered by sensory input, with that of John Lilly (1972*b*), whose data base (contemporary experiments in sensory deprivation) is conceptually similar.

contemporary evidence and theory in scientific psychology. Nor, ultimately, do I believe the model even to be necessary for the explanation of dreams.

Freud fittingly begins his model construction with several empirical generalizations:

(1) Memory "seems quite especially incapable of retaining a dream and may well have lost precisely the most important parts of its content" (1900, p. 512). Now that we know how much dreaming we actually do every night of our lives (see chapter 5), this statement seems even more correct than when Freud wrote it. Freud assumes that an active censorship is responsible for this forgetting, i.e., that the forgetting is motivated. It is not clear to me that this can be a general cause of our massive failure to retrieve our dreams (see chapter 9), although it may be a factor in selected cases. From his own assumption, however, Freud poses an interesting question: if the dream is subject to such intense *post facto* interference or censorship, how did it ever get dreamt in the first place? He concludes the conditions of sleep and wakefulness must be different, in particular, that censorship must be more relaxed in sleep than in wakefulness. Additionally, it is assumed, from Freud's dreamwork analyses, that there are more ways to evade censorship (e.g., displacements, compromise-condensations) in sleep than are characteristic of waking mental functioning.

(2) The free-association analyses also are felt to have revealed "that, when conscious purposive ideas are abandoned, concealed purposive ideas assume control of the current of ideas . . ." (1900, p. 531). This characterization of free association also is assumed to apply to the sleeping mind, where "conscious purposive ideas" are likewise absent. Analyses of the seemingly trivial or arbitrary nature of free-associative thinking also have revealed "that superficial associations are only substitutes by displacement for suppressed deeper ones" (ibid.). This characterization also is generalized by Freud to the sleeping mind, whose manifest dream products seemingly are the epitome of arbitrary or superficial logic.

(3) As in daydreams, in sleep, also, wishes seem to be potent instigators of fantasy experience.

(4) However, in the fantasies of sleep, thoughts are objectified: "their ideational content . . . [is] transformed from thoughts into sensory images, to which belief is attached and which appear to be experienced" (1900, p. 535).

Based in part on these generalizations, Freud proposes a "spatial" model of mind. The "space" is psychical space. The model's only assumption in reference to its spatial properties is that they are isomorphic with the temporal sequence in which stimuli are processed by the mind (cf. chapter 9). In Freud's schematic drawings (1900, pp. 537, 538, 541), the perceptual and motor systems are at opposite ends of a boxlike structure and the "precon-

FIGURE 4-3

Freud's Topographic Model

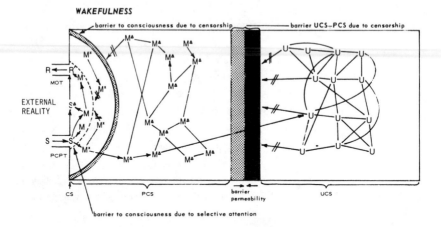

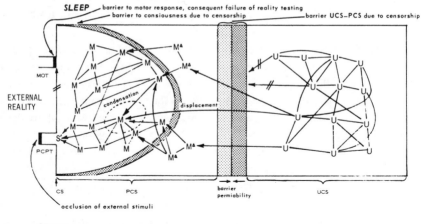

LEGEND

S   external stimulus   Sᴬ conscious association
S' percept identified as real   R' motor intention
R   motor response   →associative connection, primarily one way
—associative connection, bilateral   ⫫blocked associative pathway due to barrier
M memorial associations readily available to CS
M* memorial associations not censored but irrelevant to task at hand
Mᴬ memorial associations subject to censorship but potentially available (as via free association)
U unconcious / unavailable wishes, fantasies, etc.

scious" lies farther from the perceptual processor than does the "unconscious." I find this arrangement confusing, and have, therefore, supplied my
own schematic drawing of the topographical model (figure 4-3). My version
essentially cuts Freud's boxlike structure in half, and bends his right-hand

section back 180° so that the perceptual and motor systems now are adjacent to one another, jointly facing, to the left, external reality, in the service of perceptual-motor adjustments. The far-right-hand side of my version consists of the unconscious system, i.e., that system farthest removed from the day-to-day search for such adjustments.

As Freud notes, the topographical model is a directional one, by virtue of the presence of its sensory and motor apparatuses: "all our psychical activity starts from stimuli (whether internal or external) and ends in innervations [discharges]" (1900, p. 537). And, as we shall see, it is the directionality of their mental processing which best discriminates sleep and wakefulness. Freud's model is explicitly focused on the nature of this discrimination, which is the most basic problem of dream psychology. What *is* so different about dreaming that its products seem so puzzling to the waking mind?

We may begin a detailed consideration of the model by noting its most radical feature: consciousness, the whole topic of many earlier cognitive psychologies, is, to Freud, essentially a sensory process, turned either outward (external stimuli, somatic stimuli) or inward (psychic stimuli). Consciousness is *"a sense-organ for the perception of psychical qualities"* (1900, p. 615). As a sensory process, consciousness has no memory: "our memories—not excepting those which are most deeply stamped on our minds—are in themselves unconscious. They can be made conscious; but there can be no doubt that they can produce all their effects while in an unconscious condition" (1900, p. 539). The psychology of consciousness no longer is synonymous with the psychology of thinking; the memorial or associative structures which guide our behavior are either unrecognized (system Preconscious) or unrecognizable (system Unconscious).

With certain contemporary addenda, the waking situation, according to Freud, is something like this. The sensory system faces outward to external reality, but also is capable of sensing inner thoughts and feelings. The latter elements, however, are stratified in such a way that not all of them are equally susceptible to conscious awareness. Most eligible are those falling within a barrier of selective attention dictated by an intention in relation to external reality. Other thoughts are uncensored, but irrelevant to that intention. Still other thoughts, feelings, and fantasies are kept from consciousness by an active wish against their expression, but they are, in principle, accessible. Freud's feelings of guilt over the neglect of his wife (the "Botanical Monograph" associations) might, for example, fall here. These thoughts tend to be more loosely, i.e., diffusely, organized than those nearer system Conscious. All elements not now actually in system Cs, but potentially retrievable to it, are Pcs. Still other thoughts, feelings, and fantasies, however, have been subjected to repression, and are Ucs. These thought-elements are still more diffusely organized than those in system Pcs. Though repressed, they remain "active," i.e., press for the achievement of sensory awareness and motor expression. By and large, the fulfillment of this goal is blocked in the waking state. Because of a differential permeability of the barriers into and out of system Ucs, however, they are capable of being stimulated by certain strong impressions of the dream-day. Thus, in one of Freud's case histories, the hearing of a tale of cruel punishment stimulated the patient's childishly hostile wishes to his father (Freud, 1909). The topographic direction in that case would be Cs →Pcs →Ucs. The more usual waking outcome is Cs (sensory) → Pcs (relevant memorial associations) →Cs (motor). In either case, thought begins with a perceptual experience in system Cs, and the direction of subsequent stimulus processing is "progressive" (Freud, 1900, p. 542).

In sleep, the perceptual and motor systems to the outside world are shut down, and system Cs primarily senses thought elements derived from inner experience. The primary direction of thought, topographically, is "regressive," i.e., Ucs →Pcs →Cs. Unconscious thought-elements are able, due to the partial relaxation of the barrier separating them from Pcs thought complexes, to transfer (displace) themselves upon these complexes, and by means of them, move toward some conscious expression. Pcs thought elements of "great sensory force" (1900, p. 547) also exert an attracting force on Ucs thoughts. Within system Pcs itself, there is greater freedom of combination than in wakefulness: logical relevance no longer holds sway as gatekeeper to system Cs, nor is motivated reluctance to entertain Pcs thoughts as potent as it was. Pcs thought complexes carrying Ucs meaning are subject to displacement, and the end product of the thought process is a sensory image which condenses a number of lines of thought emanating from different complexes of this sort. The sensory image leads to no motor response, but is accepted as real (is hallucinatory), because that state of the motor system which makes action and reality-testing possible is precluded by conditions of sleep (Freud, 1917b).[13] Thus, sleeping thought *ends* where waking thought begins, with a percept which we believe to represent external reality.

The essence of Freud's topographical distinctions between waking and sleeping thought might be summarized as follows:

(1) In wakefulness, the nature of thought is dictated by external reality; in sleep, it is dictated by inner thoughts and fantasies. The mind is "turned in a different direction" in the two states.

(2) In sleep, the ways in which mental elements are organized, the rules

---

[13] It also follows from the active motor inhibition of the dream state, an hypothesis fully confirmed by recent experimental research (chapter 9), that whatever expression system Ucs achieves in sleep is relatively "harmless" (Freud, 1900, pp. 567–68).

governing their connections with one another, and their accessibility to consciousness are different than the conditions which obtain within wakefulness.

From the topographical sense in which sleeping thought is regressed, Freud goes on to propose two additional ways in which "regression" characterizes dreams. It is at this point that economic considerations begin to dictate operations within the general topographic framework evolved above. Dreams are *temporally* regressed (they begin with infantile or childhood wishes and fantasies) and they are *formally* regressed (they use "childish" means of expression). Dreaming is, in fact, "on the whole an example of regression to the dreamer's earliest condition, a revival of his childhood, of the instinctual impulses which dominated it and of the methods of expression which were then available to him" (1900, p. 548).[14]

It is, in fact, only now, while model-building, that Freud becomes fully explicit about the nature of the contents assumed to instigate, and explain, the dream: *"My supposition is that a conscious wish can only become a dream-instigator if it succeeds in awakening an unconscious wish with the same tenor and in obtaining reinforcement from it . . . . a wish which is represented in the dream must be an infantile one"* (1900, p. 553). In young children, this wish may be preconscious; in adults, it is always unconscious (repressed; hence sexual in nature or implication). Regarding those dreams in which other, more contemporary wishes seem, alone, to be fulfilled, Freud feels that "some small peculiarity in the dream's configuration will serve as a finger-post to put us on the track of the powerful ally from the unconscious" (ibid.).

The sense in which the "Irma" and "Botanical Monograph" interpretations are fundamentally misleading specimens of psychoanalytic dream interpretation now is quite clear. The preconscious wishes stressed in those interpretations were, in fact, very much like day-residues. Specifically, they were recent waking impressions either with sufficient force to remain active in sleep and establish contact with like-tenored unconscious wishes or with suf-

---

[14] In this view, schizophrenic hallucinations might be seen as formally, temporally, but only partially topographically, regressed. The endpoint of the Ucs → Pcs → Cs regression is not a sensory image, but the acoustic verbal processes which, in dreams, immediately precede the final topographic step backward.

It should be noted here that my segregation of "topographical" and "economic" models, and my conceptualization of "topographic regression," are not identical to Freud's (cf. Freud, 1915). I have made my presentation of the topographical model contain, essentially, those features of chapter VII which I feel are compatible with Freud's actual dream data-base and with contemporary models in cognitive psychology (see chapter 9). My presentation of the economic model, on the other hand, makes it the repository of those features of Freud's overall modeling which I find to be unsupported by dream data, unnecessary, and incompatible with more recent models of human information-processing.

ficient freshness to be recruitable by like-tenored unconscious wishes casting about for some disguised way of achieving representation. Behind each adult dream lies a childish, unconscious wish which "is as such quite incapable of entering the preconscious and . . . can only exercise any effect there by establishing a connection with an idea which already belongs to the preconscious, by transferring its intensity on to it and by getting itself 'covered' by it" (1900, p. 562). It is because the dream instigator is a repressed unconscious wish that the peculiar dream-work mechanisms of sleep must be invoked (1900, p. 598) and also that the dreamer's own associations are insufficient to lead us to the explanation of the dream.

On what empirical base does the postulation that the dream instigator invariably is a repressed infantile wish rest? It turns out that it is not dream data which are responsible for this hypothesis at all. Rather, the data now are being forced into the Procrustean bed of the preconceived economic model, in which only unconscious contents have the force to instigate thought sequences in sleep.

The economic model views mind as an energy system, and it is concerned with how energy is displaced, discharged, and contained. The goal of all this tension-regulation is to rid the central processing mechanism of disturbing stimuli (1900, p. 565). In sleep, external stimuli no longer are significant sources of such disturbance, and neither, it is imagined, are the recent residues traceable to such stimuli. Whatever "energy" remains in system Pcs is assumed to be invested in one major concern: the preservation of sleep. Within this model, there is only one possible source of stimuli capable of engaging the sleeping mind from its basal torpor: system Ucs. We now see why, despite its shaky empirical justification (ch. IV), Freud has been so insistent about wishes, particularly infantile sexual wishes (ch. V), as the ultimate sources of dreaming. These positions have not been required by Freud's data, but dictated by his model. Given Freud's economic model, wish-fulfillment makes eminently better sense than it does as an empirical generalization. Given this model, repressed wishes are the only conceivable stimuli sufficiently potent to engage the sleeping mind.

But what, then, is the justification of this model? Basically, it comes from Freud's researches with psychoneurotic patients (e.g., Breuer and Freud, 1895) and from an earlier, unpublished model he had developed from, essentially, that data base (Freud, 1954). Freud is candid about this relationship:

> . . . in my account of dream-psychology I have been unable to follow the historical development of my own views. Though my own line of approach to the subject of dreams was determined by my previous work on the psychology of the neuroses, I had not intended to make use of

the latter as a basis of reference in the present work. Nevertheless I am constantly being driven to do so, instead of proceeding, as I should have wished, in the contrary direction and using dreams as a means of approach to the psychology of the neuroses. [1900, p. 588]

The interrelatedness of Freud's model of dream formation and his model of symptom formation often is considered as one of the strengths of either model considered separately. Indeed, Freud makes such an argument himself (1900, p. 568-69). But, at least insofar as his energetic model is concerned, it turns out that the convergence is a rather forced one, as Freud himself acknowledges (1900, p. 606): When it comes to discussions of the role and kinds of wishes in dream formation, Freud notes that filling the numerous "gaps in the treatment of my theme . . . would involve my basing myself on material that is *alien to the subject of dreams*" (ibid., *n*. 2, italics added). Thus, when the topographical model is reformulated in terms of a distinction between *primary* and *secondary processes*, we need to understand that this shift has been dictated neither by empirical or theoretical concerns arising within the dream-domain itself. In particular, we no longer have any simple reading out of the implications of Freud's free-associative dream-explanation model, but rather an arbitrary assimilation of the data generated by that model to another explanatory context suggested by another behavioral phenomenon.

Basically, the economically-conceived primary-process model proposes that, in infancy, disturbing organic stimuli initially are disposed of by the hallucination of a suitable "experience of satisfaction" (1900, p. 565). When this hallucinatory avenue of tension discharge proves inadequate, thought and action arise as "roundabout" but "expedient" paths of tension management. This is the secondary process. The relevance of this dichotomy to sleep is that "what once dominated waking life, while the mind was still young and incompetent, seems now to have been banished into the night. . . . *Dreaming is a piece of infantile mental life that has been superseded*" (1900, p. 567). The objectification of wish-fulfillments in sleep is an infantile solution to the problem of tension management.

Whatever the plausibility of the economic model in the explanation of hysterical or other psychoneurotic symptoms, as students of dreaming we have the right to expect an independent justification in the dream case. No such justification is supplied by Freud. He rightly concludes that "if such a thing as a system Ucs exists . . . , dreams cannot be its only manifestation" (1900, p. 568). And the case for topographical generalization from neurosis to dreams, or dreams to neurosis, seems fairly solid. But Freud includes the economic model in his conclusion: "every dream may be a wish-fulfillment, but apart from dreams there must be other forms of abnormal wish-fulfillments. And it is a fact that the theory governing all psychoneurotic symptoms culminates in a single proposition, which asserts that *they too are to be regarded as fulfillments of unconscious wishes*" (1900, pp. 568–69). But this is rather disingenuous, for the dream conclusion is a forced overgeneralization from symptom-theory in the first place. And, as already has been noted, the imposition of the economic model on dream data (the energization of the sleeping mind derives solely from repressed infantile wishes) makes for none too pretty a fit with those data.

Moreover, as a number of observers recently have noted, the assumptions of the economic model—in any domain—are rather difficult to assimilate to contemporary models of explanation in psychology (see also chapter 6). All this talk of "cathexes" and "counter-cathexes," of "mobile" and "bound" "psychic energy," and so on, has the ring of an unrealistic set of hypothetical constructs rather than that of an empirically generated set of intervening variables (MacCorquodale and Meehl, 1948). The language of nineteenth-century mechanics surely cannot be taken as a literal description of the mind's operations, and, taken metaphorically, it seems equally unhelpful.

Nor is it clear that Freud really needs such a model. The energization of the sleeping mind, as well as that of the waking mind, now seems to be a "given," rather than some extraordinary circumstance requiring an explanation. Mind and brain are continuously active in sleep and wakefulness (see chapter 5 and part III). What we need to explain is not the *fact*, but the *direction*, of their activity.[15] The structures of the topographic viewpoint—which can be conceived as being either associative and/or motivational in form and which can carry "charges," i.e., be characterized in terms of their quality and quantity—are sufficient to describe the directive qualities of sleeping thought. No additional "energy source" is required. We need not look at the dream as a "safety valve" for the controlled discharge of unconscious energy during sleep (1900, p. 579). That view is quite unsupported by research on "dream-deprivation" (see chapter 5), which indicates no intensification of the conscious indicators of unconscious contents (i.e., no neurotic symptoms brought about by REM deprivation). Rather, why not simply think of the dream as a reflection of the structural situation of the sleeping mind—of the simultaneous

---

[15] In explaining dreams in terms of energizing psychic stimuli, Freud repeats the error of the earlier theorists he has criticized for explaining dreams in terms of energizing external or somatic stimuli. With them, he assumes that discrete stimuli of some sort are needed to set the sleeping mind in motion. The only point of disagreement between Freud and the earlier theorists is whether these periodically disruptive stimuli are exogenous or endogenous to mind. In both cases, mind is, in essence, passive by nature, and active only when forced to be so.

activity of a number of competing thought-elements with differential access to consciousness and different kinds of interconnectednesses than characterize the determinants of most waking thoughts? There is no need to seek explanations "in relations of energy of which we have no knowledge" (1900, p. 577).

For what is added, really, to the account of purposive or motivational structures by conceptualizing their action in terms of psychic energy? For instance, consider the following statement by Freud:

> starting from a purposive idea, a given amount of excitation, which we term "cathectic energy," is displaced along the associative paths selected by that purposive idea. A train of thought which is "neglected" has *not received* this cathexis; a train of thought which is "suppressed" or "repudiated" is one from which this cathexis has been *withdrawn*. In both cases they are left to their own excitations. Under certain conditions a train of thought with a purposive cathexis is capable of attracting the attention of consciousness to itself and in that event, through the agency of consciousness, receives a "hypercathexis." [1900, p. 594]

As far as I can see, the energy language is a gratuitous and entirely circular supplement to the structural/associative description on which it is grafted. The only points where it adds anything to Freud's descriptions is by way of its arbitrary and erroneous assumption that psychic energy in sleep is supplied only by repressed infantile wishes. It is not Freud's data which drive him from his spatial metaphors to the energetic ones of "*processes of excitation*" and "*modes of its discharge*" (1900, p. 610); it is only his attempt to establish the hegemony in the dream realm of propositions arrived at in the study of psychopathological phenomena.

From a structural point of view, there also is no inherent necessity to take dream explanations back to infantile scenes of a sexual or any other sort. There no longer is the question of these scenes alone having the power to activate the sleeping mind. Rather, it becomes an empirical question as to how far back free associations, which because of the interrelatedness of our life experiences always *can* be traced back to infancy or childhood, *need* to be traced back in order to explain particular dreams. The requirements of scientific explanation, rather than those of preconceived theory, should dictate the terms in which dream explanations are to be framed. It may be that the scientific requirements are, in certain cases, quite compatible with the explanation of dreams or symptoms in terms of repressed infantile sexuality (e.g., Freud, 1909, 1918). In other situations, infantile sexuality may be, from an explanatory point of view, a quite gratuitous and unnecessary assumption.

Conclusion: The Current Viability of Freud's Concepts and Models

Freud's topographical model (figure 4-3, p. 78), as I have presented it, is a logical outcome of the application of the method of free association to the analysis of dream experiences (figure 4-2, Schematic Outline, p. 38). It is this method which enables us to establish gradations of accessibility of mental contents to consciousness, including those for contents which we must rulefully infer from empirical association endpoints and hence designate as "unconscious." It is this same method which enables us to characterize the associative interconnections among these contents and to describe such associative mechanisms as condensation and displacement. The topographical model is an abstract representation of the stage on which we can trace out the connotative meaning of different dream images and then reconstruct the context from which, and the mechanisms by which, these dream images have been created.

As it is based on the free-associative technique, this model gives us a way to rulefully use *data* to determine roles in particular scenarios acted upon this stage. Thus, I believe it to be, in principle, a fully operational model, and hope to show below (part IV) that it can, in fact, provide the scaffolding of a rigorously empirical approach to dream meaning, dream formation, and dream explanation.

Freud's economic model, as I have presented it, on the other hand, is an arbitrary imposition on dream and associative data of other observations and of Freud's obsession with arriving at a unified, mechanical theory of dreams, neurosis, and human behavior in general. The wish-fulfillment hypothesis, the notion that repressed infantile sexual wishes instigate dreams, and the energetic characterizations of "primary" and "secondary" processes are not generated by, but are forced upon, the data in the free-association matrix. It is as if Freud is not content, as when proposing the topographic model, merely to set the stage and to identify possible actors and roles to be enacted upon it. He insists that an externally conceived script be followed, in which the infantile sexual wish always is the protagonist and preconscious thought-elements always are bit-players. It is the energy postulates of his economic model which dictate these scripts. I have tried to indicate that Freud's economic model, and its sequelae in his dream psychology, are arbitrary, unwarranted, and, ultimately, unnecessary.

As useful as the topographical model is for explaining particular dream images, I also have attempted to show that it proves unable to explain their serial order, i.e., the coherence of the manifest dream. Evidently, additional explanatory principles are required. Yet we might note here that it would not be inconsistent with the broad outlines of the topographical model to include within system Pcs a set of syntactic structures guiding dream utterance which are much like those unrecognized rules we all follow in organizing waking narratives. Freud does characterize the contents of system Pcs, and their transformations, as verbal in nature. Thus, it does not seem out of the question that some kind of coordination might be achieved between the explanation of language-behavior in wakefulness and the explanation of the "language-behavior" of dreams. Perhaps in purging Freud's dream model of its surplus, energetic meanings and making it more fully consistent with other contemporary, operational models of mind, we have facilitated this necessary rapprochement of the two disciplines which have contributed most, and have the most to contribute, to our understanding of mind—dream psychology and linguistics (see chapter 8).

CHAPTER 5

Psychophysiological Dream Research

Since 1953, the study of dreams has developed largely within the confines of a broader field most commonly known as "sleep and dream research." The linkage of dreams with objectively defined states of sleep has been the distinctive feature of this new alignment of dream psychology. The association has been, in quantitative terms, at least, an incredibly productive one for experimental dream psychology, which has undergone enormous growth from its rudimentary state at the close of the first half of the twentieth century (Ramsey, 1953).

The event responsible for this momentous alteration in the course of dream psychology was Aserinsky and Kleitman's discovery of the cyclically recurring stage of REM sleep[1] and of its correlation with reports of vivid, visual dreaming (1953). Since then, most "dream" research has made some use of Aserinsky and Kleitman's discovery. Often, the link to dreams has been implicit: subjects in an investigation are not awakened to report dreams, and may not even be humans capable of making such reports; the assumption simply is made that, since one is studying REM sleep, one also is studying the

---

[1] In practice, REM sleep is identified by the concurrence of: (a) a tonic, low-voltage irregular EEG activity; (b) almost total tonic suppression of neck and chin EMG; (c) intermittent phasic REMs. Rechtschaffen and Kales (1968) have edited a standard handbook for scoring stage REM and the several different stages of non-REM sleep.

"dreaming process" or "dreaming state." Thus Hartmann's book, *The Biology of Dreaming* (1967), is built largely around observations of REM sleep. On other occasions, the link to dreams has been more explicit: subjects are awakened during objectively defined sleep periods (in terms of EEG, EMG, or REM activity, etc.) and asked to recount their preawakening mental activity (if any). Sometimes the object of these latter studies is the further refinement of psychophysiological correlations (does the direction of eye-movement activity, for example, correlate with the direction of reported "looking" behavior in the dream?); sometimes the psychophysiological method simply defines the collection of a dream dependent variable in a study of the effects of another "psychological" variable (for instance, how do REM dreams change as a function of systematically varied presleep levels of activity or stress?).

This literature has, by now, been reviewed so many times that it hardly seems necessary to repeat the process here.[2] Indeed, it has seemed to me in recent years that review articles have proliferated at a rate almost greater than that of original research worthy of review. In any event, it is my intention here to consider the literature on inferred dreaming (the "dream state," "the dreaming process," i.e., REM sleep) hardly at all, and that on psychophysiologically labeled dream reports only in a brief and highly selective way. The exclusions are not, perhaps, quite so drastic as the previous statement implies, since various psychophysiological observations are referred to, where relevant, elsewhere throughout this volume. The question under consideration here, however, is a limited one: what research findings have been made which have immediate relevance to a cognitive model of the dream process (cf. Foulkes, 1973; Foulkes and Vogel, 1974)?

Significant Empirical Observations

The first contribution of objective, psychophysiological dream study has been the demonstration that dreaming is a pervasive human activity. REM sleep consumes roughly a fifth to a fourth of all human sleep. Young-adult subjects

[2]On sleep, see: Anthony Kales, ed., *Sleep: Physiology and Pathology* (Philadelphia: Lippincott, 1969); Frank Freemon, *Sleep Research: A Critical Review* (Springfield, Ill.: C. C Thomas, 1972); and Ernest Hartmann, *The Biology of Dreaming* (Springfield, Ill.: C. C Thomas, 1967) and *The Functions of Sleep* (New Haven: Yale University Press, 1973). On dreams, see: David Foulkes, *The Psychology of Sleep* (New York: Scribner's, 1966); Richard Jones, *The New Psychology of Dreaming* (New York: Grune & Stratton, 1970); and Allan Rechtschaffen's chapter in F. McGuigan and R. A. Schoonover, eds., *The Psychophysiology of Thinking* (New York: Academic Press, 1973). Elliot Weitzman is editing a series entitled *Advances in Sleep Research* for Spectrum Publications, Inc.,

report dreams on 80–100% of awakenings from such sleep. Non-REM awakenings produce reports of dreams (if dreams are defined as any mental activity occurring during sleep) on 20–60% of experimental trials. Awakenings during the brief sleep-onset transitional period (the so-called "hypnagogic" state) produce dream reports on 90–100% of experimental trials. Clearly, one cannot equate dreaming with REM sleep, for there is too much dream-like activity outside of stage REM. If, however, one did accept even *this cautious, conservative estimate of the incidence of dreaming, dreaming is something we each spend roughly one and a half hours doing each day.* This is probably as much time as many humans spend, for example, using or attending to speech during an average day. In studying dreams, then, we are not considering some marginal human phenomenon. We are studying a general and highly pervasive activity of human mind, one which in sheer quantitative terms must be very near the top of the list of phenomena to be explained by any general account of human experience. The evidence of recent research, then, makes Freud's choice of dreams as the basis of a general model of mind look like a not at all unreasonable one.

The next contribution of recent psychophysiological studies has been to indicate that the "state" of sleep is heterogeneous. Specifically, it has been found that there are different stages of sleep and sleep-onset, and that these stages are associated with discriminably different sorts of manifest dreams.[3]

That reports from different stages of sleep can be reliably discriminated from one another does not necessarily indicate the bases of these discriminations. We still do not have a compelling set of descriptive criteria which indicate how mentation differs across the sleep cycle. Non-REM reports, for example, often have been characterized as "thoughtlike" and REM reports as "dreamlike." But most non-REM reports are, in fact, visual rather than "conceptual" in their representational aspect, and Bosinelli et al. (1968) showed that REM/non-REM discriminations were achieved more easily on a relative, rather than an absolute, basis, since many non-REM reports met all formal

---

and more recent contributions also may be reviewed by consulting *Sleep Bulletin* (noncritical abstracts of the world's literature on sleep and dreams), *Sleep Reviews* (critical reviews of selected contributions to this literature), and *Sleep Research* (an annual compendium of the foregoing, along with abstracts of all papers presented to annual meetings of the Association for the Psychophysiological Study of Sleep), all of which are published by the Brain Information Service of the Brain Research Institute, University of California at Los Angeles. The proceedings of the European Society for Sleep Research are published by S. Karger, Basel.

[3]For example, Foulkes, 1962; Rechtschaffen, Verdone, and Wheaton, 1963; Monroe, Rechtschaffen, Foulkes, and Jensen, 1965; Foulkes and Vogel, 1965; Vogel, Foulkes, and Trosman, 1966; Foulkes, Spear, and Symonds, 1966; Bosinelli, Bagnaresi, Molinari, and Salzarulo, 1968; Pivik and Foulkes, 1968; Molinari and Foulkes, 1969; Watson, 1972; Vogel, Barrowclough, and Giesler, 1972.

criteria of dreaming (visual representations, hallucinatory quality, implausibility of content). The situation is even more complex for sleep-onset/REM discriminations, since here both species of reports generally are acknowledged to be "dreamlike." Although these two kinds of reports can reliably be discriminated from one another at better than chance accuracy, Vogel et al. (1972) found that 50% of REM reports were falsely identified by trained judges as sleep-onset reports while the same judges identified 25% of sleep-onset as REM reports. Thus, that reports from different stages of sleep can be reliably discriminated from one another does not indicate the absence of overlap in report quality among these stages. The overlap is, in fact, fairly considerable.

In line with the framework taken throughout this book, I would like to suggest the following organization of criteria which might be said to differentially characterize reports of mental activity collected on awakenings from different sleep stages:

(1) *"syntactic" criteria*

(a) *intrasentence (i.e., intraimage) organization* generally is intact in all sleep stages except during a brief period of "ego destructuralization" at sleep onset, generally, but not always accompanied by EEG stage 1 (Vogel et al., 1966)—during this period of destructuralization, there may be "incomplete" images (such as a number hanging in mid-air) or "superimposed" images (such as a train station overlaying an image of strawberries);

(b) *intersentence (i.e., interimage) organization* generally is maximal in REM sleep, from which coherent narrative reports are the general rule; at sleep onset, particularly late in the sleep-onset period, fairly lengthy narrative accounts also are common; such reports are least frequently found on non-REM arousals and during the destructuralization phase at sleep onset;

(2) *"semantic" criteria*

(a) *relatedness of dream content to everyday experience* probably is maximal during early sleep-onset, when events of the dream-day still are being mulled over (in later sleep-onset dreams, however, there can be considerable distortion); during non-REM sleep, organized narratives, if present at all, tend to be somewhat closely related to the dreamer's immediate past life (however, fragmentary non-REM reports, perhaps because contextless, can seem rather odd); REM reports generally contain at least some distortions and implausibilities—one does not expect, on a REM arousal, a literal recreation of a recent memory or the literal dramatization of a current concern;

(b) *expressive content* (images of motion, vivid color, etc., and scenarios with ego-related motoric and emotional involvement) is maximal in stage REM, can be present at sleep onset (although affect is relatively rare during the hypnagogic period), and generally is lacking in non-REM reports;

(3) *surface-representation criteria*

visual representations predominate in all sleep periods; relatively speaking, reports of purely verbal imagery are most likely to occur on non-REM arousals, and also on sleep-onset arousals for those subjects who have trouble relinquishing voluntary control of their thoughtstream as they drift off to sleep.

It should be pointed out that sleep-stage/dream-report correlations are modulated by several other factors, such as: the *amount of elapsed sleep* (generally, late-night reports are longer and more vivid than early-night reports, so that a late-night non-REM report might be as lengthy, syntactically organized, and semantically distorted as an early-night REM report); *the more intimate nature of the sleep period being sampled* (REM sleep without recent bursts of phasic eye movements may give a more non-REM-like report than REM sleep with recent REM bursts); and *dreamer personality* (both REM and non-REM reports have greater dreamlike vividness for subjects with relatively high MMPI profiles; thus the non-REM report of a high-scoring MMPI subject may be much like the REM report of a low-scoring MMPI subject). Bearing in mind these and other qualifications indicated above, consider these three reports, collected from an early-adolescent female, on the same night of laboratory-monitored sleep:

(a) *first awakening* (11:05 P.M., sleep onset, following the initial appearance of high-voltage theta EEG activity): I was dreaming about this guy who was pole-vaulting, I don't know where it was or anything. There was a guy, and he was holding a pole, and he was running down toward a thing, ready to vault. I think he was about 25, and he had pretty long hair, and—I don't know what he looked like. I wasn't in it. (Experimenter: Have you watched anybody vault, or been to a track meet, or anything like that, lately?) No. (Experimenter: Did the experience seem real at the time; did you think it was really happening until I woke you up or did you know all along that you were just making it up in your mind?) I thought it was really happening. (Experimenter: Did you have any feelings that you can remember in this?) No.

(b) *second awakening* (3:43 A.M., REM sleep of 12 minutes' duration, characterized by recent phasic [REM-burst] activity): I dreamed we were on a bus that was going to [basketball] tournament, or, no, it was going back from the tournament, and we were talking about the people that had lost money at tournament. We just—somebody said somebody lost some money, and somebody said somebody else did. (Experimenter: Did this look like the bus you really came back from tournament on?) Yeah. (Experimenter: OK, who was in this bus?) A bunch of girls, I don't know who they were exactly. (Experimenter: They were made-up characters?) Well, I think they were people I knew, they just weren't recognizable. (Experimenter: So is the situation more or less like the situation you really were in when you came back on the bus?) Yes. (Experimenter: When you really came back, was there any discussion of people losing money?) No. (Experimenter: Who, in specific, was telling about this? Were you?) Yeah, I was doing some, and other people, I don't know who they were, though. (Experimenter: OK, what did you say?) I said somebody lost some money, but I can't remember who. (Experimenter: In the dream you said, "I can't remember who"?) Yes. (Experimenter: At the time you were dreaming this did it seem that these things were really happening, or did you know you were just making them up in your mind?) I thought it was really happening. (Experimenter: Did you have any feelings in the dream?) No.

(c) *third awakening* (5:47 A.M., stage 2 non-REM sleep): I was dreaming about a piece of pineapple. All I could see was a chunk of pineapple, and it had skin on it that seemed like bark on a tree. (Experimenter: Could you see anything besides the pineapple?) No. (Experimenter: Were there any people?) No. (Experimenter: Were you in it?) No. (Experimenter: At the time you saw the pineapple did you think it was really there, or did you know this was just a picture you were making up in your mind?) I thought it was really there. (Experimenter: How big a chunk was this?) About two inches long. (Experimenter: Did you have any feelings when you were seeing this?) No.

Like most representative "examples," these reports partly do, and partly do not, conform to the idealized descriptions which they are intended to illustrate. General syntactic features are portrayed rather more typically than semantic ones. Here the REM report seems most faithful to everyday experience, although the lost-money theme does distort the recent memory which is its basis. There is no indication of a specific life-history reference for the more fragmentary sleep-onset and non-REM reports, although only the non-REM report is intrinsically bizarre (bark on a pineapple).

The most significant observation concerning the *content* of REM dreams, first made in a systematic way by Snyder (1970), is its general ordinariness. It usually is not difficult to find connections between REM dreams and the concerns of daily life. One rarely gets the impression that dreamers are helplessly in the grips of distortions reflecting affects or impulses which they cannot manage. Dreams generally display ego competencies at least in proportion to their representation of conflicts. Interestingly enough, this seems especially true of children's dreams[4], where our expectation might have been quite different.

[4]For example, Foulkes, 1967, 1971, 1977; Foulkes, Pivik, Steadman, Spear, and Symonds, 1967; Foulkes, Larson, Swanson, and Rardin, 1969; Foulkes and Shepherd, 1972a; Foulkes, Shepherd, and Scott, 1974.

Freud's "id-psychology," of course, prepares us for some use of recent material in dream construction, but it seems that it is psychoanalytic ego psychology (see chapter 6) which better prepares us for the major role current waking preoccupations play in the narrative organization of many children's dreams. The evidence makes these preoccupations look like much more than "some cheap material always ready to hand" (Freud, 1900, p. 237), and their role look more like that of a tune-calling ego capitalist than that of mere entrepreneur for a capitalist id (Freud, 1900, p. 561).

Systematic examination of comparable waking and dream variables further indicates the continuity of waking and dreaming thought (Foulkes, 1970). One instance of this continuity already has been mentioned: subjects whose waking mentation is prone to intrusion by bizarre ideation (as indexed, for instance, by the MMPI), have both REM and non-REM dreams of a relatively bizarre sort. An even more instructive example, perhaps, is Trupin's finding (1976) not only that there was a positive correlation between waking-and dream-assessed "ego level" (Loevinger and Wessler, 1970; Loevinger, Wessler, and Redmore, 1970), but also that the absolute level of ego functioning observed in dreams and wakefulness was identical.

The inner, ego-structural determination of dreams is further supported by the results of experiments in which systematic manipulations are made of presleep stimuli (films, drugs, etc.) or circumstances (social experience, activity level, stress, etc.). While statistically significant effects sometimes are observed in such experiments (generally fitting, again, the pattern of waking-sleeping continuity [Foulkes, 1970]), these effects seldom are large. Despite recent claims to the contrary (Garfield, 1974), it is not easy to deliberately manipulate dream content (cf. Foulkes and Griffin, 1976). The specific content of REM dreams has proved to be largely refractory to outside control.

Moreover, the manner in which presleep or sleep stimuli are incorporated in REM dreams (when they are at all effective) is most revealing. A five-year-old sleeping in our laboratory (Foulkes et al., 1969) once got his wormlike, soft-plastic electrode chain wrapped around his neck. We became aware of this when, four minutes after he entered a REM period, he screamed aloud. He did not awaken, so we immediately initiated an experimental awakening. The dream report was that he was in the family car and that a brother put crawly "caterpillar worms" on his sister's leg. The chain was around his neck, but the stimulus was displaced, without dream affect (despite the behavioral scream), to his sister's leg. This example always has impressed me as indicating how early in life it must be that the dreamer can successfully manage disturbing stimuli during sleep. Examples of this sort also indicate the essential correctness of Freud's position that the fate of disturbing external stimuli is to be ignored, or, failing that, denied, by the dream narrative and that, in any event, such stimuli never suffice to explain the dreams with which they are associated.

The cyclic regularity of REM sleep (REM periods terminating 60-90 minute non-REM periods) also argues against the dream as being instigated by occasional external (or somatic) stimuli of any sort. Moreover, experimentally controlled external stimuli have not been observed to initiate REM periods. The sources of dream content, as Freud indicated, must lie not in extrinsic stimulation but in the programs of the dreamer's own mind.

Studies of the effects of external stimuli sometimes can be used to characterize the central processes operative during stage REM, however. Berger (1963), for instance, found that the most frequent mode of dream incorporation of auditory stimuli was "assonance"—i.e., mediation by phonemic, rather than semantic, similarity. This supports Freud's description (1900, p. 206) of the alliterative tendencies of dream thought, as well as the notion that phonemic codes are particularly prominent in the generation of particular dream images (see chapter 9).

It has been demonstrated that sleep "pathologies" such as nightmares (Fisher, Byrne, Edwards, and Kahn, 1970) and somnambulism (Jacobson, Kales, Lehmann, and Zweizig, 1965) typically are *not* associated with stage REM. That is, their explanation is not integral to the explanation of typical stage-REM dreams.

In general, studies of the effects of experimentally induced deprivation of REM sleep have failed reliably to indicate deleterious psychological consequences of such deprivation (Vogel, 1975)[5]. Whatever advantages may be conveyed by REM sleep, or its associated REM dream, it does not appear that they are critical to the organism's gross adaptation to the task and social-emotional requirements of its environment.

However the findings of REM-deprivation research are evaluated, moreover, they cannot indicate the functions of dreaming. As we have seen, dreaming is not limited to stage REM. Furthermore, REM-deprivation studies are extremely difficult to conduct at the human level without eliciting a whole host of confounding variables (see, for instance, the discussion by Foulkes, Pivik, Ahrens, and Swanson, 1968). REM-deprivation research, then, is neither a conceptually nor a methodologically suitable strategy for determining dream function.

---

[5] Early studies (Dement, 1960), still widely cited, suggested that personality dysfunction was a consequence of REM deprivation. This no longer is a credible position. The best-controlled and most extensive of recent REM-deprivation experiments (Vogel, Thurmond, Gibbons, Sloan, Boyd, and Walker, 1975) suggests, in fact, that REM deprivation alleviates the symptoms of endogenous depression.

Shortcomings of the Available Evidence

Despite the genuine advance some of the foregoing data represent in the search for better dream explanations, they have not led to any fundamentally new insight on crucial issues in dream psychology. These issues, as Freud identified them, include: the deep-structural sources of dream content; the transformational/associative processes which "work over" these sources and, more generally, which characterize the sleeping mind; the basis on which only certain experiential sources are chosen for representation in manifest dream imagery; the most appropriate methods for, and results of, inserting the dream in a waking-life dreamer context; and the functions of dream experience. This list includes the major questions of both dream-process psychology—how does the mind work in sleep?—and dream-interpretation psychology—how can we determine what dreams mean?

What is it that is lacking in currently available research data? What is it which renders these data insusceptible of answering questions so fundamental to the goals of dream psychology? The answer to both questions, I think, is that today's "sleep-and-dream" dream researchers neither utilize nor collect free associations. Their dream observations most often consist either of ratings (e.g., Hauri, Sawyer, and Rechtschaffen, 1967) or of content analyses (e.g., Hall and Van de Castle, 1966) of the "manifest content" of the dream experience. But Freud's model indicates that such manifest-content data are insufficient either to reconstruct the processes of mind by which the dream is created or to determine the meaning and significance of any particular dream. To achieve these goals, the model stipulates that the dream report must be supplemented by the dreamer's free associations.

I am in agreement with Freud's model on these points. Free associations do provide the most reasonable way to recreate the thought/motive matrix from which the dream emerged. By generating a personal context for the dream, they also do provide the most reasonable way to assess the meaning of the dream.

Vogel (1973; Foulkes and Vogel, 1974) has, I think, most clearly illustrated the importance of free associations to any comprehensive dream analysis:

> A man who is a subject in a sleep laboratory experiment reports the following dream: "I am riding a bicycle." Imagine that we, the researchers, want to find the experiential sources of this dream, its mode of construction, its meaning, and its function. We use the methods commonly employed in dream research for the past twenty years: the dream is

rated and content analyzed according to criteria which do not require information as to who dreamed the dream or when. Using these criteria, we note that the dream has a relatively realistic or plausible theme and that it contains only the dreamer, who is an actively participating character manifesting no affect as he performs gross locomotor activity in connection with a vehicular object. We note no aggressive or sexual themes, and conclude that it is rather prosaic in quality, seeming not to touch on any deep concerns of the dreamer's life. Not having systematically manipulated the subject's presleep behavior, for this is not an experiment on the effects of presleep bicycling on dream content, we know little of the sources of the particular image the dream contains. Since this is the only dream the subject has reported dealing with bicycling or travel, we have learned little about the organization of mentation during sleep. As we have not collected associations to the dream, we have few clues as to its meaning. And, since we know little of our research subject's life history—at most we have given him a few psychological tests—we know nothing of the function his dream might serve for him.

In point of fact, we, the researchers, probably are not very interested in this dream per se. For us, it is only part of a dream pool collected from this same subject, perhaps as he moves from one experimental condition to another. Its final place in our data is as a fractional contributor to a mean or median or percentage reflecting the effect of some manipulation on some dimension of dream experience occurring in one of these conditions.

Suppose, however, that instead of using approaches which depend on publicly observable knowledge of the manifest dream, we ask the subject what comes to his mind about bicycles. In abbreviated form, his reply is this: "Bicycling brings two things to mind. First, it is my son's hobby and he is going away to college in the fall. I want to spend more time with him and share with him some of the things he likes to do before he goes off to make his own way in life. The second, darker association is that my father died less than a year ago of heart disease. He was an exerciser—he had a stationary bicycle. I think I need to exercise more strenuously to avoid his fate."

From the associations, it is clear that the bicycle dream was connected with the dreamer's deepest feelings about the two most important males in his life. Had we not asked for private, individual associations, rather than the public ones of "dream judges," we would have had no knowledge of this. Had we wondered about the dream's experiential sources, we would have thought in terms of bicycles and travel rather than of fathers and sons. We would have had no knowledge of the association paths leading from bicycle to the whole constellation formed around father and son. Without the knowledge of the dreamer's life history, we would have completely missed its significance in his emotional life. Herein may lie some clues as to why contemporary dream research has so little to tell us about the nature of the dream as an organized and meaningful psychological experience. [Foulkes and Vogel, 1974, pp. 14-15]

But *why* has contemporary dream research rejected Freud's main contribution to the scientific study of dreams—free association? Paradoxically, because it is thought to be "unscientific." Misguided readings of often-mistaken canons of current "scientific psychology" denigrate "subjective" contents (even the dream report has its "objective, psychophysiological markers"), idiographic study, purely "descriptive" research strategies, and attempts to "interpret" observations. However, it must be acknowledged that it also is true that no reliable, ruleful way ever has been developed for organizing the material collected in free-association sessions and for coordinating this material with dream and waking-life observations so as to implement the goals of dream-process and dream-interpretation psychology. Thus free-association dream psychology, at present, may well be "unscientific" in its detailed application.

Is it *inherently* so, however? Clearly not. There is nothing unscientific about collecting free associations and classifying and organizing them according to rules. The current "unscientific" status of free-association utilization in dream psychology simply reflects the fact that "objective" students of dreaming, myself included, have been sufficiently in the sway of the canons of contemporary psychology never to have considered it worthwhile to attempt to develop a reliable procedure for coding and using free-associative material.

The very limited success of psychophysiological research conducted *without* free-associative evidence now indicates, however, that it is imperative that we develop such procedures. We have gone about as far as we can without them, and that is not very far. Part IV of this volume presents one reliable procedure for using free-associative data to determine the personal meaning of dreams and to implement the goals of Freud's dream-process psychology. Almost certainly, this procedure is not the best one which ultimately will be devised. But it is a beginning.

It is an important beginning, for *where free-associative data are incorporable within an objective study of dreams, it should be possible to address the major problems identified by Freud, to effect a rapprochement of clinical and experimental method in dream psychology, and to integrate Freud's cognitive-*

symbolic conceptualization of dream processes and dream-meaning with psychophysiological techniques of dream-collection and dream-labeling.

More particular applications of the specific procedure proposed below to classical problems of dream psychology are considered in chapters 15 to 17. For the present, it may simply be noted that a reliable procedure for coding and utilizing free-associative data makes it possible to rulefully reconstruct the presumed matrix from which the dream issued and the presumed operations of the dreaming mind which created it. It also makes it possible for us to operationalize Freud's critical insight that the meaning of the dream is not its significance to us but its significance to the dreamer.

Summary

The evidence reviewed in this chapter suggests that, however useful it may be as a method of dream collection or observation, psychophysiology cannot, at present, be expected to make any substantial contributions to the explanation or interpretation of dreams. In this respect, the current situation of dream psychology is not unlike that when Freud wrote *The Interpretation of Dreams* (1900). In a reductionist scheme of science, there still is no more basic or "scientific" discipline by whose bootstraps our contemporary understanding of dreams will receive a much-needed lift.

The fundamental difference between contemporary psychophysiology and the study of dreams is the centrality of meaning to the latter discipline. As I have interpreted him in chapter 4, Freud was not so much concerned with establishing the material conditions in which dreams transpire as he was with elaborating a symbolic context in which dreams would "make sense" as psychological acts and from which they presumably emerged. By 1900, if not earlier (cf. Freud, 1954), Freud clearly saw meaning as the major problem of dream psychology. *The Interpretation of Dreams* is fully responsive to this conceptualization. That is, it is a cognitive or symbolic account of dreams. Any attempt to assimilate Freud's concerns to an asemantic neural model (e.g., McCarley, 1976) simply misses the point of Freud's efforts. Such misunderstandings are not surprising, for as Edelson has remarked, there is a kind of "language" barrier separating psychophysiologists from psychoanalytic (and other) dream theorists: what "makes psychoanalytic theory seem so peculiar and unscientific to most other scientists, since they study the intrinsic characteristics of objects and their relations" is that dream cognition involves the study of "objects and events that *stand for* other objects and events" (1975, p. xii, italics added).

It is not my position that a biological perspective is, by its very nature, forever barred from making substantial contributions to dream psychology. Rather it is simply my impression that the psychophysiology of today is inadequately geared to mesh very effectively with the major concerns of dream theory. But, as will be seen later, when a biological perspective is applied *directly*, rather than *reductively*, to human symbolic behavior—e.g., the study of language dysfunction in relation to brain damage (Luria, 1973)—there are, even now, some potentially exciting implications for dream psychology. Superficiality becomes a real problem only when, as most often has been the case, very simple neural models generated in asemantic observational settings are uncritically generalized to higher symbolic functioning.

If dream psychology still finds itself bereft of substantial support "from below" (psychophysiology), is it, then, necessarily still as lonely a scientific venture as it was in Freud's day? That certainly no longer needs to be the case. Today's intellectual climate provides substantial "lateral" support systems for dream psychology which were utterly unavailable to Freud. In recent years, especially, major advances have been made in cognate branches of "symbolic science" which I think should and do have considerable significance for dream psychology. If our situation today is that we still have precious little brain-data on which to build better dream theories, it also is one in which we have a wealth of newly discovered mind-data and of newly elaborated mind-theory which should prove invaluable in this same quest. To mention only the most obvious of these "symbolic" sources, we now have a systematic experimental approach to cognition ("cognitive psychology"; e.g., Neisser, 1967) and a complex model of linguistic competence ("transformational-generative grammar"; Chomsky, 1957, 1965). Furthermore, in Noam Chomsky (1928-   ) and in Jean Piaget (1896-   ), we have contemporary scholars of mind whose brilliance clearly rivals that of Freud himself. These newer accounts of the workings of the waking mind, should, on the logic of chapters 1 to 3 and on the evidence of this chapter, have a great deal to say about the workings of the sleeping mind. It is the purpose of the chapters of part III to attempt to systematize some of the implications for dream psychology of the recent work in these and other symbolic disciplines.

PART III

EMPIRICAL

FOUNDATIONS FOR

A CONTEMPORARY

MODEL OF

DREAMING:

OBSERVATIONS FROM

COGNATE SYMBOLIC

DISCIPLINES

CHAPTER 6

Psychoanalytic Ego Psychology

The Language of Psychoanalysis

The development of psychoanalysis since Freud has been painfully slow and is yet quite incomplete. Moreover, much that passes for "development" within psychoanalytic theory is so trivial or so unrelated to observation as to give the impression that psychoanalysis, like its most recalcitrant patients, is fixated at a very early stage of growth. The undoubted successes of psychoanalysis as a cultural institution have not been paralleled by—have, in fact, probably impeded—its growth as a science of human behavior. The dominant picture within the movement itself is stagnation, if not decay. Some observers have gone so far as to suggest that any successful revisions of analytic theory will have to come from those who "lack commitment to any institutionalized form of it" (Hilgard, 1966, p. 549). Despite this gloomy picture and prognosis, however, there has been some significant change of direction within the psychoanalytic mainstream, and the body of its received theory has been sufficiently attractive to command the continuing attention of a number of gifted scholars.

I propose here to review, quite briefly, two important new directions within psychoanalytic theory, both of which render it more likely to provide an adequate empirical and formal base for a contemporary model of dreaming. I also want to discuss several interesting attempts at formalizing analytic theory in a cognitive terminology.

The first of the two theoretical innovations is the relatively greater role assigned "ego" factors in psychological development. To some, but not all, contemporary analytic theorists, these ego factors are "autonomous"—i.e., can arise and function without the mediation of unconscious instinctual forces. Hartmann spoke of such processes as comprising a *"conflict-free ego sphere"* (1939, p. 8), which differentiates developmentally *beside*, rather than *from*, the instinct structures of the "id."

Holt (1967) has detailed some developmental implications of Hartmann's viewpoint for dreamlike (primary-process) thinking. Primary-process thinking cannot be present in the neonatal period. Piaget's research (see chapter 7) suggests that the capacity to image absent objects is a developmental achievement of the period preceding the child's second birthday. Both primary- and secondary-process thinking, therefore, are overlays of more primitive sensorimotor structures. Both, then, must be conceived themselves as emerging organizations of perceptions, memories, and so on. "Primary" and "secondary" processes describe different, but parallel, evolutions of mental structuration. One important implication of this theoretical revision is that the classical analytic dilemma (chapter 3) of how to have an "impulse" interact with a "thought" rests on a false premise—namely, that the former is a primitive mass of libidinal energy while the latter, alone, is a synthetic mental structure.

The ego is a component of Freud's structural model (Ego, Id, Super-Ego; 1923*a*). The precise relationship of this model to the topographic model of *The Interpretation of Dreams* is somewhat controversial. Some see the structural model as a replacement for the topographic one (e.g., Rapaport, 1960), while others do not see the two models as intersubstitutable (Blanck and Blanck, 1974, p. 22). It *is* clear that the terms of the two models are not meant to be equated. Specifically, Ego is not to be identified as system Cs, nor Id as system Ucs. A major motivation behind the elaboration of the new model was, in fact, the recognition that structures with (ego) *functions* of external adaptation might or might not have the *quality* of consciousness, and therefore that the access of a structure to system Cs might not be among its most important functional or systemic properties. The structural model essentially takes a "what does it do?" point of view toward a mental structure, whereas the topographic model takes a perspective of "how can we get at it?"

The proposal of Hartmann (1939) and others is that certain ego structures determine behavior in a manner which is relatively free of contemporary or historical dictation by instincts. Transposing this position to the variant of

Freud's topographical model presented in chapter 4, it might be read as saying that the dream-determining structures "discovered" through free association, or hypothesized as syntheses of free-associative products, need not be instinctual wishes. This would, of course, be consistent with the viewpoint of chapter 4 that the specification of dream instigators be left open to empirical investigation in any particular case, and it also would be consistent with that chapter's reinterpretation of Freud's own evidence and logic regarding the "primacy" of wish-fulfillment. The use of Freud's method of discovery should not commit one to some invariant function for the products of discovery. Investigation of the functional or systemic properties of the observed/ hypothesized products is an independent question.

In this sense, the structural and topographic models remain somewhat different in their focus and purpose. My conception of their interrelatedness is that a topographic model, because it can be operationally based on a well-specified method, provides a valuable empirical foundation for the structural model, whose functional questions are inherently more abstract and unwieldy. The difficulty in having the structural model "replace" a topographic one is that one then is committed to proposing functions for structures whose discovery no longer is rooted in empirically reliable operations. Ego, Id, and Super-Ego, for instance, are high-level theoretical abstractions representing giant conjectural leaps on Freud's part (cf. Schafer, 1976, pp. 64–66). On the other hand, the systematization of Freud's discovery-method of free association can lead, initially, to the identification of low-level structures and, ultimately, to more reliably identified and empirically useful high-level ones.[1]

The essence of contemporary psychoanalytic ego-psychology is, as I understand it, a concern with identifying persisting endopsychic representations of the world and of ourselves in relation to that world (Blanck and Blanck, 1974). Therapy, within this framework, has the goal of changing or reinforcing such inner structures. I hope to show below (part IV) that, beginning with an operationalization of Freud's topographic model, it is possible to reliably identify object relations and drive structures of the sort currently of interest to ego-oriented psychoanalytic therapists. I believe that this operationalization also should greatly facilitate the systematic study of the structural integration of mind—the concern underlying Freud's "structural" model.

---

[1] Schafer objects to the psychoanalytic concept of structure altogether. He says that it betrays an "archaic" metaphor "picturing mind as a matter of places, currents, quantities, barriers, and interactions—in short, as a spatial entity . . ." (1976, p. 162). While this charge is appropriately directed at certain psychoanalytic formulations of structure, it does not invalidate the operationalization of Freud's topographic model given in chapter 4. In the latter case, the concept of structure is no kind of "metaphor" at all. Schafer's total dismissal of "structure" on the basis of prior ill use is, I think, symptomatic of his general tendency to give up valuable parts of the baby as he flushes out decades of dirty bathwater.

The second innovation in recent psychoanalytic theory to which I wish to call attention is the shedding of the quasi-physical language ("energy," "libido," etc.) of Freud's economic model. A number of theorists (e.g., Kardiner, Karush, and Ovesy, 1959; Loevinger, 1966; Edelson, 1975; Schafer, 1975, 1976), have come to see that Freud's essential psychological insights (topographic/structural formulations of mind and a dynamic model of human motives and their conflicts) stand independent of the particular "physico-chemical and biological language," as Schafer puts it (1975, p. 41), which permeate, especially, Freud's economic model. While such perceptions have by no means yet carried the day within psychoanalysis itself, they have special appeal for those outside the movement proper, for they purge analytic theory of precisely those components which are most difficult to assimilate to current thinking in either brain-science or mind-science.

Edelson (1975), among many others, stresses the difference between two levels of Freud's theorizing—a "metapsychology," or abstract explanatory theory, in which he awkwardly borrowed the languages of nineteenth-century physical and biological sciences, and a "clinical theory" in which he (a) kept closer to actual observables and, hence, (b) used an explanatory language faithful to the symbolic character of human experience. In the one case, he aspired to achieve for psychology explanatory models parallel in form *and content* to those used in other late nineteenth-century sciences, as he understood them. In the other case he was guided more by his observations than by any particular concept of what "real science" was supposed to be like. Freud's particular models of "real science" now seem quite dated, and so too, it is argued, are the psychological theories he constructed to match these models. Where, on the other hand, Freud remained faithful to the imperatives of his symbolic data, his observations remain as cogent as ever. This argument, of course, is quite consistent with the relative evaluation I have given (in chapter 4) of the last two chapters of *The Interpretation of Dreams*. I have tried to justify the proposition that it is the data-bound sixth chapter which is Freud's greatest achievement, rather than, as conventional analytic wisdom would have it, the abstract and extrapsychologically derived formulations of his seventh chapter.

Edelson rightly emphasizes Freud's relative lack of any available "scientific" alternatives to physical/chemical/biological language as he developed his theories. There was, at the time, no coherent body of observation or theory in linguistic or other symbolic realms—none, that is, until Freud himself published *The Interpretation of Dreams*. But Freud understandably was reluctant entirely to trust his own reasoning at this point. At critical moments, he apparently felt the need to relate his symbolic or information-processing observations back to energy-discharge processes.

It is a familiar failing of psychological theories that they are greatly constrained by current understandings of how the nervous system handles inputs, understandings which invariably are relatively primitive in relation to the patent richness of human experiential or behavioral outputs. In such situations, it becomes the responsibility of the psychologist to impress upon the neural theorist the facts that *these are* the outputs the organism achieves, that the nervous system clearly mediates such outputs, and that any psychobiological theory must comprehend such organismic mediation. To sell experience short by trying to fit it to any neural model less comprehensive than this is a great error. That it is an understandable one—psychologists today harbor feelings of scientific inferiority in regard to their anatomical/physiological/biochemical elder brothers and sisters as profound as those felt by Freud—makes it not one whit less erroneous. There is nothing in the laudable goal of analogously structured theories in the several sciences which requires that adequate observations in one context be reduced to inadequate models formulated in another context. Until neural sciences comprehend the myriad everyday miracles performed by our mind/brain, psychology shall have to go it alone, and hope that, in the process, it can broaden the perspectives of brain theory to the point where such theory meets psychology halfway in its quest for reasonable psychophysiological correlations.[2]

If neither classical mechanics (energy and its transformations) nor more recent physical models (neurotransmitters and their sites, single nerve cells and their projections) can give us a very useful "language" for describing or explaining human experience, in what terms shall we think of, say, dream experience? No one has considered this problem as carefully as Roy Schafer (1968, 1973, 1975, 1976), who has proposed that psychoanalytic theory be recast within the framework of an "action language." In this action language, "each psychological process, event, experience, or behavior" is to be regarded as an "activity," or "action," and is to be described in terms of an action verb and attendant adverbial modification (1976, p. 9). The avoidance of substantive terms or adjectival modifiers is intended to free psychoanalytic theory from its tendency toward the reification of metaphorical terminology. To Schafer, *everything* is action—there are no causes apart from the action world, no qualitatively unique processes which set action (or thought) in motion.

Schafer sees his action language as superior to the language of traditional analytic metapsychology, which "is committed to and organized around one basic assumption . . . that it is necessary to postulate psychic energy for ex-

---

[2]Cf. Lashley (1930): "Psychology today is a more fundamental science than neurophysiology. By this I mean the latter offers few principles from which we may predict or define the normal organization of behavior, whereas the study of psychological processes furnishes a mass of factual material to which the laws of neural action in behavior must conform" (quoted by Marshall, 1974, p. 358).

planatory purposes" (1976, p. 79). He effectively shows that that assumption is, in fact, neither necessary nor useful in a psychoanalytic explanation of human experience. Although acknowledging Hartmann's many successful reorientations of Freud's own theory, Schafer faults both Hartmann and Freud for their adherence to the notion of psychic energy in particular, and for their reliance on natural-science models more generally. The major consequence of both Freud's and Hartmann's theoretical choices is said to be the exclusion of *meaning* from the core of analytic theory. Action-language, on the other hand, puts us squarely within the realm of "the purposive, meaning-creating, choice-making person" (1976, p. 98). It also avoids the nominalization of an emotional concept such as anger, considering it instead as a way of acting, and it avoids the nominative use of terms like "self," "conscious," and so on.

But, in giving up the various undoubted physicalistic and anthropomorphic excesses which have characterized psychoanalytic metapsychology, Schafer also seems to want to give up more—something which was very near and dear to Freud's own heart—namely, the possibility of causal explanations of behavior. Psychoanalysis, Schafer says, at best *redescribes* behavior in a way that makes it comprehensible: "Control, prediction, mathematical precision are beyond our reach" (1976, p. 205). His action-language alternative to the metapsychology of forces and underlying motives no longer gives the causes of, but only the reasons for, particular behaviors.

This line of retreat seems to me unwarranted. It is one thing to reject particular implausible proposals of "physicochemical," or "substantial," causes; it is quite another to forsake causal analysis altogether. To use a computer-programming analogy, surely knowing something about an organism's programs has potential predictive value in relation to its treatment of given inputs. I shall hold (chapter 17) that there is, in fact, the possibility of obtaining even a certain kind of *dream* prediction—of the general motivational structure of a dream, if not of its specific surface forms. And, as will be seen in chapter 10, it does not seem quite so impossible as Schafer imagines that a human's intentions, purposes, and so on—i.e., her or his programs—can be assigned some substantial or material base (Luria, 1973).

It is a valuable contribution for Schafer to have freed psychoanalysis from its own peculiarly archaic notions of causal forces, but it seems an unwise step beyond to act as if, when person X behaves in some characteristic way, there is no central nervous system program guiding this behavior, and that, therefore, it is fruitless to attempt to isolate this program, either behaviorally or neurally, so that it might be used for subsequent predictive purposes, It is, for these reasons, not at all clear to me that Schafer is correct in his suggestion that symbolic or psychological sciences are inherently nondeterministic, aiming only for "intelligibility" (1976, p. 227), or in his position that a sharp dichotomy can be drawn between "natural" and "interpretive" sciences (1976, p. 362).

In stating that psychoanalysis gives reasons, and not causes, Schafer indicates that reasons are "personal meanings" and that such meanings are incompatible with causal analysis (1976, p. 369). In essence, he feels that a mediational, symbolic, nonbehaviorist approach to human experience cannot be "scientific," at least in the ordinary understanding of that term. Perhaps because he has reached this conclusion, relatively little attention has been paid by Schafer to the formalization of his "action language." Broad outlines and nether boundaries are sketched, but Schafer has, to date, given his readers little of the real substance of a "new language for psychoanalysis."

The approach of this book incorporates the working hypothesis that "private meanings" *can* be assimilated to a scientific causal analysis. Like Schafer's publications, this book proposes a new "language"—a "language-language," rather than Schafer's "action-language." Unlike Schafer's works, it tries to provide a systematic syntax and semantics for its language. I am committed to the proposition that this language, or something like it, may make it possible not only to understand, but also to predict personal meanings, at least at a generalized and somewhat abstract level. In what I take to be the spirit of science, I propose that the possibilities of this language, or some similar one, be examined before we conclude, as Schafer has, a priori, that personal meaning and causal explanation are inherently incompatible.[3]

Although it evolved quite independently of Schafer's action-language (1975), the language to be described in part IV of this book is, in a number of ways, analogous to his. We both distinguish what I would call structures (his "active verb") from what I would call dynamic modifiers (his "adverb"). It is not clear that his sensible avoidance of nominalization in reference to psychological processes is meant to extend to object representations. His action-language translations tend to be of rather anonymously directed behaviors, e.g., "He makes sure never to think of how sensuously he engages in competition" (1975, p. 44), whereas the action-encodings I shall describe invariably are mapped out to a world of represented others, who seemingly must be considered "noun" elements for whom adjectival descriptors are the appropriate dynamic modifiers. We both describe actions, structurally, in their active-voice, definite forms. We both treat emotional terms as dynamic modifiers of our basic structural concepts (e.g., Schafer's translation of "It

---

[3] At least in part, some of Schafer's more vigorous exceptions to the possibility of a causal analysis of behavior seem to stem from his clinical identification. Like many of the earlier dream theorists who seemed to disagree with Freud on substantive grounds, Schafer simply seems less interested than Freud in what is genuinely explanatory, and more concerned with what is likely to be a useful terminology for therapeutic interaction.

makes me feel happy" into "I think of it happily" [1975, p. 45]). More crucially, we both have agreed that "we shall give up the idea that there are special classes of processes that prepare or propel mental activity, i.e., classes that are qualitatively different from the mental activity they prepare or propel" (1975, p. 46), and that it is senseless to postulate a "mindless drive" interacting with "phenomenal thought" (1975, p. 47).

One difference between the two language systems is Schafer's at least verbal disallowance of motivational constructs; my system makes an important distinction between what Schafer earlier (1968) referred to as *representations* (associational structures or cognitive maps of what goes where and with what) and *regulations* (action tendencies conceived within such an inner world of representations). Id, for Schafer, is seemingly reduced to adverbial status, while for me, it is retained in certain basic regulative "verb" structures themselves. This difference may be less significant than it might at first seem, for what Schafer seems to be objecting to is merely the notion of nonrepresentational motives, rather than of motives per se. The motive structures I will propose are representational and are coordinate with, though not identical to, nonmotivational thought structures.

I do, however, see the verb-adverb ("action") choice of Schafer's language as reflecting a basically different theoretical option than the subject-verb-object choice of my language. Curiously, in this respect, Schafer's language is faithful to at least the spirit of some of the earlier psychoanalytic concepts he otherwise rejects. It gives us no "agentive I" (Schafer, 1973) and no external world as the object of our actions; it merely leaves us with an "inner propulsion." Moreover, there is the question of whether, if language rather than action is really to determine our modeling, we shouldn't rely on the most basic and universal of linguistic units, the sentence, rather than upon some arbitrary selection of its component elements.

In this context, two other recent attempts to reformulate the language of psychoanalytic theory are of special interest (Gass, 1975; Suppes and Warren, 1975). Gass notes Freud's progression (e.g., 1895 to 1900) from neurophysiological modeling to more frankly psychological conceptualizations and characterizes the unit of Freud's basic psychological model as a "sentence." Each such sentence embodies one of a limited number of propositions, with the following components: (1) ego—the wisher; (2) object—the wished for; (3) organ—the "path" by which ego meets object; and (4) drive reduction—the pleasure accompanying wish gratification. Gass proposes that psychic propositions can be written in terms of:

I = subject, wanter
W = "want," whose increments in strength are indicated by repetition

of the W term and whose form can be either → or ←, active or passive

P = "pleasure" or hedonic state (+P = pleasure, −P = pain)

Ob = "object"

Or = "organ," the means (an internal means, i.e., erogenous zone, through which satisfaction is to be obtained)

Hence, "I badly want to take pleasure from the world through my body" translates as

$$WWW(I- +P \rightarrow Ob,Or).$$

The direction I → Ob,Or can be reversed, making I, in effect, the object of the sentence.

While Schafer tends to conceive levels of mind as misleading metaphors, whose only substantial meaning is adverbial ("consciously," "preconsciously," and "unconsciously" are modes of action, much like "competently" or "recklessly"), Gass retains a topographic (and structural) layered model of mind. For Gass, there is an "unconscious ego" which puts a proposition in a form capable of passing censorship and becoming preconsciously sayable; there is a further censorship barrier between the preconsciously sayable and the consciously said; and still a further censorship barrier between the consciously said and the overtly spoken. Beginning at the sayable, the model moves forward in roughly analogous fashion as Chomsky's deep structure → surface structure → phonetic realization (1957). The addition is a uniquely Freudian unconscious, which tells us, as Chomsky does not, *why* we want to say what we say.

Similarly, in Chomskyan fashion, Gass is concerned with identifying the transformations which operate on deep propositions as they move to overt expression. He identifies four such transformations:

reflexivity (a subject/object reversal)

reversal (a verb change—e.g., love to hate)

sublimation (an object or means substitution)

repression (sentence suppression or distortion under the influence of "dream-work" "operators")

Again, although the system I will describe evolved independently of this model, there are numerous similarities between them, the full extent of which only will become evident later in part IV. However, two points of contrast can be identified between the two systems: (1) Like Schafer's, Gass's language is intrapsychic rather than interpersonal—as he says, "In my sentences the id is speaking to the ego" (1975, p. 28) rather than, as in the system of the present book, to the external world; (2) Gass's notational system is quite complex and awkward—for instance, a conflict my system describes as $(E \rightarrow X)$ $(E \prec X)$—("I want pleasure from, and power over, your body") is described by Gass as WWWsex$(I-+P \rightarrow Ob,Or)+$WWpres$(I-Pow \rightarrow Ob,Or) \equiv$ WWpWs$(I-+P \rightarrow PowOb,Or)$!

Suppes and Warren (1975) also present a propositional/sentence model of psychoanalytically conceived contents. Specifically, they propose a propositional unconscious (cf. chapter 3), in which propositions either "represent" or are unconscious thoughts and impulses. Like Gass, they are concerned with the transformations between unconscious propositions and their conscious analogues. Their specific focus is, in fact, demonstrating that the variously proposed "defense mechanisms" of psychoanalytic theory can be reduced to different kinds of propositional transformations. Thus, given a general actor-action-object form for an unconscious proposition,[4] a simple shift in object might define *displacement*, an "opposite" verb form might define *reaction formation*, while the substitution of another for a self-subject might define *projection*. In like manner, Suppes and Warren generate twenty-six other defensive transformations. They note that there is precedence in Freud (1911*b*) for considering unconscious contents as propositional and the transformation of such contents as involving mechanisms of defense. In addition, fifteen "mechanisms of identification" are distinguished in which transformations substitute self for other.

Suppes and Warren indicate that they are not certain that their model can dispense entirely with energetic concepts. In a very tentative way, they propose that one may think of energy as being "attached" to unconscious propositions. In a complete treatment of defensive transformations, then, one would need to attend to the fate not only of the original proposition (p), but also of the quantity of its associated energy (e). In *denial*, for instance, (e) remains "blocked" at an unconscious level, whereas in *displacement* it attaches itself to the transformed object of the original unconscious proposition.

Certain other classical defenses require treatment which extends beyond simple propositional transformations. *Undoing*, for example, implies:

E loves X, at time t;
E hates X, at time t'.

[4]Suppes and Warren specifically choose this terminology instead of subject-verb-object to emphasize the independence of the concept "proposition" from any linguistic embodiment.

Regression also introduces the notion of temporal/semantic labeling of the contents of propositions—it is said to be present when any transformed actor-action-object predates the term it replaces in the experience of the person in question. *Repression* is identified simply with the topographical operation of placing any proposition in the unconscious, i.e., rendering it unaccessible to awareness.

The similarities of the Suppes-Warren model to my own are, once again, considerable, although, once again, the reasoning evolved independently. Both systems consider that psychologically significant contents are encoded propositionally (although my system does assimilate "proposition" more directly to a linguistic frame of reference). Both models propose that there is a need to supplement propositional structures with dynamic/energetic features and to distinguish structural and dynamic transformations. Both formulations are explicitly interested in mathematical realizations (algebraic operations for Suppes and Warren, digraph theory for me), and both are concerned with the hierarchical organization of propositions (although only the digraph approach begins to formalize such concerns). Both systems consider pairings of propositions (which, in succession, define *complex transformations* for Suppes and Warren, but, in simultaneity, *conflict* in my system).

There is, however, by no means an identity of the two approaches. Suppes and Warren's model is explicitly directed to a limited class of behaviors, while mine presumably could apply to all mental/action phenomena. In this regard, I have found it necessary to distinguish associative and interactive propositions. It is, presumably, interactive or motivational propositions whose impulsive power renders them subject to defensive transformations, while associative linkages provide a means through which such transformation might be achieved. This distinction helps to resolve a problem recognized by Suppes and Warren, namely, specification of the conditions in which a proposition moves for conscious expression (they simply assume *all* propositions do so move, which makes sense only if they are talking about a subset of motivationally active propositions).

In addition, Suppes and Warren do not supply a semantic analysis, indicating which verb classes, for example, should be considered "opposites," nor do they formulate rules for translating behavioral data into systemic propositions. Nonetheless, the two approaches are remarkably similar in their general intent, and, I think, supplement each other in mutually beneficial ways. My system provides an empirical realization for their model, i.e., rules in terms of which psychological data can be put into a form such that the Suppes-Warren model applies. Their system, on the other hand, beautifully formalizes the defensive transformations presumably operative in "dream-work" (cf. chapter 4); it provides a taxonomy of transformations which should be immediately applicable to the dream case.[5]

The Psychoanalysis of Language

Freud once admitted that "we should be better at understanding and translating the language of dreams if we knew more about the development of language" (1910, p. 161). As we have seen, *The Interpretation of Dreams* applies linguistic analogies to dream formation and dream interpretation. The whole business of psychoanalysis-as-therapy is conducted in a largely verbal medium. In his studies of dream reports, myths, and slips of speech, Freud ceaselessly circled about the phenomena of language. Yet, curiously, Freud never formulated a systematic psychoanalytic model of the most prevalent form of waking symbolic behavior (Thass-Thienemann, 1973*a, b*).

This failure to develop a coherent account of language is disappointing not only because it makes for an incomplete psychoanalytic model of human symbolic functioning, but also because it has deprived the rapidly developing science of linguistics of any deep psychological base. Linguistic theory tends to be silent on how to conceptualize why people want to speak and why they want to say the things they do. Psychoanalytic evidence and reasoning clearly should prove relevant to such questions.

When a psychoanalytic approach *has* been taken to language, it is not surprising that semantics, rather than syntactics, most often has been the focus. Thass-Thienemann, for example, accepts Jean Paul's view of language as a "cemetery of dead metaphors" (1973*a*, p. 183) and employs etymological analyses to explore collective prehistory, much as Freud used dream symbolism to explore the preverbal history of a given individual. Thass-Thienemann also holds that etymological histories reveal a layer of unconscious meaning which still infects even the most banal utterances of

---

[5]Highly similar to the Suppes-Warren proposal are K. M. Colby's computer simulations of defense mechanisms (e.g. Colby and Gilbert, 1964). Here, too, the basic unit is the proposition, which carries a dynamic charge; and here, too, defense mechanisms are categorized in terms of the elements which they change in the original proposition. As a dynamic component, the program includes a *Danger* monitor, whose reading is responsible for the selection of that particular defense mechanism which best balances the reduction of the charge of the original proposition with successful evasion of anxiety. Considered as plausible models of human central processes, however, these programs have a number of significant deficiencies, as has been discussed by Boden (1974).

In later versions (e.g., Tesler, Enea, and Colby, 1968; K. M. Colby, 1975), Colby maps concepts into digraphs as nodes according to their semantic relations (cf. chapters 14 and 15).

the contemporary speaker. These meanings are related to anxieties over the themes of birth, sex, and death. Essentially what Thass-Thienemann is doing is to map a psychoanalytic view of significant human experiences into human semantic organization. It is a valuable, and lavishly detailed, account. It establishes, I think, beyond any reasonable doubt, the relevance of general psychoanalytic theory to a meaningful segregation of semantic classes. A similar effort is detailed below in chapter 11.

Laffal (1973) also has developed a set of semantic classes on the basis of "psychological" (although not psychoanalytic) criteria (e.g., "tornado" is classed as DAMG-[damage] –rather than as a metereological phenomenon). Syntactic use is largely ignored. Where words represent the same concept (e.g., *true, truth*), Laffal feels that their grammatical form is irrelevant. His "concept dictionary" sorts some 23,500 words into 118 different content categories. However, it seems to me that many of his categories (e.g., AGGR-[aggression] and DAMG-) could be collapsed on theoretical grounds. Laffal's strategy essentially is to start with everyday linguistic complexity and to expand the number of semantic categories until they fit his texts. My strategy (and Thass-Thienemann's, as well), on the other hand, has been to start with a (psychoanalytic) theory of human experience which suggests a very limited number of semantic categories and to broaden category widths until the categories comprehend all of the textual material.

The "structuralist" (see chapter 7) Jacques Lacan has written extensively (e.g., 1957, 1966), if somewhat obscurely, on language and psychoanalysis, insisting that language is *the* subject matter of psychoanalysis. Freud's system Ucs, for example, contains not impulses but ideational material structured in a linguistic form. To Miel, Lacan's "most startling conclusion" is that "*the structure of the unconscious is the structure of language*" (1966, p. 108). For Wilden, Lacan demonstrates "the less than obvious fact that psychoanalysis is a theory of language" (1968, p. 310). My view is that Lacan certainly has revealed linguistic aspects and implications of psychoanalytic theory, but that he has not introduced any effective method or model to pursue his discoveries. Indeed, Edelson (1975) justifiably doubts the seriousness of Lacan's interest in relating traditional linguistic concerns to the basic structure of Freudian theory.

The most serious attempt by far at relating psychoanalysis to language is Edelson's (1972) own thought-provoking integration of Chomskyan grammar (see chapter 8) and Freudian dream theory. Edelson anticipates and develops many of the major themes of this book. He gives a persuasive reading of *The Interpretation of Dreams* as a symbolic, linguistic analysis of dream mentation. He sees the possibility of developing "a general theory of symbolic function" by relating Freud's theory of night-time's most prominent symbolic activity to Chomsky's account of day-time's most prominent symbolic activity (1972, p. 210). Needless to say, such a "general" theory might constitute the needed extension of psychoanalytic theory to fill in the linguistic gaps noted by Thass-Thienemann (1973*a*).

In general, Edelson is impressed by the parallel between the transformational-generative grammarian's distinction of deep and surface structure and Freud's topographic distinction of unconscious ideation and conscious representations. In both cases, intervening processes (transformational rules; dream-work mechanisms) transform deep "kernel" structures into just one of their many possible surface realizations. *Freud's dream-work mechanisms are the transformational rules of the grammar of dreams.*

From this perspective, Edelson holds that the basal structures of thought are unchanged in sleep:

> The state of sleep alters not the thought processes, but the processes by which symbolic forms are generated to represent these thought processes. (These formulations imply that "secondary process thought" and "primary process thought" signify differences in the symbolic representation of thought and not differences in thought itself.) [1975, p. 235]

Some role in explaining differences in dream/speech realizations is assigned to pictographic factors—the component which assigns images to surface structures cannot work in the same way as the component which assigns words to them. But the major assumption is that it is transformational rules which differentiate sleeping from waking utterance. "The only 'thinking' that is different in sleep is the dreamwork" (1975, p. 244). *Differences between dreams and waking utterance are explained by the different transformational grammars of their respective states.*

For two reasons, I find this last argument difficult to accept. First, as Edelson approvingly notes, Freud tended to consider the dream as a kind of sleepy *bricolage*, a patchwork of whatever raw materials happen to be at hand. This is reflected in the topographic model, where the quantity and interrelatedness of latent but active dream-thoughts are increased in sleep, as compared to waking thought, whose background is organized in a more single-minded way by a regnant intention or purpose. It seems strange to say that the transformations necessitated by this vastly altered underlying thought matrix are responsible for differences between waking and sleeping mentation and to ignore the differences in basal conditions themselves. As I have read Freud (chapter 4), in sleep we have more and different things to say, as well as different ways of saying them. If Edelson's point is simply that the form of unconscious and preconscious dream determinants remains propositional, then one can readily agree that this must be the case, for it is an assumption of his model. But he seems to be saying something more than that, namely that base grammar and semantics are largely irrelevant in explaining the peculiar properties of dreams. Despite supportive quotes from Freud (e.g., 1900, pp. 506-7, *n*. 2), that position seems to me rather unFreudian as well as inherently implausible.

Second, there is something disturbing about how Edelson reaches his conclusion. Ultimately it is by fiat, supported by a seemingly persuasive formal analysis and by citations from Freud. What is lacking is a methodology to render this critical question of dream psychology (how are dreams different from waking thought/utterance?) susceptible to empirical analysis. In part IV, I will propose such a methodology.

Granting, for the moment, that dream-work mechanisms are as critical to the resolution of this question as Edelson believes, how does he characterize them?

> The criteria governing choice of a set of images for use in constructing a manifest dream will include the following: (1) each image will be capable (compared with possible alternatives) of allusion to a maximum number of semantically interpreted deep structures—the latent thoughts —to be represented by the dream; (2) the set of images will contain (compared to possible alternative sets) a maximum density of nodes, where processes of allusion arising from each image intersect.
>
> The first criterion is concerned with the economy of means for assigning a perceptible representation of meaning. The second is concerned with providing a means for assuring the recovery (from the perceptible representation of a derived surface structure) of the theoretically determinate underlying meaning of the dream. [1975, p. 262]

These statements are noteworthy in two respects: (1) representational processes of condensation are emphasized. But it can be shown (see chapter 15) that structural condensation is a necessary consequence of the altered basal conditions of sleep. You can't have a large network of meanings underlying particular images without having something which looks like "allusive economy." Thus we once again are driven to consider the differences between wakefulness and sleep not just in terms of transformation operations, but also in terms of the contents on which they operate. (2) Disguise operations of displacement are neglected. Elsewhere (1975, p. 257), Edelson sees displacement as a very secondary factor in dream formation, as "almost an inevitable result of a process of condensation (and not necessarily of a motive to censor or disguise)." But, once again, one feels that this deemphasis is more by fiat than by evidence. It evidently is a major problem to reconcile a linguistic model where representation is paramount with a dream case where it might be secondary. Ergo, dreams are representational. But Freud seems to have proposed that the fundamental intent of dream representations is different from that of waking utterance. In the latent dream thoughts we have propositions we both do and do not want to utter. Given Freud's persuasive illustrations of this possibility, it hardly seems fair to legislate it out of substantial existence because it is not a tidy fit to transformational-generative grammar. Once again, one feels that the basal character of the dream case, i.e., its possible difference with that of the speech case, has not been given sufficient attention.

What I have been describing as "basal" differences, Edelson sees as differences affecting only the final, pictographic-selection component. Different memories are available in sleep, so that image selection follows different lines than word selection. But, in Freud's model, it is not merely the final step of image selection, but the whole underlying preconscious/unconscious thought matrix which assumes different properties in wakefulness and sleep. In linguistic theory (e.g., Chomsky, 1965), deep structures are defined as containing all the information needed for semantic interpretations. It seems reasonably clear to me that Freud would want to say that it must be at that kind of level, too, that waking and sleeping states should be differentiated.

I am not persuaded, then, that it is only in terms of its unusual transformations (in a positive sense) or of its absence of transformational constraints (in a negative sense) that the dream differs from language. Nor is it self-evident to me that the defensive components of Freud's model, which radically but systematically shift whole lines of meaning, find analogies in Chomsky's transformations, which preserve a common semantic kernel. Evidently the superficially appealing parallels between deep and surface structure, on the one hand, and latent and manifest content, on the other, are, when taken too literally, somewhat misleading. The received wisdom of Chomsky and of Freud just don't match up very well. Edelson's theoretical integration is highly instructive, but ultimately unsatisfactory. The next, and hopefully more productive, theoretical step should be to match dreams, regardless of what Freud says about them, with language, regardless of what Chomsky says about it. Obviously neither figure can or should be totally ignored in this analysis. But neither should the obvious deficiencies of their respective theories be overlooked. We need not, for example, as Edelson does, accept Freud on the primacy of the wish in sleep (cf. chapter 4). Nor need we accept Chomsky's obviously incomplete and probably inadequate semantic model (cf. chapter 8).

Empirically, the next step clearly should be the derivation of methods, to bring all of this high-flying formal analysis down to earth. Since 1972, Edelson (1975) has become more concerned with developing analytic methods to supplement his theoretical interests, but, unfortunately for the present discussion, in the area of literary analysis rather than that of dream psychology. His interest in poetry (Wallace Stevens's *The Snow Man*) *is* better suited to his Chomskyan sources—a large part of the fascination here is in *how* the poet says what he does—and to his own clinical and interpretive interests. Still empirically unexplored, however, are the explanatory questions raised by Freud—*why* do we say (or dream) the things we do?

CHAPTER 7

Structuralism

General Tenets

Structuralism is a contemporary intellectual movement especially prominent in the French-speaking world. Among those figures most often considered (and considering themselves) as structuralists are Claude Lévi-Strauss, Jean Piaget, and Jacques Lacan. An effective popularization of the movement has appeared (Gardner, 1972). It remains somewhat difficult, however, to determine precisely what it is that discriminates "structuralists" from "nonstructuralists" or from scientists or scholars more generally. There is more consensus on who the structuralists are than on what it is that unites them.

As Wood points out, structuralism seems to be more of a "perspective" than anything else. He goes on to define this perspective in the following terms: ". . . a sense of system where we thought there was only the reign of chance, a glimpse of rules where we hadn't even seen that there was a game" (1976, p. 32). Structuralists have investigated such seemingly primitive phenomena as cultural myths and the language and thought of the child, and have demonstrated that, below surface chaos, there is an underlying order or structure. Structuralists, in other words, have done for other personal/cultural phenomena what Freud did for dreams.

Gardner's account of the structuralists' method is that:

> whatever the complex phenomenon under investigation . . . the structuralist treats it like a foreign language which must be deciphered; through careful observation, and the performance of appropriate experiments,

he determines the basic "words" or units, the syntax, and the meaning of the foreign behavior, and describes it in terms which other scientists can comprehend. In addition, he adopts procedures which can be followed independently by other scientists. [1972, pp. 6-7]

It is clear that, both in metaphor and method, Freud's great work on dreams anticipates the major tenets of contemporary structuralism.

The preceding quotation suggests a more restrictive definition of structuralism: "the projection of a model from linguistics on to a range of other disciplines" (Wood, 1976, p. 33). In this sense, it is not quite so clear that Freud was a self-conscious structuralist, although it is the burden of my treatment of him (chapter 4) that he was, at the least, an unwitting one. Edelson is more explicit. Freud, he says, was "the progenitor and prescient exemplar of constructive structuralism" (1972, p. 250).

The term "constructive" indicates another assumption of the contemporary structuralist. Mind is seen as critical to the understanding of behavior. Behavior is mind externalized. The structures underlying behavior are those of mind. Mind here is conceived not just as an inference from behavior, which would make the structuralists' assumptions tautological, but as a "real," universal set of brain structures/processes. We behave in response to a reality which is the construction of the structural/functional principles of our central nervous system. Our behavior is isomorphic with this reality, hence with a set of biologically given principles of cognitive functioning.

Freud, of course, also stressed our active role in creating the reality to which we respond. The paranoid creates threats to which her or his behavior then becomes a sensible response. But it was *The Interpretation of Dreams* which most tellingly illustrated the constructivist properties of the structures of our mind. Our dreams are *our creation*, Freud showed, not just something that "happens" to us. We must accept responsibility for the features of our dream-world: we made them. The heart of Freud's efforts in *The Interpretation of Dreams* is a "structuralist" effort to understand the principles of mind by which we perform such creation.

A final assumption (for our purposes) of contemporary structuralism is that the operations of mental structures can be expressed in formal models of an abstract symbolic and/or mathematical sort. It is only in this respect that Freud's dream psychology might be considered "transitional" to structuralism, rather than structuralist per se (cf. Gardner, 1972, p. 41). Although Freud must have used diagrammatic or other abstract devices in formulating his dream-work concepts, the published model is largely verbal. In this sense, the content of my chapter 15 may be seen as an implementation of the final stage of Freud's structuralist analysis of dreams.

Of the structuralists mentioned, Lacan already has been considered. It remains to consider the anthropologist Lévi-Strauss and the "genetic episte-mologist" Piaget.

Claude Lévi-Strauss

Lévi-Strauss's work has consisted of a search for the deep structures of human mind revealed by such cultural artifacts as myth and kinship terminology. Explicitly influenced by Freud, Lévi-Strauss wants to know the mental elements and rules of combination which underlie the creation of such artifacts. His findings stress the binary oppositional (e.g., endogamy vs. exogamy) and relational (analogical, comparative) nature of mind. Language cannot help but reflect and reveal this nature, as well as infect other cultural institutions with it.

> Verbal categories provide the mechanism through which *universal* structural characteristics of human brains are transformed into *universal* structural characteristics of human culture. [Leach, 1970, p. 36]

Myth is an especially fertile field in which to study the master "language" of human cognition, because myth is a kind of "social dream," minimally constrained by current sense data. Myth also is dreamlike in its use of concrete symbols to represent abstract concepts (e.g., raw = Nature; cooked = Culture). Lévi-Strauss wants to penetrate beneath the surface banality and illogic of mythological stories to discover their underlying nonrational, concrete-sensory "logic" or "language." Freud, of course, also thought that myth had such a latent structure. But Lévi-Strauss wants to make the determination of that structure less a matter of brilliant guesswork and more the inevitable outcome of disciplined analysis. His intent, that is, is parallel to mine in the area of "personal" dreams. He claims to have laid bare the transformations by which myth represents a limited set of interpersonal relationships (e.g., friendship, hostility) among a limited set of social categories (e.g., kinship and age classes) in terms of such concrete forms as interspecies relationships and sensory contrasts (e.g., sweet versus sour).

A major criticism of Lévi-Strauss's analyses, however, has been that they still are essentially intuitive rather than ruleful or intersubjectively reliable. One wonders about the long-term merit of this criticism, recalling the unjust wholesale dismissal of Freud on the same grounds. Although it does not seem that Lévi-Strauss himself has evolved a formal set of methods which the dream psychologist simply can "plug in" to her or his particular structural concerns, an impressive degree of formalization already has been achieved in applying his logic to culturally significant cognitive processes (B. N. Colby, 1975).

Although Lévi-Strauss clearly has been influenced by modern structural linguistics (Lévi-Strauss, 1958, ch. II), it is important to note that he is not a simple linguistic "imperialist." That is, it is his view not so much that language organizes experience as that experience has, socially, invented language in its own image so that, personally, language nicely fits the facts of experience. Ultimate attention is directed not so much to language as to the mind which creates and assimilates it. In this respect, Lévi-Strauss's views seem not unlike those of Chomsky (chapter 8). Linguistics is appealing to structuralists like Lévi-Strauss perhaps more because it is a model of a symbolic discipline which has achieved a high degree of formalization than because its subject matter is thought to be fundamental.

As so often is the case, the very grounds on which Lévi-Strauss most often has been criticized can, from another perspective, be evaluated favorably. If Lévi-Strauss, in fact, has not achieved the formal rigor of Piaget in methodology or theory, then neither has he been forced to pay the costs of that rigor. Unlike Piaget, his work indicates a wholesome appreciation of the affective/ motivational qualities of human experience and an openness to the thought of other students of mind.

Jean Piaget

Piaget, on the other hand, however substantial his accomplishments within the domain he has chosen to study, has achieved what is, by contrast, a relatively bloodless and closed formal model of mental operations. He is, seemingly by temperament, relatively uninterested in the kinds of phenomena which fascinated Freud, and at some pains to dissociate his enterprise from that of Freud. Piaget's domain is the acquisition of scientific and logical reasoning. From a psychoanalytic perspective, the subject matter is a certain set of ego functions, highly valued in contemporary Western culture, which exist within a conflict-free sphere of ego functioning. More critically, one might say that the subject matter is the mind abstracted out of the person.

For a variety of reasons, some intrinsic and some extrinsic to the logic of the development of psychology, Piaget now is the central figure of scientific psychology, certainly the leading influence on developmental psychology.

He is a prolific, but difficult, writer. His work has spawned numerous popu-larizations, the most thorough of which is one by Flavell (1963). But the latter work is sufficiently difficult that it, in turn, has spawned even more popular popularizations (e.g., Phillips, 1975)! It is not my intention here to distill Piaget's system one further time. Rather, after a superficial overview of Piaget's general goals, methods, and conclusions, I want to focus on what Piaget has had to say about two topics of particular interest in the present context: dreams and "mental imagery."

Piaget's general goal is to trace out the ontogenesis of human knowledge, "knowledge" defined in terms congenial to Western science and philosophy. He wants to establish that such knowledge is not acquired haphazardly, but according to a program of invariant stages of mental development which presumably reflect invariant sequences of central nervous system capability. Within each such stage (a *period*, to Piaget), thought has a unique underlying structure which Piaget hopes to isolate by the presentation to the child of particular problem situations and a search for the pattern underlying the child's response to them.

Thought begins, Piaget holds, as action, or, more precisely, as a series of sensory-motor coordinations. The *sensorimotor period* characterizes, roughly, the first two years of life. Although primitive by adult standards, the "reason-ing" of this period soon becomes surprisingly versatile. The child's behavior is guided by intentions or *schemata*; it shows a means-ends distinction and the ability to detour on the path to a goal; it is sensitive to the meaning of events, rather than to their physical characteristics; and it includes deliberate experi-ments on objects to discover their properties and meanings. Objects are responded to as if they had the quality of permanence, and their visible dis-placements are attended to with much interest. A major limitation of the reasoning of this period, however, is its total dependence on direct encounters with environmental inputs. It is little more than intelligent *behavior*.

Piaget's observations of the sensorimotor period clearly demonstrate that many fundamental structures of thought precede the onset of speech (see also Vygotsky, 1934). Even at later ages, Piaget observes that the structure of a child's practical understanding of a problem may not be mirrored in her or his verbal description of it. Signification begins, Piaget feels, with motor mimicry, but first becomes internalized with the formation of images. Only later are words assimilated to an already ongoing symbolic system.

At about age 2, the child passes from purely behavioral manipulations of the world to the possibility of mental ones as well. Thought becomes representa-tional. "Mental" experimentation is feasible. As already noted, it is not pri-marily the acquisition or use of words which marks this transition, but rather the first evidences of the utilization of concrete imagery. Words do become increasingly important, however, because they are the medium through which the parents are able to socialize the child's thought.

In this *preoperational period*, however, thought is not guided by coherrently formulated inner plans. It is very susceptible to direction, and distraction, by current perceptual configurations. A "centration" on any given stimulus configuration, once established, tends to be irreversible. Thought also is "egocentric" in that it is difficult for the child to "center" her or his thought around any perspective other than her or his own. (A major problem in Piaget's description of this period is that it neglects the child's acquisition and use of ruleful syntactic structures. The child's language, at least, becomes highly, internally organized during the preoperational period. But Piaget is little interested in language per se. Cf. chapter 8.)

The period of concrete operations, first achieved at ages 5-7, marks the beginning of the organization and rationalization of inner representations. Thought becomes systematic; the world begins to be organized propositionally. "Operations" are recurrently useful and widely applicable programming routines. The grade-school child, for example, now performs arithmetic solutions not by rote memory, but as the end product of a series of simple computational routines. The routines at this age are "concrete" in that they operate on data rather than upon each other. The concrete-operational child is unlikely to be "lost" in her or his operations. When a problem presents itself, children "operate." When it doesn't, they don't. On the other hand, the child now can decenter, reverse, and take another's perspective in a way the preoperational child cannot. Piaget has formalized his concept of concrete operations in terms of a qualitative mathematics of his own invention, whose basic concept is a *grouping*.

The development of the capacity for more abstract thought, for the application of operations to other operations, and for "losing" oneself in these operations, comes, at least to certain children living in "sophisticated" and scientifically oriented societies, at about the ages 12-15. This marks the beginning of the *period of formal operations*. These are the developments which, in turn, make science and philosophy possible. One now can live in a world of the purely "as if?" or "what if?" Propositions are formed not only on the basis of sense data, but also on the basis of other propositions. Propositions begin to become hierarchically interrelated. Piaget formalizes these operations in terms of the mathematical concepts of *lattice* and *group*.

If the *structures* (plans, programs, operations, schemata, etc.) which guide behavior are systematically variant over time, the *functions* of thought are, to Piaget, invariant. These functions are: *adaptation* (relating thoughts to the world) and *organization* (relating thoughts to one another). Also invariant is the tendency toward equilibration of two mechanisms of adaptation: *assimila-*

tion (the modification of inputs to conform to structures) and *accommodation* (the modification of structures to conform to inputs). It is the ebb and flow of these latter two processes which is, in some sense, held responsible for the saltatory nature of the child's achievement of logical reasoning. That is, assimilation and accommodation are evidently meant to serve some sort of explanatory role. I doubt their value at that level, and, in general, see Piaget more as a *descriptive* developmental psychologist, a judgment in which Flavell (1963) seems to concur.

Several remarks also should be made regarding Piaget's conformity to the general "structuralist" program which introduced this section. Piaget clearly is no kind of linguistic imperialist. Indeed, it seems, as Phillips (1975, p. 174) has remarked, that for Piaget language is a kind of "epiphenomenon" of cognitive development, at least until the stage of formal operations (Piaget, 1963). As Phillips also remarks (ibid.), Piaget has focused, especially in recent years, much more upon the development of "physical and quantitative thinking" than on that of "language and associative processes." It also should be noted that Piaget's mathematical formalizations are more "ways of thinking" about mental operations than they are formulae for translating observable behaviors into modular terms (Flavell, 1963, p. 189). That is, Piaget's precision lies more in his models themselves than in the extent to which they directly map into observables. Piaget is perhaps even more likely than Freud to get lost in the world of his own formal operations.

Dreams, along with play and imitation, are anomalies in Piaget's general process of adaptive equilibration. Dreams and play are almost pure cases of assimilation, i.e., the schemata of mind freely impose themselves on, but are unchecked by, external reality. Imitation, on the other hand, is almost pure accommodation, in the sense that the external world is copied in a highly literal way. Here it is the inner schemata which are sacrificed to reality, rather than vice versa. Since Piaget has defined intelligence as a form of equilibrium toward which structures tend (1947), dreams, play, and imitation are not conceived by him as especially "intelligent" behaviors (although the development of imitation is considered "essential" to the rise of symbolic functioning at the end of the sensorimotor period [Piaget, 1963]).

Another puzzling feature of play, dreams, and imitation for Piaget is that they are not stage-dependent behaviors—their incidence spans across the various periods of mental development. In Piaget's equilibration scheme, they are "nondevelopmental" changes (Flavell, 1963, pp. 65-67). Within any developmental period, there are essentially unpredictable disequilibria of both the play/dream and the imitative mode.

With respect to these anomalies, Piaget offers no real explanation. They exist, and Piaget describes them. It is tempting to think that these formal cognitive anomalies might have been more sensibly integrated with general mental development had Piaget's model of that development been more sensitive to affective and motivational factors.

In Piaget's major book on play, dreams, and imitation, he suggests that play and dreams proceed "by relaxation of the effort at adaptation and by maintenance or exercise of activities for the mere pleasure of mastering them and acquiring thereby a feeling of virtuosity or power" (Piaget, 1951, p. 89). "Sheer-pleasure-of-experiencing-it" explanations tend to be tautological, and "fictional-" (or hallucinated-) control explanations work out to be a subspecies of them: "sheer pleasure of creating it." Thus, Piaget here does not give a particularly convincing statement of *function* for either dreams or play. Later, in discussing "symbolic" games—those implying the mediation of some representational processes—Piaget suggests additional functions for "distorting assimilations" such as play and dreams: wish-fulfillment, compensation, and the "liquidation" of conflicts (1951, p. 112). But these explanations seem more to be tacked onto his regular developmental model than to be deductions from it. One still looks in vain for a novel but cogent conceptualization of dream function growing directly out of Piaget's formal cognitive approach to dreams.

Elsewhere we are told that the "function" of symbolic assimilative distortions is the assimilation of reality to the ego (1951, p. 135). But this, of course, is the *definition* of such distortions, not an independent statement of their function. Finally, we are told that, in the distorting assimilations of *play*: " . . . the ego is revenged, either by suppression of the problem or by giving it an acceptable solution" (1951, p. 149). This statement seems unsatisfactory, simply because it does not, as a rule, fit the facts of the *dream* case. Why, then, is play, as Piaget acknowledges, more easily controlled than the dream? Piaget speaks of the prevalence of "affective schemas" (1951, p. 205*ff*.) in sleep, but, once again, this seems an ad hoc solution, because it grows out of the necessities of the dream case rather than out of any integrated account of affective or affective-cognitive development.

It is clear that Piaget wants a formal explanation of dream quality rather than a content-oriented explanation such as Freud has proposed. There is dream symbolism not because certain contents must be repressed or are in such-and-such a state, but because sleeping thought takes the form of egocentric assimilation. But, once again, the explanation proves to be only a redescription—if we infer that sleeping thought is an egocentric assimilation on the basis of its content, we cannot turn that inference around to explain the content in question.

Nor is it clear why, if on Piaget's model, assimilative distortions are prevalent in childhood because there are no logical thought structures to which reality can be assimilated, such egocentric distortions persist, are indeed enhanced (see chapter 5) in the dreams of adults. How and why is it that the adult mind returns to a more primitive egocentrism during the state of sleep? Piaget's answers here (1951, pp. 199, 209) turn out to be surprisingly like Freud's: in sleep there is a loss of contact with reality, a consequent increase in thought determination by "repressed tendencies," and a consequent inability of affective life to be accommodated to reality. One clear flaw in Piaget's research strategy emerges at this point: in focusing on the child's march toward the possibility of formal operational thought, little or no attention has been paid to the successive refinement and elaboration of prelogical thought (Flavell, 1963, p. 442).

And so it goes. Piaget's intentions are very clear: to explain dreams in terms of the functional invariants of accommodation and assimilation. But it is not clear that these latter concepts have genuine explanatory value in *any* context. As applied to the dream case, they prove to be tautological. Arbitrary solutions, not growing out of Piaget's formal model, are then supplied. But their arbitrariness is obvious, and they still do not explain all that needs explaining. Piaget's brave try at a contentless explanation of dreams is a failure. But it is an instructive failure for the cognitive view of dreams, because it reveals that only a well-worked-out, "warm-blooded" model of cognition (cf. Flavell, 1963, p. 441)—one which deals integrally with motives and feelings—can do the job which needs doing.

Curiously, the mental-formalist Piaget has no convincing explanation of the serial, dramatic organization of the dream. Discussing the "disorganization" of play, Piaget remarks that this "can be reduced to assimilation. . . . reality is being assimilated to the whims of the ego instead of being thought in accordance with rules" (1951, p. 149). For Piaget, then, fantasy, as opposed to "serious" thought, is relatively ruleless. The assimilating ego is a collection of whims. This makes it rather difficult to comprehend the cohesiveness of the dream narrative.

It may be that, here, as well as throughout his account, Piaget is handicapped by generalization of his data, which are based mostly on observations of the *play* of 3 youngsters, to *dreams*, for which he has admittedly much less data. Play can be relatively, or almost totally, "disorganized." There is however, something about the (adult) REM state, something with which Piaget does not come to grips, which almost invariably makes its mentation highly structured and cohesive. It is an achievement which seemingly calls for more than a passive explanation. Piaget's statement (1951, p. 176) that "the few dreams we have been able to collect bear a remarkable resemblance to symbolic games" might be true for children of the ages studied by Piaget, but it is not a very substantial foundation for a general theory of dreams, since our dreams are remarkably more cohesive than most young children's symbolic play.[1] Accepting a general dream-play parallel, we might better look for an explanation of our own dreams to a rule-bound, chess-playing ego than to one which whimsically pronounces that now dolly will take a walk.

In fairness to Piaget, several points need to be made. First, Piaget does recognize Freud's major contribution:

> It must be emphasized that Freud's contribution is essentially a new technique [free association], and that . . . this technique continues to be the only systematic method so far discovered of exploring the "unconscious" schemas. [1951, p. 182]

Second, Piaget takes exception to Freud at a number of the same points that I have (chapter 4) and that the psychoanalytic ego-psychologists do (chapter 6): for example, Freud's "substantialist language" of energy, and so on (1951, p. 186). Third, Piaget recognizes the necessity that Freud's contributions be coordinated with those of general cognitive psychology rather than forming "a realm apart" (1951, p. 208). In his own discussion of "affective schemas," Piaget attempts to begin this process of assimilating Freud to the schemata of his own system. The major problem with this incorporation is that Piaget himself doesn't have a very highly developed set of theoretical structures for the affective/motivational domain of experience.

With respect to these last points, it should be noted that several authors have suggested unifications of psychoanalytic ego psychology with Piaget. Flavell (1963, p. 414), for instance, observes that Erik Erikson's (1963) version of psychoanalysis nicely complements Piaget's developmental model. More systematically, Wolff (1960) has fused Piaget's sensorimotor theory with an ego-psychoanalytic model of infancy. He sees in Piaget's sensorimotor schemata a model for the autonomous ego functions of Hartmann and others. Wolff's account leaves off, however, just at the point of interest to cognitive dream psychology, i.e., just when, at about age 2, Piaget observes both dreams and speech emerging.

As Wolff (1967) later has observed, the methodology of Piaget and that of psychoanalysis have been complements of one another. Piaget is concerned with the child's response to external stimulus variation in conditions of intrapsychic equilibrium. Psychoanalysis classically has been concerned with the behavior of the child in circumstances of internal disequilibrium. Psychoanalytic ego psychology shares both of these concerns, and might well be the vehicle of their coordination.

[1] Cf. Piaget's assumption that children's play and "the dreams of both children *and adults*" (1951, p. 211, italics added) are all of one piece.

Piaget himself, however, has not left us entirely uninformed about how he might handle a cognitive/conative integration. He speaks of the affective aspect of behavior as supplying "the energy necessary for action" by the way in which it attaches values to goals, while the cognitive aspect of behavior is structural (1947, p. 4). Thus, "every action involves an energetic or affective aspect and a structural or cognitive aspect, which, in fact, unites the different points of view" (1947, p. 5). On the *affective* side, there are both internal regulations of energy ("the subject's reaction to his own actions" [1947, p. 4]) and external regulations of energy ("the value of the solutions sought and of the objects concerned in the search" [1947, p. 6]). *Structurally*, there are maps of the routes "between subject and object. It is this structuring of behaviour that constitutes its cognitive aspect" (1947, p. 5).

These two aspects are

> inseparable although distinct. They are inseparable because all interaction with the environment involves both a structuring and a valuation, but they are none the less distinct, since these two aspects of behaviour cannot be reduced to one another. [1947, p. 6]

Or, as Piaget later states, "feelings express the interest and the value given to actions of which intelligence provides the structure" (1951, p. 205). For Piaget, then, motivational forces inhere in cognitive structures, as they do in action, because such structures represent action (elementary schemata) or are internalized action (operations). Affective schemata are not separate entities, but merely intellectual schemata described from their affective point of view (1951, p. 207). In a certain sense, one might classify schemata where persons are the other party, in contrast to those where objects serve that role, as being especially affective, but, Piaget notes, affective schematic considerations clearly extend into the object realm, and, in the end, schemata "are all both affective and cognitive" (ibid.).

This sketch of how affective/motivational psychology might be integrated with cognitive/structural psychology provides, I think, a valuable set of leads for those who now would attempt such integration. In part IV, an attempt will be made to pursue these leads. The main discrepancy between Piaget's account and my own will be in my segregation of a group of cognitive structures without explicit motivational implications ("associative sentences"). This segregation, however, effects another kind of integration—that of Piaget, who sees all cognitive structures as having an action (hence motivational) base, with Lévi-Strauss, who sees relatively more passive perceptual operations (e.g., perceiving opposites) as the basis of cognition (cf. Gardner, 1972, pp. 192-93).

I will argue that both kinds of structures are needed, and that neither by itself can encompass the whole range of cognitive structures.

In concluding this brief survey of Piaget's work, it may be useful to consider his general position on the relations between perception, imagery, and thought. Piaget's association of dreaming with play focuses on functional and content similarities. But, from a representational viewpoint, dreams also have been likened to perception and are said to take place in the form of "mental images." What can we glean from Piaget's treatment of perception and imagery which might be useful to dream psychology?

Piaget's basic position is that perception must be considered as a different process from imaging, and that imaging must be considered as a different process from thinking. For Piaget, "intelligence and perception, both resulting from sensorimotor activity, represent two related but distinct aspects of knowledge of reality" (Laurendeau and Pinard, 1970, p. 10). Intelligence develops not out of perception, as analogical as their operations often may seem to be, but out of the reasoning of the sensorimotor period. Perception remains, in many respects, an inferior, more primitive, and more limited basis of knowledge. It is fooled (perceptual illusions), where mind knows better. It tends to be irreversible and inflexible (it is difficult to "undo" an illusory perceptual structure), whereas, for Piaget, reversibility is exalted as the key to higher mental operations. Thus, a sharp distinction may be drawn between our perception of space and our schematic representation of it. (The former, for example, greatly predates the latter, and its development is not imagined to occur in a series of stages but to be a more continuous process of adaptation.)

And yet, in the final analysis, it is clear that Piaget does not want a total separation of perceptual development and intellectual development. As Flavell notes, Piaget imagines that "a number of perceptual phenomena . . . appear to be crude sketches or first drafts of better structured intellectual phenomena to come" (1963, p. 233). As an example, he cites the obvious analogy of perceptual constancy (e.g., in shape constancy, the child *perceives* an object as having a constant shape no matter from what angle it is viewed) to schematic conservation (e.g., the child *knows* that a mass of clay contains the same amount of material whether it is shaped as an elongated sausage link or as a compact sausage patty). While the precise genetic relationship is obscure, Piaget (1963) more generally imagines that symbolic phenomena arise as internal "imitations" of nonsymbolic phenomena.

Both *percepts* and *mental images* are classified by Piaget as *figurative* aspects of knowledge, and are contrasted with *operative* knowledge. Figurative knowledge consists of momentary perceptual, imaginal, or other imitative configurations. Operative knowledge consists of the operations by which these configurations are actively reconstructed as mental schemata. Percepts, images, and so on, supply data; operations transform these data to produce the vastly more flexible conceptual organizations of thought (Piaget and Inhelder, 1966; Laurendeau and Pinard, 1970).

Imaging, on the other hand, is sharply contrasted with *perceiving*. The image is not a temporally extended percept nor a reactivated percept. It is a *construction* which presupposes *mental operations*, "the motor winding the film" (Piaget and Inhelder, 1966, p. xv). The image is not a copy of reality but a schematic reconstruction of reality. The process of conjuring an image is not a perceptual process but an internal "imitation" of a perceptual process. Images thus are symbolic representations rather than faded or reactivated percepts. Moreover, there is no substantial evidence that the child uses images until he or she enters the preoperational period, until, that is, he or she becomes a symbol-using organism.

The meaning of images resides, then, in their representational or symbolic context rather than in the objects they "depict." Piaget and Inhelder explicitly employ a linguistic framework in speaking of images; in addition to image semantics, there also is image syntactics and image morphology. And, indeed, the way in which they have freed imagery from perception makes it seem that there should be little difficulty in aligning conceptualizations of iconic representation with those of verbal representation.

A fundamental derivation of Piaget and Inhelder's theory is that, if mental imagery (excepting, perhaps, eidetic imagery) is conceptual rather than perceptual, then the child should only be able to image what he or she understands, rather than anything which has been perceived. This derivation is supported by the empirical observation that kinetic "reproductive images" (images of movement of familiar objects) do not appear until the point at which unfamiliar kinetic images also appear (ages 7/8), despite the child's extensive prior *perceptual* experience of familiar movement. What seems to be critical to the appearance of kinetic imagery, the authors feel, is the development of a set of *symbolic operations* for dealing with object transformations, seriation, and so on.

Piaget and Inhelder have provided a fairly persuasive body of evidence for viewing images as symbolic or conceptual, rather than perceptual, phenomena (cf. chapter 1). As such, images serve a similar role as linguistic symbols (1966, p. 379). This naturally raises the question, "Why sometimes images, and why sometimes words?" The authors' answer seems to be that, in general, words are more flexible, have a wider range of applicability, and, because they are conventional, better lend themselves to social control. Images, however, remain useful for less abstract and more personalized meanings;[2] they are needed, in particular, where it is necessary to think about particular experiences one has perceived but cannot describe very well. Language, on the other hand, better suits our requirements for dealing with generalities.[3]

Characteristically, Piaget and Inhelder have studied the use of images only in problem solving, and not in play or dreams. Consequently, one must feel some reservations about the direct applicability of their evidence and theory to dreams. (Is it, for example, correct that the child's *dream* images are static until ages 7 or 8? That seems unlikely [Foulkes and Shepherd, 1972a; Foulkes, Shepherd, and Scott, 1974]. There even is serious doubt that the Piaget-Inhelder account accurately describes the child's accession to kinetic imagery in wakefulness [Marmor, 1975].) Nevertheless, the general logic of their argument is persuasive at several key points: images are symbolic constructions; as such, they must share properties of other symbolic constructions ("inner speech"); and their preferred range of application probably differs systematically and predictably from that of other symbolic constructions.

[2] Piaget and Inhelder speculate that images may somehow serve a similar role for the preoperational (ages 2-7) child as operations do for the operational child (i.e., "internal" as well as external perceptual configurations may "guide" thought). Might this mean that, as Freud would have it, when one is thinking "in images," this period of childhood is especially susceptible to evocation?

[3] Reversing this argument, one might propose that when cognition is "forced" into an imaginal mold, as during REM sleep, it will tend to deal with particularities and private meanings (connotations).

CHAPTER 8

Linguistics and Psycholinguistics

In the past two decades, Noam Chomsky has been responsible for a reorientation of linguistic theory as profound as that earlier effected by Freud in dream psychology. Chomsky has described his own contributions in writings of varying, but generally difficult, accessibility (e.g., Chomsky, 1957; 1965; 1972). He has been fortunate, however, in attracting a number of excellent interpreters of his work and its relevance to nonspecialists (e.g., Lyons, 1970; Greene, 1972; Leiber, 1975).

Chomsky's field is grammar. Now, it must be admitted at the outset that "grammar" is not one of those terms to which our minds are likely to be fondly attuned. Our socialization into formal grammar is likely to have been a mixture of repetitious description (e.g., "diagramming" sentences) and pedantic prescription (e.g., the occasions for "will" versus those for "shall"). For Chomsky, the study of grammar ultimately is conceived as a descriptive discipline, but as a more systematic and theoretically exciting one than our past experience may have prepared us for. A grammar of a language is a specification of a "device" (1957, p. 11), or minimal set of rules, which generates all the grammatically acceptable sentences, while not generating any grammatically defective sentence, in that language. Formulating such a grammar becomes much more than a matter of surface description of what people are saying or of arbitrary prescription of what they should be saying. It involves the search, through a combination of observation, intuition, and model building and testing, for the most efficient explanatory system for a particular language.

If, as Chomsky imagines, the underlying structure of this system will be reasonably similar, whatever the particular language studied, then the search for an adequate grammar is, in fact, the attempt to characterize those structures of brain or mind which must be responsible for the form of human language. In view of the possible centrality of speech—both interpersonal and internal—to human cognition (see chapters 9 and 10), Chomsky's goal is a fundamental one for any human symbolic psychology. He wants to characterize the mind capable of generating speech, much as Freud wanted to characterize the mind capable of generating dreams. In both cases, moreover, there is the strategic use of a particular subject matter—language, dreaming—to attempt to frame a model of mind more general than the particular observational base selected. The ultimate subject matter, in both cases, is mind itself.

The observational bases of the two theorists are remarkably appropriate to this goal, and remarkably similar. In speech and dreams we have *the prime instances of human intellectual creativity, and ones in which practically all human beings participate.* We are forever saying things we never said before and dreaming things we never thought before. The achievement is so effortless, so "unconscious," that we tend to take it for granted. But it clearly requires explanation. For both Chomsky and Freud, there is the passion to show that the infinite diversity of our everyday creativity as speakers and dreamers can in fact be explained in terms of a finite and small set of rules.

As revolutionary figures in their fields, Chomsky (e.g., 1972) and Freud (e.g., 1900) share, moreover, a number of orienting assumptions. Both have reacted to the inadequacy of simple mechanistic models prevalent in their fields, models based on a few elementary processes suggested by the experimental disciplines of their day. Both acknowledge the symbolic complexity of human experience and are concerned with characterizing the symbolic systems of the human mind. Even in the shape of their new conceptualizations there are striking parallels. Both figures have identified, beneath the level accessible to everyday awareness, a deeper level required to explain the surface phenomena of interest to them, and, as a result of this new insight, both have faced a problem previously unarticulated in their field: what are the relations, the transformations, between deep structures and surface realizations? Finally, Chomsky and Freud have faced the same methodological problems. For both speech and dreams, only the surface phenomena are available for observation. Simple introspections of speakers and dreamers as to how they create are uniformly useless. In both cases, the available data, collateral observations and intuitions, and formal modeling must be used to attempt to reconstruct, symbolically, the generative act.[1]

In view of numerous parallels in intent, observational base, assumption, analysis, and method, it does not seem inappropriate to consider the possibility of parallels at the level of resolution. For example, can an explanatory model of dreaming be built around the explanatory models of modern transformational-generative grammar (cf. Edelson, 1972)? Can explanatory models in linguistics be assimilated to those of dream psychology? Are the formation and transformation rules creating and modifying deep structural components in the two cases analogous, or even homologous?

In *Syntactic Structures* (1957), the revolutionary analogue of *The Interpretation of Dreams*, Chomsky considers three possible candidates for a language-generating "device." (It should be noted Chomsky intends that "device" apply to what, in computer terminology, would be considered "software," i.e., programs, rather than to "hardware," i.e., computers themselves [Leiber, 1975].) The first possibility considered is the "finite-state-machine," or Markov-process model. It is, essentially, a surface model of language, in which left-right word sequences are generated on the basis of momentary sequential probabilities, or habit strengths: $A \rightarrow B \rightarrow C \rightarrow D \rightarrow E$, etc. The device generates only words, or "terminal" elements; it does not generate abstract structural descriptions of those terminal elements, and, since each element generated is, by definition, terminal, it cannot be rewritten in any other form. It is a device without an overriding plan, and without memory; it simply moves from its present state to the next one, and from that one to a still further one, on the basis of relative probabilities attaching to the paths open to it at the current state. It is, in essence, an attempt to account for language without recourse to mentalistic concepts (cf. Skinner, 1957).

Chomsky quickly demonstrates the implausibility, and then the logical impossibility, of the left-right, finite-state-machine explanation of language. In what Leiber calls "Chomsky's axiom," it is shown that "a natural language consists of an infinite number of sentences" (1975, p. 44). With an infinite set of possibilities, the probability attaching to any one sentence combination

---

[1] "Chomsky, like Freud, wants to find out something about the inner, essentially unconscious, structure of the mind—and not through direct neurophysiological investigation but through postulating structures that underlie and explain the complicated human activity that we can look at directly" (Leiber, 1975, p. 68).

must be infinitely small. Hence, it is difficult to see how sequential probabilities could be useful in sentence generation. As Greene notes, the explanation would have to be "wildly uneconomical" (1972, p. 15).

But Chomsky's *coup de grace* is his demonstration that the finite-state-machine *cannot* generate certain kinds of "nested dependencies" which occur in grammatical sentences of the form:

"The man who said that the watermelons are ripe, is coming today."

In this sentence there is a dependency between a word to the left of the comma (man) and a word occurring to the right of the comma (is) which a simple word-flow-chart model cannot accommodate. Since this sentence *is* grammatical, the model is inadequate.

Chomsky's criterion that a grammar must generate all the grammatical, but no ungrammatical, sentences is called the *weak generative capacity* of a grammar. But Chomsky feels a grammar also should meet the criterion of having a *strong generative capacity*, that is, it not only should generate acceptable strings of terminal elements, but it also should give them valid structural analyses. We are likely to feel, for instance, that

(the man) (said) (that) (the watermelons) (are ripe)

is a better structural analysis than

(the) (man said) (that the) (watermelons are) (ripe)

A satisfactory grammar, Chomsky feels, should give us some kind of structural analysis of grammatical sentences (for our intuition tells us sentences do have structural units), and that analysis should correspond to our intuitions as to the structural units in question. The finite-state-machine device, of course, does neither. The second generative model Chomsky considers, however, the phrase-structure grammar model, gives us structural descriptions of general validity.

The language-generating device of the phrase-structure grammar model clearly does more than simply bump along from word to word, response to response. Here, one can envision a hierarchically organized plan, or set of structures, corresponding to the constituents of grammatical analysis. The parsing of a sentence according to its phrase structure can be represented as a tree diagram (Chomsky, 1957, p. 27):

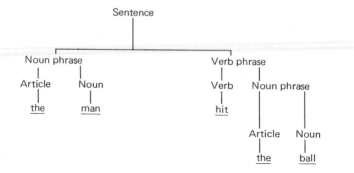

The tree is a structural description of the sentence. The diagram nicely suggests the mentalistic implication that phrase-marking structures "underlie" or "over-arch" the surface texture of a sentence (for supporting evidence, see Garrett, Bever, and Fodor, 1966).

The associated phrase-structure grammar might, then, consist of the following rules (Chomsky, 1957, p. 26):

(i)   Sentence → Noun phrase *plus* Verb phrase
(ii)   Noun phrase → Article *plus* Noun
(iii) Verb phrase → Verb *plus* Noun phrase
(iv)   Article → the
(v)   Noun → man, ball, etc.
(vi)   Verb → hit, etc.
(Where → means "can be rewritten as")

Using these "rewrite" rules, it is easy to see a series of steps by which one could generate "the man hit the ball." For instance, successive applications of rules (i), (ii), (iii), (iv), (v), (vi), (ii), (iv), and (v) give us this *derivation* (1957, p. 27):

Sentence
Noun phrase *plus* Verb phrase
Article *plus* Noun *plus* Verb phrase
Article *plus* Noun *plus* Verb *plus* Noun phrase
the *plus* Noun *plus* Verb *plus* Noun phrase
the *plus* man *plus* Verb *plus* Noun phrase
the *plus* man *plus* hit *plus* Noun phrase

the *plus* man *plus* hit *plus* Article *plus* Noun
the *plus* man *plus* hit *plus* the *plus* Noun
the *plus* man *plus* hit *plus* the *plus* ball.

By virtue of the fact that it is not limited to relationships between adjacent words, a phrase-structure grammar *can* generate grammatical sentences with nested dependencies. As it also assigns structural descriptions with some intuitive appeal to sentences, phrase-structure grammar seems to approximate both the weak and strong generative criteria for evaluating grammars. Nonetheless, Chomsky ultimately rejects the notion that a phrase-structure grammar is all there is to language generativity. Why?

First, because there are some intuitions of language-speakers which are not captured in the phrase-structure grammar's tree diagrams. We are likely, for instance, to feel that "the man bit the watermelon" and "the watermelon was bitten by the man" are closely related sentences, but phrase-structure analysis is not very sensitive to this similarity. Second, because it proves very cumbersome to resolve via phrase-structure grammar rules the structural ambiguity of a phrase like "old dogs and wine" ([old] [dogs and wine]?) ([old dogs] and [wine]?). Third, and most importantly, because there are certain sentences whose structural ambiguity simply cannot be resolved at all by a phrase-structure analysis. The most familiar example of such a sentence to transformational-generative grammarians may be: "The shooting of the hunters was awful." A phrase-structure analysis of this sentence cannot discriminate its two potential meanings: that the hunters were shot was awful; the shooting done by the hunters was awful.

To meet these objections, Chomsky proposes a two-level model of language generation: a basal phrase-structure grammar which generates simple "kernel" sentence structures (active voice, declarative, affirmative) and a set of transformation rules which operate, in a prescribed order, to effect various combinations and reorderings of the kernel elements. The transformation rules differ from phrase-structure rules in that they rewrite, not a single nonterminal element, but a whole structural description or a string of nonterminal symbols. For example, in rough form, the *passive* transformation is:

Noun phrase 1 *plus* Auxiliary *plus* Verb *plus* Noun phrase 2 →
Noun phrase 2 *plus* Auxiliary *plus* be *plus* en *plus* Verb
plus by *plus* Noun phrase 1

i.e., the man *plus* is *plus* biting *plus* the watermelon (is transformed to) the watermelon *plus* is *plus* being *plus* en *plus* bit *plus* by *plus* the man. This solution enables Chomsky to provide a structural description of active and passive sentences which matches our impression of their similarity. Both derive from the same kernel construction; they differ only in their transformational history.

Similarly, analysis of the sentence "Tom T. Hall loves old dogs and wine" might implicate two kernel structures of the form:[2]

>   Noun phrase—Verb—Noun phrase;
>   T. T. Hall loves old dogs;
>   T. T. Hall loves old wine;

which by a deletion transformation,

$$A + B + C + D \text{ } plus$$
$$A + B + C + E \rightarrow$$
$$A + B + C + D + and + E$$

achieves its surface form. Or, alternatively, the kernel structures subject to combinational transformation might be of the form:

>   T. T. Hall loves old dogs;
>   T. T. Hall loves wine.

The point is that at the deeper structural level underlying the surface form the two cases can be discriminated and that this is a clear advantage of the two-level analysis Chomsky ultimately accepts. It can readily be seen that exactly the same considerations will apply to the case of "The shooting of the hunters was awful."

Thus the essence of Chomsky's 1957 model turns out to be this: a base-level phrase-structure grammar generates kernel structures by a small number of rules; these kernel structures are operated upon by a small number of trans-formational rules, some obligatory (subject and verb must agree in number) and some optional (sentence can be active or passive), which join and/or rearrange base-generated structures to produce more diversified and complex surface structures; the surface structures are then converted, by a series of "morphophonemic" rules, into phonetic realizations. The total number of rules required by a combined phrase-structure/transformational model is far smaller than that which would be required by a phrase-structure model alone.

---

[2]For simplicity, the example which follows imagines the base structures to be sentences. It should be borne in mind, however, that the base output is a tree-structure and *not* a sentence. Transformations operate on structural descriptions, not on sentences.

The economy is achieved through the fact that transformation rules operate on hierarchically superior tree-structures rather than on separate but interdependent elements of those structures.

Chomsky's 1965 book, *Aspects of the Theory of Syntax*, presents a revision of the *Syntactic Structures* model which is now known as "the standard theory." The 1965 grammar consists of three components. One, the *phonological* component, is, for our purposes, equivalent to the morphophonemic rules of the 1957 version. The other two components, however, are either altered (*syntactic* component) or novel (*semantic* component).

The syntactic component consists of base rules and transformational rules. The base rules consist, in turn, of a phrase-structure grammar and a lexicon. The phrase-structure grammar rewrites nonterminal structural descriptors; the lexicon rewrites them as words in the language to be explained. The lexicon is conceptualized by Chomsky in a way which recognizes "semantic" classes which affect syntactic usage: transitive versus intransitive verbs, animate versus inanimate nouns, and so on. Both groups of lexical entries and single lexical entries require some kind of labeling to indicate contexts in which their usage, according to simple phrase-structure rules alone, would generate ungrammatical sentences. Chomsky wishes to avoid generating sentences such as "The eggs elapsed" and "Mike handed redness to Sam" (Kimball, 1973, p. 67). A separate lexicon achieves this goal more economically than a phrase-structure grammar generating words as output. The phrase-structure grammar generates the "slots into which items from the lexicon can be inserted" (Greene, 1972, p. 62). The transformational rules are equivalent in general intent to those of the 1957 version (some differences are noted in the next paragraph).

The semantic component takes the output of the syntactic base and, by means of a "dictionary" and a series of "projection rules" for meaningfully combining dictionary entries, "interprets" that output. Chomsky himself has contributed little detailed analysis of this component. It is important to note that, at least in 1965 (various hedges having surfaced since then), Chomsky imagined that the output of the syntactic base contained *all* the information necessary for semantic interpretation. This implies, correctly, that he saw the transformational rules as preserving meaning. This, in turn, necessitated some revision in the conceptualization of phrase-structure grammar and of transformation rules: the former now include the generation of markers for such features as negativity, and negativity has been deleted as a transformation. If we leave the base output as a structure of the rough form "T. T. Hall likes watermelon wine," and let "not" be an optional transformation, then clearly the base output will *not* contain all the information needed for an interpretation of the "surface-structure" for "T. T. Hall does not like watermelon wine." The output at the syntactic base also obviously must be more complex than the "kernel structure" envisioned in 1957 if it is to resolve all semantic ambiguities. The new phrase attached to this no-longer-necessarily-simple output is "deep structure." Deep structure is, more clearly than kernel structure, a potentially semantic, as well as a syntactic, concept.

From a syntactic point of view, the deep structure is the tree diagram on which transformation rules originally operate, and "surface structure" is the tree structure of the final transformation derivation. The province of grammar is, for all the grammatical sentences in a language, the generation of pretransformational and posttransformational outputs—deep and surface structures—and the formalization of rules relating these structures.

Leiber (1975) makes the point that the seemingly semantic additions of Chomsky's *Aspects* model were necessitated not on semantic grounds but on syntactic ones. In general, it has been Chomsky's unwavering intent to keep the construction of grammatical models independent of semantic issues (e.g., 1957, ch. 2). At least in part, this position seems to reflect Chomsky's feeling that, if the door is opened to any semantic consideration, in will rush all the endless controversies of the various symbolic disciplines. By staying in a purely formal syntactic mode, Chomsky hopes to avoid these controversies and to permit formal linguistics to make an elevating and clarifying contribution to topics hopelessly mired down in the bogs of human psychology (Leiber, 1975, pp. 162, 177).

It is clear that grammaticality and meaningfulness can be distinguished. Chomsky's famous "Colorless green ideas sleep furiously" (1957, p. 15) has at least some elements of grammaticality, but no meaning at all. We are, every day, exposed to many agrammatical fragments which clearly convey meaning. Moreover, Chomsky refuses to identify his grammatical distinctions, e.g., Noun phrase/Verb phrase, with semantic ones, e.g., actor/action. In "watermelon wine is liked by T. T. Hall," for example, "watermelon wine" = Noun phrase, but $\neq$ actor. (At a *deep-structure* level, of course, the equation of actor = noun phrase, action = predicate might be possible.) Also, as now seems apparent, certain transformations do, in fact, alter meaning while preserving grammaticality. For example:

> everyone in this room knows at least two languages;
> at least two languages are known by everyone in this room.

It is the implication of the latter, but not the former, that the two languages known are known in common.

However justified—syntactically or semantically—the rules of the standard, or 1965, version do seem to bend toward semantic concerns more than those of the 1957 version. But it clearly is not the case that this greater explicit incorporation of semantics in the grammatical model has satisfied very many linguists. It is, by consensus, semantics which has been the area of Chomsky's least compelling theorizing.

In his 1957 version, Chomsky did not elaborate a separate semantic component. Meaning derived from choices of optional rules, both at the phrase-structure (e.g., Noun → watermelon, Noun → kumquat) and transformational (e.g., the passive transformation) levels. While this model of meaning proved unsatisfactory to Chomsky, it did at least accord with the typical speaker's intuition that semantics and syntactics cannot be clearly separated from one another. In the *Aspects* model, Chomsky does elaborate a more semantically adequate base model, but, in the minds of a number of revisionists known as "generative semanticists," he has made a curious choice at just this point. Rather than having a semantically conceived generator, Chomsky postulates a syntactic generator whose output is read for its meaning by an interpretive component situated outside the main lines of his original model. The benign neglect this component has received from Chomsky himself suggests a process of incorporation by isolation. The generative semanticists suggest, by contrast, an incorporation of the sort effected by a primitive tribe when a stranger is welcomed as their new tribal chief. While the contributions of this group (George Lakoff and others) have not been accepted by Chomsky, they are enough within the same tradition not to have suffered definitive rejection, either. The Chomskyan alternative is neither sufficiently well characterized nor so clearly superior to allow a resolution of the grounds of contention. The controversy continues (surely proving, if nothing else, that Chomsky's apprehension that semantics is the linguists' quagmire was a valid one).

Leiber presents the generative semanticists' case in the following terms:

> ... if some semantic features of sentences can be specified in their syntactical deep structure why can not all such features be specified? Why split the syntactic and semantic components at all? Why not equate ultimate syntactic deep structure with semantic representation? Or, more speculatively, why not take the system of semantic representation to be something like the familiar predicate logic (with perhaps a few additions), and the base to be such a system supplemented with a relatively small number of "atomic predicates," or semantic primitives, universal to human thought? [1975, p. 122]

Thus, the first operation of this language model would consist of the generation of formulae/sentences/structures combining semantic primitives. These formulae then would be the input to a component putting a particular formula into some form considered grammatical in the natural language in question. The main problem attaching to such a solution is the allegation of arbitrariness which can be directed at any particular specification of its semantic details (Leiber, 1975, p. 129). Kimball complains that any such solution would have to be achieved "by brute force" (1973, p. 126). By this, he presumably refers to the lack of techniques or rules for specifying semantic deep structures.[3]

Psychologically, however, a generative semantic model is much more plausible than Chomsky's (Anderson and Bower, 1973, ch. 5). This observation leads us to these two questions: is Chomsky's model meant to be a real-time, "psychological" model of language usage and can psychology systematically supply more input to Chomskyan and generative-semantic language models so that these models can be more realistic approximations of human linguistic behavior?

The question of formal modeling versus actual performance is dealt with by transformational-generative grammarians in terms of distinctions between competence and performance and between language and speech. A natural language consists of an infinite collection of all grammatically appropriate sentences in that particular language. Speech, as we all know, is something else. Through inexperience, fatigue, indolence, and sheer stubbornness, among other contributing circumstances, our utterances often fall outside this grammatical class. Chomsky surely is correct in his understanding that a model of language should not have to incorporate all those factors which cause deviance from the grammatical norm. However, on the other hand, this does not isolate language modeling from psychology altogether, say on the example of a "pure" mathematics conceptualized as a realm of knowledge independent of knowers, particularly when language is, for Chomsky, a way of reconstructing the mind which generates it.

Chomsky recognizes this dependency of language modeling on psychology:

> . . . at several levels the linguist is involved in the construction of explanatory theories, and at each level there is a clear psychological interpreta-

---

[3]The problem of specifying semantic deep structures is one also faced, of course, in dream psychology, where, in principle, it has been solved via the free-association technique. That technique, formalized into a reliable procedure, might be of value in the study of conventional language as well. Or, if it is not literally applicable, its underlying principle—namely, that the resolution of semantic questions demands more data than does the resolution of syntactic questions—probably is. It will not be sufficient to examine one textual sentence. "Context," either as generated by the surrounding text or by free association, will need to be considered.

tion for his theoretical and descriptive work. At the level of particular grammar, he is attempting to characterize knowledge of a language, a certain cognitive system that has been developed—unconsciously, of course—by the normal speaker-hearer. At the level of universal grammar, he is trying to establish certain general properties of human intelligence. Linguistics, so characterized, is simply the subfield of psychology that deals with these aspects of mind. [1972, p. 28]

The problem is that the extent of this dependency, here clearly verbally acknowledged by Chomsky, seems not always to be recognized in the practice of transformational-generative grammarians. In recent years, largely thanks to the Chomskyan stimulus, a separate discipline has arisen in psychology known as psycholinguistics (e.g., Slobin, 1971). The psycholinguist studies the acquisition and use of language. The question has arisen of how the psycholinguist's findings are to be incorporated in theories such as Chomsky's. Various "experimental tests" of Chomsky's models have, for instance, indicated that these models underestimate the significance of semantic factors (Slobin, 1971; Greene, 1972). Developmentally, it has been observed that meanings (object pairings, categorizations) are acquired before verbal grammar (Brown, 1976; Miller, 1976). On the basis of such evidence, Locke (1976) has proposed that the child uses meaning to learn language, rather than language to learn meaning.

One might imagine, then, that transformational-generative grammarians would have attended to these suggestions of a conceptual/developmental priority of meanings. If so, one would be wrong. As Greene nicely illustrates, the typical response of contemporary grammarians to the contrary evidence of psycholinguistic research has been a retreat to the position that the psycholinguist has it all wrong: their field is *not* a subdiscipline of psychology, but, rather, is a purely descriptive account of the best set of formal rules capable of generating grammatical sentences which "accord with native speakers' intuitions about grammatical relationships" (1972, p. 95). The processes *actually* used by speakers and listeners—that's another topic altogether. It never was *intended* that these formal grammars be identified with structures of the mind (Sanders, 1974, p. 13). This response, of course, seems more than a little disingenuous. It is difficult, for instance, to accept the following statement by one of Chomsky's apologists at absolute face value:

Neither the earlier nor the later version of transformational grammar is presented by Chomsky as a psychological model of the way people construct and understand utterances. The grammar of a language, as conceived by Chomsky, is an idealized description of the linguistic *competence* of native speakers of that language. [Lyons, 1970, p. 94]

If the statement is taken literally, it surely makes Chomsky's efforts much less interesting, and much less relevant, than generally is imagined. Instead of a worldly model, we have merely a wordy one.

Regarding the competence/performance distinction, Greene notes that

it is very difficult not to slip into the assumption that, if a language user's intuitive knowledge is best described by a set of rules, then these rules must in some way be represented in his mind. . . . [1972, p. 96]

It also is difficult to believe that mind-data should not, in turn, be allowed to guide the reconstruction of this set of rules. And yet Chomsky regards it as "absurd" to consider his model a model of performance:

In fact, in implying that the speaker selects the general properties of sentence structure before selecting lexical items (before deciding what he is going to talk about), such a proposal seems not only without justification but entirely counter to whatever vague intuitions one may have about the processes that underlie production. [1972, p. 157]

Precisely. But, is the absurdity that the critics have not well understood Chomsky, or that he has failed to heed them? Why must "a theory of performance" "have to incorporate the theory of competence" (ibid.), but not vice versa? One can think of no other "subfield" of psychology in which competence models are so utterly distant from performance data.

I agree with MacCorquodale's (1970) argument that Chomsky's disavowal of performance concerns "leaves the competent speaker with nothing to say" (Greene, 1972, p. 192). One recalls Tolman's (1938) rats, lost in cognition at the maze's choice point. It seems to me incumbent upon a model with the mind-characterizing ambitions of Chomsky's that it be at least potentially framable in terms coordinate with those of some language of intentions or actions. I do not accept MacCorquodale's choice of a nonmentalist behaviorism as the ideal language for this purpose, but will instead propose below (part IV) a neopsychoanalytic model in which such coordination might be achieved. But, to coordinate intentions with execution, it must be recognized that, whatever the particular model chosen, we are expanding "formal" models of language to ones with a heavy semantic commitment at their logical *and temporal* base.

It is well to remind ourselves that it is not just the requirements of a theory of motivated action which suggest semantic priority. It also is the evidence of psycholinguistic research. For example:

> ... subjects confuse in their memory a sentence like *John liked the painting and bought it from the duchess* with other sentences such as *The painting pleased John and the duchess sold it to him*, which have different deep structures but similar semantic representations (Johnson-Laird and Stevenson, 1970). This has been interpreted as evidence that the level at which people process semantic content is even more abstract than a particular deep structure configuration.
>
> It might seem to follow from the foregoing discussion that what is required is neither a *one-level* theory, concentrating only on surface structure, nor a *two-level* deep and surface structure theory, but rather a *three-level* model incorporating semantic representation of "ideas," deep structure syntactic relations and surface structure final ordering of words. [Greene, 1972, p. 181]

If we accept the notion that an "abyssal" semantic level is required in language modeling, how shall we characterize that level? And how are we to avoid the charge of total arbitrariness in achieving these characterizations? Are there, perhaps, *psychological* data to lend some weight of reality to our choices? I believe that there are.

A third criterion Chomsky proposes for evaluating a grammar (in addition to weak and strong generative capacities) is *explanatory adequacy*. This criterion seems "psychological," in the sense that it specifies that a grammar must conform with plausible fact and theory relating to language acquisition in the child. The fact and theory must characterize what is universal, rather than particular, in language acquisition. They must address themselves to the issues of how it is that almost all humans achieve linguistic competence and that this competence is so parallel in form that we can, in each case, describe it as "linguistic" and mean, approximately, the same thing.

Chomsky's *use* of this criterion, however, has been such that the relevance of psychological observation and theory has been drastically minimized. He repeatedly emphasizes the "enormous disparity between knowledge and experience" (1972, p. 78). That is, children of almost all degrees of intelligence, however poorly organized and unsystematic the linguistic "reinforcement contingencies" they face, develop grammatical competence. This observation has suggested the somewhat controversial position that linguistic competence is mediated by a set of "innate" structures requiring only the priming action of very minimal and defective sorts of linguistic input. This position pushes the explanatory adequacy criterion in the direction of being synonymous with agreement with a rationalist model of linguistic structures. What seemed to have been a "psychological constraint" on linguistic modeling is, effectively, no longer that at all.

As Luria (1974–75) has pointed out, however, Chomsky seems to have overreacted to the clear failure of a particular species of behaviorism (Skinner, 1957) to account for language acquisition. From the observation that schedules of reinforcement cannot account for linguistic competence (Chomsky, 1959), Chomsky seems to have concluded: (a) that the development of linguistic competence is not mediated by experiential inputs and other developing competencies and (b) that, therefore, psychological observation of the infant and child has little direct relevance to linguistic modeling. Luria's counterproposal, the general tenor of which I agree with, is that

> ... "deep syntactic structures" as well as "deep semantic structures" should be looked on as the reflection of objective external relations having an objective significance as well as a long preverbal history which should be carefully studied in order to leave no room for the assumption that they stem from "innate rational schemes." [1974–75, p. 384]

The preverbal child has, as Piaget observes, already structured its world. It is not as if linguistic organization arises out of an organizational void. In fact, as Bloom (1970) and McNeill (1970) have pointed out, the propositional base of language is manifested earliest; it is not a generalization from linguistic experience, but a precondition of speech development. Since the verbal child will use language in a context of perception and action, it seems quite unparsimonious to assume that the underlying organization of language, perception, and action will be greatly different. At the adult level, it seems quite reasonable to imagine that these three systems will constantly feed back to one another to correct any significant discrepancies which develop among them. Ontogenetically, however, it seems most plausible to imagine that it is developing sensory and motor organizations which either, in a passive way, constrain, or, in a more active way, help to organize, linguistic competence. What this position means for the explanatory adequacy criterion is that a grammar of language should be in accord with "grammars" of perception, action, and motivation.

Bower's excellent review (1974) of the perceptual achievements of the infant begins to suggest some structural components of the child's perceptual "grammar": the dichotomous organization implied by the primacy of figure-ground relationships and, later, of subject/object discriminations; the egoistic frame of reference implied by the fact that movement or change of position is perceived relative to some representation of self; the grouping of environmental events by "common fate," or change of position, relative to self; the relatively later and more slowly achieved organization of events on the basis of their static proximity; the early acquisition not only of the segregation of objects as units in a visual field but also of the assignment of ego-relevant properties to them (is it graspable?); and so on. These "grammatical" competencies clearly suggest both syntactic and semantic components whose structures must feed into the development of linguistic competency.

Likewise, Piaget's description of the sensorimotor accomplishments of the child suggest a grammar of action and intention. The "invariant function" of assimilation, as a descriptive statement, implies the apprehension of a set of external events to which the infant's behavior is directible. Accommodation implies that behavior is, in turn, directed by these events. Sensorimotor development is environmental/self interaction of a servomechanistic form in the service of efficient adaptation. From initially undifferentiated perceptions and responses, those features of the environment with significant ecological implications for ego are perceptually segregated out and differentially responded to. Piaget himself says that sensorimotor schemes "prefigure" linguistic classes and relationships (1963, p. 124). Action logic precedes, and prefigures, verbal logic.

To this relatively "cold-blooded" account of the development of sensorimotor schemata received from experimental sources, moreover, we might add a psychodynamic notion of a developing grammar of motivational schemata (cf. Wolff, 1967). The world is a bundle of satisfiers, hurters, and frustrators; ego can, in turn, explore, attack, retreat, cuddle, complain, and so on. Action and movement, of varying degrees of affective quality, dominate.[4] The early development of intentionality, described by Piaget, suggests that "motives," as well as simple reaction patterns, are organized well before language comes on the scene.

These various observations and theoretical statements regarding infancy have, I submit, direct relevance to the formulation of an adequate explanatory model (in Chomsky's sense) of language. They suggest, for example, that the sentence, as a syntactic unit, is a direct outgrowth of the semantic, ecological requirements of infancy: I act on you and you act on me; this object goes with this object; this object has these properties. If this is the case, then one might be able to formulate, on the basis of early developmental data, a set of semantic primitives (only later feeding into linguistic

---

[4]It is, incidentally, these ecological requirements of developing cognition, and their dynamic consequences, which render inherently implausible any proposed base semantic organization, such as that of Reid (1974), which holds that only nouns, and not verbs/actions, have base representation.

syntactic structures) in such a way as to counter the argument that these primitives merely represent arbitrary armchair speculations of the adult philosopher, superimposed by "brute force" on the language-learner's mind. A set of such primitives, which I believe to be not implausible psychologically, is suggested later in the context of a dream "grammar" (chapter 11).

The primitives I will propose rest on two fundamental dichotomies suggested by developmental evidence: the moving versus the static basis of representational structures; and propositional (structural) versus modality (dynamic) organization (cf. Fillmore, 1968). In the first instance, there is the developmental suggestion that static environment contingencies are perceptually registered more slowly, and following a more halting course of development, than are moving ones. Bower (1974) reports, for example, that infants at one week of age perceive distance and changes of distance, while static perceptual groupings are not effectively organized until the end of the first year of postnatal development. The grouping operation which first develops and continues in later life to be used most efficiently is that of "common fate"; it depends upon the situation of either a moving self and a stationary object array, or a moving object array and a stationary self. There is also, of course, the massive evidence that the infant is a "doer" rather than a passive spectator/cogitator.

The second dichotomy rests on the distinction between the child's perceptual identifications (object perception) and her or his perceptual characterizations (a "good" object). It also derives from a psychoanalytic theory of development which suggests the "conative" task of characterization is as strong a developmental requirement as the "cognitive" one of identification. From the point of view of this theory, the structural/dynamic distinction attempts to accommodate, in a linguistic/propositional format, the dichotomy between psychic structures and mental energetics.

The intention of chapter 11 is to formalize, along lines suggested by Chomsky's model of syntactic organization, a Freudian theory of generative semantics. (Freud is a "generative semanticist." He attempts to frame a real-time, "psychological" model of the semantic structures underlying both action and thought. And, as already noted, he supplies a method for identifying these structures.) If these structures can be coordinated with the requirements of perception, action, utterance, and thought, as I believe they can, we then will have a way of thinking about language and motives, about syntactics and semantics, which might be a helpful input from psychology to linguistics.[5]

[5]To anticipate the subject matter of chapter 11, the base I will be proposing is a phrase-structure semantic grammar with the following rules:

1. $S \rightarrow S_I, S_A$
2. $S_I \rightarrow N_A V_I N_E, N_E V_I N_A$

It may seem curious to propose that any kind of dream grammar could have relevance to language. As I have tried to make clear, however, there are a number of formal parallels between the two cases: together, dreams and language are the most highly creative "ordinary" achievements of the human mind; neither can be accounted for by currently popular behaviorist, i.e., nonmentalist, models of explanation in psychology (it is, in fact, the *organization* of dreams, rather than their status as "conscious experiences," which has led to their neglect or denigration by behaviorists). There surely are differences as well between the two cases: the constraint of successive presentation in verbal utterance versus the possibility of simultaneous presentation (of a "sentence" as a particular image) in dreaming; the conventional and limited vocabulary of speech versus the personalized and practically limitless number of pictographic symbols probably available to the dreamer; and so on. But the differences seem, at this point, more matters of detail than fundamental. And, of course, there is the overriding similarity that both dream pictures and speech sounds are employed to construct organized, meaningful, i.e., motivated, narratives.

Since Freud's investigations of dreaming, the centrality of motivational factors in dreaming has been unmistakable. Freud attempted to show that many of the surface peculiarities of dreaming could be derived from the intersection of incompatible motive structures. This directed our attention to the peculiar situation underlying dreams: the person who is motivated both to "utter" and "not utter" X, or who is simultaneously motivated to "utter" both X and *not X*. In the case of literal utterances of the sort studied by the linguist, on the other hand, it has perhaps been more easy to imagine that motives can be taken for granted. Since we are studying competence, thereby excluding linguistic "slips" in which we say one thing but "really mean" another, the postulation of motives would be redundant: we say X because we *meant* to say X. It also would be tautological, because no separate access to meaning is provided except through the utterance itself. It is quite understandable, therefore, that the necessity of always linking utterance to motive or intention would first have become apparent in the dream case, and that

---

3. $N_A \rightarrow F, M, Si, Pm, Pf, Sp, C, Sy$
4. $N_E \rightarrow E$
5. $V_I \rightarrow ⊛, \rightarrow, \leftarrow, -<$
6. $S_A \rightarrow NV_A N, VV_A V$

7. $N \rightarrow N_A, N_E$
8. $V_A \rightarrow ⇕, =, = \ldots \square$
9. $V \rightarrow V_I, V_A$

The terminal elements of the system are F, M, Si, Pm, Pf, Sp, C, Sy, E, ⊛, →, ←, —<, ⇕, =, and = . . . □, and will be introduced more fully in chapter 11. The nonterminal elements are S (sentence), S_I (interactive sentence), S_A (associative sentence), N_A (noun, alter), N_E (noun, ego), V_I (verb, interactive), V_A (verb, associative), N (noun), and V (verb). The system actually may be closer to "correlational grammar" than to any Chomskyan grammar (E. von Glasersfeld, "The Yerkish language and its automatic parser," in D. M. Rumbaugh, ed., *Language learning by a chimpanzee: The LANA project.* New York: Academic Press, 1977. pp. 91–130).

a model implementing this necessity would first have arisen there, where the method of free association does provide conventional and independent access to such motives and intentions.

The plain fact is, as Vygotsky put it long ago, that:

> thought itself is engendered by motivation, i.e., by our desires and needs, our interests and emotions. Behind every thought there is an affective-volitional tendency, which holds the answer to the last "why" in the analysis of thinking. A true and full understanding of another's thought is possible only when we understand its affective-volitional basis. [1934, p. 150]

The same argument applies, of course, to speech. No explanation of linguistic behavior can be complete until some provision has been made for determining and encoding its "last why." Dreams, which flaunt their motivational base, have the general virtue for cognitive psychology of every mental exaggeration: they highlight processes which unobtrusively permeate more regular forms.

It remains to be seen, of course, whether linguistics and dream psychology really can do each other any favors. No one can pretend to a priori insights as to whether dreaming and language are as similar genotypically as they are phenotypically. We can only imagine, and adopt as a working hypothesis, that two phenomena so superficially alike in so many ways derive from common, rather than independently evolved, structures. But we do well, also, to recall that the phenomena themselves are not precisely parallel.

The simultaneous presentation of propositions in dream images, for instance, implies that the syntactic components (e.g., the transformational rules) concerned with intrasentence serial order must serve a different role, if any role at all, in dream construction. The order problem in dreams is *between* sentences (i.e., images). This is a problem largely neglected by contemporary linguists, whose breadth of coverage rarely exceeds the single sentence. Halliday (1967), however, has made an attempt to describe syntactic rules for the organization of semantic content across sentences in discourse. His work raises the possibility that some of the "thematic" integration of dreams could be explained in terms of a series of syntactic constraints on adjacent sentences. Basically, Halliday describes a method of parsing in which "given" and "new" semantic content is marked; it seems reasonable to assume that those interpropositional structures we call "narratives" will feature certain syntactic constraints pertaining to "new" and "given" elements. (Alternatively, of course, one might simply imagine that each dream episode is, from a Chomskyan viewpoint, a potentially gigantic complex sentence, containing a hierarchical order of nested constituent simple sentences.)

Whatever the difficulties which may lie ahead, however, it does not seem unreasonable to begin a serious and systematic consideration of the possibility of a true grammar of dreams. It surely will prove unproductive to continue treating dreams, in our research and in our theory, as ungrammatical strings of cognitive or affective elements. Dreams are phenomena with many organizational and structural parallels to language. It is time, then, to begin the process of relating the conceptualizations, methods, and models of the two fields to one another.

CHAPTER 9

Cognitive Psychology

Modern cognitive psychology is a systematic attempt to characterize the structures and processes by which humans process sensory input. Its method is not introspective description but the experiment whose performance data implicate a certain structure or process. Historically, its development owed a great deal to models—mechanical and conceptual—of information processors, and the terminology and reasoning of information theory still saturate the field. As it deals with the "fate" of sensory input (Neisser, 1964), cognitive psychology is largely concerned with human *memory*—i.e., with the kinds of post-stimulus representations we create and their organization. Its major contribution has been the systematic separation, on the basis of careful experimental evidence, of different forms of mental representation and of different levels at which such representations are processed. The classic introduction to the field is Neisser's *Cognitive Psychology* (1967). Other surveys include those of Posner (1973), Klatzky (1975), and Norman (1976).

As I have indicated in chapter 4 (figure 4-3, p. 78), Freud's topographic model makes certain assumptions about the waking treatment of sensory input. Its application to dreams is the suggestion that waking information flow is directionally reversed during sleep. Since cognitive psychology can supply us with a much more differentiated and soundly based model of waking information processing than was available to Freud, it should prove useful to reexamine Freud's concept of topographical regression in light of current evidence and theory on waking cognition. I would like to think that Freud would not have been displeased at this kind of reevaluation, for, as he once said ". . . dreaming is another kind of remembering, though one that is subject to the conditions that rule at night and to the laws of dream-formation" (1918, p. 51).

In this chapter, I will give a brief and highly selective account of that recent work in cognitive psychology which seems to me to have the most direct relevance for a cognitive model of dreams. The order of presentation is more or less chronological. I begin with the efforts of George Miller et al. to formulate a unit of psychological analysis compatible with the symbolic complexity of human experience—including, presumably, dreams. The argument then shifts to a more comprehensive plane, with an examination of Ulric Neisser's and others' models of waking information processing. The focus here is not so much on the fine detail of the waking model as such, but rather on those features of it, which, when topographically regressed, might have explanatory value in regard to dream experience. Examination then is made of a recent cognitive model of long-term memory, the deep-structural repository of Freud's "essential dream-thoughts" and the point of thought origination in a topographically regressed, dreaming mind. Finally, brief consideration will be given to recent studies of the free-association technique on which Freud erected his whole model of dream processes.

George Miller et al.: A New Unit of Cognitive Analysis?

George Miller was responsible for the introduction both of information theory and of transformational-generative grammar to cognitive psychology. His most important general contribution probably is his collaborative book, *Plans and the Structure of Behavior* (Miller, Galanter, and Pribram, 1960). In reaction to a long tradition within "the psychology of thinking" (Vinacke, 1952; Johnson, 1955), Miller et al. stressed the need for cognitive concepts with action implications. Drawing mostly on computer technology and theory they provided psychology with a new unit of behavioral analysis, the TOTE (*t*est-*o*perate-*t*est-*e*xit) routine. It was their idea that such an information-processing unit might replace the venerable but thoroughly shopworn concept of the reflex arc, the implicit basis of the psychological analyses of both classical psychoanalysis and classical behaviorism. TOTE was to be a unit fully consistent with the symbolic level of human functioning.

Input arrives at a TOTE unit's test phase, where it is subject to comparison, evaluation, and so on; when some incongruity is detected with the organism's current/desired state, an operation, or action, routine is initiated to move the organism toward that state; when the test operation indicates the desired match, the through-put exits the TOTE unit. Test is a representation ("image") unit, while Operate provides the action. The feedback loop between the two is an essential servomechanism controlling both thought and behavior. A *plan* is a hierarchy of TOTE units, with special elaboration of the operate phase (the authors' examples most often are of the execution of planned motor skills). Plans specify the order in which sequences of operations are performed.

Language enters into the TOTE unit in several ways. The subjective representation of plans is largely verbal ("first I'll do x, then y, then check it out, then . . .") More important, however, is the fact that, with the acquisition of grammaticosemantic plans (à la Chomsky), it now becomes possible to have plans generated by other plans rather than by "raw experience" itself. Language gives us the capacity for "metaplans." Plans are by no means an exclusively human prerogative; metaplans are. The authors clearly side with Soviet, rather than American, behaviorists in their insistence that language acquisition is responsible for a qualitatively different and more complex mediation of behavior ("the second signaling system"; see chapter 10). Miller et al. wax most enthusiastic about language: "Almost nothing we could say about the psychological importance of language could be too extravagent . . ." (1960, p. 143). They consider speech to be "controlling" of "all the psychological processes in a human being" (ibid.). And yet there is some hesitation to literally equate laws of grammar with laws of thought (1960, p. 155).

At a single stroke, Miller et al. seemingly resolved a number of the conceptual difficulties of reflex-arc psychology: how to deal with intentionality; how to explain the serial organization of behavior (cf. Lashley, 1951); how to account for the hierarchical (including grammatical) organization of behavior; and how to incorporate linguistically guided behavior, with its infinitely wider range, within a framework of behavior control shared with nonlinguistic organisms. Nonetheless, despite forging a considerable consensus for their criticism of reflex-arc models in psychology, Miller et al. were not successful in their sponsorship of TOTE as a replacement for such models. It is interesting to speculate why.

The basic answer, I think, is that TOTE leaned too heavily on computer-programming analogies and was not sufficiently well conceptualized within the natural language of psychology (or of humanity, which may be the same thing). In their tentative search for neuropsychological correlates, for example, the authors propose the following equation:

$$\frac{\text{plan}}{\text{mind}} = \frac{\text{program}}{\text{computer}} = \frac{\text{X}}{\text{brain.}}$$

Part of the difficulty in solving for X, I think, is that only the central term is moderately well understood. The plan/mind term is suggested by analogy to the middle term, but is not well-enough characterized in its own unique language—the language of human symbolism—to make its meaning very clear or to render it very useful in solving the term on the right. In riding two horses at once—transformational-generative grammar and information theory—TOTE gives full rein only to the latter. But that alternative is an *analogy* to human experience, while language *is* human experience. The authors are committed to the proposition that linguistic analysis may be the model for hierarchically and serially organized human behavior, but TOTE is not, basically, a linguistic unit. It is something we can map into programming routines in computers rather better than we can into human beings (cf. Leontiev, 1975).

As a potential natural language unit, TOTE does have some suggestive features: the segregation of a passive/associative/comparative test phase from an active/motivational/planful operate phase and the attachment of a dynamic, evaluative function to test units. And Miller et al. do have some interesting observations to make of sleep (dreams seem not to have attracted their attention): there is a close connection between consciousness, volition, and speech; at sleep onset we stop making plans, and inner speech and volition wane. "In sleep we are about as planless as we can get" (1960, p. 64). The implication seems to be that, when we dream, i.e., when consciousness "returns" in a major way, there is a restoration of inner speech as its necessary precondition.

But, by and large, and for reasons already indicated, Miller et al.'s positive program for the reformation of psychology has fared less well than their criticism of earlier models. It is to other lines of its development that we must turn to find cognitive psychology's more productive foundations for a contemporary cognitive model of dreams.

Ulric Neisser: A New Version of Topographical Regression?

Neisser's (1967) analysis has had greater staying power because it is more of an inductive generalization from research evidence and because programming analogies never overshadow psychological realities. Neisser's basic characterization of human information processing is that it proceeds by "analysis by synthesis"; that is, in analyzing input, the mind is forever reconstructing it. What is rejected emphatically is the idea that mental representations are copies of sensations; neither perceptions nor images nor memories are scaled-down residues of the original input—all are the products of active, constructive processes of mind.

At an elementary level of analysis of visual inputs, Neisser distinguishes two sorts of constructive processes: one is quick, crude, wholistic, and works in parallel; the other is deliberate, detailed, attentive, and sequential. The first process gives us, for example, the elemental units of perception, tells us what we might attend to. Following these preattentional processes, a more sequential focal-attention process fleshes out these elemental abstractions with full-scale perceptual structuring and supplies "meanings" from *schemata*, derivatives of past experience. All perception, Neisser feels, is a constructive cognitive process. Dreams, which Neisser likens to waking perceptions, clearly are cognitive acts; there is no possibility of treating their "perceptions" as veridical copies of any recent stimulus input. And yet dreams only show, in their characteristically exaggerated way, what is true of perception in general.

As also is true for the dream case, the constructive nature of waking perception can be based not only on generative, but also on serial-organizational, criteria. Visual perception always is an integration of inputs from serial glances or "snapshots." It has continuity over time. This fact implies an integrative process which persists across the span of successive glances at least long enough for us to perceive the world in a smoothly continuous way.

The preattentive representation of visual inputs, *iconic memory*, might itself facilitate this integrative process. Whether or not this is so, the experiments underlying the "discovery" of iconic memory provide an excellent illustration of the nonintrospective base on which cognitive psychology posits mental systems or processes. Sperling (1960) made a tachistoscopic presentation of a 3×3 matrix of letters. At various brief exposures, subjects could identify only 4 or 5 letters. However, when, after a display was terminated, a tone indicated a particular row to be reported, subjects often could report all 3 letters in the row. This seems to imply that for a brief period following the display the subject has access to the *complete* visual array. The time period is on the order of a second. "In short, Sperling's results demonstrate the existence of a form of immediate visual storage that is highly accurate but that decays very rapidly" (Klatzky, 1975, p. 29). As shown by "backward masking"— when, during a 1–2 second delay between the display and the signal of which row to report, a circle appears in the place of a letter, that letter is "erased"— iconic memory is highly susceptible, after a very brief interval, to interference by other visual input.

As Freud noted years ago in his paper on the mystic writing-pad (1925*a*), the requirements of adaptation are that we need an immediately reusable receptive system, but also a system which "holds" past impressions at least momentarily. Freud's solution was to divide these two functions "between two different systems (or organs of the mental apparatus)" (1925*a*, p. 228). Iconic memory is the most immediate holding mechanism of our visual-information processing apparatus.

Neisser wants to equate perception with the schemata which integrate successive glances or snapshots rather than with the latter themselves. This clearly makes perception a constructive process rather than something "given" by environmental inputs. It also raises the possibility, in the case of dreams and hallucinations, that schemata can be activated from storage as well as by environmental inputs. Dreams have the integrated properties of schematically guided perception. In specific reference to dreams Neisser states that "it is reasonable to conclude that all types of imagery do involve a process of visual synthesis, of construction, much like the one used to attend to objects and to integrate successive snapshots in ordinary vision" (1967, p. 153). That is, the images of dreams are not "retrieved" from some ancient filing cabinet of visual memory for later display, but they are reconstructed by the same processes which are responsible for integrated waking perceptual experience.

Similar processes are operative in auditory perception, whose "sensory register" is called by Neisser "echoic memory." Listening also is considered a constructive process. Rapid visual and auditory processing probably works in parallel, rather than through a common processor (Griffin, 1973). In correlation with the requirements of serial speech perception, preattentional echoic memory seems to persist for at least twice as long as iconic memory, and to be less readily "erasable" by subsequent inputs. Neisser stresses the role of inner speech in the attentional analysis which integrates discrete echoic data. The constructive attentional process of auditory perception is inner speech: we produce "linguistic forms" (1967, p. 217) (but not necessarily covert articulation) to match the filtered outputs of echoic memory. Furthermore, at a level one step removed from simple auditory perception, "active verbal memory," or "short-term memory," seems temporarily to "store" both visual through-puts (generally translated to verbal form[1]) and auditory through-puts by the recycling and organizing process of "rehearsal." Recycled long enough, such contents may pass into long-term memory. Rather than viewing short-term memory as a set of "structures," however, it is probably preferable to simply imagine a rehearsal process intervening between perceptual identification and long-term storage.

[1]It is clear, however, that at least some visual coding is possible in short-term memory, even if that is not the most typical coding strategy (Klatzky, 1975, ch. 7).

The importance accorded inner speech in auditory attention and in active verbal memory has an implication for language use. Since the understanding of language is constructive, the generative mechanisms identified by Chomsky also must be involved in language reception. In general, Neisser works to assimilate Chomsky's structures to general psychological analysis by demonstrating similarities in perceptual and linguistic analysis. For example, he uses the case of perceiving a point on a moving wheel to show that visual perception is hierarchically ordered and that "constituents" of this organization (e.g., figure/ground) can be identified (1967, p. 254). That we cannot understand a sentence until a constituent structure is generated for it is, of course, compatible with Neisser's more general model of perceptual analysis by synthesis or construction.

Other authors have separated different levels of information processing in terms of their preference for different coding strategies. These strategies are indicated by typical errors of identification in conditions of iconic storage, rehearsal, and long-term storage (Klatzky, 1975). For example,

BAT-RAT

is a likely error in an iconic memory experiment, whereas

BAT-PAT

building less on iconic similarity and more on phonetic similarity, is a likely error in a "short-term memory" experiment. In recall of terminally stored material, however, a likely error might be

BAT-BALL

i.e., semantic strategies dominate in long-term storage.

Much of the experimental effort of cognitive psychology has focused on immediate or short-term processing mechanisms. Thus Neisser's characterization of long-term storage is more tentative. He feels that "remembering," like "perceiving," involves at least two stages: a crude, wholistic one (labeled "primary process"!) and a more analytic, sequential one ("secondary process"!). The secondary process is guided by what he calls "executive routines."

One of the great advantages for psychological theory of the development of computing devices has been its demonstration that it is not unreasonable to assign self-regulating routines to devices as complex as Homo sapiens. All psychology students are taught to reject little-people-inside-the-person as explanations of behavior, and also they generally are taught that Freudian concepts like ego and censor are prime examples of such homunculi. Drawing on analogies to computer-software technology, however, Neisser insists that humans must have metaplans, or programs, which regulate other programs. He explicitly suggests (1967, p. 294) that Freud's dream censorship, for instance, might be conceptualized as an executive routine. This would not be explanation by an unanalyzed homunculus, however, for the properties of such an executive routine could be specified.

With respect to precisely what it is that long-term memory stores, Neisser suggests that it is in the nature of constructive recollection that we remember "how to," rather than "what." That is, action sequences are more directly elicitable than any particular products of such sequences. We remember "how to" use an automobile jack, but also "how to" recreate a picture of an old friend's face and "how to" recite a childhood poem.

In remembering such events, active verbal memory—i.e., selective rehearsal, organization and reorganization—receives input from long-term storage rather than from receptor systems. But it is not imagined that this limited "topographic" reversal radically alters the central processing systems of mind: they operate similarly whether "input" is from perception or memory.

This last observation provides a framework in which to consider more systematically the current applicability of Freud's model of topographic reversal during sleep. To his great credit, and unlike most other cognitive psychologists, Neisser does see dreaming as a major problem for cognitive psychology and Freud as a major cognitive theorist. Neisser's own model of dreaming seems to be something like this: active processing of input from storage (and to a very limited extent, from perceptual systems) goes on during REM sleep; the processes involved include the same constructive, synthetic, and selective mechanisms which operate on sense inputs in wakefulness; due perhaps to a weakening of the strength of waking executive routines and/or to the institution of other executive routines, dreaming is characterized by multiple, parallel processing to a greater extent than is waking thought; the result of the outputs of the several simultaneously operative processors may or may not be sensible, useful, and so on. The discontinuous or illogical nature of dream thinking is, at least in part, attributed to motivational intrusions.

This model is remarkably similar to Freud's topographic one, as I have presented it in chapter 4. Unfortunately, I believe the similarity extends to one major known limitation of Freud's model: Neisser shares Freud's unwillingness to acknowledge fully the synthetic nature of the dream product. Like Freud, he underestimates the serial, narrative organization of the dream, which must reflect the operation of executive routines like those operative in narrative formation generally, applied here to multiple-processor outputs generated during sleep.

Another possible difficulty is that Neisser's approach to imagery is a "functional" rather than a "phenomenal" one (Neisser, 1968). This approach certainly is appropriate to, and has been convincingly argued for (e.g., Pylyshyn, 1973), that part of cognitive psychology concerned with the uses of representation in external adaptation. It is less helpful to dream psychology, however, where imagery is the dependent variable and where one of the things we most need to explain is how, in the dream, merely "knowing about" X passes into a sensory-like "experiencing of" X. How is it that the object reconstructions of sleep become uniquely "real" to us?

> You can obviously say or think "triangle," without a triangle in front of you. You can picture a triangle, visually or tactually. Most people find it easier to say triangle than to picture one. The closer you get to the raw sensory experience, the harder it is to generate the response from within. There may, in fact, be a sensory stage that is wholly out of reach for most people. The higher [i.e., more schematic] levels of reconstruction seem more commonplace in ordinary experience than the lower ones, *except in dreams.* [Brown and Herrnstein, 1975, p. 437, italics added]

The question is how helpful Neisser's functional account is in discriminating "lower" levels of perceptual reconstruction, including dream imagery, from more schematic ones. The dream problem is to explain why REM images are regularly so literal. From a general topographic viewpoint, we must imagine, with Freud, that a deficit of incoming sensory stimulation in sleep (also, in psychosis, sensory deprivation, etc.) permits the "degeneration" of abstract verbal or spatial schemata into more literal perceptual constituents.

It does not seem, then, that topographically regressing Neisser's model would produce results much different from those found in Freud's model of dreaming. In both cases, one might imagine information flowing "backward" in sleep, resulting in "sensory-like" images. The newer model does, however, make explicit some interesting explanatory possibilities only latent in Freud's version.

One of the most peculiar properties of dreams, for instance, is the fact that "the subject does not relate what is happening to memories of his past life and of the normal world, so that the dream is 'discontinuous' with the rest of his experience" (Green, 1968, p. 15). This lack of critical reflection, this failure to bring past experience to bear upon the interpretation of dream images, is perhaps more understandable if we imagine that the active verbal processes which ordinarily interpret visual displays are, in the dream case, already "loaded" with the task of *creating* them. It is interesting to note that, even in the imaginative production of daytime visual narratives from storage, critical reflection can be, at least for the moment, absent (Foulkes and Fleisher, 1975).

Another peculiarity of dream thought, noted by Freud (1900, e.g., pp. 206, 326-29), is its susceptibility to nonsensical clang associations and semantic reversals. If we imagine that phonetically or acoustically biased short-term memorial processes characterize the immediate predream generator, then the dream's reliance on phonetic puns is not nearly so surprising. Nor, more speculatively, would the "black-white," "love-hate," etc., reaction-formation reversals of dreams be so surprising: at an automatic, almost non-semantic, level, the word "black" most often does trigger off the word "white." Although there clearly is a semantic relation between the two terms, it is not "meaningful," and it seems to introspection that their connection for the adult mind is more at the superficial level of an acoustic "relatedness."

A major deduction of the model would be the dependence of dreaming on inner-speech processes. It is the attentional, organizational mechanisms of active verbal memory which would have to critically intervene between long-term stores and visual images. It is this deduction which suggests the feasibility of constructing "a grammar of the image" (Reid, 1974), particularly a grammar of dream imagery. The suggestion is that this grammar is derivative of the grammar for speech and therefore that its constituents should reflect those of ordinary grammar. It is on this premise that the grammar of this book is constructed (see chapter 11).

Is there any direct evidence to suggest an integral relationship between inner speech and perception in dreams? As it so happens, there is. Jakobson (1973, p. 39) reports that:

> the inhibition of visual dreams connected with encoding disorders of language (Anan'ev, 1960, p. 336) has rightly been interpreted as a breakdown of that code which provides the transition from verbal to visual signals. (Žinkin, 1959, p. 475)

Likewise, consider the account by actress Patricia Neal of her recovery from three strokes. At six months following the strokes, little recovery of syntactic organization was observed and "her sleep was dreamless . . ." (Farrell, 1969, p. 90). Even as inner and external speech patterns were returning to their pre-stroke norms: " 'I haven't had a single dream since this thing happened to me' Pat remarked as we sat down to dinner one night. 'Not *one* dream . . .' " (ibid., p. 157).

These claims might be viewed with some skepticism, in view of the illusory claims by many normal-speaking subjects that they "never" dream; brought into the laboratory and awakened during REM sleep, such subjects *do* recall dreams (Goodenough, Shapiro, Holden, and Steinschriber, 1959). The independent assertion of the same claim in the same circumstances does seem somewhat remarkable, however. Even stronger evidence, I believe, comes from the case of C. Scott Moss, himself a dream researcher at the time he had a stroke. Here, clearly, is an ideally sensitive observer of his own dream experience.

Moss reports that, for a four-month period following his stroke:

I did not recall a single dream. This struck me as a curious state of affairs since for years I had been interested in the study and meaning of dreams; however, my stroke apparently impaired either the ability to have dreams or my capacity to remember them. I lay down each night for seven or eight hours of uninterrupted sleep. It was as if during the day-time I had no words to express what was happening and at night I had no dreams—it was a complete and total vacuum of self-speech . . . . [1972, p. 9]

The possibility of faulty dream recall seems less plausible than the one of faulty dreaming, for

. . . even today I hold many waking memories from my period of hospi-talization and the first few months when I had no words to describe these events even to myself, but at the same time do not remember hav-ing dreamed at all during these four months . . . . as I recovered my in-ternal verbalizations, the memory of nocturnal mentation began to recur. [ibid.]

Moss's impression, conveyed to me in personal correspondence (1975), is that "perceptual imagery in sleep was totally absent." While REM-awakening data are needed to tie down this relationship of defective inner speech and defec-tive or nonexistent dream imagery, Moss's observations surely are among the most significant ones yet made on the process of dreaming, and they are in striking accord with a cognitive-topographical model of the conditions under-lying dream formation.

Another feature of dreams which Freud (1900, ch. VII) felt must have significant implications for their psychological explanation is the ease with which they are forgotten. Recent research has established that REM dreams are indeed generally forgotten unless spontaneously or experimentally termi-nated by a period of wakefulness (e.g., Wolpert and Trosman, 1958). This process of forgetting is so regular, so reliable, that it seems unpromising to at-tribute it to "repression," which is itself a poorly understood and unreliably demonstrable effect. The explanation more likely derives from "cognitive" factors.

It seems likely that active verbal memory, or rehearsal, mechanisms are sufficiently engaged during REM sleep in following their own dream-narrative creations to permit the kind of serial organization REM dreams patently have. That is, some "shadowing" of the perceivable dream is required for its construction as a coherent narrative. However, as indicated earlier, we might imagine that the requirements of dream construction itself are sufficiently demanding that other tasks habitually performed by active verbal memory become strictly secondary considerations during stage REM. These other tasks include not only critical reflection, but also a systematic enough effort at rehearsal so that imaginal content is prepared for long-term storage. Thus recall generally is available on REM arousals for specific dream episodes or for interrelated series of such episodes, but, unless the active verbal memory processes of a waking mind supervene, these dream episodes are lost to long-term retrieval. It should be stressed that, on the present model, it is not so much that the mind is "waking" but that wakefulness means it no longer is encumbered by the constructive task with which it was occupied during sleep.

Thus, it does not seem to me impossible that the cognitive psychologist's waking model of information processing might be "topographically regressed," as Freud put it, and some features of dreaming explained thereby. As compared to the waking model Freud turned on its head, the present one rests more upon careful experimental data than on assumption. And this version of topographical regression has the great merit that it seems susceptible to certain forms of experimental verification.[2]

[2] It should be made clear that Neisser is *not* responsible for the particular dream model sketched in above. The model is my construction from inputs supplied by him and other sources. Hence, the inaccuracies and deficiencies of the model are my responsibility alone.

It also should be noted here that Neisser has offered a revision of his 1967 information-processing model in a book which became available only after the present volume was in press, namely: U. Neisser, *Cognition and Reality* (San Francisco: W. H. Freeman, 1976). The newer account, foreshadowed in Neisser (1975), is a perceptual-cycle model in which *schemata* direct *exploration* sampling *objects* modifying *schemata*, and so on. It differs from the earlier model primarily in its change from a closed inner-information-processing system only initially dependent on stimulus inputs to an open perceptual cycle which is continously interactive with real-world objects. The modification makes Neisser's cognitive model more consistent with perceptual models developed by J. J. Gibson.

Neisser now refuses to identify the schema, or *any* particular portion of his tripartite cycle, as a percept. Perception is a *continuous process* of dynamic interaction of schemata, exploration, and objects. Neisser's disavowal of the schema as percept also follows from a rejection of the phenomenal account which asserts that we "read off" our own perceptual imagery. Adopting Gibson's point of view, Neisser holds that we see objects in the world rather than replicas in the mind. But this sensible denial that we *see* mental *replicas* is extended to the denial of a distinct phenomenal status for those *representations* we *use* in perceiving the world.

Neisser allows that schemata can become detached from the rest of the perceptual

One of the nicest qualities of Neisser's theorizing is his openness to considering the limitations of current cognitive psychology. Freud's models of mind contained not just processes and systems but also contents and motives. Neisser (1964, 1967) distinguishes the task of cognitive psychology (how sensory inputs determine experience and performance) from that of what he calls "dynamic psychology" (how motives determine experience and performance). Cognitive psychology takes motives for granted or considers them as *constants* in its analysis. Neisser recognizes the equal validity of beginning with motives as *variables*.

Taken by itself, the cognitive approach is weak as explanation:

> If what the subject will remember depends in large part on what he is trying to accomplish, on his purposes, do not predictions become impossible and explanations *ad hoc?* If we give no further account of these purposes, how can we tell what he will think of next? [1967, p. 304]

The problem is not so much that its models are "cognitive" as that, at present, cognitive psychology's models are relatively contentless:

> ... a really satisfactory theory of the higher mental processes can only come into being when we also have theories of motivation, personality, and social interaction. The study of cognition is only one fraction of psychology, and it cannot stand alone. [1967, p. 305]

---

cycle. In fact, such detached schemata are thought to underlie "all so-called higher mental processes" (1976, p. 133). The most familiar form assumed by the detachable schema is that of the mental image. Since Neisser's model does not characterize such schemata as percepts, how does it characterize them? According to Neisser's revised account of mental imagery, schemata are perceptual *anticipations*, preparations for specific kinds of information acquisition. Detached schemata lead, not to perceiving, but to the "fundamentally different" (1976, p. 131) higher mental process of imagining. "Imagining and seeing are fundamentally different . . . . The experience we have when [schemata] do stand alone is imagining, not seeing" (ibid.).

Neisser's current view, then, rejects the idea that a visual image is a "percept" formed in a topographically regressed manner in a linear system. He asks why, if this were the case, "images and percepts are not systematically confused with one another. How does the subject know whether the present content of his consciousness originated with an external stimulus? . . . [W]e almost always know this, *at least when we are awake*" (1976, p. 129, italics added). Neisser answers his own question with the observation that imagining and perceiving normally are not confused "because the latter involves the continuing pickup of new information" (1976, p. 130). Or, as Freud (1917b) put it, when we are awake we can use motor activity to test the reality of our perceptual experience.

Neisser himself observes, in a footnote (1976, pp. 31–32), that dreams present some difficulty for the position that it is the full, real-world interactive perceptual cycle, rather than its internal schema, which is to be identified with perceptual experiencing. But he seems not to appreciate the full extent of this difficulty. *The fact is that, despite the absence both of real-world objects and of real-world explorations, we have perceptual experience during sleep.* That is, in the absence of a complete, interactive perceptual cycle, we do experience detached schemata, or mental representations, as if they were percepts. Neisser (1967) acknowledged this fact; it is unclear how Neisser (1976) can ex-

As laudable as Neisser's sentiments are, I cannot help but feel that his way of stating them is part of the problem, rather than its solution. That is, the implication seems to be that it is the task of other specialists, in other disciplines of psychology, to round out the cognitivist's account. But cognitive psychology is not a "fraction" of human psychology, it is its *core*, and it is that core itself which needs elaboration of its semantic dimensions rather than passive borrowings from other fields.

John Anderson and Gordon Bower: A New Mental Semantics?

The functional treatment of imagery has led to at least one significant experimental finding. Certain kinds of images are highly effective mnemonic devices. Neisser (1975) cites the case of the facilitation of an X-Y memorial connection by the device of imaging X *in* Y. His particular example is "shark *in* crib." It is not effective to separately imagine a shark and a crib. The ele-

---

plain it. In fact, it seems as if a linear model of imagery as perceptual "backfiring" is better able to explain the phenomenal data of sleep than is Neisser's current model of the image as a detached perceptual anticipation. The current model simply amplifies the problems I have ascribed to the older one in accounting for the sensory-like quality of dream experience.

Neisser's revision has been framed in the service of the laudable goal of making cognitive models increasingly real-world relevant. But there is confusion here, I think, between according real-world objects a coordinate *theoretical status* with mental representations of those objects, on the one hand, and making a cognitive theory more readily *congruent* with real-life experience, on the other. Paradoxically, Neisser's revision is a less realistic account than his earlier statement. Quite to the contrary of everyday observations, we now are presented with a person whose sole goal seems to be efficient information acquisition. Neisser specifically rejects Piaget's notion of assimilation as a counterpart to the accommodation of cognitive structures to reality (1976, p. 66). The young child is not distorting the world in the service of already existent inner-systemic structures; he or she merely is accommodating less efficiently. A parallel from small-group research (Bales, 1951), however, suggests that Neisser has given mind an external "task" orientation without realizing that any system established for external purposes soon develops internal needs of its own, needs which come to distort its task mission in systematic ways. It is difficult to see how, in the absence of such a recognition, one could begin to account for the content of dreams, or, for that matter, for much of everyday life experience.

By no means, however, are all of the features of Neisser's revision unpromising bases for an account of dreaming or uncongenial with the particular model of dreaming developed in this book. For example, in refutation of the criticism that Neisser has relegated motives to an extracognitive status, he now explicitly characterizes motives as general cognitive schemata rather than as "alien forces that bring otherwise passive [cognitive] systems to life" (1976, p. 56). The revision also contains an increased recognition of the parallel organization of perception and action. Schemata are not only plans for action but patterns of action. The concept of "cognitive map" is elaborated to describe the embedding of perceptual schemata in higher-order schemata which synthesize information inputs and guide behavioral outputs. It is interesting to note that, in Neisser's characterization, such maps always include a representation both of ego and of world (1976, p. 117).

ments must be interrelated if facilitation is to occur. Neisser reports that all subjects told to imagine "shark *in* crib" experience memorial facilitation, regardless of whether they claim to have seen "an internal representation which bears a close correspondence to the sensory experience which . . . [might have given] rise to it"—Posner's definition of imagery (1973, p. 18). Thus the demonstration seems to have little to do with phenomenal imagery. I take it, rather, as saying that the natural unit of the cognitive system is a relational one. Information put in that form is better assimilated than is information which does not fit a relational mold.

Anderson and Bower (1973) reached the same conclusion on the basis of their study of long-term semantic storage. For dream psychology, such storage is as basic a starting point as iconic or echoic memory and pattern recognition are for traditional cognitive psychology. Thus the dream model to be presented in chapter 11 is especially concerned with the semantic organization of the dreamer and of the dream. In this context, Anderson and Bower's model of waking semantic organization merits attention.

Their theory is called HAM, for *h*uman *a*ssociative *m*emory. It is conceived within what the authors call a neo-associationist framework, a tradition quite removed from Neisser's constructivism. And yet, at a critical point, it deviates from associationism proper (hence the "neo") in the direction of rationalism and structuralism, particularly perhaps in the direction of Chomsky. The basic unit of long-term memory, the authors assume, is neither the single item of input nor the stimulus-response bond: it is the mentalistic notion of a "proposition." What we store are propositions about our world and our relationship to it.

HAM imagines that both auditory and visual inputs are parsed into propositions on their way to long-term memorial encoding. A linguistic parser works on the output of auditory holding mechanisms (and, secondarily, on that of visual holding mechanisms); a perceptual parser works on the output of visual holding mechanisms (and, secondarily, on that of auditory holding systems). The holding systems, or "buffers," are short-term memorial processes. The parsers analyze inputs into binary graph structures or tree diagrams. To use the authors' own favorite example, the auditory input "In a park a hippie touched a debutante" is parsed as

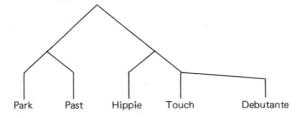

Park   Past   Hippie   Touch   Debutante

Each propositional tree has two sides: the left branch is the *context subtree;* the right branch is the *fact subtree.* In terms to be developed here (see chapter 11), the fact subtree is a *sentence structure,* while the context subtree contains *dynamic* or *means modifers.* The fact subtree asserts a relationship; the context subtree qualifies it. Thus, although Anderson and Bower specifically avoid phrasing their propositional concept in linguistic terms—to make certain that it is understood that the unit encodes perceptual as well as linguistic data—it is compatible with the kind of linguistic/propositional units developed in chapter 11.

It is highly instructive, I think, to note how similar units independently evolved in two quite different contexts. Anderson and Bower's choices were made after perusal of the experimental and theoretical literature of their field. They were made in full recognition of how important unitizing choices are:

> The most fundamental problem confronting cognitive psychology today is how to represent theoretically the knowledge that a person has: what are the primitive symbols or concepts, how are they related, how are they to be concatenated and constructed into larger knowledge-structures, and how is this "information file" to be accessed, searched, and utilized in solving the mundane problems of daily living. The choice of a representation is central, since how one handles this issue causes widespread effects throughout the remainder of his theoretical efforts .... a good structural representation of the problem already constitutes half of its solution [1973, p. 151]

The "deep grammar" of HAM consists of a set of rules describing input trees which HAM will accept for storage. The "receptiveness" of long-term memory to material from active or short-term memory generally is considered to be as important to long-term coding as is the sheer amount of rehearsal the material has received (Klatzky, 1975, ch. 5). Among the most basic rewrite rules of HAM's deep grammar are these:

proposition → context, fact
fact → subject, predicate
predicate → relation, object
context → time, location.

In its deep grammar rules and its formalization of propositional trees, HAM is a significant achievement in the conceptual organization of the phenomena of semantic memory.

In terms of the topographical model suggested earlier, one might imagine that, in dream formation, propositions are "parsed back" into images. Therefore, in any meaningful dream analysis, images must, in turn, be reparsed into propositions with structural and dynamic features characteristic of HAM's propositional trees. I believe that the scoring system for dreams described in part IV meets this criterion.

Incidentally, a question arises in this and other topographic models: why isn't there more regression to *auditory* imagery? Why, particularly if the immediately preceding step is primarily speech mediated, isn't the final step of regression simply a set of hallucinated speech realizations? Only guesses can be hazarded here. One might be that speech *is* "action," and that inner speech is an important mechanism in the regulation and control of human action. Freud's (1900) protection-of-sleep may require more passive realizations, ones less likely to spill out "behaviorally." In this regard, it is especially interesting that, although in nonlinguistic organisms muscle tone is diminished in stage REM all over the body, in humans it is reduced most perceptibly in those muscles of face, chin, and neck which are most strongly implicated in speech realizations (Berger, 1961; Jacobson, Kales, Lehmann, and Hoedemaker, 1964).

Although Anderson and Bower readily admit that we have images, and although they are inclined to view imagery in more "sensory" terms than Neisser (1967), they note that HAM does not permit the permanent storage of pictorial representations. HAM stores tree-diagram interpretations of perceptual inputs. Under conditions of topographical regression, these interpretations presumably are used to reconstruct perceptual representations.

HAM lacks a set of rules for assigning propositional trees to either auditory or visual inputs. The authors' examples—e.g., the hippie and the debutante—have been worked out intuitively.[3] Clearly the most difficult, and still the least successful, part of the construction of the dream model to be presented in part IV has been writing rules of data/model correspondence. Yet the model does have a set of rules for such correspondence, which, if far from ideal, are at least workable (cf. appendix B).

There are a number of likely possibilities as to how the propositional contents of long-term storage are interconnected. Tulving (1972) has discriminated *episodic* memory (stored information relating to temporally ordered events: "first I did this, then that, then this happened . . .") from *semantic* memory (this, "logically," goes with that: this is an instance of that or this is a class of which that is a member). Anderson and Bower (1973) feel that their

---

[3]Frederiksen (1975), however, has provided a ruleful alternative procedure for representing the structure of knowledge acquired from linguistic or nonlinguistic inputs.

distinction of context (particularization) and fact (timeless) covers Tulving's dichotomy. The same argument, of course, might apply to my dream model's dynamic/structural distinction. However, it also is possible to coordinate semantic memory with the relatively unordered associative sentence (A goes with B = B goes with A) and episodic memory with the sequentially ordered interaction sentence (A hit B ≠ B hit A). The dream model's lexical class/ subclass orderings would correspond to Anderson and Bower's hierarchical organization of classes. Its associative/interactive distinction, however, may not be precisely identical to any distinction in HAM, although it may be like Frederiksen's (1975) state/event dichotomy. This distinction, moreover, has the further provocative feature that it puts motives *in* memory, rather than just having them act on or through it (cf. Frederiksen's provision for "procedural" as well as "structural" memory).

Fundamentally, the interrelatedness of long-term stores is best conceptualized at present as a matter for empirical investigation. With the selection of appropriate analytic units, and with rules for coordinating such units with linguistic/perceptual inputs/outputs, memorial organization moves into that select class of psychological problems which effort alone may solve.

The Method of Free Association

Freud proposed the use of "free association" to determine the associative context in which the dream presumably was generated (1900). Recent research by cognitive psychologists Matthew Erdelyi and Ralph Haber confirms that "free association" can, in fact, result in the recovery of previously unreported memorial contents.

Haber and Erdelyi (1967) had 30 subjects view an historical scene (a gathering of people and objects around a cotton gin) for a .1 second exposure time. The subjects next indicated, by drawings, their recall for the picture. Members of an experimental group (n = 20) then "mentally concentrated on the picture" while fixating on a blank projection screen and said aloud whatever words came to mind. For each experimental subject, the first 12 of these self-generated cues were recorded by the experimenter on cards, which then were used as stimuli for further free associations (no longer limited to single words). Then subjects gave 10 discrete word associations to each stimulus card. The entire free association procedure took about 35 minutes. The control group (n = 10), meanwhile, had been playing darts. Both groups then were asked to redraw the original stimulus. Each member of a "yoked-control" group (n = 10) was shown the original drawing of a yoked experimental group subject and asked to copy it; the subject then went through the free-association tasks and redrew the stimulus to which he originally had been exposed. This group thus knew as much of the stimulus as experimental subjects "consciously" knew at the time of their first drawings. Judges reliably rated drawings for their degree of correspondence to the original stimulus. In addition, each subject's 132 discrete word associations were reliably rated for their relevance to 7 key elements of the original stimulus.

The results indicated that the second drawings of experimental group subjects were in significantly greater correspondence with the original stimulus than were their first drawings. This was not true for subjects in either control group. The difference between the experimental and the yoked-control group is taken to indicate that experimental subjects were not simply filling in plausible correlates of the material of the first drawing, but were adding elements recovered from their brief exposure to the original stimulus.

The authors then analyzed whether the 7 items, in terms of whose relevance free associations were judged, had appeared in either or both of a subject's drawings. An item appearing in both drawings was called "conscious"; an item appearing only in the second drawing was called "preconscious"; while an item appearing in neither drawing was either "unconscious" or "unregistered." The free-association relevance scores for such items were ordered as follows: conscious, preconscious, unconscious/unregistered. The superiority of the emission of preconscious to unconscious/unregistered elements suggests that the particular content of the free-association procedure may have been responsible for item recoveries in the second drawing. Unconscious and unregistered contents were segregated on the basis of data from the yoked-control group, which obviously could not have registered the original stimulus. Since there were significantly fewer unconscious/unregistered associations for the yoked-control group than for experimental group, it seems clear that the latter group's unconscious/unregistered associations also must have contained a genuinely "unconscious" component. Employing these latter criteria, the magnitude of emergence of different kinds of contents in free associations is ordered in the following way: conscious, preconscious, unconscious, unregistered. Thus subjects' free associations were most likely to reflect already available contents, but they also included significant components relating to previously inaccessible memories and they included memories which continued to be inaccessible in deliberate attempts at recalling a previous experience.

The authors conclude that:

> the experiments support certain key notions of Freud. The hypothesis
> that below-conscious psychic material continues to influence and mani-
> fest itself in a variety of behaviors is naturally one of these. Another
> concerns the Freudian therapeutic technique in which fantasy produc-
> tions of varied types (including primarily free associations) are the basic
> tools for achieving this necessary clinical recovery. The present study has
> experimentally demonstrated that genuine recoveries of below-conscious
> material can and in fact do occur as a result of intervening word-associa-
> tion experiences. [1967, p. 627].

In a second investigation, Erdelyi (1970) employed a 4 X 3 matrix of
discrete objects (a cat, a TV set, etc.) as the original stimulus. He essentially
replicated the findings of the first study. In the latter experiment, however, a
third drawing was solicited, under the instructions that subjects should freely
guess missing matrix elements when they didn't think they could recall them.
No control-experimental group difference emerged in these third drawings.
This would seem to indicate that the efficacy of the free-association technique in both the first and second experiments was attributable to its effect
on the subjects' willingness to respond, rather than upon their actual sensitivity to originally perceived material. A further study, employing signal-
detection methodology, confirmed that free association does not increase
signal sensitivity as such. The conclusion was that the free association technique "increases the extent to which information is outputted from memory
storage, [while] the input traces in memory storage do not themselves become intensified" (1970, p. 111).

Erdelyi takes this last finding to be a refutation of Freud, although
which Freud it is hard to ascertain, as no reference is made to any of Freud's
writings. Freud's characterization of the method of free association in *The Interpretation of Dreams* (1900) certainly seems consistent with Erdelyi's findings. In free association, Freud writes, two changes are induced in the patient:
"an increase in the attention he pays to his own psychical perceptions and the
elimination of the criticism by which he normally sifts the thoughts that occur to him" (1900, p. 101). These are "response strategies" of precisely the
sort Erdelyi found to be effective. At any rate, whatever the mechanism
might be, the major upshot of both investigations is that *free association
works*, i.e., it does increase the reportability of "preconscious" and "unconscious" impressions genuinely connected with a prior stimulus.

Conclusion

Posner defines thought as *"the achievement of a new representation through the performance of mental operations"* (1973, p. 147). The definition rests on his distinction between mental representations (e.g., images, inner speech) and operations (e.g., laws of association, combinatorial routines). It is clear from this definition that dreams are, or should be, in the very mainstream of the psychology of cognition. Posner (1973) and Klatzky (1975), however, hardly consider dreams; only Neisser (1967) has embraced dreams as an integral concern of cognitive psychology. The neglect has been mutual, of course: few dream psychologists have made any significant use of the concepts or findings of cognitive psychology.

The most striking implication for dreams which I see in cognitive psychology is the suggestion of the considerable interdependence of verbal and visual codes of representation. In particular reference to Freud's concept of a topographic reversal during dreaming, it seems to follow that dreams must be the creation of a syntactic mechanism, a "parser" which ordinarily assigns linguistic constituents to visual inputs but which, during sleep, assigns visual constituents to verbally coded propositions.

Many glib generalizations have been drawn in recent years about the two halves of the brain, following the pioneering observations by Sperry (1968) of the effects of surgical disconnection of the cerebral hemispheres in humans. In the sharp dichotomies which have been drawn between right- and left-hemisphere "thinking" (nonlinear versus linear thinking; perceptual/spatial versus verbal reasoning; intuitive versus intellectual thinking—see Ornstein [1972]), dreaming naturally has seemed to be a function of the right side of the brain. But what is interesting in this regard is that cessation of dreaming has been reported after right-hemisphere damage (Humphrey and Zangwill, 1951), after hemispheric disconnection (Bogen, 1969), and after left-hemisphere defects affecting language behavior (Moss, 1972). This patterning of observations only makes sense if it is assumed that linear, verbal, intellectual thinking is integrally involved in dreaming. Moss's observations, in particular, are not even consistent with the interpretation that the right hemisphere "dreams," while the left only "tells us about it." Without linguistic input to the right hemisphere, Moss's observations suggest, the allegedly autonomous processes of nonlinear, perceptual, intuitive thought simply do not occur.

This notion of verbal/visual interrelatedness makes much more sense than the various "two-mind" hypotheses now in the air. The requirements of adaptation surely are such that integration, rather than autonomy, of cognitive mechanisms and processes must be the general rule. Such integration may be difficult to keep up to date while mental processes are "on line," however—that is, while they are handling externally generated informational inputs. It is tempting in this regard to speculate that REM sleep may be a major mechanism by which subtle integrations can be achieved between verbal and perceptual analyzers and generators. The subtlety would be consistent with the general failure of gross behavioral tests to indicate a clear-cut function for stage REM (e.g., Vogel, 1975), although the hypothesis also does suggest some directions in which future testing might be carried out. So far as I know, the hypothesis is not inconsistent with any strong physiological data. (Berlucchi [1965] has reported a *lessening* during stage REM of electrical activity in the callosal bridge between hemispheres, but this is in the cat, a non-linguistic species whose brain manifests quite different functional and even anatomical hemispheric differentiation than our own.)

The hypothesis *is* consistent with Berger's observations (1969) that: (1) mammals are both the only vertebrates reliably showing REM sleep and the only vertebrates with immediate interhemispheric integration in visual functioning (stereopsis, binocularly coordinated eye movement); (2) there is a positive correlation, across species, between the proportion of sleep time spent in stage REM and the percentage of partial decussation of optic tract fibers at the optic chiasma (the structural basis of stereopsis). These observations suggest that REM sleep arose in conjunction with new requirements of interhemispheric integration, and that these requirements first were manifested in visual-system operations, as a function of the partial representation in both hemispheres of the visual field of a single eye. Berger, however, speculates only that REM sleep continues to have oculo-motor integrative functions. However, the lateral specialization of the *human* brain assumes a striking new dimension: that of language. It seems reasonable to propose that: (1) this specialization creates new requirements of *visual/verbal* integration; (2) these new interhemispheric integrative requirements will be assumed by mechanisms (e.g., REM sleep) already selected by evolution to handle other, more primitive interhemispheric integrations.

Thus the hypothesis of verbal/visual interconnectedness during dream generation may have some implications for the heretofore elusive goals of specifying REM and dream *functions*, as well as its more immediate implications for dream *analysis* and *explanation*. Its plausibility surely suggests, once again, the need for students of visual and verbal narratives to begin sharing theories, methods, and findings with one another.

CHAPTER 10

Soviet Psychology
and
Neuropsychology

At a time when American behaviorism was enforcing a peripheral-reductionist view of human thought (Watson defined thinking as "habits which . . . [are] exercised implicitly behind the closed door of the lips" [1930, p. 225]), Soviet psychologists were receiving encouragement from Pavlovian theory to conceptualize distinctively human accomplishments in more distinctively human, and biologically central, terms. Both schools were committed to an "objective" psychology, and both stressed the centrality of inner speech in explaining human thought. The Soviets, however, employed their greater theoretical license to initiate a series of wide-ranging investigations whose value only recently has been fully recognized by American scholars, the history of whose own approach to thinking turned out to be less than productive.

The Pavlovian message certainly was a mixed one, for Pavlov could be quite hostile toward purely psychological interpretation (e.g., Pavlov, 1932a). Nonetheless, in addition to recognizing elementary unconditioned and con-

ditioned reflexes, Pavlov described a new psychophysiological possibility at
the human level:

> ... there is added, possibly especially in the frontal lobes, which are not
> so large in the animal, another system of signalisation, signalling the first
> system—*speech*, its basis or fundamental components being the kines-
> thetic stimulations of the speech organs.
>
>   Here is introduced a new principle of higher activity ... abstraction.
> ... [1932*b*, p. 113-114]

Of these new "abstractions," Pavlov wrote:

> ... it is precisely they which constitute our superior and specifically
> human intelligence. Speech is a real conditional stimulus to human
> beings, as real as the others, which are common to animals as well; but
> this one stimulus is far more inclusive than any other. In this respect,
> there is no comparison, qualitative or quantitative, between speech
> and the conditional stimuli of animals. [quoted by Cuny, 1962, pp.
> 84-85]

The tone clearly is most unWatsonian.

Beginning in the 1930s and continuing up until today, a group of
gifted Soviet investigators has accepted Pavlov's challenge to characterize
the speech-mediated signal system of the human brain/mind. Like Pavlov,
they have been especially concerned that this signal system, and the human
accomplishment it permits, be anchored both in objective behavioral observation and in neurophysiological data.

L. S. Vygotsky

L. S. Vygotsky (1896-1934) was foremost among the pioneers of this approach.
He was especially interested in the ontogenesis of speech. Unlike Freud and
the early Piaget, Vygotsky (1934) saw thought as social in origin. The child's
earliest "thoughts" are communicative acts. Egocentric thought develops
later, when externalized thought-forms are directed to the realm of inner
experience in the form of self-with-self "dialogues." Internal speech is a
natural sequel. From internal speech develop, in turn, both autistic and
logical kinds of thinking. The psychological interiorization of speech—its

direction toward inner experience—precedes its physical interiorization, which becomes progressively more abbreviated and schematic in form over the course of human development. On Vygotsky's model, then, autistic thought is "a late development, a result of realistic thought and of its corollary, thinking in concepts . . ." (1934, p. 22). One might expect, then, that such thought—e.g., dreaming—would be propositionally structured in a manner betraying its origin in speech acts.[1]

Vygotsky acknowledges that, both phylogenetically and ontogenetically, intelligent behavior precedes speech and is separable from it. The infant babbles "speech" sounds and "intelligently" uses tools; these are as yet unconnected behavioral attainments. At about age 2, however, a momentous, if partial, unification of these two functions is effected: the child discovers symbolization by sound. At this point, there is a qualitative shift in the course of human development: relationships now are established at high levels of generality. Such relationships were necessarily lacking in the more concretely bounded perceptual and motor organizations of infancy. The nature of abstract thought is relational: "Every thought tends to connect something with something else, to establish a relationship between things" (1934, p. 125). And, since thought "comes into existence" (ibid.) through words, these relationships must be grammatical ones.

Vygotsky distinguishes realized speech and its inner base, however, in a manner suggestive of that followed by Chomsky (1957) years later. External speech does *not* directly reflect the structure of inner thought. Speech has the function of communication; thought has that of programming behavior and structuring experience. Because of these different functions, the structuration of the two phenomena is not identical. Speech must be explicit and complete; thought often is abbreviated and condensed. Thus the syntax of speech is more elaborately organized than the abstract or "kernel" forms which characterize thought. This implies, of course, that a series of transformations is required to elaborate our thoughts into words.

It should not be assumed, however, from the fragmented nature of its syntax that inner speech is "simpler" than external speech. Vygotsky points out that inner speech, precisely because it is not at the mercy of others' external signals, can be deliberately planned, and thus often becomes very complicated.

The most typical form of abbreviation in inner speech, Vygotsky feels, is the omission of reference to ego. Since "speaker" and "listener" are identical, the "speaker" need not explicitly refer to its implication in any described

[1] And also that, as we already have seen to be the case (chapter 5), autistic thought would become better differentiated over time: adults' dreams being more "dreamlike" or autistic than children's dreams.

event: the "listener" already implicitly understands this perspective. This situation commonly leads to condensation of propositional content to "predication": only the predicate is "voiced," and inner speech has "an almost entirely predicative syntax" (1934, p. 145).[2] But syntax itself, Vygotsky believes, is less important than in external speech; "inside," semantic factors predominate. Thinking is accomplished "in pure meanings" (1934, p. 149).

Vygotsky notes several semantic "peculiarities" of inner speech which sound remarkably like the semantic peculiarities Freud identified in the associative matrix underlying the dream. For example, in inner speech "sense" overshadows "meaning." This seems to be Vygotsky's way of saying that connotative meanings dominate denotative ones. Connotative meanings prove, moreover, to be much more fluid than denotative ones: as one's context changes, so does the "sense" of one's inner speech. Inner speech also is characterized by "agglutinization," which proves, I think, to be identical to Freud's concept of condensation—i.e., one term can carry the sense of many. The senses of words also can combine in dynamic composites. Thus a single inner word can become "so saturated with sense" (1934, p. 148) that we would be quite at a loss to explain its role by means of any simple utterance in external speech. To "explain" our thoughts, we need to transform "the predicative, idiomatic structure of inner speech into syntactically articulated speech intelligible to others" (ibid.).

Thus Vygotsky's account of a qualitatively unique, abbreviated, predicative, semantically based inner speech would not lead us to equate the structure of external speech with that of thought. Levels are discriminated, much as they are by Freud and Chomsky. The understanding of inner thought does not routinely follow from superficial analysis of its external forms. Since one can express the "same" thought in different words, or different thoughts in the same words, thought units are not identical to speech ones. And yet, *historically*, human thought represents a progressive refinement of speech, leading ultimately to a realm of "pure meanings," which lie behind even inner speech itself (1934, p. 149). The nature of thought is to be found in its linguistic history. Thus, the task for "pure psychology" is to characterize the peculiarities of this increasingly internalized and schematic form of speech, while for neuropsychology it is to identify those high-level speech centers whose action must mediate our most distinctively intellectual acts—including, I would assert, dreaming.

Vygotsky sees the representational properties of words—their generality

---

[2]In the dream model proposed below (chapter 11), an ego term always is included in interactive propositional codings. It is possible that this convention makes explicit what is, in real-time processing, merely implicit.

and abstractive properties, in particular—as leading linguistic creatures to "realities" and serial orderings literally inconceivable to nonlinguistic creatures. He rejects the Gestaltist hypothesis that perceptual organization determines mental organization. However, in drawing a sharp line between perceptual and conceptual organizations, Vygotsky seems to have underestimated the ecological pull on linguistic creatures to coordinate their perceptual and conceptual realities and therefore to have neglected the opportunity afforded by dream study to examine how these two realities can mesh with one another.

As the quote from Vygotsky toward the close of chapter 8 indicates, he was strongly aware of the need to coordinate motivational analysis with the study of thinking. Thoughts do not "think themselves." One needs to consider "the personal needs and interests, the inclinations and impulses, of the thinker" (1934, p. 8). Meaning itself is both cognitive and conative: "every idea contains a transmuted affective attitude toward the bit of reality to which it refers" (ibid.). In the Soviet system, moreover, there is the possibility of granting more than verbal fealty to conation's role in thinking. Since behavior is directed by inner-speech programs, and since affective attitudes inhere in mental concepts themselves, a common language exists for coordinating thought and impulse, denotation and connotation.

A. N. Sokolov

Sokolov's (1972) work is largely within the theoretical tradition set forth by Vygotsky. It is important because it carries Vygotsky's ideas beyond their original base of informal developmental observation and into the experimental laboratory, with its possibilities of measurement by subtle instrumentation and experimental control of relevant variables.

For Sokolov, as for Vygotsky, inner speech begins as an implicit copy of external speech, but becomes progressively more schematic as a result of the difference in functional circumstances between it and external speech. Sokolov conceptualizes the abbreviated structural elements of inner speech as *semantic complexes*. An example of a semantic complex might be the way we use a few key words in skimming a text in order to arrive quickly at a notion of its sense: these few words, for our purposes, carry the meaning of the whole. It is imagined that similarly efficient abbreviations are regularly employed in inner speech.

To demonstrate the importance of inner speech in human information processing, a number of experiments have been performed by Sokolov and other Soviet investigators in which inner speech has been interfered with, either through mechanical devices clamped on organs of articulation or through the presentation to the subject of extraneous verbal tasks. Sokolov reports his own findings as typical of experiments of the second kind, which "load" not only the articulatory apparatus but also central speech centers. At first, there is a "sensory aphasia" for inputs. Subjects whose speech systems are engaged in repeating verses known by heart cannot identify words spoken to them.

> This state quickly fades away, however, and is replaced by instantaneous amnesia: an extremely rapid forgetting of a text heard or read, resulting in a considerable reduction of the volume and accuracy of perception and memory, and speed of reading and problem solution. Later on, as the enunciation of extraneous verbal material becomes more automatized, internal (concealed) articulation of words is gradually reinstated, and the subjects, despite the preoccupation of the speech apparatus with the continual enunciation of word series or syllables learned by heart, grasp and retain the meanings of the words perceived and manipulate them correctly by means of concealed articulation of certain generalizing words. Moreover, along with the rudimentary articulation of the key words, all subjects noted during these experiments the appearance of vivid visual images which are usually absent under normal conditions and which they use here as a means for comprehending and retaining the meaning. [1972, p. 54]

These results are interesting on several grounds: (1) the necessity of, in some degree, actually *articulated* inner-speech reproductions to the understanding of speech; (2) the increasingly abbreviated forms which inner speech reproductions can assume; (3) a reliance on "semantic complexes" to achieve this abbreviation; and (4) the ability to translate words to "pictures" and to use these pictures as word-surrogates in intellectual tasks when speech generators are otherwise occupied or unable to function.

Clinical observations by Soviet investigators seem to Sokolov to be compatible with his experimental findings. Aphasia is reported to involve disturbances of inner speech. Hence aphasics perform better when working aloud than silently, and are especially handicapped by mechanical interference with external articulation. One of Luria's motor aphasics is quoted by Sokolov as saying:

> . . . if I repeat it aloud, I understand. Then I can figure it out right away . . . I can't understand what it is that helps . . . When my tongue

is clamped, it seems as if the words are there, yet it's impossible to connect them. [1972, p. 63]

Sensory aphasics, on the other hand, in whom inner speech is less impaired, "retain the capacity for abstract operations and for an understanding of logicogrammatical relationships" (1972, p. 64); their problems arise more at the level of acoustical analysis.

As Vygotsky suggested, Sokolov finds inner-speech representations to be qualitatively different than external-speech realizations. Inner speech is not just a "de-voiced" external speech, but a radically different structuring of speech components. The "language of 'semantic complexes' " uses "a very abbreviated and generalized code" (1972, p. 71), which generally is purely verbal but which occasionally, as we have seen, also can use visual images. Such abbreviations were evident, for example, in the think-out-loud protocols of subjects solving problems or translating texts from foreign languages. In the latter situation, certain "key" or "generalizing" words served as "reference points" or semantic "landmarks in the process of understanding" (1972, p. 80). *These semantic keys generally were either nouns or verbs*, with other verbal forms not directly conveying the elemental structure of semantic meaning: "in the initial stages of textual understanding, nouns and verbs, i.e., words designating objects and actions, play the role of semantic reference points" (1972, p. 87). The elemental semantic complex is seen by Sokolov as the "principal structural element of inner speech" (1972, p. 88). Inner speech, in turn, is essential not only in recognizing inputs but also in organizing and retaining them as logicogrammatical schemata.

With specific reference to dreams, Sokolov suggests that their peculiar susceptibility to forgetting stems from the fact that such logicogrammatical organization cannot be supplied for the dream's images. On awakening, however, such linguistically mediated organization can be given, and the dream can be fixed in memory (1972, p. 118). Sokolov does not explicitly identify the conditions responsible for the absence of effective inner-speech processes during dreaming sleep. Following Pavlov's theory, presumably they might simply reflect the passive, or inhibitory, nature of sleep itself. An alternative hypothesis, however, has been presented above (chapter 9): that, in the act of *creating* the dream, the speech apparatus has been "interfered with," or "overloaded," just as surely as it has in Sokolov's experiments with extraneous verbal tasks. Since Sokolov has found that it is the retention of novel or difficult tasks which is most susceptible to interference by articulatory distractors, it should be especially difficult to recall creatively unfamiliar REM-dream scenarios without active organization by inner-speech mechanisms.

And yet the serial organization of the dream, as also noted earlier in chapter 9, must require at least some short-term shadowing by inner-speech mechanisms. There *is* a coherent dream scenario which binds together the separate incidents of the dream. It is especially interesting in this regard to note that, although REM-burst imagery is relatively unreflective, moments of REM sleep between actual REM bursts do seem to be characterized by more self-reflective thought and verbal imagery (Molinari and Foulkes, 1969; Foulkes and Pope, 1973). It has been suggested that it is in these moments that discrete visual images are synthesized into a coherent narrative (Molinari and Foulkes, 1969). Schwartz and Lefebvre (1973) also have observed frequent "microawakenings" during stage REM which could momentarily liberate inner-speech processes from their immediate dream-generative role.

Among the especially valuable results of Sokolov's researches is the electrophysiological verification of the role of abbreviated inner speech in cognitive tasks. A variety of recording techniques (of micromovements of the tongue, of action potentials in various articulatory sites, of integrated electromyogram [EMG] activity from articulatory mechanisms, etc.) established the correlation of speech-mechanism activation with intellectual performance. Action potentials from the tongue and mylohyoid muscles, for instance, preceded actual phonation in mental arithmetic solutions by a half second or so; they were more marked for difficult problems and for slower problem solvers. The last observation suggests the abbreviation process described earlier, and, by extrapolation, helps to explain the case of those simple or automatic tasks for which inner-speech mediation was not detectible at a peripheral central-nervous-system level.

Sokolov reports that even in all but the most elementary of perceptual reasoning tasks, speech musculature is reliably involved. In dealing with items from Raven's Progressive Matrices, for instance, Sokolov's subjects had to choose from one of six alternatives a drawing D which matched drawing C as drawing B matched drawing A. The response mode was nonverbal (pointing to the correct alternative). Some EMG activation was found during solutions in the speech musculature, but not at a control site, in all subjects studied. Sokolov concludes that inner speech is "a necessary component of thought activity in general" (1972, p. 219), i.e., of "visual" thinking as well as of "verbal" thinking. He notes that GSR and EEG measures did *not* correlate well with problem difficulty nor, presumably, with processes of mental analysis and synthesis. The speech measures alone showed the required relationship. Sokolov thus feels that "concrete" or visual thinking in humans most generally is better described as "verbal-concrete" (1972, p. 233). Verbalization directs the analysis and synthesis of imagery much as it does of words, and is intimately related to perceptual functioning.

It should not be imagined, from this account of Sokolov's work, that he feels that proprioceptive speech mechanisms are all that there is to inner speech. Motor-speech mechanisms of a peripheral sort are imagined to stimulate the second signal system of the cortex as well as producing a facilitatory state of generalized cortical arousal. It is, finally, cortical mechanisms, rather than peripheral ones, which are basic to inner speech. These high-level motor mechanisms are the means through which voluntary, intentional control is exerted over human behavior and experience. It is merely expediency which focuses Sokolov's research attention on peripheral motor mechanisms. These are the only available recording sites for intact humans. Fortunately, the bodily interiorization of inner speech proceeds slowly from the outside inward, so that all but the most routinized or abstract forms of inner-speech mediation still may be recorded at peripheral sites. The ultimate fate of inner speech, however, is to be driven "upstairs," to become abstract cortical motor programs independent of peripheral articulatory accompaniment, however abbreviated or schematic. And one's ultimate interest, therefore, must be in the precise nature of this cortical fate. To pursue this topic, however, it is necessary to move from the electrophysiological recording experiment with the normal human subject to the analysis of the effects of brain damage on human intellectual/linguistic performance.

A. R. Luria

Neuropsychology takes advantage of the fact

> that mental functions which cannot be studied selectively under laboratory conditions in the healthy individual may break down in a circumscribed manner as a result of brain injury or disease. Nature herself performs the experiment and its consequences are open to scientific scrutiny. The study of mental disorders as they are manifested in the clinical setting can, therefore, provide valuable information about the working of the healthy mind . . . . [Williams, 1970, p. 11]

No neuropsychologist has more boldly made use of the field's data in sketching out the workings of the normal human brain than A. R. Luria (1902-1977). His book, *The Working Brain* (1973), is one of the few genuine classics of modern psychology. If, at times, it seems to overreach its data base, it is a refreshing contrast to the timidity of mainstream American neuroscience in its willingness to address itself to such issues as intentionality, self-regulation, consciousness, and the neural bases of higher cognitive functioning. It would, of course, be well beyond the scope of the present volume to present a detailed accounting of all of Luria's ideas about the workings of the human brain. I would, however, like here to summarize that part of Luria's data and modeling which seems most relevant to the conceptualization of dreaming as a motivated, serially integrated, linguistically planned higher cognitive process.

According to Luria, brain function can be analyzed in terms of three major systems: one (largely subcortical) system which regulates cortical tone or states of arousal; one (largely lateral and posterior cortical) system which receives, processes, and stores information; and one (largely frontal cortical) system which programs behavior and experience.

Certain cerebral zones also participate in the regulation of cortical tone. The medial and mediobasal aspects of the cerebral hemispheres do not seem to have informational or action-guiding functions, but, rather, have energetic or dynamic ones. Thus, with lesions in these zones, patients retain the grammatical and semantic structuring of their speech behavior, but speak disinterestedly. Perhaps as a result of this "energetic" change, it sometimes also is observed that general reality orientation is lost, dreamlike confabulations emerge, and associative linkages become increasingly fluid and arbitrary.

The parallel between these latter changes and those observed in REM dreaming suggest some of the contributions the state of REM sleep may introduce to the mental apparatus by way of altered mediobasal brain functioning. We imagine crimes occurring, but are unconcerned. We are unable or unwilling to discriminate being from seeming. We are unable or unwilling to suppress distant and wild associations. More generally, Luria's observations supply a neuropsychological base for my dream grammar's discrimination of intellectual and action structures from dynamic modulation. The two functions do seem to have separate cerebral representation.

A distinctively human information-processing system seems to be anatomically mediated at the boundary of the parietal, occipital, and temporal cortices of, especially, the left cerebral hemisphere. It is here that the inputs of the several sense systems are fitted to common structural molds provided by language. Thus, visual syntheses become verbal ones; visual organizations become logicogrammatical ones; and so on. The anatomical area in question is present only in the human brain. Interestingly enough, it is a slowly maturing one, becoming only fully functional at about age 7, that is, at the age when Piaget identifies the stabilization of concrete operational thinking and at which Bruner (1966) sees the child extending her or his hitherto precocious syntactic structures to the totality of her or his experience.

Luria describes the organizational principle of this "tertiary" intermodal sensory analyzer as being "spatial" in form (1973, p. 147). One of the major effects of lesions to this area is, in fact, a disturbance in finding one's bearings in any system of spatial coordinates. However, disturbances also appear, especially in left-hemispheric lesions, in "logical, 'quasi-spatial' relationships" (1973, p. 151), specifically in *"logical-grammatical structures"* (1973, p. 152).

Even more precisely, there is no general interference in the understanding of *events* (e.g., A hit B), but there is deterioration in the understanding of more static *relationships* (e.g., A is below B). This fascinating observation of two neuropsychologically discriminable "forms of grammatical construction" (1973, p. 312) provides some justification for my dream grammar's distinction between *interactive* and *associative* structures. In terms of Freud's model (1900, p. 311), the distinction might be akin to that between "essential dream-thoughts"—dynamic motive structures—and "intermediate and linking associations." That is, we might conceptualize Freud's dream-thoughts as frontal motor programs which periodically infiltrate and temporarily reorganize more static associative structures in the parieto-temporal-occipital cortex.

It also is interesting, in line with earlier suggestions (chapter 8), that there seems to be a structural linkage between spatial and grammatical organization, as if the latter were a kind of metaphorical extension of the former.

Tertiary sensory-zone lesions generally do *not* interfere with executive or planning functions. The lesioned patient seems well enough to know what he or she wants to do; the problem is that operational routines involving spatial or relational sensory synthesis may not prove adequate to implement the plan. Disturbances in the associative components of thought sequences, then, are separable from, and do not imply, disturbances in the planful organization of intelligent behavior.

Lesions to the tertiary sensory integrator seem to mimic REM dreaming in one significant effect: *paraphasia*—the inability to suppress morphologically, semantically, or phonetically related but inexact associations. "Semantic schemes" (1973, p. 157) are disturbed, such that there is difficulty in finding the right names for associative items. Interestingly enough, this name-finding difficulty appears to be mainly restricted to *objects* rather than to *actions* or *qualities*. The strong implication is, once again, of a static or noun-centered associative network in the tertiary sensory zone, with a differential cortical representation of the interactive and dynamic aspects of experience. I think this observation further supports the associative/interactive distinction of my dream grammar.

The observation also suggests the possibility of a more precise characterization of what is, and what is not, "crazy" about dreams. Is the distortion of dreams mostly at the level of noun or object representations, with verbs and affective modification represented in a relatively more straightforward way? It does not strike us as unusual, for instance, that, in the "Irma's Injection" dream, Freud (1900, p. 107) is concerned about Irma's health, that he wants consultation with other physicians, and that he wants to displace his responsibility for Irma's continuing symptoms to other persons or circumstances. What *is* curious is the imprecise characterization of people, visible symptoms, and palpable remedies (e.g., "propyl, propyls . . . propionic acid . . . trimethylamin" [ibid.]). Freud himself certainly felt that the affective contents of dreams were more straightforward than the ideational ones, i.e., had undergone less distortion (1900, ch. VI).

It also is interesting that disturbances in the visual representation of objects seem to be an integral part of this faulty name-finding syndrome. Patients can neither draw objects nor describe their details. Luria proposes that parieto-temporal-occipital tertiary-zone lesions may produce "a defect of the visual representation of the object requiring to be named, thus disturbing the visual basis of the naming process" (1973, p. 160).

It is significant, also, that Luria has identified a cortical region directly implicated in word-image association. The posterior left temporal region evidently integrates auditory and visual analyses. Lesions to this region result in the failure of words to evoke visual images. If, for example, an object is named, the patient cannot draw the object in question, although he or she can copy a reproduction of it perfectly well. It seems, then, as if the left hemisphere is specifically programmed to convert words to images, a function undoubtedly of great significance in dream formation.

The semantic and semantic-visual defects described above are seen *only* in left-hemisphere lesions. Parallel right-hemisphere lesions do not interfere with logical-grammatical comprehension, although they have their own pattern of perceptual and spatial symptoms. It seems to be the left hemisphere in which visual/verbal integration generally is achieved. This makes Moss's (1972) loss of dreaming in conjunction with that of inner speech seem much more comprehensible (cf. chapter 9). Although the right hemisphere may be involved in elementary perceptual presentations, it seems not to participate in syntheses involving speech mechanisms.

At the level of human voluntary behavior, the motor programs of Luria's third system, i.e., *intentions*, are verbally formulated, first in external speech and later in inner speech, and are mediated largely by the frontal granular cortex. This cortical zone Luria considers to be a *"superstructure above all other parts of the cerebral cortex*" (1973, p. 89). Lesions to this zone lead to a loss of complex, serially ordered behavior routines and to the appearance of unplanned and disorganized behavior sequences.

Anatomically, the frontal areas in question are most highly developed in humans. Functionally,

> the chief distinguishing feature of the regulation of human conscious activity is that this regulation takes place with the close participation of *speech*. Whereas the relatively elementary forms of regulation of organic processes and even of the simplest forms of behaviour can take place without the aid of speech, *higher mental processes are formed and take place on the basis of speech activity*. [1973, pp. 93–94]

In patients distractible because of subcortical lesions, for instance, but with a relatively intact frontal cortex, the attentional deficits often can be compensated for by voluntary, verbal control. Patients with frontal lesions, on the other hand, are irremediably distractible—the possibility of deliberate verbal self-regulation no longer exists.

It is interesting to note that electrical changes in frontal activity (Grey Walter's slow EEG "expectancy waves") accompany verbalized anticipation in a variety of test situations. During REM sleep, EEG "sawtooth" waves with a frontal representation regularly precede bursts of rapid eye movements. Might this reflect a verbal program being translated to an experience of visual imagery? Foulkes and Pope (1973) found sawtooth bursts to be accompanied by what subjects experienced as a relatively major change in the direction of their REM-dream narrative.

With large frontal lesions, the formulation of stable intentions to guide behavioral operations becomes difficult, and the patient is unable to adhere to any given program. Unlike operational deficits (following posterior or premotor lesions, for instance), these disturbances are neither noticed nor the occasion for attempts at correction. Verbal commands can be retained and, at least at some level, understood. The difficulty seems to be that speech—either the commands of another or one's own inner speech—no longer is an effective stimulus to planful activity. Verbally formulated intentions no longer guide the flow of behavior. Behavior, in fact, no longer "flows" but jerks along, impulsively and distractibly, to no particular end.

While Luria feels that there is some equipotentiality (Lashley, 1929) in frontal tissue, he also finds some anatomical specialization of function. Left-lateral frontal lesions are most closely associated with the intentionality deficits described above. Basal lesions, as already noted, are more likely to be correlated with affective disturbance. Medial lesions lead to a disturbance of cortical tonus, and hence to dreamlike associative and reality-testing dysfunctions: memory traces are not discriminated on the basis of their task relevance, and confabulations emerge.

It should be evident from an analysis of most REM-dream specimens that the lateral-frontal function of *planful* organization of verbally formulated narratives is generally intact. In "Irma," for example, a clear set of dreamer intentions (Irma is well; if not, I am not responsible, but I want her well) over-arch the whole narrative structure (Freud, 1900, ch. II). Affective and associative functions, however, may be somewhat less well preserved. Neuropsychologically, it is tempting to characterize the dream as a relatively functional frontal integrative system coping with sleep-disinhibited basal-affective and posterior-associative systems.

In this regard, the contrast with schizophrenia is significant (e.g., Bleuler, 1911; Arieti, 1974). In one critical respect, the schizophrenic is *not* "a waking dreamer" (cf. Freud, 1900, p. 90). Schizophrenic thought disturbance extends to an interference with planful integration. In dreams, planful integration generally is maintained, albeit in the face of a somewhat unwieldy set of affective and associative contents. Of these contents, it might be said that Pavlov's "Law of Strength" (Luria, 1972) no longer holds as well as it does in wakefulness; stimuli are not elicitable strictly on the basis of their importance but in a somewhat more indiscriminate fashion. However, this loss certainly is less than total, for the dreamer's world is by no means as chaotic as that of the patient with extensive tertiary temporal-parietal-occipital damage (ibid.). The dreamer's functions must *all* be relatively intact; it only is being suggested here that some are slightly more so than others.

Although Luria seems not unsympathetic to Chomsky's analysis of language, he does, as befits his interest in real-time psychological modeling, place verbally formulable motives or intentions as initiators of expressive speech sequences:

> ... narrative expressive speech or expression begins with an *intention* or *plan*, which subsequently must be recoded in a verbal form, and moulded into a speech expression. It is clear ... that both these processes call for the participation of the *frontal lobes*, an apparatus essential for the creation of active intentions or the forming of plans ...
>
> ... patients with a marked frontal syndrome, in whom general aspontaneity and adynamia are accompanied by a well-marked "aspontaneity of speech"... [manifest] absence of ... spontaneous expressions .... The aspontaneity of speech ... cannot be regarded as an "aphasic" disorder. It is more of a special form of general aspontaneity. By contrast, the type of speech disturbance which I shall now describe

occupies a definite, although special, place among the aphasic disorders. This type of speech I describe as dynamic aphasia. . . .

The transition from the general plan to narration requires the re-coding of the plan into speech, and an important place in this process is played by *internal speech* . . . providing what is known in syntax as the "linear scheme of the sentence." [1973, pp. 318–19]

Luria goes on to say that this transition is effected effortlessly both by normals and by patients with left-temporal or left-posterior lesions. Even if the words selected are inappropriate, the "general intonational and melodic structure of the sentence" (1973, p. 319) is maintained, showing that the linear sentence scheme is operative. But, with certain forms of left-frontal lesion, the narrative schemata themselves are lost, i.e., there is dynamic aphasia.

These patients can repeat words and they can name objects. It is not that they suffer from any defect in elementary plan formulation, for, even when a plan is provided to them ("describe this picture"), they still are at an expressive loss for words. With external linear props (empty cards represent-ing subject, verb, and object), they can formulate simple sentences. But when the props disappear, so too does the possibility of linear sentence formation. EMG recordings indicate implicit speech in the prop-present, but not in the prop-absent, condition. These observations demonstrate the critical role of inner speech in translating general plans into verbal narrative structures.

Although Luria himself is silent on problems of dream generation and tends to denigrate the possibility of organization within dreams (e.g., 1973, p. 44), it does not seem implausible to imagine that inner speech also must operate to produce the linear narrative structure of humanity's other great form of narration—dreaming. If this line of reasoning is even approximately correct, it has momentous implications for dream interpretation and explana-tion. It means that the "deep structure" underlying dream imagery is linear, verbal in form, and grammatical in structure. It implies that a satisfactory dream analysis must take us back to the elemental grammatical structures responsible for dream narratives, and, through them, to the verbal plans and intentions of the dreamer. The dream model presented in the next chapter thus can be viewed as a preliminary attempt to work through some implica-tions of neuropsychological data and theory on narrative creation.

PART IV

SSLS: A MODEL OF

DREAMING AND

A METHOD OF

DREAM ANALYSIS

CHAPTER 11

A Scoring System for Latent Structure (SSLS)

In conjunction with additional scoring rules given in appendix A, this chapter will describe an objective procedure for coding and analyzing dream and free-associative material so as to implement the two great goals of Freud's dream psychology: the characterization of how the mind operates in sleep and the determination of the meaning of dreams. This procedure is the Scoring System for Latent Structure (SSLS). Any data-reduction scheme makes assumptions about the data, and, the more comprehensive the analytic scheme, the more inclusive these assumptions must be. SSLS's aim is to be comprehensive. Thus, it makes a sufficient number of assumptions about what dreams are and about how they are generated to be considered a model of dreaming.

But the model is only latent in the succeeding discussion; the focus is on scoring operations. I feel that this approach is entirely appropriate for a field in which theory has tended to soar well above any empirical moorings. My goal here is to present a model defined in terms of rules of observation and rules for the organization of observations. These rules may be controversial, but at least they are explicit.

The model is meant to be "empirical" in another sense, as well. It has been framed in such a way that I believe it to be consistent with the best-established evidence of clinical (chapter 4) and experimental (chapter 5) studies of dreams, as well as with findings and theories currently favored in cognate symbolic disciplines (chapters 6-10). The aim has been to provide a model which, although compatible with the classic accounts of dynamic dream psychology, also is consistent with the more contemporary approaches of other disciplines devoted to the study of mind. In this sense, the material of parts II and III is indispensable to understanding the content of this and succeeding chapters. Although extensive cross-referencing will not be provided, choices made in the design of the scoring system either rest upon, or are supported by, data discussed in the earlier chapters.

Goals and Derivation of the Scoring System

Goals

As a content-analysis technique, SSLS attempts to establish a reasonable and orderly set of rules for the analysis of the "private meaning" (Foulkes and Vogel, 1974) or latent content (Freud, 1900) of dreams. Any number of systems have been developed for scoring the "public meaning" (manifest content) of dreams (most notably Hall and Van de Castle's [1966] general content-analysis scheme, but also various ordinal rating scales in wide use [e.g., Hauri, Sawyer, and Rechtschaffen, 1967]). It now is clear, however, that such systems have not permitted achievement of the major goals of dream study, and cannot do so, because of their relative neglect of private meaning (see chapter 5).

To say that SSLS deals with *private* meaning means two things: (1) In the analysis of *dream-report statements* themselves, persons, objects, places, and events are not always taken at face value. Thus, SSLS would score the dream-report statement "the old man became ill" not as an uncaused misfortune accruing to an elderly stranger but as an aggression by the dreamer toward the father. In addition to such conventional transformations, manifest dream-elements also are subject to recodification in SSLS on the basis of contextual information contained in the dream itself. Thus "house" = "mother," where the dreamer says the house "belonged" to mother. Even at the level of the manifest dream report, then, SSLS goes beyond public meaning.[1]

[1] In this sense, it is like what Hall and Van de Castle (1966) have called their "theoretical scales," but which neither they nor others have developed into a comprehensive

(2) SSLS also permits the derivation of private meaning through its analysis of the dreamer's *free associations* to manifest dream-report statements. It does this, first, merely through its provisions for coding free-association material in the same manner as dream material, and, second, by allowing recodification of the dream on the basis of contextual information supplied in the free associations. As did Freud,[2] SSLS considers free associations to be the *ultimate* basis for ascribing private meaning to any dream.

Moreover, as Freud clearly saw, it is only when free-association analysis is performed that *both* major goals of dream study can be fully approached: finding out something about the *dreamer* (which also is possible, to a lesser or greater degree, when analysis is restricted to manifest dream statements) and finding out something about the *process of dreaming* and the underlying *structure of the dream* (which can be achieved only when free associations are available). In dreamer psychology, free associations are used to isolate connotative meanings of dream elements, which, in turn, suggest something of the nature of that particular dreamer's meaning systems. In dreaming or dream psychology, these same associations are used to construct a more general model of how manifest dream content derives from its underlying structure and of the intervening transformations involved.

"Dreaming" or "dream" (rather than "dreamer") *psychology is, in fact, the primary focus of SSLS.* It is not intended that SSLS simply be another (but hopefully better) system of content analysis. Rather, the ultimate goal is to address still larger gaps in the concerns of contemporary dream psychology, namely, dream structures and dream processes. By what mechanisms is the foreign-to-waking-consciousness dream product created? How does the mind work in the state of sleep? What are the underlying structures of sleeping thought? The contribution of present-day dream research to answering these questions is quite unspectacular (see chapter 5). Thus, SSLS is advanced, also, and primarily, as an objective procedure for dealing with the *structures* from which and the *processes* by which the dream is formed. It is intended to facilitate the description and empirical study of these phenomena.

To achieve these latter ends, SSLS clearly must go beyond the mere reduction of dream and free-association statements to some common, psychologically meaningful language. It also must provide reliable ways of organizing

---

system for coding all manifest dream-report statements. At the level of the dream-report statement, SSLS derives private meanings either from contingencies the dreamer describes within the dream report itself or from the logic and general findings of earlier analyses of dream experience (chapters 4 and 5).

[2] "... both in practice and in theory the first place continues to be held by the procedure .. which attributes a decisive significance to the comments made by the dreamer, while the [arbitrary] translation of symbols ... is ... an auxiliary method" (1900, p. 360).

its translated statements so as to reveal their underlying structure and so as to suggest the transformational processes operative between underlying and surface structures. SSLS provides such techniques (chapters 13-15). These techniques are sufficiently formalized to permit the use of mathematical operations (digraph analysis) in the hypothecation of "deep" psychic structures and in the definition of transformational processes lying between these structures and the surface-level structures of the manifest dream.

Because both private meaning and dream structures and processes are areas of weakness in current dream psychology, SSLS returns to the methodological innovation—free association—of that dream psychology—Freud's—whose greatest strengths lie just in these same areas (see chapter 4). As we have seen, contemporary dream researchers do not routinely collect free associations; hence they neither can perform private-meaning dream analyses nor can suggest the structures or mechanisms involved in dream formation (chapter 5). The crucial methodological omission stems, in part, from the fact that there are "some very real difficulties in arriving at intersubjective agreement on how associations are to be organized" (Foulkes and Vogel, 1974, p. 22). That is,

> rules for introducing order into the dream's network of potential meanings have never been specified in such a way as to provide high rates of intersubjective agreement on the validity or priority of potential meanings nor on the particular unconscious factors which might be involved. Foulkes and Vogel, 1974, pp. 19-20]

SSLS attempts to provide such rules.

Clinicians or theorists may object that, in attempting to formalize methodology in areas heretofore left to intuition, many valuable insights are likely to be lost. This undoubtedly is true. The point is, however, that unless reliable schemes are developed for dealing with private dream meanings and with dream structures and processes, objective dream research will remain largely isolated from such issues altogether, while theorists will be unable to establish those linkages with dream research which ultimately can only clarify the nature and utility of their own work.

It is claimed that SSLS *is*, in principle and in fact (see appendix B), *reliable:* that is, that it spells out rules of sufficient precision and clarity that different observers will be able to achieve rough agreement on analyses of individual dreams. It may be objected that there is no proof that this agreement relates to anything truthful about dreams or dreamers (i.e., it doesn't yield *valid* data). This is a question of the *utility* of the analyses, which only can be established through subsequent research with the system. Undoubtedly, at a minimum, SSLS will, as a result of future experience, require revision; at worst, it may prove only to have been an instructive failure. In either case, it still may have achieved the goal of focusing attention on the necessity of devising methods to bridge the chasm currently separating dream "researcher" from dream "analyst," and reliable-but-unimportant statements from unreliable-but-important ones about dreamers and their dreams.

The remainder of this chapter is devoted to a description of SSLS as a system of *content analysis*, while succeeding chapters will illustrate its application to dream and free-associative material (chapter 12) and demonstrate how SSLS's content analysis permits the subsequent isolation of underlying dream structures and of the transformational processes presumably operative in the formation of the manifest dream (chapters 13–15). The description of particular techniques will, at times, be somewhat complicated. This is inescapable. It seems unlikely that any simple way exists to unravel either the secrets of the sleeping mind or the problems currently besetting dream analysis—or even, as in the case of the present work, to attempt to approach such goals. In the present chapter, an effort has been made to restrict consideration to the essentials of the content analysis. More detailed, supplementary scoring rules are given in appendix A.

Methodological Derivation of the Content Analysis

The present system derives from the Scoring System for Children's Dreams (SSCD) of Foulkes and Shepherd (1971). Methodologically, SSLS attempts to reconcile two levels of analysis found in the earlier system—a comprehensive and lengthy enumeration of content categories (characters, settings, actions, outcomes, etc.) not unlike that of Hall and Van de Castle (1966) and a brief set of rating scales yielding one overall score per dream per scale. Extensive application of SSCD (Foulkes and Shepherd, 1972*a, b*; Foulkes, Shepherd, and Scott, 1974) led to the feeling that the content-analysis results were too numerous and too diffusely arrayed, but the rating data too few and compact, to adequately reflect the inner structure of dream events.

The present system, in addition to its attention to latent or private meanings, tries to find a middle ground between these two levels of summarization, a level where essential nuances of dream structure are retained but not overwhelmed by a mass of ephemeral data. It might be more appropriate to rephrase the beginning of the previous sentence in this way: "The present system, *because of* its attention to latent or private meanings, *can achieve* a middle ground. . . ." That is, it is the collapsing of manifest-content categories on psychodynamic grounds which permits the more compact and orderly presentation of dream structure in the present system. Or, alternatively, it is the expansion of rating scales to encompass more essential psycho-dynamic content which permits the more informative presentation of dream structure in the present system.

Theoretical Derivation of the Content Analysis

It will be evident from what already has been said that many theoretical assumptions are built into the coding system of the content analysis. It is self-evident that this must be so. Specifically, SSLS derives from a number of tenets of Freudian dream psychology (Freud, 1900; chapter 4). From Freud, it takes the basic distinction between manifest-dream content and latent associative structure, the idea that through latent-content analysis the dream can be interpreted as meaningfully related to the dreamer's own life (person psychology) and the idea that latent → manifest transformations indicate laws of mental organization during sleep (dream-process psychology). Acceptance of the latent-manifest distinction implies, further, acceptance of Freud's idea that dream distortion is symptomatic either of motive conflict or of a multitude of associative terms which must accept a single representation.[3]

Moreover, as the sample treatment of a dream statement above suggests, a number of conventional symbolic equations proposed by Freud (e.g., old man as father) have been incorporated in SSLS. These equations originally rested upon a system of universal semantic categories, representing primary human motives and encounters. All the richness or complexity of adult life was said to be rooted in, and reducible to, these semantic bases. SSLS accepts this general notion of a universal semantic system, deriving from basic motives and environmental contingencies experienced in childhood (although not necessarily Freud's characterization of the motives or contingencies in question).

There are still further parallels between SSLS and Freudian theory, as will be noted below. It is important, however, to understand *why* these assumptions have been drawn from Freud's system. It is not because SSLS is an attempt to operationalize all of Freud's dream theory. As discussed earlier (chapters 4 and 5), a number of features of that theory now seem to be of questionable utility. They are not incorporated in SSLS. Wish-fulfillment, for example, is not the root assumption of the content analysis, nor is a dream analysis considered incomplete should there fail to be an infantile or sexual determinant.

What *has* been accepted from Freud's system is a broad framework, a

---

[3] Although not necessarily accepting the idea that all dream elements, or even dreams, are so distorted (cf. Foulkes and Vogel, 1974, p. 13).

way of thinking about dreams and their meaning, rather than all specific hypotheses of his general theory of dreaming and human development. In terms of the discussion in chapter 4, *what has been accepted is Freud's free-association model of dream interpretation/explanation.* What has been accepted has been accepted not because Freud said it, but because it still seems today to provide the single most useful way of approaching dream phenomena.[4] That, of course, is an assumption, an orienting assumption. It is, however, also a working hypothesis, in the sense that SSLS, or better variants thereof, may prove not to generate useful data for person psychology or dream psychology. If so, the orienting assumption is challenged, and one begins again from a different orienting assumption to see if matters are improved thereby.

With this broad picture in mind, we now may turn to the more specific assumptions built into SSLS's content analysis and to the description and justification of its categorical structure.

An Outline of the Scoring System

What Is Scored

It is assumed that *every* statement in the dream report and free-association protocol (with a few minor qualifications detailed in appendix A) is important and should be scored. Nothing is considered self-evident or too trivial for analysis. This is consistent with the verbal form of most theories of dream interpretation, if not always with practice purporting to implement these theories. It is considered a methodological advantage of SSLS, in contrast to clinical practice, that the analyst is not free to pick and choose elements for analysis according to whim, intuition, or theoretical preconception. It *is* allowed that scoring of some dream statements may prove to be more productive in some contexts than the scoring of other dream statements. In fact, for the ascription of motives or meanings to the dreamer, explicit provision is made for the separation of presumably relevant material from presumably irrelevant material (the distinction between "interactive sentences" and "associative sentences" discussed on pages 201-7). But no material of

---

[4]In this sense, the system may be considered to embody one person's summary of the best thinking and evidence available on the nature of dreams and dreaming—or, alternatively, that person's idea as to the assumptions which would have to be embodied in an empirically defensible contemporary theory of dreams.

possible relevance is simply suppressed, and the utility of SSLS's presumptions of probable relevance is open to empirical verification.

Units of Analysis: Verbs and Verb-Defined Sentences

SSLS's conceptual unit of analysis is "relationship." The dream is a cognitive act, and like other cognitive acts, it is assumed to proceed in terms of linguistically shaped propositions or relationships (chapter 2). In the dream case, these relationships are thought to be capable of grammatical summarization in the form: subject-verb-object. In fact, *SSLS's operational unit of analysis is "sentence,"* i.e., relationships are coded in linguistic units. But it should not be assumed that "relationship" (sentence, proposition) has been selected as a unit of dream analysis merely on the basis of generalization from the study of other cognitive phenomena. As has been suggested in chapter 2, the selection also rests on dream phenomenology itself.

The form of the manifest-dream experience is perceptual pluralism (different characters and objects) and interrelatedness. Manifestly, dreams are not solipsistic. They are not a direct form of self-awareness. They are like what Lilly calls the "projection of external reality equivalents from storage" rather than like what he describes as the ego expanded "to fill the subjectively appreciated inner universe" (1972*b*, pp. 33, 34); i.e., they are more akin to the forms of ego's interactions with external reality than they are to its inner realization of satori.

Controversy may arise when the question is asked whether this pluralistic, dramatic form of dream "expression" is to be taken literally (we really *are* concerned with external reality), or whether it hides a higher-level solipsism or monism. For some theorists, for instance, the dream ultimately is thought to be solipsistic in the sense that it portrays the activity of different selves or self-components, rather than extra-self relationships (e.g., Jung's [1948] interpretations at a "subjective" level). SSLS does not make this assumption (although it permits the translation of its relational codings, according to the interpreter's frame of reference, into intrapsychic form). It retains the manifest interpsychic form of dream experience, permitting (and implicitly favoring) the interpretation of such experience in interpersonal terms. The preference is to follow, at least initially, the way dream experience itself is organized, rather than to immediately reinterpret it in some other form.

It is largely on the same grounds that wish-fulfillment plays no conceptual role in SSLS. As Freud (1900) himself acknowledged, wishes often are difficult or impossible to discern in the manifest dream. Thus, to remain faithful to dream experience itself, we cannot *begin* our analyses with wishes or their hypothetical drive for fulfillment. (It *is* possible, however, to interpret SSLS's relationships in wish terminology [wisher/moving-toward/wished-for-object], should the analyst's theory so dictate.)

The selection of relationship as a conceptual unit of analysis has one implication which may not be immediately apparent and which deviates from much conventional practice in dream interpretation. This is that the form of a relationship is as important as the parties so related. Discussions of "dream symbolism" often seem to center about the decoding of nouns—persons or objects. Who or what do they mean? The system described here demands equal attention be given to the verb—*how* are these persons or objects related to the dreamer or to one another? In analyzing his own dream of the "Botanical Monograph," Freud (1900, pp. 169-71; see also pp. 51-53 herein) devotes much attention to the meaning of "botanical monograph," but scarcely any at all to the nature of his relationship to that monograph: "I *had written* a monograph on a certain plant." Is it at all important that he here describes a creative or productive act on his part? This system assumes that it is.[5]

In fact, relationships are categorized by SSLS on the basis of their relational form, or "verb" term. A relationship is either "interactive" or "associative," depending on its verb code. Interactive relationships can be:

Moving Toward, symbolized as →
Moving From, symbolized as ←
Moving Against, symbolized as —<
Creating, symbolized as ⊚→

Associative relationships can be:

(Role) Equivalence, symbolized as =
Means, symbolized as = ... □
With, symbolized as ⇕

Thus, the most basic conceptual categories underlying SSLS's analysis rest on verb/relational, rather than noun/static, criteria.

The first three interactive verb categories are modifications of the "Approach," "Avoidance," and "Attack" categories of SSCD (Foulkes and Shepherd, 1971), and originate in Horney's interpersonal revision of psychoanalysis

---

[5]Freud apparently considered his creative relationship to a monograph as self-evident and not worthy of further analysis. Others, however (e.g., Riesman, 1954), have not agreed and thus have given us different interpretations of the same dream material. This difference, it is believed, highlights the significance of SSLS's convention that *all* material in the dream report be scored.

FIGURE 11-1

Interactive Relationships*

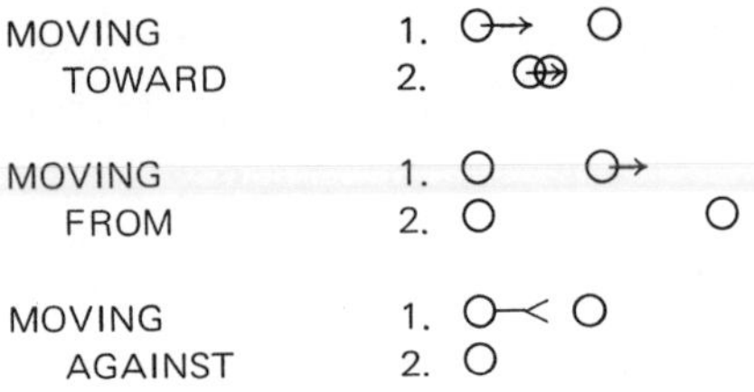

MOVING TOWARD	1. O→ O
	2. ⊕
MOVING FROM	1. O O→
	2. O O
MOVING AGAINST	1. O—< O
	2. O

*After Horney, 1945.

CREATING	1. ⊙→
	2. O O

(1945; see figure 11-1). These three categories are theoretically neutral, however, in the sense that one also can think of them behavioristically (approach, avoidance, and aggression being familiar terms to comparative psychologists), in terms of orthodox analytic theory (Eros, conflict, and Thanatos), in terms of trait theories of personality (e.g., needs for Affiliation, Harmavoidance, and Aggression), and so on.

Horney's suggestive scheme has been broadened here to include a relationship perhaps bordering between interaction and association. The scientist is not merely "associated with" her or his theory; she or he *creates* it. The mother is not merely "with child"; she is *making* it. One may begin here with a simple situation of association, but the end-product of an *active process* is a *dynamic separation*. Diagrammatically, we have the case at the bottom of figure 11-1. As the figure illustrates, an alternate label for the creation process, one commensurate with the labels attached to other interactive relationships, might be "separating from." This label is useful in that it indicates, for example, what kinds of parental behavior would be "creative" and what kinds might be considered "movement against" the child. Even the case of material creation—e.g., painting, carpentry, and so on—has this aspect of separation— an idea, plan, or program achieves an empirical realization outside of its locus of origin.

Thus, whenever something/someone is created, discovered, produced, thought up, or formed where it did not exist before, the relationship of agent to object is one of creation rather than either the dynamic relationship of movement toward or an associative one of contiguity. Besides allowing scope for creative principles in psychic functioning, the Creating category also may

FIGURE 11-2

Creation and Aggression

1.	O		1.	O	O
2.	⊙→		2.	O—<	O
3.	O	O	3.	O	

Creating	Moving Against

be seen as a logical complement to the destruction of the Moving Against interactive-verb category (see figure 11-2).

One clear line of "perceptual" demarcation between all these interactive verbs and any associative verb is the presence of "relative movement" in the former, but not in the latter, case (cf. figures 11-1 and 11-3). In *(Role) Equivalence*, A temporarily *is* B, not simply moving toward B (figure 11-3, 2a). In *Means* relationships, the same sort of relatively static "role" assignment is made: some person, object, etc., in a *relatively fixed* relationship to an actor is the means through which the actor sustains some other relationship (figure 11-3, 2b).[6] The most general associative relationship, *With*, subsumes a variety of relatively static relationships of temporal or spatial contiguity: "together with," "reminds me of," and so on (figure 11-3, 2c1). Even its more "active" form, i.e., "moving together with," preserves the concept of absence-of-relative-movement (figure 11-3, 2c2). Thus, there is, on the basis of the presence or absence of relative movement, a way of separating the relative-static (associative) from the relative-moving (interactive) components of complex statements of relationship.[7]

SSLS's interactive sentences are assumed to represent dreamer motive structures, wishes (Freud, 1900), intentions (Luria, 1973), or behavioral programs (Lilly, 1972b). SSLS's associative sentences are conceptualized as components of a more purely "cognitive" representational network which exists apart from motive structures, but which is susceptible to intrusion from, and reorganization by, such structures.

[6] In a more abstract sense, this is true even when the "means" changes hands: e.g., "I brought her flowers." The flowers are a means, fixed in their association with the interpersonal relationship. "Means" sentences describe something more general than the ordinary understanding of instrumentality: they include *any modification which applies to a relationship as a whole* (a flowery getting-together of X and Y), rather than to any unit thereof (flowery I, flowery approach, flowery her). In this context, the role of flowers is fixed.

Note that, in line with its general interpersonal orientation, SSLS generally ascribes movement to persons rather than objects. Hence: I approached her, via flowers; rather than: flowers came to her, via me.

[7] It will be recalled (chapter 10) that a neuropsychological basis has been adduced for the associative/interactive distinction.

FIGURE 11-3

Associative Relationships

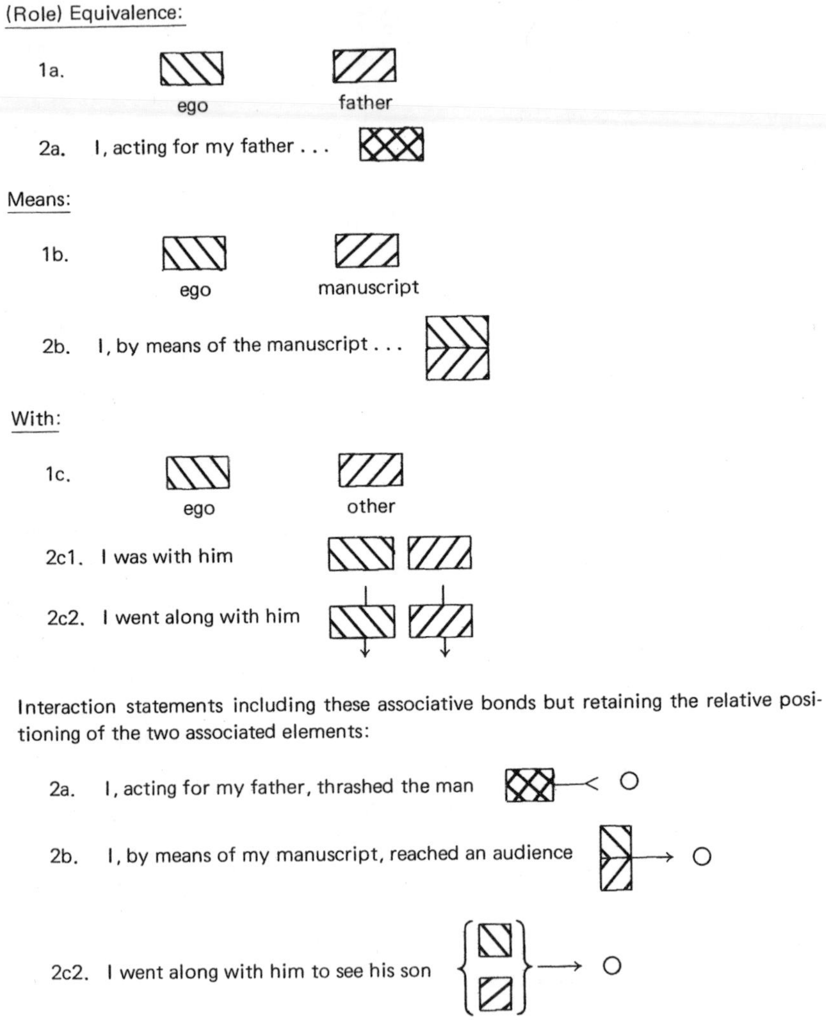

(Role) Equivalence:

1a.   ego   father

2a.   I, acting for my father . . .

Means:

1b.   ego   manuscript

2b.   I, by means of the manuscript . . .

With:

1c.   ego   other

2c1.   I was with him

2c2.   I went along with him

Interaction statements including these associative bonds but retaining the relative positioning of the two associated elements:

2a.   I, acting for my father, thrashed the man

2b.   I, by means of my manuscript, reached an audience

2c2.   I went along with him to see his son

The specific form of the interactive-associative distinction represents SSLS's answer to the major question to which psychoanalysis and all other comprehensive attempts at understanding human behavior have addressed themselves—what is the relationship between motives and thought? SSLS's answer is that *they both are cognitive processes*, that is, *they both are representational in nature and linguistic in form*; that *they both are abstract*, in the sense that behavioral programs or intentions are high-level ("tertiary," in

Luria's terminolgy) syntheses of a motoric sort while "associations" are high-level ("tertiary") syntheses of perceptual/symbolic organization; and that *they are in almost continuous and dynamic interaction with one another*; for example, one's intentions at any given moment select, direct, and organize perceptual/associative mechanisms but also are being continuously modulated by perceptual/associative feedback. More generally, it seems likely that SSLS's interactive-associative distinction, because it is framed in the context of a ruleful organization of the primary behavioral datum of human psychology—language—might be a valuable operational contribution to the problem of motive-thought interaction.

In terms of the theory of dream processes, SSLS's interactive sentences correspond to Freud's (1900) "essential dream thoughts" or "important impressions," while SSLS's associative sentences represent the "indifferent" associative network through which these stimulating elements pass, and in which they are transformed, in the construction of the manifest dream.

In terms of the requirements of dream interpretation, SSLS's interactive sentences represent the dreamer attributes we wish to know, and SSLS's associative sentences are the means by which we can achieve such knowledge. Specifically, SSLS's interactive sentences represent motive structures. But the motive structures of the manifest dream may not be identical with those originally active in dream formation. By tracing back along the associative pathways leading from the manifest dream, however, we may be able to uncover these underlying motive structures. Operationally, SSLS permits the rewriting of manifest-dream interactive sentences on the basis of such associative data. Specifically, whenever an impersonal alter-entity appears in an associative sentence with a given character, then any interactive sentence containing the symbol generates a *transform* interactive sentence containing the character. For instance, if a dreamer associates to the dream element, "I kissed a rose," that his mother's maiden name is Rose, then the associative sentence linking rose to mother permits a transform of the original interactive sentence to "I kissed (moved toward) mother." Rules specifying permissible directions for such transformations are discussed below (pp. 229–35). What deserves notice here is that *SSLS's associative (specifically, its "With") sentences provide an objective and reliable basis on which the private meaning of dream symbols can be imputed.*

The nearest that psychoanalytic literature comes to a recognition of the necessity of distinguishing associative relationships from interactive ones is in its discrimination of *identifications* from *object–choices*: in the one case, the child acts *as if it were* the parent, while in the other, sexual *union* with the parent is the goal. However, one typically also finds, especially in the writings of more recent psychoanalytic theorists (see chapter 6), some more general recognition that not all self-related persons and objects need be invested with libido, that is, that there can be "positive" relationships without a unifying (libidinal) aim. In this sense, SSLS recognizes the existence of associative processes which could be considered, at least in principle, and at any one moment in time, the counterpart to the contemporary psychoanalyst's libido-free sphere of ego-functioning.

It is assumed that the seven forms of relationship (i.e., Moving Toward, Moving From, Moving Against, Creating, Equivalence, Means, and With) are exhaustive and mutually exclusive. That is, any dream or free-association textual unit can be classified into one of these categories and there is one best fit among these categories for each such unit.[8]

These assumptions represent a considerable degree of seemingly arbitrary structuring of the unlimited nuances of intra- and interpersonal relationships. In defense of this semantic reduction, however, these points may be made: (1) As already noted, structuring and systematizing inevitably entail progressive losses of detail for particular events so ordered, but can offer compensatory increases in organization and clarity of material. (2) That the particular structure advanced here is not entirely arbitrary is suggested by the fact that portions of it have been advanced, albeit in different terminologies, by several observers or systems of psychological theory. (3) Its arbitrariness, i.e., lack of dependence on dreamer-produced associations or dream context, always is subject to the check of those associations or that context—within the system itself, one can rescore codings based on the initial assumptions of the system in those cases where the dreamer indicates, either in related segments of the dream or within his associations, that relationship A_1 is, for him, akin to relationship B rather than to relationship A_2. (4) The ability of SSLS to handle all interactive-relationship statements within its mutually exclusive categories is suggested by experience (Foulkes and Shepherd, 1972*a*, *b*; Foulkes, Shepherd, and Scott, 1974) with SSCD (Foulkes and Shepherd, 1971), in which similar categories have been used (albeit nonexhaustively) with dream interaction data. (5) Actually, the Means associative sentence allows the coding *within SSLS* of many more than four interactive verbs. For example, different nuances in the detail of *how* ego approaches object can be

---

[8]Obviously, critical to the understanding of this statement is the definition of a raw-text unit. This is considered in appendix A (pp. 363–75), where mode detailed rules are given for textual translations. At present, we simply may say that a *textual unit* is the smallest part of a text which sustains the scoring of any relationship, i.e., which can be coordinated with the operational unit of the scoring system. At this level, the portion of the statement above referring to exhaustiveness is circular. It becomes more meaningful when it is shown (as is done in appendix A) that all relationships asserted in the text can be coded into one of SSLS's seven categories of relationship-form.

encoded in the Means sentence which "modifies" an interactive sentence: ego, might, for instance, approach object with work or with candy, on a jet plane or on a bicycle, with speeches or with money, and so on.

And, finally, of course, the assumptions SSLS makes regarding the basic forms of human relatedness are not entirely "arbitrary," because they rest upon the most detailed examinations yet undertaken of the life history and motives of the human dreamer—those conducted under the auspices of psychoanalysis or psychodynamic psychology. The results of these investigations have suggested that it may be possible to specify a set of universal semantic categories—a limited set of significant others and of ways in which we conceptualize our relationships with these significant others.

Thus, *an SSLS sentence* is defined as *a coded proposition in which one SSLS verb relates two SSLS nouns to one another.*[9] If the SSLS verb (the middle term of the statement) is an interactive verb, the sentence is an *interactive sentence.* If it is an associative verb, the sentence is an *associative sentence.*[10] The first term of the sentence is the *subject* of the sentence; the last term of the sentence is the *object* of the sentence.

Grammatical Constraints on SSLS Sentence Formation

SSLS's grammar imposes certain restrictions on the nouns which can be employed *in its interactive sentences.* These restrictions are imagined to correspond to grammatical constraints typically operative in dream formation, i.e., in the underlying phrase-structure semantic grammar of dreams (see chapter 8). They are so fundamental in their implications that, before considering the assumptions made in forming particular noun classes, we first must consider the rationale underlying these principles of noun usage in interactive sentences.

The dreamer must be either subject or object in every interactive sentence, but cannot fill both roles in the same sentence. That is, the dreamer is considered to be a party to each dream interaction, but *self-self "interactions" are not permitted.*

The requirement that the dreamer be scored in every interactive sentence rests on a basic orienting assumption, adopted, once again, from Freud:

> Dreams are completely egoistical. Whenever my own ego does not appear in the content of the dream, but only some extraneous person, I may safely assume that my own ego lies concealed, by identification,

---

[9] In textually infrequent cases, all three terms can be verbs: e.g., "the act of creation reminds me of the sexual act" = Creating/With/Moving Toward.

[10] To facilitate the separate analyses of interactive and associative sentences, the latter always are encoded in brackets, while the former are written without brackets.

behind this other person; I can insert my ego into the context . . . my ego may be represented in a dream several times over, now directly and now through identification with extraneous persons. [1900, pp. 322–23].

The assumption is compelling, given the conditions under which sleeping thought operates: isolation from thought-monitoring by others and from the directive influences of their actual, imagined, or implied presence (Allport, 1954, p. 5). It also gains plausibility from the dreamer's relative inability to sustain abstract, conceptual forms of thinking ("formal regression"—Freud, 1900, p. 548). Given these circumstances, it seems relatively unlikely that sleeping thought would be well restrained by socially established and socially enforced barriers against self-centering, or that it would be greatly concerned with abstract ideological issues. Moreover, those who have studied dreams most systematically since Freud's time (e.g., Hall, 1953c) generally have found that assumption of egoism to be supported by their observations. Thus, SSLS assumes that the dreamer is located in at least *one* pole of every scored interactive relationship.[11] In so doing, it rejects the humanist position (e.g., Fromm, 1951) that the dreamer can be sufficiently concerned in a disinterested way with a relationship between any other X and any other Y that he or she dreams about it without considerable projection of ego into at least one of the related entities.[12]

Dream texts can, however, contain third-party (X-Y) interactions in which the ego (E) seemingly is uninvolved. SSLS assumes that such an X-Y form is the surface outcome of a transformation which has obscured E's involvement in the underlying structure by substituting X or Y for E. The traditional explanation offered for such a transformation is that ego's role in the underlying structure is too threatening or threatened to pass directly into surface representation. The user of SSLS is not committed to that particular explanation (whose validity SSLS can, in fact, independently evaluate—see chapter 15), only to the principle that X-Y surface forms reflect an ego-obliterating transformation of underlying X-E or E-Y structures, that is, to

---

[11] This, it is believed, is what Freud means by "complete egoism." By contrast, one may distinguish "absolute" egoism, in which the self would be represented at *both* poles of all dream relationships (Jung, 1948).

[12] This latter rejection is one of the more controversial principles of SSLS. While rejection of absolute egoism in coding does not preclude the later collapsing of categories so as to achieve solipsistic interpretations, failure to preserve X-Y interaction as separate in initial codification *does* seem to preclude later interpretations of altruistic concerns for third-person relationships. However, as we shall see, SSLS does hedge a bit here and permits the encoding of some relevant X-Y interactions within its Means associative sentences.

the principle that the underlying rules of dream formation generate "kernel" sentence structures invariably including E.

The task of the dream analyst in the face of X-Y textual propositions, then, is to undo the work of ego-obliterating transformations. A manifest alter-alter proposition must be returned to its hypothetically original ego-alter form. Thus SSLS must provide rules for converting alter-alter textual interactions to ego-alter systemic ones. Furthermore, these rules must be justified as being reversals of transformations plausibly occurring during dream construction.

SSLS begins with the assumption that it is the dreamer who creates the dream. That is, despite the ego-alien, involuntary phenomenological quality of dream experience, it is assumed that the only viable scientific position is to hold the *dreamer* responsible for the dream experience. This is the position taken by Freud (1900) in framing his topographical model of mind operations. John Lilly takes exactly the same position with respect to the subjective phenomena observed in the "human biocomputer" under LSD-25:

> *In the absence of external excitations coming through the natural end organs the perception systems maintain . . . activity.* The excitation for this activity comes from other parts of the computer, i.e., from program storage and from internal body sources of excitation. The self-programmer interprets the resultant filling of these perceptual spaces . . . *as if* this excitation were coming from outside.
>
> . . . It is convenient for me to assume, as of this time, that these phenomena all occurred within the biocomputer. I tend to assume that ESP cannot have played a role. At the moment this is the position which I find to be most tenable in a logical sense. I do not wish to be dogmatic about this. [1972*b*, pp. 31–32, 52–53]

The implication of this assumption about the origin of the dream for the location of ego in X-Y dream interactions is that *whatever is done in a dream is something the dreamer has made happen; therefore, other things being equal, it is something for which SSLS assigns the dreamer grammatical responsibility.* Other things equal, the dreamer is made the *subject*, rather than the *object*, of the interaction.

In addition to having a logical, causal rationale, the assignment of ego to the subject role in third-person interactive sentences also finds support in more purely psychological considerations. Whereas waking life circumstances may force us into passive interaction roles, in dreams these circumstances are attenuated, and we are free to be active initiators rather than passive recipients (even though our active role sometimes may be obscured by dream distortion). Indeed, it seems likely that one of the functions (i.e., effects) of dreaming is the transformation of passively received waking impressions into actively controlled experiences (Freud, 1931, p. 236; Foulkes, Shepherd, and Scott, 1974).

In practice, the "active-voice" rule described above is modified by "identification" rules which align ego with persons of like age and sex. These age- and sex-similarity factors are the "other things" which must be "equal" before the rule of active voice applies. Specifically, we now restate the latter rule as follows: *whenever characters X and Y are of the same generation and sex, then X-Y interactions are scored E-Y.*

What happens when X and Y are of the same generation, but not of the same sex, as one another? SSLS's general rule proscribing third-person inter-actions means that ego must be located at one pole of such age-concordant but sex-discrepant X-Y pairs. SSLS assumes, in such cases, that E is "identi-fied" with the character of like sex as hers or his, whether that character is in an initiating or in a receiving role in the X-Y interaction.

The logic behind this convention is that sex role is so salient an aspect of self that self-projection will follow this principle, rather than the principle of active voice, where the two are in conflict. There is considerable evidence that concerns with sexual identity and sex-role enactments *are* of critical signifi-cance in the ontogenesis of dreaming (e.g., Foulkes, Pivik, Steadman, Spear, and Symonds, 1967; Foulkes, 1967; Breger, 1969; Foulkes and Shepherd, 1972a; Foulkes, Shepherd, and Scott, 1974). The developmental evidence for "bisexuality" in dreams, on the other hand, is weak. (This is not to deny that bisexuality exists, nor its critical importance to those persons with one gender but another gender identity, but only to state that its scope may be pervasive only in special cases best omitted in a coding system intended for general application.)

Where X and Y are of the same sex, but not of the same generation, as one another, assignment of E to X or Y depends on what that sex is in rela-tion to E's own sex. (1) Where X and Y are of the same sex as E, but of dif-ferent generations (e.g., a father-male peer relationship for a male dreamer), E is identified with the character of his own generation (or with the younger generation in interactions between scored parent figures and scored infant/child figures). In these cases, peer and child characters are felt to be enacting ego's own role in relation to parental authority. The assumption is that ego's ontogenetically prior role (e.g., passivity/dependence to parent figures) is more likely to be represented in dreams with intergenerational interaction than is the developmentally later accession by ego to an adult role and status relative to others. (2) Where X and Y are of different sex than E, and of dif-ferent generations from one another (e.g., a mother-female peer relationship for a male), E is identified with the initiating character, X, rather than with the receiving character, Y, in X-Y interactions. That is, reversion is made to the principle of active voice. Active voice is imagined to be a stronger determinant of dream identifications than any tendency to identify with cross-sex peers.

Finally, there is the case where X and Y are discrepant both in generation and in sex (e.g., a mother-male peer relationship, or a father-female peer relationship). Here some choice obviously will have to be made between the age-identification principle and the sex-identification principle in assigning E a role in X-Y relationships. SSLS's choice is identification of E by sex-similarity.

As previously noted, the evidence for frequent cross-sex identifications in dreams is not persuasive. On the other hand, it seems well-established that dreamers can and do identify themselves as punitive adults (Freud's "superego" [1923a] or Berne's [1972] "controlling parent"), admirable adults (Freud's "ego-ideal" or Berne's "nurturing parent"), troublesome infants or small children (Freud's "id" or Berne's "rebellious child"), or happy and carefree infants or small children (a nostalgic Freudian ego-id amalgam or Berne's "natural child"). A critical feature of normal development for many theories and according to numerous observers is, in fact, an identification with an age-discrepant but sex-concordant adult. The ontogenetic dream data cited above also generally are supportive of the idea that such a process exists and that it can be of crucial significance in deciphering dream content.

In summary, where:

(1) X and Y are concordant for age and sex, E = X (principle of active voice);

(2) X and Y are concordant for age but discrepant for sex, E = whichever character is of her or his own sex (principle of sex identification);

(3) X and Y are discordant for age but concordant for sex, and that sex is the same as E's, E = whichever character is of her or his own generational status (principle of age identification);

(4) X and Y are discordant for age but concordant for sex, and that sex is opposite to E's, E = X (principle of active voice);

(5) X and Y are discordant both for age and sex, E = whichever character is of her or his own sex (principle of sex identification).

Various possibilities for parental-peer interactions fitting principles (3), (4) and (5) are coded, for illustration, in figure 11-4.

In mitigation of the arbitrariness of the conventions enumerated above and the assumptions they encode, it should be noted that E's role *always* is

FIGURE 11-4

Role Assigned E in Intergenerational X-Y Interactions

Where E = O→,		Where E = O+,	
X = mother, and Y = peer		X = mother, and Y = peer	
Y = O→	Y = O+	Y = O→	Y = O+
then	then	then	then
E = Y[1]	E = X[3]	E = X[1]	E = Y[2]

Where E = O→,		Where E = O+,	
X = father, and Y = peer		X = father, and Y = peer	
Y = O→	Y = O+	Y = O→	Y = O+
then	then	then	then
E = Y[2]	E = X[1]	E = X[3]	E = Y[1]

[1] identification by sex
[2] identification by age
[3] identification by active-voice principle

open to discovery through linkages established in her or his associations to the dream or through contextual analysis of the dream. Thus where a male dreams: "I was with A. She was berated by a male, B," E is assumed to be identified ("contextually") with A, thus to be the object of the berating. Or where E free associates to the dream "B berated A" that "I always kind of identified with her there," E again is located with A rather than with B, in the B-A interaction. Thus, following Freud's dictum (1900, p. 360), associational or contextual data *always* are given priority in coding *when they are available.* Assumptions need to be made, however, when such supporting data are lacking, assumptions based on general principles which seem to have been confirmed in observation of many other dreamers much of the time. The scope of the rules we have been discussing—i.e., active-voice and identification rules—consists *only* of cases where more direct data on E's role are lacking.

Associative sentences are exempted from the rule prohibiting third-person (X-Y) sentences. This exemption is justified in several different ways. On dramaturgical grounds, if we adopt an analogy which has wide relevance to dreaming, indeed to all of human existence (Goffman, 1956), it seems that a certain amount of stage-setting must be permitted before a drama can, itself, take place. We assume that it is in the action—the dramatic exchanges of the dream—that the dreamer is most likely to become identified with dream characters, as a token of her or his enhanced involvement in the scenario. A similar degree of egoism need not necessarily characterize the setting of the stage for the drama. Consider a textual sentence with two clauses: "Because

A was associated with B, A attacked C." The independent clause of the sentence is an action statement, and it is assumed that ego is identified here with A or C. The dependent clause of the sentence merely qualifies our understanding of the major statement. Here, it is assumed, the dreamer is not so much "creating a story-line" as "formulating a dictionary," in this entry of which he or she explains that "by A, I also mean B." In these latter formulations he or she necessarily will posit direct connections between third parties, connections which need to be understood exactly as they are stated.

While the motives (interaction propensities) which generate the dream always are considered to be important (ego-relevant), the associational network through which they "pass," or in which they lie, contains elements selected precisely for their "indifferent" (i.e., ego-irrelevant) quality (Freud, 1900). Relationships within this fabric connecting dream instigators to dream products must, necessarily, be capable of assuming more varied form than those within the dreamer's basic motive structures. Freud's final resolution of the age-old problem of the significance versus insignificance of dream impressions is precisely this—the motives which generate the dream always are significant and always implicate the dreamer, while the connective tissue separating these motives from their ultimate expression or disguising their manifestation in the dream need be neither significant nor ego-cathected.

SSLS follows Freud in distinguishing these two aspects of dream phenomena and in proposing constraints for the one which need not apply to the other. In terms of its own model, it is clear why SSLS cannot permit interactive sentences, which are assumed to represent dreamer *motives*, to exist in alter-alter form. Associative sentences are not motive constructs, and hence are exempt from this proscription.

On purely methodological grounds, exemption for associative sentences from the ban on direct third-party statements is required so that the evidence of the dream and associations can be used intelligently in writing interactive-sentence transforms (determining private meanings). Consider the sequence:

(a) I hit X;
(b) X goes with Father.

Where the second, associative, sentence cannot be coded directly (i.e., where ego must be inserted in it as either subject or object), we are unable to decode the first reasonably. If ego must, in sentece (b), be identified with Father, we get the translation of (a) that "I hit myself." If ego must, in sentence (b), be identified with X, we get a translation of (a) that "Father hit X." Neither of the possibilities is the most reasonable reduction of (a), namely, "I hit father," which *does* follow when association statements are allowed to stand in the form: "X associated with Y," with neither X nor Y = ego. Thus, *With* associative sentences must be exempt from the proscription of third-person relationships if they are to be of use in determining the private meaning of dream symbols.

Unrestricted *Equivalence* and *Means* sentences also are desirable, because an X-Y exclusionary rule would entail significant losses of dreamer meaning, to the detriment of SSLS's overall analytic program. *Equivalence* indicates a *With*-relationship of ultimate strength (identity). Clearly, if either Equivalence or With statements could not be preserved intact, it would be impossible to characterize the transformations involved in creating the dream (i.e., it would distort the *association-path* analyses to be described [chapter 13]). This same consideration applies to Means sentences. In the latter case, there is an additional advantage to not observing the third-person exclusionary rule. Since a Means sentence most often qualifies an interactive sentence (X interacting with Y through means Z), it can preserve the integrity of the textual interactive relationship which was submitted to the third-person rule in the interactive sentence itself.

In this sense, the Means sentence permits us "to have our cake and eat it too." It allows us to avoid some of the potential disadvantages of always stating interactive sentences in a restricted form. Furthermore, it serves this role in a manner which remains faithful to the dreamer's own texts as well as to our model of the dreaming process.

As we have discussed at some length, SSLS restricts its interaction sentences such that ego must appear in them. SSLS also demands that ego fulfill only *one role* in *any* sentence, interactive *or* associative. Ego can be either subject or object, but not both. The rationale underlying this demand is partly conceptual, partly methodological.

Conceptually, despite Jung's "interpretation on the subjective level" (1948), in which all characters are assumed to be aspects of the self, it seems, *prima facie,* unlikely that genuine ego investments in social reality can so easily be shed during sleep. It surely is instructive, even should Jung's analysis be partly correct, that the dreamer "explores herself or himself" using referents from external reality. It does not seem plausible that these referents could be used without a significant contamination of the hypothesized self-analysis by relationships with and among the referents in question.

Methodologically, self-self relationship statements are difficult to verify. Moreover, unless one has a reliable catalog of different self-systems, it is hard to know what such statements mean: which self is doing what to which other self? As is well known, psychology has no such catalog, no agreement on the nature of our inner world. Hoping to avoid fatal submersion in these troubled waters, SSLS has opted for the reliability, verifiability, and convenience of focusing on real-world externalizations of internalized behavioral predispositions. This is not a *denial* of the multifaceted complexity of human nature, but an *apprehension* of its *concrete externalizations.*

"If you want a moonlight night, Chekhov advised, write that on the dam of the mill a fragment of a broken bottle flashed like a small bright star" (Gray, 1962, p. 2). Self, like moonlight, is best described by its manifestations in the familiar "external reality" immediately at hand. Thus SSLS pitches its motivational variables at quite a different level than does classical psychodynamic theory: in place of private constructs, we have public relationships. The advantages in clarity and verifiability are enormous, and the loss of meaning need be quite small, for intrapsychic constructs are (or should be), after all, posited on the basis of real-world observations.

What is one to do, then, with texts which assert self-self relationships, e.g., "I hate myself"? Such textual statements receive *no* structural translation to SSLS, but become *dynamic modifiers* (see Dynamic Analysis, pp. 238–42, of adjacent interactive sentences. To illustrate the logic of this convention, consider the following pair of assertions:

1) I hate myself (for)
2) having left Mother.

Basically, SSLS proposes that the first assertion is a modifier of the second, thus giving us one, *modified* ego-alter interactive sentence: "Hateful/hated I left mother."[13]

Noun Categories

Now, having considered the grammatical restrictions SSLS puts on the *use* of nouns in interactive sentences, we need to consider the nature and logic of SSLS's noun *categories* themselves. Simplification of the infinite diversity of dream content is inherent in any system of content analysis. We have observed the drastic form reductiveness has assumed in SSLS's treatment of verbs. A similar though much less drastic reduction has been imposed on dream subjects and objects. As general principles of character categorization, SSLS has relied upon the familiar dimensions of age, sex, and familial relationship.

In forming its particular noun categories, SSLS once again has taken its cue from Freud. One of the major contributions of *The Interpretation of*

---

[13] Suppose, the reader may ask, the *entire* dream report is "I killed myself." Here, by convention, the dream report is scored as a "defective" sentence (see Dynamic Analysis, pp. 238–42) of the form: —< . . . . That is, the aggression is considered scoreable, but not the subject or object of the aggression.

Dreams (1900) is the demonstration that behind the many different characters who appear in dreams, as fictitious (if the dreamer cannot identify them) or trivial (if her or his relationship with them in waking life is incidental) as they sometimes may seem, stand the truly significant persons in the dreamer's current waking life or developmental history. The orienting assumption is that

> . . . what we dream is either manifestly recognizable as psychically significant, or it is distorted and cannot be judged till the dream has been interpreted, after which it will once more be found to be significant. Dreams are never concerned with trivialities; we do not allow our sleep to be disturbed by trifles. [Freud, 1900, p. 182].

Therefore, the classification of dream characters involves identifying the generally most significant relationships within the life-span of the person in contemporary Western society. (It is recognized that persons or classes of persons not *generally* significant may be specifically so for certain dreamers; while such characters are not ignored and can be identified by SSLS, they are not deemed of sufficient general significance to warrant the elaboration of separate categories on their behalf. The aim is for that degree of categorical simplification which stops just short of significant general distortion of the instances being classified.) The system identifies significant persons as follows: *mother* [symbolized: M], *father* [F], *sibs* [Si], *spouse* [Sp], *male peers* [Pm], *female peers* [Pf], *children* [C], and, of course, the self *(ego)* [E]. There also is a residual *symbolic* [Sy] category.

This reduction scheme now will be justified not only in terms of whom it includes, but also in terms of whom it excludes. All persons older than the dreamer by a generation (or more) are classified as parents.[14] Here we follow the logic and findings of Freud's dream analyses, the logic being that developmental considerations point to the parents as the prototypes for all future relationships with older persons and indicate that all such future relationships will draw heavily upon their immensely significant historical precursor, and the findings being that Freud established that kings, queens, older strangers, paternal or maternal contemporaries, aunts, uncles, grandparents, and so on, did seem to stand for parents in the dreams he subjected to detailed analysis.

[14]Note that age-criteria employed in "vertically upward" character classification are relative to the dreamer's true age. Thus in a father-uncle interaction where ego is identified with father, uncle is not a peer, as he would be to father, but a "father" figure as he would be to the dreamer. However, when the dreamer assumes a childlike role, his child-peers are scored as peers, not as children. The child category is reserved, therefore, for cases where the dreamer maintains his true generational status, and relates to a child. These two rules assume that, when ego regresses, so too does the whole world, but that when ego "progresses," the dreamer's world remains as it is.

By the same criteria, institutionalized authority figures (e.g., policemen, male doctors, priests, bureaucrats) and nurturance figures (e.g., nurses, female doctors) of a still wider potential age range are classifed, respectively, as "father" and "mother."

Following the same general lines of reasoning and evidence, sibs are identified categorically, although for many adult dreamers in American society, they will no longer be figures of contemporary significance. Historically, sibs are part of the miniature drama from which many of life's later scenarios derive, and relations with sibs often are seen to be important prototypes for peer relationships, as in school or work settings.

"Spouses," or lived-with (by the dreamer or a like-sex peer) opposite-sex peers, are separated out from opposite-sex peers in general, since, on the sheer face of it, living with someone, including the potential sharing of parenthood, creates a special relationship of peculiar intensity.

It is possible for the user of SSLS to reduce contemporary peer relationships to the primitive family situation (e.g., same-sex peers = sibs, spouse or opposite-sex peers = opposite-sex parent). However, such reduction is not obligatory, not built into the system: within the system itself, such reduction transpires only when contextual dream or association data permit the scorer to associate contemporaries with family members according to certain rules. Put another way, the system also is open to the possibility that contemporary relationships with like- or opposite-sex peers can be legitimate objects of dream concern in their own right, *relatively* untouched by their supposed historical prototypes. This is entirely consistent with Freud's own work, in which dreams (e.g., "Irma's Injection"; Freud, 1900, ch. II) often were not traced back to infantile determinants but productively analyzed nonetheless.

Taken together, Peer M, Peer F, and Spouse are broadly representative of a horizontal dimension of relationship, in which social ties must be established through some degree of sharing and mutuality, in which heterosexual (and homosexual) tendencies generally are worked through, and in which that intimacy which is the special province of intragenerational cohorts can be established. Vertically, as we have seen, "upward" relations to older persons are conceptualized as involving problems of authority versus freedom and nurturance/dependency versus autonomy, and are assumed to turn about generic parent figures. The "Children" category reflects an emphasis from "adult" psychology, in which downward vertical relationships also can be inherently significant. The child nurtures the adult but the adult also parents the child.

In justifying the separate "Children" category (persons a generation or more below the dreamer), two points need to be made, the first to those who would exclude it altogether, and the second to those who might wish separate categories for one's own children and other children. (1) It is recognized that children in dreams can stand for the "child" in the dreamer. Perhaps for the young, and nonparents more generally, that most often is the case, and children appearing in dreams should be routinely so interpreted. It seems, however, unduly restrictive to immediately classify all self-child interaction as solipsistic. Parenting is one of the most significant roles in adult society, and, like pairing, it has its own special set of conflicts, compromises, and joys. SSLS permits the user the option of collapsing all ego-child relationships into ego-ego ones; it also allows the user the option of treating such relationships *sui generis.* (2) As with vertical relationships upward, it is considered that the diversity of vertical relationships downward can be greatly simplified. Parenting is parenting, whether it is the mother or the father with their own child, teachers with students, or the nurse holding a newborn. As all relationships upward are, in some important sense, to mothers and fathers, so too all relationships downward are to "one's own children," whether they fit that biological/sociological definition or not. Younger persons can be seen generically as the objects of one's wish to live on, through the seeds (whether sperm/egg or knowledge/culture) one plants.

No one, it is supposed, objects to the idea of a self (*ego*) category. "The chief character in almost every dream is the dreamer himself. He is an active participant in many of the events that take place, and when he is not participating he is observing what others are doing" (Hall and Van de Castle, 1966, p. 52). The only apology offered for this category is for its lack of differentiation: why does it lack an id, ego, and super-ego; an animus and anima; an internalized parent, adult, and child; and so on? In part, as already discussed, it is felt that the analyst who wishes to can see such entities objectified in categories already present in the system. Beyond this, as also already discussed, the identification of significant subselves is at present too controversial and unresolved a matter to permit their encoding into the categorical structure of the present system. (There are, however, two respects in which SSLS *does* permit the coding of "subselves:" social roles—e.g., physician—enacted by the self and body parts of the physical self. In this sense, SSLS does permit the scoring of some self-self relationships of a relatively overt sort. See appendix A.)

Much the same sort of justification is offered for the gross lumping together of animals/creatures, body parts, material objects, and ideas— everything, in short, which cannot be classified in the previously enumerated subject/object categories—into a residual class of *symbolic* entities. While this may seem a gross evasion of theoretical responsibility, it would, in fact, be totally incompatible with the nature and goals of SSLS were it to offer an arbitrary set of rules for the immediate translation of all manifestly "symbolic" dream elements into its other noun classes. That the constituents of the present symbolic category often are not to be taken at face value is clearly recognized by the category label. But the writing of a priori transformation rules is not a satisfactory way of reducing these symbolic constituents. Besides being theoretically indefensible, it would add inordinate complexity to the system and reduce its appeal for those many dream students who would not share the author's conviction about what a set of appropriate symbol translations might be.

As a system devoted to the discovery of "private" meaning, then, SSLS can provide no general set of symbol translations. It cannot *prejudge* symbol meanings. What it can, and does, do is to provide a convenient way to *discover* the private meaning of dream symbols in particular cases. As has been noted earlier, With sentences permit the writing of transforms of interactive sentences (see also pp. 229–35). Where an SSLS associative sentence, as scored either from the dream text itself or in the free-association material, aligns some symbolic noun X with some element representing an SSLS character category, then any SSLS interactive sentence relating ego to X generates an interactive-sentence transform in which ego is related to that character category. Thus "I climbed a hill. My mother was at the top of the hill" leads to these *raw scores:*

Ego/moving toward/symbol(A) (Interactive);
Mother/with/symbol(A) (Associative);

and to this interactive-sentence *transform:*

Ego/moving toward/Mother (Transform).

Thus SSLS provides a systematic framework in which we may actually implement the principle most generally given only lip-service by dream theorists (including, to some extent, Freud, particularly in later editions of *The Interpretation of Dreams*). This principle is that a dream symbol should be deciphered on the basis of information about its dreamer rather than on the basis of suppositions about dreamers in general.

SSLS's treatment of "symbolic" entities is not entirely free of a priori assumptions, however. It appears clear, from clinical phenomena in general and from the study of dreams in particular, that animals or animate creatures often "stand for" significant other persons or for different aspects of the self. This evidence has been discussed elsewhere (Foulkes, Shepherd, and Scott, 1974) in the context of relatively frequent occurrences of animal imagery in children's dreams.

SSLS thus proposes several general a priori principles for translating animal or animate characters. (1) Where animals or creatures are clearly humanoid in portrayal, they are treated as humans. Specifically, this means that when *age* and *sex* classifications are noted for animal characters in relation to each other, these characters are categorized following rules applied to humans, and ego is located according to rules for human interaction. Thus "Uncle Donald Duck" is "father" if he punishes nephew "Louie," and following rules elaborated above, for a male dreamer (see figure 11-4), this interaction would be coded Father-Self.

(2) Where animals or creatures are intermixed with human characters, but not specifically assigned age/sex roles relative to members of their own species or class, they may be assigned human character roles on the basis of *size* relationships. Thus, for example, it seems clear that very large undomesticated animals often are used by children to symbolize parent figures (Morris, 1967). When human characters interact with such animals or with other creatures grossly larger than themselves, it is assumed that these animal/creatures are parents. "The elephant attacked me," for instance, is scored as a parent-ego aggression. If animals or creatures interact among themselves, size relationships also can be used to establish human identifications. "The elephant attacked the mouse," for example, is considered a parent-child aggression, and it would again be scored as a parent-ego aggression.[15]

(3) Where animals are explicitly described as *pets* or are members of species commonly considered as housepets in Western society, they are considered as *ego* symbols in an SSLS *interactive sentence* if the other noun with which they share a raw-text interaction also is symbolic, but not a pet. The principle here is the well-established identification of humans with pets. *Otherwise, the rule of "active voice" discussed above is used to locate ego in textual statements of interaction between two manifestly symbolic creatures, objects, concepts, and so on.* That is, with this level of noun disguise, ego's responsibility for dream interactions is assumed to be generally capable of direct representation. (In *associative sentences*, of course, pets retain their symbolic classification.)

(4) By convention: (a) *cows* and lactating animals, but not "cattle," are scored as M; (b) *subhuman primates* always are scored as human characters; (c) *horses* and *snakes* are considered as male, and thus as impermissible ego-identification figures for female dreamers in *interactive sentences*, unless

---

[15] Although contextual "he," "she," "him," "her," etc., references sometimes will be present, it may not always be possible to identify the sex of creatures in such interactions; where sex cannot definitely be ascertained, the larger creature is scored simply *Parent* [P], rather than Mother or Father, and the smaller creature is assumed to be of the same sex as the dreamer, e.g., ego is identified with the latter.

there is some specific indication to the contrary. The basis for these conventions is fairly obvious, and supporting evidence has been discussed by Morris (1967).

There are, of course, in addition to circumstances where the above principles can be employed, many other dreams where animals or creatures will be mapped into human categories via transforms of interactive sentences. As in other coding areas, identifications of animals or creatures by means of the dreamer's own comments are considered to have conceptual and empirical *priority* over those generated by any of SSLS's a priori assumptions.

The justifications for having any a priori coding principles for animals at all are: (a) the fact that certain impressive regularities *have* been observed in earlier studies of dreaming and symbol formation, regularities of sufficient strength to permit the tentative formulations embodied in these principles, always subject, of course, to revision on the basis of dreamer-generated data; and (b) the practical need not to leave the analyst totally in the dark when these latter data are absent, i.e., not to have the seemingly inexplicable symbolic category overfull when there is at least some indication of what some exemplars within it might stand for.

Yet, considering the class of *symbolic* nouns more generally, it clearly is desirable, as already has been noted, not to elaborate more than a few a priori principles to guide their translation into other subject/object categories. SSLS's initial aim is for effective coding of most dreams, but, inevitably falling short of that goal, more for a situation in which important elements are unlabeled than for one in which they are arbitrarily mislabeled. Thus, even though there is evidence to support a degree of generality for some conventional Freudian translations within this domain (e.g., enclosures as female genitals, elongated objects as male genitals), *SSLS offers no rules for the translation of objects or concepts.*

With animals and living creatures, it is clear that they are intended as actors in an interpersonal sense. They already have been mapped into an interpersonal action field, as it were, and only their precise placement there is in question.[16] Using principles generally employed within that same field for their particular placement seems an eminently reasonable convention.

For object or concept classification, however, new questions arise. Are objects always to be considered symbolic of interpersonal concerns? As they stand at some greater manifest distance from such concerns than do animals or other living creatures, a positive answer here would seem more arbitrary than in the case of animals.

---

[16] Animal-human or animal-animal relationships are assumed, in contemporary Western civilization, generally to be lacking in *intrinsic* interest to the dreamer, though exceptions clearly may exist. Thus animals usually must stand for some other actors in the interpersonal field where ego *does* invest its energy, attention, and interest.

One advantage of the "symbolic" category, in fact, is that it permits the analysis of dream concerns which are *not* exclusively interpersonal in charac- ter. Thus SSLS allows the possibility of relatively independent ego-investments in mastery of the material world and in ideals which transcend particular encounters with other human beings. Analysts may collapse "symbolic" relations into other categories according to rules of their choice if that reduc- tionism is demanded by the theory under which they are operating. This reduction is not built into the present system, however, in accord with its general principle of beginning with what-seems-to-be, and in view of persuasive reasoning and some evidence in favor of the proposition that social-mastery may be but a particular case of world-mastery in a larger sense.

However, it is clear that objects or concepts also *can* be used as symbols for interpersonal referents. In such cases, SSLS does, in a sense, offer "guide- lines" for *interpretation*, even if it forgoes writing a priori translation state- ments for specific classes of objects or concepts. These guidelines are found in the coding of *relationships* involving objects. Thus, if elevator is not imme- diately defined as a "feminine" symbol, its nature may be revealed by its relationship to ego. "I entered the elevator" would be coded an ego-object interaction, but of the Moving Toward (or penetrative) mode. While this is not a precise translation of an orthodox Freudian symbol-transformation statement, it is apparent that not all of the symbol's "Freudian" meaning has been lost in its SSLS translation, either. As noted earlier, SSLS pays relatively more attention to relationships, and relatively less to the noun classes so related, than most other interpretive systems. In the case of noun symbolism, this leads to examining symbols-in-use rather than symbols-at- rest. Not only does this way of proceeding partially obviate the construction of a cumbersome set of rules for many different classes of nouns; it also provides a contextual check on meaning which is not provided by flat state- ments such as "guns are penises."

One final point needs to be discussed in the context of symbol-scoring: *where is E to be located in apparent symbolic-X or X-symbolic third-person interactive sentences?* Obviously, many of the rules evolved for the more general class of X-Y interactions will not apply here, since objects (concepts, creatures) will be lacking age and sex characteristics. The rules applied in such cases are as follows: (1) In "negative" (Moving From or Moving Against) relationships where X is scored as a parent, E is identified with the *symbol* (Father hit the rock [ego]; the rock [ego] hit father), on the grounds that such a transformation, in the reverse direction (i.e., ego to rock), is needed to conceal E's role in a negative act within the original family context. The reason parental interactions have been selected out for special consideration is the assumption that negative feelings toward or from the powerful-but-necessary figures of early childhood are highly repressed (thus we have the conventional idealization of parents in waking life). Hence, when negative feeling forms one part of a sentence stem whose other identifiable part is a parent, we assume that E will be in a highly distorted role, viz., the symbol.

(2) In negative relationships in which X is not scored as a parent, E is identified with X if X is of like sex as E and with the symbol if X is of unlike sex as E.

(3) In "positive" (Moving Toward or Creating) relationships, E always is identified with X if X is of the same sex as E or with the symbol if X is of different sex than E.

Underlying the latter two rules (and other conventions presented earlier) is an assumption of *economy of distortion*. It is assumed that E's egoistic involvement in a dream sequence will be distorted in a smaller, rather than a larger, number of ways. (Stated from the viewpoint of a *theory* of dreaming rather than from that of a hypothetical *description* of the dream process, this is the same as saying that the theory will follow the principle of parsimony— it will make fewer, rather than more, assumptions about the phenomenon it seeks to explain.) It further is assumed that the basic *form* of the relationship is, as SSLS has coded it, relatively undistorted, and that the *symbol* is, by definition, likely to be quite distorted. Since the assumption of egoism mandates that E be located *somewhere* in the interactive sequence, we then consider the *third term* involved.[17]

If that third-term person is similar to (like-sexed as) E, we have, following the rules above, to assume only that the person is a very mild distortion of E ("like father, like son") and that the object is a heavy distortion of someone or something. On an alternative rule identifying E with a cross-sex person, on the other hand, we would have to assume heavy distortion concealed in the symbol *plus* one of the following implausibilities:

(a) E is identified with a culturally proscribed opposite-sex role in a Moving Toward ("sexual") transaction;[18]

---

[17]In general, it is assumed that SSLS's verbs can be taken at face value. The reasoning here is partly conceptual, partly methodological. Conceptually, following Freud, SSLS's verbs stand for the basic moving forces of human nature. As primordial givens, they are less tractable than one's associative mapping of a later-comprehended external reality. Clinically, instinct reversals are seen less often than instinct displacements, i.e., it is more likely that the instinct remains, with a variable object, than that it is transformed, with an invariant object.

Methodologically, SSLS's four interactive verbs already represent such a massive reduction of everyday interaction that transformations across its verb-category boundaries imply a much more radical reordering than do transformations across its noun-category boundaries. Observationally, there *are* relatively few nontrivial verb transforms in SSLS scoring in comparison to noun transforms—i.e., the dreamer's own statements give us little data to support the idea of frequent verb intersubstitution.

[18]Cf. my earlier comments on dream bisexuality, p. 210

(b) E is identified with a cross-sex role in a creative transaction, in the face of a strong sex-typing of creative roles (Mead, 1949); or

(c) E is identified with a cross-sex role in a withdrawal transaction, when the bases of attraction *and repulsion*, particularly at the peer level, are strongly sex-typed.

That is, if sex-typing of behavior is as pervasive as it seems to be, and if its scope extends into dream life, as it seems to (Foulkes, Shepherd, and Scott, 1974), then identification of E with a cross-sex character seems less likely in cases (2) and (3) on page 223 than does identification with a (manifestly) unsexed symbol.

As is true of SSLS's other assumptive principles of dreamer semantics, these rules also are subject to check, and correction, by dream context and dreamer associations. Where these latter materials give rise to appropriate interactive-sentence transforms, such transforms have priority over any and all of the rules given above. Thus, if Father is moving away from a spider, E = spider, but if a male dreamer's Father is moving away from (by an associative sentence) *Mother's* spider, then E = Father.

Summarizing SSLS's treatment of dream symbols, then, SSLS generally fails to provide the kind of detailed translation rules one finds in many dream books (e.g., Gutheil, 1951). It relies on the symbol dictionary in the dreamer's head—as revealed in the dreamer's associations—more than on the one likely to be on our bookshelf. Thus, where associations are not collected, its dream analysis is likely to be minimally revealing. But, as we have seen, SSLS's "message" is that associations are necessary for effective dream analysis. Something else besides the dream text is required. SSLS provides rules for dealing with that "something else," so that it can be coordinated with the analysis of the dream text.

Even the most scrupulously collected associations will not always do the job, however. In part, this may be handled by adopting a convention that allows symbol transformations developed within analyses of other dreams from the same dreamer (i.e., in the same "dream series"—Hall and Nordby, 1972) to be generalized back to the dream in question, providing that certain contextual and temporal criteria are satisfied. But, beyond that, it may be the greater part of wisdom to recognize the limits of our power to interpret dreams reliably and to forgo "complete" analysis rather than succumbing to the temptation that we must "know everything." It is in the resistance to that temptation that recondite areas of psychology, such as dreams, are most likely to be brought within the framework of scientific understanding. It surely is in the yielding to such temptation that dream psychology most often has lost its basis in any kind of intersubjectively verifiable reality.

In general, then, SSLS attempts, in its determination of the meaning of "symbolic" nouns,[19] to follow the logic of Freud's most essential contribution to dream psychology:

> Freud's major discovery was that the interpretation of dreams can be achieved in relation to private information derived from the dreamer's own thought processes. He took seriously the working hypothesis of psychological determinism and searched for predream thoughts, wishes, and feelings which caused the dream to be dreamed as it was. In this effort, he introduced his great methodological innovation, the use of free association to elements of the manifest dream, allowing him to relate manifest dream content back to those waking predream experiences which gave the dream its meaning. Freud recognized that the thoughts elicited in free association were not apt to be identical to those active in dream formation, but argued that it was plausible to consider them as not unrelated to thoughts or experiences which might have played an antecedent role in relation to the manifest dream. [Foulkes and Vogel, 1974, p. 19]

Failing to find symbol translations in these sources, SSLS turns to a finite number of assumptions (egoism; identification by sex, age, size, and cross-species similarity; the greater likelihood of variable age- than sex-identifications; an active-voice principle underlying dream identifications; examination of object symbols "in use"; the need to distort negative feelings toward, about, or perceived-as-coming-from those family figures upon whom the dreamer, as a child, was so dependent; and economy of distortion). These assumptions, while most often explicitly derived from Freud (1900), are nonetheless consistent with what might be called a more general psychodynamic viewpoint. Since it is theories adopting this viewpoint which have had the greatest success in dealing with dream content, it is these theories with which SSLS must attempt to retain some compatibility.

Lexical Classes Within Noun Categories

We now have considered the rationale underlying the discrimination of nine noun categories (i.e., mother, father, sibs, spouse, male peers, female peers, children, symbolic, and ego) by SSLS. It may be objected that this degree of categorical simplification is too drastic, particularly for nouns.

[19]"Symbolic" is used now in its wider sense and not merely as synonymous with SSLS's cateogory, *Symbolic*. That is, in the wider sense in which the Uncle Donald Duck who punishes nephew Louie is symbolic, even though SSLS classifies him as *Father*.

While in some sense aggression, however softly it is expressed, is still aggression, dreamers may attach fundamentally different connotations to relationships with two or more different persons in a given noun class. They may, for instance, see the world as containing both good and bad fathers, or both supportive and frustrating female or male peers. To the retort that, psychologically, these intracategory discriminations represent a defensive splitting-off of elements which, at some ultimately deep level, are fused, e.g., the good-bad father or the approachable-unapproachable sex-object, the reply can be made: maybe so, but at the reality level where dreamers live, it makes a fundamental difference in our *interpretations*—i.e., our predictions about how dreamers *behave*—whether they're dreaming about father$_1$ or father$_2$, female-peer$_1$ or female-peer$_2$. Moreover, in attempting to recreate the associative processes assumed to be active in *dream formation* (which has been stated as the primary goal of SSLS), it surely should be kept distinct whether the dreamer is associating to or from one or the other of these good-bad or approachable-unapproachable persons. Can SSLS afford to lose track of these significant characterological discriminations the dreamer reveals to us?

The answer clearly is no, it can't. One of the major problems in classical psychodynamic interpretive systems arose at just this point—their bias in favor of the deeper-fused entity rather than the behaviorally discriminative one, i.e., their preference for simplicity over complexity in dreamer and dream characterization. To implement its own goals, SSLS must make adjustments of earlier methods so as to profit from these mistakes of application. To this end, *SSLS permits the formation of lexical classes within its non-ego noun categories*. The categories themselves are retained, and where it is desirable to treat all older males—good, bad, and indifferent—as one, this clearly can be done. The noun category is the operative unit. But, where it is desirable to discriminate among older males, this too can be done. The lexical class is the operative unit.

At present, SSLS suggests that lexical classes be formed inductively, and on a case-by-case basis. This is not to deny the possibility that, at some later time, it will be appropriate, either within particular dreamers or across dreamers in general, to standardize lexical classes. For example, the symbolic category, as a starter, might contain lexical superclasses corresponding to discriminations we already have made informally—i.e., animals, other creatures, material objects, ideas and concepts, and so on. Lexical classes might then be formed within each superclass—e.g., animals might be classified as either pets, barnyard, native-undomesticated, or exotic (cf. Foulkes and Shepherd, 1971). Until many more dreams have been studied with SSLS, however, there will be no firm empirical base on which to decide what lexical classes are sufficiently general to deserve systemic codification. To facilitate discovery of ultimately useful lexical classes, then, SSLS sacrifices the immediate reliability which could be achieved with an arbitrary assumption of appropriate lexical units.

Rather than supplying hard and fast rules as to how to form lexical classes, this introduction to SSLS can only indicate, illustratively, the way in which it now seems best to proceed (see, especially, the coding of Freud's "Botanical Monograph" dream, chapter 12). Nevertheless, certain suggestions can be tentatively advanced. For character categories, separate lexical coding should be given to each discriminable character unit, although larger classes can be formed on the basis of group identity. Thus, for peer-males (Pm), consider the following dream:

I was lecturing to a class of young men (Pm_1). One of the students, a very tall boy (Pm_{1A}) stopped me after class to ask me for my lecture notes. He was with another youth, dressed as if he were an auto mechanic (Pm_2).

Our Pm lexicon for this dream report would read:

Pm_1—students;
  Pm_{1A}—tall student;
Pm_2—auto mechanic.

As the example illustrates, lexical-class identity within an SSLS noun category is indicated by subscripts (first numbers, then letters), and these are assigned in the order of character appearance in the scored text.

For the symbolic category, the SSLS analyst necessarily must work at a more intuitive level, trying to be sensitive to all major details of the dreamer's text and bearing in mind that the association-process analysis will require that all transitional elements in an association chain be coded. The best illustration of how symbol analysis might proceed in any particular case is, again, the analysis of "Botanical Monograph" given in chapter 12. Here, we consider only a brief specimen:

The man walked up to the bush. Nearby was a single flower, pale yellow. That reminds me of a pale yellow rose I once gave my girlfriend. She has a yellow dress she's always wearing when we go out.

The lexicon for the symbolic (Sy) category for this report might be:

Sy_1 (botanical) Sy_2—(apparel)

$_{1A}$—bush $_{2A}$—dress

$_{1B}$—flowers

   $_{1B1}$—dream-flower

   $_{1B2}$—waking-rose

Note that lexical entries are *standard grammatical nouns,* and that the adjective "yellow" does not figure directly in the formation of any SSLS lexical-class. (Grammatical adjectives most often are *dynamic* modifiers of nouns in SSLS rather than *structural* elements themselves within SSLS sentences [see Dynamic Analysis, pp. 238-42]).

SSLS's goal is, where possible, to restrict its lexical classes—i.e., its nouns—to persons, places, and substantial "things." While, in trial scorings, we have found it necessary to form classes such as "verbal" (e.g., jokes, puns), "psychological" (e.g., dreams, memories), the preference is for restricting SSLS noun classes to palpable entities, such as "writings" (e.g., books, letters) and "residential" (e.g., house, trailer). Thus, for instance, where "game" refers to a boxed entity containing a board, pieces, pointers, and so on, it legitimately is categorized as a member of a "recreational object" noun class; however when "game" (as in "I liked the game") clearly is a reification of an activity, then an activity should be scored, and nouns should be restricted to palpable accompaniments of the activity. For instance, "I liked soccer" would, in the context, "I was playing soccer," be scored:

$$E \rightarrow Sy_{1A1};$$
$$[\overset{+}{E} = E(Sy_{1A2}) \boxed{\rightarrow} Sy_{1A1}];$$

translated as

Ego (as ball)/moved toward/goal;

Approving I/was agent by which/ball/moved toward/goal.

That is, "soccer" is a shorthand designation of a set of activities rather more than it is a label for an entity; "soccer ball," however, is a legitimate entity, as is the place, "goal." (In the context of "I was watching a soccer match," "I liked soccer" would be scored:

$$E \rightarrow Sy_{1A1};$$
$$[\overset{+}{Pm} = E(Sy_{1A2}) \boxed{\rightarrow} Sy_{1A1}];$$
$$E \rightarrow \overset{+}{Pm};$$

translated as

> Ego (as ball)/moved toward/goal;
> Players/were agent by which/ball/moved toward/goal;
> I/(approved of) moved toward/players.)

The exceptions seem to arise in cases where the abstract noun is not even roughly synonymous with an activity: to like a theory is not to like theorizing. The general act of theorizing has issued in a discrete "product" which, although not a material essence, can be imagined in that form. It is this "product" of activity which is the object of regard, rather than the activity per se.

Obviously, hard and fast distinctions cannot be drawn between entities and activities, as can be verified by the unsuccessful efforts of traditional grammarians to give satisfactory definitions of "noun" and "verb." Is "winter" a "thing" an "activity," or what? SSLS simply states the general rule that, in the more blatant cases of reification in texts, ones where activities can be scored plausibly, this latter course be followed. This rule, it is imagined, must take us closer to the "concrete" language of dream experience itself than would a slavish adherence to the abstract forms sometimes found in reports of that experience.

Transforms

As already has been noted, a With (but *not* a Means *or* an Equivalence) sentence can be used to generate transforms of *interactive* sentences. This can be done only where the lexical class in the With sentence *is identical to* that in the interactive sentence. For example, where

1) I went into the new school = $E \to Sy_{1A}$;
2) My old school reminds me of Jill = $[Sy_{1B} \updownarrow Pf_1]$;

the identity of lexical superclass (Sy_1, "scholastic") is not sufficient to permit writing a transform of sentence 1) such that: $E \to Pf_1$. Or, where,

1) I went into the school $[Sy_{1A}]$ = $E \to Sy_{1A}$;
2) A school book $[Sy_{2A}]$ reminded me of Joe = $[Sy_{1A2A} \updownarrow Pm_1]$;

the "partial" identity of the Sy entries, i.e., their common element Sy_{1A}, is not sufficient to permit writing a transform of sentence 1) such that: $E \to Pm_1$. The reasoning in each of these cases is that, were the related two symbols meant to be functionally equivalent, no discriminations of the sort embodied in the dreamers' narratives would have been present.

Also, using the same reasoning, transforms are not written on the basis of translations requiring more than one "stage." For example,

1) $E \rightarrow Sy_{1A}$;
2) $[Sy_{1A} \updownarrow Sy_{2A}]$;
3) $[Sy_{2A} \updownarrow F_1]$;

does *not* yield the transform of sentence 1) that

$E \rightarrow F_1$.

That a two-stage translation is required to replace Sy_{1A} with F_1 suggests the possibility of some discrimination of F_1 and Sy_{1A}, since the presence of the intermediary, Sy_{2A}, cannot be justified, following the "economy of distortion" principle, where a simple replacement of F_1 with Sy_{1A} was intended. (Prohibiting two-stage translations, where there is some intermediary term, does not imply a prohibition of two-*step* translations, i.e., the simultaneous one-stage translation of a noun and verb in the same interactive sentence on the basis of two separate With sentences.)

Transforms are *routinely* generated by With statements only within *the same association chain* (as defined in chapter 13). Across chains, or dreams, interpreters are free, of course, to make substitutions, but at their own risk. That is, they must have reason to believe, in the face of a manifest episodic discrimination by the dreamer, that "other things" still are "equal."

Transforms *also* are routinely generated, however, from any free-association chain back to the dream *chain* (and not merely to the sentence) which generated it. This is illustrated below.
Dream-text sentence:

	Raw Scores	*Transforms*
The rock crushed me	$Sy_1 \overset{+}{\prec} E$	$\overset{+}{F} \overset{+}{\prec} E$

Associations to the above sentence:

Rock? I guess I always thought
of my powerful father as being
kind of like a rock. $[Sy_1 \underset{-}{\overset{+}{\updownarrow}} \overset{+}{F}]$

Note the notational system. Transforms are written in a separate column from Raw Scores. The Transform column is to the right of the Raw Scores column, which, itself, is to the right of the text being scored.

The above example involved the substitution of one noun for another in an interactive sentence on the basis of their sharing a With sentence. Verbs also may be substituted on the same basis. Specifically, where any two interactive verbs are joined by ↕ , any interactive sentence containing one of the verbs may be used to generate a transform containing the other. Thus [⊙→ ↕ →] leads to rewriting all appropriate ⊙→ interactive sentences as → interactive sentences and of all appropriate → interactive sentences as ⊙→ interactive sentences. These transforms *supplement* (but do not *replace*) the Raw Score sentences, and are written with the preceding notation: *also*. The bidirectional nature of the substitution in the verb case reflects the judgment that SSLS's verb classes are equally basic, i.e., there is no more fundamental term to which any SSLS verb should be totally reduced (cf. fn. 17). The statement [⊙→ ↕ →] thus implies free intersubstitutability, rather than reduction.[20]

SSLS's noun classes, on the other hand, are not judged to be equally basic. Therefore, noun transforms are neither necessarily bidirectional nor necessarily nonreductionist. Some directions of noun transformation are impermissible. F, for example, is never replaced by Sy; we are striving for greater, rather than lesser, interpersonal relevance, and F clearly is more relevant in this context than is Sy. Similarly, based on a judgment of the interpersonal relevance of associated nouns, sometimes noun transforms simply replace an existing sentence, whereas at other times they supplement it. For example, E → Sy is replaced by E → F where [Sy ↕ F], while E → Pf may be supplemented, but not replaced, by E → Sp where [Pf ↕ Sp]. SSLS thus strives for reductions to more basic interpersonal situations in the dreamer's life history, but not at the expense of obliterating other interpersonal situations of potential relevance to her or his daily life situation.

---

[20] *Structural* transformations also can be made when the verb With is associated (by means of itself) with an interactive verb, e.g.: [↕ ↕ →] or [→ ↕ ↕]. There are further restrictions on such transformations, however: (1) because the verb With has so many different uses, transforms are restricted to cases where there is some indication of verb communality over and above belonging to the same global verb class—specifically to cases where dynamic modifiers are identical (thus [↕̇ ↕→] leads only to interactive rewrites of appropriate associative sentences containing the verb ↕̇); (2) because the goal of writing transforms is to characterize dreamer motives, such rewrites only are generated for sentences of the form: [E ↕ . . .], i.e., sentences which, when rewritten, will link *ego* to a person or symbol via an interactive verb; (3) because the goal of writing transforms is to characterize dreamer motives, only associative sentences (meeting the above criteria) are rewritten as interactive ones, and never vice versa.

Dynamic transformations also are made. For example, the sentence [→ ↕ ↠] leads to unidirectional transformation of appropriate → sentences as ↠ sentences (and not to the rewriting of appropriate ↠ sentences as → sentences). That is, such transformations never *delete* dynamic signs, but can only *add* them. More complex cases of dynamic transformation (those involving different verbs in their associative sentence base, e.g.: [⊙̇→ ↕ →]) are discussed in Transforms, pp. 402–5.

Specifically, the following rules govern the *when* and *how* of noun transformation:

(1) Where a With sentence links an Sy with C, Pf, Pm, Sp, Si, M, or F, any interactive occurrence of that Sy is *replaced* by the character term associated with it in the With sentence. For example,

    1) $E \circlearrowright Sy_{1A}$;
    2) $[Sy_{1A} \updownarrow Sp]$;

results in

    IT) $E \circlearrowright Sp$.

But a character term never is replaced by Sy.

(2) Where a With sentence links C with Pf, Pm, Sp, Si, M, or F, any interactive occurrence of C is *replaced* by the character term associated with it in the With sentence. For example,

    1) $E \circlearrowright C$;
    2) $[C \updownarrow M]$;

results in

    1T) $E \circlearrowright M$.

But no other character term ever is replaced by C.

(3) Transformations are permitted among lexical classes *within* any given character category. These transformations are bidirectional, i.e., $[Pf_1 \updownarrow Pf_2]$ leads to supplementary (*also*) transforms of Pf_1 interactive sentences to Pf_2 ones and of Pf_2 interactive sentences to Pf_1 ones.

(4) $[Sy \updownarrow Sy]$ sentences never generate transforms, however.

(5) No transform ever is written if it reduces an interactive sentence to E-E form, i.e., no interactive sentence noun can be replaced or supplemented in a transform by E. Thus:

    1) $E \rightarrow Sy_{1A}$;
    2) $[Sy_{1A} \updownarrow E]$;

does *not* lead to

    1T) $E \rightarrow E$;

since, as discussed earlier, such a transform would not clarify any interpretive situation.

(6) Associative With sentences involving characters from within the peer stratum—Pm, Pf, Sp—generate transforms as follows:

[Pf ⇕ Pm] or [Pm ⇕ Pf] —supplement (*also*) interactive Pm's with Pf's
and Pf's with Pm's
[Sp ⇕ Pm] or [Pm ⇕ Sp] —supplement (*also*) interactive Pm's with Sp's
[Sp ⇕ Pf] or [Pf ⇕ Sp] —supplement (*also*) interactive Pf's with Sp's

The bias of these rules is a reduction toward the (presumably) more basic (Sp) relationship. Thus:

1) E → Sp;
2) E → Pf;
3) [Pf ⇕ Sp] ;

leads to

Raw Scores	Transforms
1) E → Sp	
2) E → Pf	*also* E → Sp
3) [Pf ⇕ Sp].	

No peer-level noun is ever reduced to (replaced by, supplemented by) an Sy or C noun. Any With association of a peer-level noun with a parent-level noun (i.e., [Sp ⇕ M], [M ⇕ Sp], [Sp ⇕ F], [F ⇕ Sp], [Pm ⇕ M], [M ⇕ Pm], [Pm ⇕ F], [F ⇕ Pm], [Pf ⇕ M], [M ⇕ Pf], [Pf ⇕ F], and [F ⇕ Pf]) results in a supplementary (*also*) transform of interactive sentences with the peer-level term to the parent-level term, but not vice versa. For example

1) E → M;
2) E → Sp;
3) [Sp ⇕ M] ;

leads to

Raw Scores	Transforms
1) E → M	
2) E → Sp	*also* E → M
3) [Sp ⇕ M].	

The same logic applies to With relations linking Pm, Pf, or Sp and the category Si: Si supplements Pm, for instance, but not vice versa.

(7) For With sentences involving members of the family of orientation, the following transformation rules apply:

[Si ⇕ F] or [F ⇕ Si] —supplement (*also*) Si interactive sentences with F
ones
[Si ⇕ M] or [M ⇕ Si] —supplement (*also*) Si interactive sentences with M
ones
[F ⇕ M] or [M ⇕ F] —supplement (*also*), bidirectionally, interactive sentences having one parent category with interactive sentences bearing the other parent category

No family-of-orientation figure ever is reduced to (replaced by, supplemented by) Sy [rule (1) above], C [rule (2) above], or Pm, Pf, or Sp [rule (6) above].

The noun transforms permitted, and proscribed, by SSLS obviously encode certain theoretical assumptions. These include:

(1) *A bias to historical explanation.* Later-developing relationships, e.g., especially C, but also Pm, Pf, and Sp, reduce to historically earlier ones, but not vice versa. SSLS thus shares Freud's (1900) bias to historical reduction, rather than other dream theorists' bias to "contemporary significance" (e.g., Fromm, 1951; Perls, 1969).

Sherwood (1969) has discussed types of explanations used in areas of psychology such as dream analysis. Explanations in terms of *origin* and *genesis*—the precipitating and contributing causes of an event—have an historical bias. Explanations in terms of *function* and *significance*—the effects and contemporary meaning of an event—do not share this bias. Much of the controversy surrounding the different "schools" of dream theory seems to involve not so much differences in theoretical assumptions as different degrees of interest in these two broad classes of explanation. Freud, for example, in his applied papers on dream analysis (1911*a*, 1923*b*, 1925*b*), clearly seems to recognize that a "scientific" concern for historical antecedents may be out of place in a "therapeutic" environment. Those who refute Freud, on the other hand, do not seem to be denying historical antecedents for the contemporary problems reflected in the dream so much as the value for the patient of such historical reduction (e.g., Fromm, 1951; Perls, 1969). It may well be true, they seem to say, that the patient's problems with co-workers historically were his problems with "father," but the situation to which both therapist and patient now must apply themselves is the contemporary one.

SSLS is developed in the spirit of Freud's *The Interpretation of Dreams* (see chapter 4)—Freud the "scientist," the "archaeological psychologist"—

rather than in that of Freud the "therapist," the "consulting psychologist." It takes a different "presumption of interest" (Sherwood, 1969) than do those currently popular theories of dreaming which stress the contemporary or anticipatory role of the dream in the dreamer's life.

(2) *The critical importance of family life.* Among those historical relationships singled out as basic—i.e., more reduced-to than reduced-from—are early ties to parents and siblings. The justification for considering the child's relationships to parents and sibs as prototypes for later social behavior has been discussed above. SSLS also assumes that the more basic of contemporary relationships is that to spouse rather than that to friends and acquaintances. The ego-mate relationship is thought to be the only one regularly occurring in Western society which approaches the psychodynamic complexity and intensity which early family life has for the child.

(3) *Openness to alternative hypotheses.* Despite the choices noted above, SSLS's noun transforms generally *supplement*, rather than *replace*, the original ("raw") scores. That is, although "symbol" reduction is not carried out from the past/familial situation *toward* the contemporary/nonfamilial one, manifest references to the present are *not suppressed* in reductions in the other direction. These references remain as valid interactive sentences, and as potential bases for characterization of the dreamer's current life situation. Thus, SSLS attempts to maintain an at least partially open stance toward different theoretical perspectives on dream phenomena.

The two points at which it becomes *relatively* closed are in translations of Sy and C nouns. Here character or other-character transforms *replace*, rather than supplement. For Sy nouns, SSLS simply takes a frankly interpersonal approach, a bias toward characterizing the dreamer's significant motives in terms of her or his relations with other people rather than with material or nonsubstantial reality. In the case of C nouns, SSLS's position is that, for most dreamers, "child" seems more likely to represent ego's childish investments in others than ego's progeny. (Were the system likely to be applied extensively to the elderly, rather than to young-adult research subjects, this convention might have to be altered.)

Structural Analysis: A Brief Summary

We have been proceeding at a somewhat difficult level. I have tried to present a rationale for the general form of SSLS's content analysis without going into the fine detail of all of the scoring rules themselves (see appendix A). Yet one cannot understand something's theoretical basis without knowing what that thing is itself. Thus, much detail inevitably has crept into the discussion, perhaps so much that the theoretical justification has been obscured. Therefore, let us now briefly recapitulate the main features of the argument.

SSLS is meant to be applied to all statements in (1) the manifest-dream report and (2) the dreamer's own associations to that report. (It is the burden of SSLS's structure that provisions generally must be made to collect associations in any research which will use the system.) SSLS is based upon the principle that these are the only two generally reliable sources of information about the meaning of a dream and that both are required to interpret all but the simplest dreams.

The conceptual unit of analysis, following the apparent form of dream imagery itself, is *relationship*. While relationship can be interpreted intrapsychically, SSLS prefers to follow the ego-alter form generally conveyed by the dreamer in her or his description of dream interactions, and the ego-alter or alter-alter form of her or his descriptions of static relationships.

The operational unit of analysis is an SSLS *sentence*, and the model guiding the analysis is a linguistic one. Sentences are classified as *interactive* or *associative*, depending on their verb. Interactive verbs describe motivated interaction; four categories are discriminated on the basis of dream data, psychodynamic theory, and logical considerations. Associative verbs describe relatively static contingencies among noun (or verb) elements; three categories are discriminated on external semantic and internal pragmatic grounds. The seven verb categories are assumed to be exhaustive and mutually exclusive.

Observations of the dreamer and the psychophysiological state in which dreams occur suggest that the dreamer should be considered partially implicated (i.e., present, either as subject or object, but not both) in every interactive sentence. When this implication is not immediately verified in the manifest dream, SSLS supplies rules for locating the "disguised" ego.

The associative-sentences network surrounding interactive elements is exempt from the egoism rule applied to interactive sentences. Associative sentences portray the private, connotational meaning of dream elements, and SSLS provides a technique for using them to generate *transforms* of otherwise incomprehensible interactive sentences in the dream.

It is claimed that dreams relate to significant "objects" in the real world. Psychodynamic theory has been used to identify and justify eight SSLS *noun* classes of significant persons. SSLS also contains a ninth, residual category, in which significant others or the self generally are assumed to be present in disguised form. The system provides a few general rules for deciphering these disguises, but generally allows that symbol translation is best accomplished on the basis of the evidence of the particular dream and dreamer at hand, or, failing this, that it is best left simply undone. The simplification entailed in reducing all parties to relationships into only nine noun categories is mitigated by the possibility of forming separate *lexical classes* within any such category. Figure 11-5 summarizes SSLS's verb and noun categories and the symbols used in their scoring.

FIGURE 11-5

Scoring Categories

CATEGORIES	EXAMPLES	SYMBOL
Verb		
Interactive		
Moving Toward	loving, unifying, penetrating, "getting into," helping, etc.	→
Moving From	withdrawing, isolating from, neglecting, dissociating from, etc.	←
Moving Against	being hostile toward, destroying, hurting, stealing, uprooting, etc.	—<
Creating	producing, discovering, thinking up, nurturing, developing, etc.	⊙→
Associative		
With	associated with, near to, reminiscent of, being with, moving with, being like, etc.	↕
Equivalence	role equivalence; being (at least momentarily) identical to	=
Means	serving as the means/medium through which some relationship is sustained	= . . . □
Noun		
Father	father, old man, uncle, grandfather, males in authority roles	F
Mother	mother, old woman, aunt, grandmother, females in nurturing roles	M
(Parent)	(scored only when parent sex is uncertain)	(P)
Sibling	siblings	Si
Spouse	spouse, peer of opposite sex lived with in sustained, unique relationship	Sp
Peer Male	males of approximately same generational status as dreamer	Pm
Peer Female	females of approximately same generational status as dreamer	Pf
Children	males/females of inferior generational status to dreamer	C
Ego	self	E
Symbolic	animals/creatures; material objects; concepts, ideas; etc.	Sy

FIGURE 11-5 (Continued)

SAMPLE SENTENCES	TRANSLATION
F → E	Father moves toward me (loves me, helps me, etc.)
← M, E	Mother moves from me (withdraws love from me, etc.)
Si ─< E	My brother threatens me (hits me, kills me, etc.)
Sp ⊙→ E	My wife nurtures me (helps me develop my potential, etc.)
[Pm ↕ E]	My friend is with me (goes with me, is like me, etc.)
[Pf = E]	This woman is me
[Sy = E →| Pf]	I approach her with flowers (by means of a car, etc.)

Inevitably, SSLS makes assumptions about the structure and content of particular dreams which are not based on those dreams or on associations to them. In defense of these assumptions, it can be said that: (1) these are expediencies, clearly acknowledged as such; (2) they usually are of a sufficiently general character as to retain compatibility with diverse theoretical orientations; (3) they are based on experience, unfortunately not as systematic as one might wish, but on experience, nonetheless, with other dreams and dreamers; (4) they are subject to modification in particular instances as the data of those instances dictate; and (5) they are subject to revision, should an unusually large number of such discrepant instances materialize.

Dynamic Analysis: A Brief Introduction

As heretofore described, SSLS is a system for coding motivational or associational structures from dream or free-association protocols. But these protocols contain more material than that which asserts such relationships. For example, identical *structural* scores would be offered for the following two textual sentences:

1) I hit the old man = E ─< F;
2) I, feeling quite anxious about the whole thing, viciously and mercilessly hit the weak, feeble, old man = E ─< F.

Clearly, were the scoring system merely to code *structures*, it neither would be exhaustive in the technical sense nor satisfactory from a psychological point of view.

Freud's psychoanalytic theory contains both structural and dynamic models of behavior and experience. On the one hand, he discusses certain long-term structures guiding behavior (e.g., his topographic, structural, and genetic models [Rapaport, 1960]); on the other, he also is vitally interested in the fluctuating energetics of behavior (e.g., his dynamic and economic models [ibid.]). If SSLS is to do justice to Freud's dream theory (as well as to its own data) and to provide anything like an adequate psychoanalytic model of symbolic behavior, it must code dynamics as well as structures.

The extra material in sentence 2 is, in fact, coded by SSLS, in the form of *dynamic modification* of interactive (or associative) sentences. Thus, the complete SSLS scoring of the two sentences above is as follows:

1) $E \prec F$;
2) $\underline{E} \overset{+}{\underline{\prec}} \underline{F}$.

"Anxious" I in sentence 2 is Ego-minus; "viciously and mercilessly" hitting is Moving-Against-plus; and "weak and feeble" old man is Father-minus. More generally, nouns are scored dynamically as plus or minus as various textual modifiers enhance or detract from their referent's suitability to consummate or sustain the relationship in question, and verbs are scored dynamically as the strength of the relationship is enhanced or diminished by adverbial modifiers in the text or by textual statements in which the dreamer attempts to distance herself or himself from the relationship (e.g., "it was kind of hazy," ". . . had a long-ago feeling to it," etc.).

SSLS assumes, then, that dynamic aspects of behavior regulation, including affect, are modifiers "attached" to behavior-regulating or -organizing structures (cf. pp. 123–33 and pp. 184–90). By this convention, SSLS conveniently relates energetics to structures of the sort envisioned in its underlying model. Also by this convention, SSLS provides a coherent way of scoring a variety of linguistic phenomena, such as adverbial and adjectival modifiers and tense, which appear in dream or free-association protocols. The convention, moreover, seems not to be inconsistent with electrical stimulation data (Penfield, 1958) indicating that "feelings" about an event generally seem to be cerebrally "stored" "in close connection with" the representation of that event and with phenomenological observations that feeling and event representations do, however, remain separate, i.e., can become dissociated (e.g., the disturbances of affect in schizophrenia discussed by Bleuler, 1911).

Within dream theory itself, Fromm (1951) makes a useful distinction between qualitative and quantitative dream interpretations. By a qualitative interpretation he seems to mean the imputation to the dreamer of certain psychic structures, e.g., "this dreamer has a conflict between his hatred of his father and his love of his father." By a quantitative interpretation, he seems to mean the imputation to these structures of a given level of strength as vectors in the conflict situation, e.g., "this dreamer's intense hatred of his father now gives rise to overwhelming guilt feelings."

Fromm notes that qualitative interpretations of single dreams are likely to be more reliable than quantitative ones. That is, psychic structures are defined as relatively stable personality characteristics, while the "force" attached to these structures is assumed to be subject to fluctuation over time. The latter is an empirically plausible assumption in regard to dreams, since the level of dream expression of a "drive" is known to be related to recent experiences of waking satiation/deprivation of the drive and to recent experiences of dream expression/inhibition of the drive (Foulkes, 1970).

SSLS's relationships (its sentences, its structures) are thought to reflect what Fromm describes as "qualitative" features of the dream. That is, the following paired sentences from a hypothetical male dreamer are assumed to involve the same "structures":

    1) The woman was *very pretty*. She was *naked*. I approached her.
        (I approached the [very pretty] [naked] woman) = $E \rightarrow Pf$;
    2) The woman was *very ugly*. I approached her *anyway*.
        (I approached the [very ugly] woman) = $E \rightarrow Pf$;
    1) I *slowly began to* hit the woman, *but weakly and ineffectively.* = $E \prec Pf$;
    2) I hit the woman *viciously and mercilessly.* = $E \prec Pf$.

Obviously, however, we would infer a different strength of drive or defense "quantity" in the case of the two sentences comprising each pair. Considering the first pair of sentences, we have the contrasting cases of a relatively uninhibited act (it is encouraged by the woman's dreamer-portrayed suitability) versus a relatively inhibited one (it proceeds in the face of her dreamer-portrayed adverse suitability). A similar contrast may be made with respect to the second pair of sentences: a relatively inhibited act (reluctantly performed) versus a relatively uninhibited one (willingly performed).

From the italicized phrases we want to infer the relative strength of the "inhibitions" and "excitations" which now have attached themselves to the underlying structures of heterosexuality and heterosexual aggression, i.e., to the underlying situation of heterosexual relationship. SSLS encodes such dynamic modifiers of structures (sentences) in a manner already indicated. Thus,

1) The woman was very pretty. She was naked. I approached her. = $E \to \overset{+}{Pf}$;

2) The woman was very ugly. I approached her anyway. = $E \to \underline{Pf}$;

1) I slowly began to hit the woman, but weakly and ineffectively. = $E \underset{}{-\!\!\!<} Pf$;

2) I hit the woman viciously and mercilessly. = $E \overset{+}{-\!\!\!<} Pf$.

Note that + signs are written above the sentence position they modify, but that − signs are written below the sentence position they modify.

Dynamic scores also give SSLS a reasonable way to resolve certain textual material involving intransitive verbs. An intransitive verb such as "run," when it has a manifest or clearly implied indirect object, presents no scoring problems. For example,

$$\text{He ran to me} = Pm_1 \to E.$$

Sometimes, however, there will be no such object. A minimal dream account, for example, might be

I was running.

Since it is unclear whether the running was *to* or *from* some person, place, or thing, even the verb form is indeterminate. This would be scored as a *defective sentence* of the form

$$\overset{+}{E}\ldots\text{[21]}$$

i.e., "active ego."

[21] Defective sentences always are indicated by three dots following their single scoreable term. (Where two terms are given by the text, the third is routinely supplied, yielding a grammatically complete sentence. Thus, a female dreamer's "I was shot" =

$$Pf_1 -\!\!\!< E$$

where Pf_1 is entered in the lexicon as "shooter," assumed, in the absence of contradictory data, to be of like sex as the dreamer. Or, "I was walking someplace" =

$$E \to Sy_{1A}$$

where Sy_1 = geographical, and Sy_{1A} = place-walked-to. Footnote 13 gives an example of a defective sentence containing only a verb.)

Where "I was running" is *not* the entire dream report, but is followed, for example, by "Then I was thinking of Italy," the dynamic score would become a modifier in the adjacent, structurally complete SSLS sentence

$$[\overset{+}{E} ¢ Sy_{1A}]$$

i.e., active-running I/thinking of/Italy.

Scoring rules for dynamic modifiers are given in appendix A (pp. 405-18). Less attention is given here to dynamic scoring than to structural scoring partly because, at present, analysis and synthesis is better worked out (chapters 13-15) for structural than dynamic scores. Nevertheless, it *is* worth noting here that the *potential* scope of SSLS as a system of analyzing symbolic behavior exceeds that suggested by the mostly structural exercises which follow.

It is not entirely pragmatic considerations, however, which dictate the relative neglect of dynamic scores in SSLS scoring at this time. Or, rather, the pragmatic considerations are not, themselves, without theoretical justification. It seems to me that relatively too much attention in the past has been accorded the dynamic, energizing, or affective aspects of dreams and their associations. As a result, we have failed to see the dream as a cognitive event; it has been relegated to the curiosity shop of motivational psychology. It is to redress this imbalance that SSLS focuses on structures, both cognitive *and* motivational, but with both kinds of structures conceived in cognitive terms. And, as a research strategy, it seems wise first to focus on *what is there*, and then to worry about the questions of *in what quantity* or *with what affective charge*.

The Collection of Associations to the Dream

SSLS assumes that associations will have been collected following one of several techniques described by Freud (1923b). Collectively these methods are called *free association*. "Free" obviously is not intended in any absolute sense ("random"?; "undetermined"?), but indicates that the *guide* of the association process (i.e., the therapist, experimenter, or perhaps, the dreamer herself/himself) is establishing conditions conducive to a free flow of thoughts and to an open reporting of these thoughts. It further is assumed that: (1) an attempt will be made to have the dreamer associate to the entire dream, or, in the case of long dreams, to their major thematic elements; and (2) that the associations themselves will not be limited to single terms or phrases, but will be of the form $A \rightarrow B \rightarrow C \rightarrow D; A \rightarrow E \rightarrow F \rightarrow G \rightarrow H \rightarrow I$; and so on, where A is the stimulating dream element.

Specifically *proscribed* are both features of Jung's (1948) alternate procedure, *amplification*. Amplification consists of: (1) enforcement of a series of single associations ($A \rightarrow B, A \rightarrow C, A \rightarrow D$), rather than permitting a series of associational trains to each manifest dream element; and (2) supplementation of dreamers' associations with those produced by analysts, on the basis of their immersion in the fields of literature, religion, mythology, and so on.

The material elicited by Jung's directed-association procedure seems better calculated to determination of the *significance* of the dream than of its *origin* or *genesis* (Sherwood, 1969); i.e., it meets the goals of dreamer psychology better than those of dreaming or dream psychology. The material elicited by Jung's "supplementation" procedure is absolutely unacceptable. It is the admission of such out-of-court evidence by theorists of all persuasions which has so perilously undermined the entire field of dream interpretation by making it seem a personalistic art form rather than an attempt at scientific explanation.

Explicit rejection of amplification in the second sense does not deny the ultimate importance of inserting dreams within the context of other information about the dreamer than is gleaned from associations. It is to insist, rather, that such information: (1) must come from operationally defined and reproducible assessment of dreamers themselves; and (2) must be joined together with dream analysis according to operationally defined and reproducible procedures. SSLS's *immediate* concern is the analysis of the dream itself, rather than the correlation of dreams with nonassociative dreamer data. The analytic scheme for dreams does, of course, have implications for the organization of case-history data and for the integration of dream data with a dreamer life-narrative (Sherwood, 1969). These are discussed in chapter 16.

It does seem desirable, however, to *begin* analysis by keeping dream and case-history data separate. There is a tendency on the part of many dream analysts to blur the lines between dreamer associations and their own associations formed on the basis of their case-history constructions. Any such infusion of extra-dream-generated data into the dream analysis itself defeats one's later purpose of making an independent evaluation of how the interpreted dream correlates with such data. The logical ordering of dream/case-study analysis, it seems to me, is: (1) analysis of dream and association data; (2) analysis of case-history data; (3) correlation of the products of (1) and (2).

One problem which arises when SSLS is applied to free associations or dreams collected without prevision of such analysis is that the referents of some textual terms or phrases may be obscure (e.g., certain of Freud's associations to "Botanical Monograph"—see chapter 12). Clearly it is desirable that dream collectors and association guides be aware that the data they are collecting will have to be reduced to the SSLS format, and that they press, in a nondirective way (Kahn and Cannell, 1957), for clarification of potentially ambiguous material. This caveat merely restates the more general scientific rule that you collect more usable data when you know the use to which you will put it.

One conceptual difficulty many observers perceive in utilizing free associations to determine dream meanings is that it is not clear "how we know where to stop—where is the right solution" (Wittgenstein, 1966, p. 1). You may think that the data you have collected satisfactorily resolve the dream, but, suppose you had collected more associations—wouldn't those data, too, lead you to the same sense of satisfaction, but by way of a different interpretation?

I don't see that this is a problem either unique or fatal to dream interpretation via free associations. One's conclusions or explanations *always* are relative to the particular observations at hand. Wittgenstein assumes (as Freud mistakenly has encouraged him to do) that there is one "right" interpretation, and that the analyst's goal is to find that interpretation. But, as we have seen (chapter 4), interpretations always are *relative*—relative to one's interests and puzzlements, and relative to one's observational base. There is *no* one "true" interpretation or explanation, of dreams or anything else.

The question Wittgenstein raises is, moreover, itself susceptible to empirical analysis. Let us systematically compare different free-association strategies (e.g., spontaneous/brief associations versus these plus elicited/extended associations). Which technique generates the "better" data for some particular interpretive purpose, e.g., predicting dreamer behavior or explaining puzzling elements of the manifest dream? Is it true that associations forced along to some preconceived endpoint (Freud's wish, an interpersonal motivational referent, etc.) generate "better" data for any of these purposes than do associations "spontaneously" terminated by the dreamer? While much remains to be learned about the free-association process and its most appropriate form and role in dream psychology, these are questions in principle susceptible to empirical resolution. It does not seem to me, then, that dream interpretation or explanation by way of free associations is, from a scientific point of view, inherently flawed or any more objectionable than any other data-based interpretive/explanatory scheme.

CHAPTER 12

Freud's "Botanical Monograph": A Specimen Analysis

Introduction

At this point, it becomes impossible to further describe SSLS without a complete analysis of some particular dream. Freud's dream of the "Botanical Monograph" (Freud, 1900, p. 169) has been selected for this purpose. This dream, and Freud's analysis of it, are reproduced in chapter 4.

"Botanical Monograph" is, superficially, a simple dream, containing only 48 words in English translation. Thus, it lends itself readily to specimen analysis. Yet, as has been shown elsewhere (Foulkes and Vogel, 1974, p. 21), "Botanical Monograph" also is rich in terms of its potential "meanings." Thus, its analysis will introduce some of the problems which arise in scoring difficult material as well as providing a test case for determining whether the system yields results commensurate with the impressionistic results generated by other, less formalized analyses of the same dream.

"Botanical Monograph" has been selected, rather than Freud's own choice as a specimen dream, "Irma's Injection" (Freud, 1900, p. 107), not only because it is "simpler" but also because its associations seem to be given in an order in which they might spontaneously have occurred to Freud (they seem less "worked-over" for didactic presentation than the "Irma" associations). "Botanical Monograph" also figures at least as prominently as "Irma" in Freud's discussion of dream-work mechanisms and could be considered Freud's own specimen dream for those parts of his theory dealing with dream processes.

It is recognized that Freud's associations as given in the section of *The Interpretation of Dreams* from which this analysis proceeds are not exhaustive (Freud also discusses the dream elsewhere in the book; he does not draw out his associations to his "screen-memory" paper [Freud, 1899], which surely are relevant to the general trend of dream associations [cf. Foulkes and Vogel, 1974, p. 21]; and he does not discuss some related material now generally familiar to students of his life [see, e.g., Grinstein, 1968]). Nonetheless, the associations dealt with here are sufficient for illustrative purposes, and their analysis yields results probably highly consistent with still more thorough analyses which could be made of the same dream.

The SSLS Analysis

	Raw Scores	Transforms
The Dream		
(X-1) I had written a monograph	$E \circleddash Sy^+_{1A}$	$E \circleddash \overset{+}{P}m_{7C}$ (E-4)
(X-2) on a certain plant.	$[Sy_{1A} \updownarrow Sy^+_{2A}]$	
(X-3) The book lay before me	$[Sy^+_{1A} \updownarrow E]$	
(X-4) and I was at the moment turning over a folded coloured plate.	$E \overset{+}{\rightarrow} Sy^+_{1A1}$	
(X-5) —	$*[\overline{Sy_{1A1}} \updownarrow Sy_{1A}]$	

*Starred sentences are written in accordance with rule (5) described in appendix A, pp. 383–87. Note also that in the dream and free-association text, brackets contain

	Raw Scores	Transforms

The Dream

(X-6) Bound up in each copy
     was a dried specimen of
     the plant, $[\overset{+}{Sy}_{1A} \updownarrow \overset{+}{\underline{Sy}_{2A}}]$

(X-7/8) as though it had been
       taken from a herbarium. $\overset{\leftharpoonup}{=} E, Sy_{2B}$ $\overset{\leftharpoonup}{=} E, F_{3C}$ (C-12)

                              $[Pm_1 \equiv \boxed{\leftarrow} E(Sy_{2A}), Sy_{2B}]$

The Free Associations
(to X-1/2)

(A-1) That morning I had seen
     a new book $[E \overset{+}{\underline{\updownarrow}} \overset{+}{Sy}_{1A}]$

(A-2) in the window $[Sy_{1A} \updownarrow Sy_{3A1}]$

(A-3) of a book-shop, $[Sy_{3A1} \updownarrow Sy_{1A, 3A}]$

(A-4) bearing the title $[Sy_{1A} \updownarrow Sy_{1A2}]$

(A-5) *The Genus Cyclamen–* $[Sy_{1A2} \updownarrow Sy_{2C}]$

(A-6) evidently a monograph
     on that plant. $[\overset{+}{Sy}_{1A} \overset{+}{\updownarrow} \overset{+}{Sy}_{2C}]$

(A-7) Cyclamens, [I reflected,]
     were my wife's favourite
     flowers $[\overset{+}{Sy}_{2C,2D} \overset{+}{\updownarrow} Sp_1]$

(A-8) (my wife) $[E \updownarrow Sp_1]$

(A-9/10) and I reproached
       myself ($E \prec E = \underline{E}$) for
       so rarely remembering
       to bring her flowers, $E \rightleftharpoons Sp_1$

                              $[\overset{+}{Sy}_{2D} \equiv E \boxed{\rightarrow} Sp_1]$

(A-11) which was what she
     liked (she liked the
     bringing, i.e.,
     bringer).– $Sp_1 \rightarrow E$

(A-12/13) The subject of
       (my) "bringing
       flowers" $E \rightarrow Sp_1$

                              $[\overset{+}{Sy}_{2D} = E \boxed{\rightarrow} Sp_1]$

(A-14) recalled an anecdote $[\overset{+}{Sy}_{2D} \updownarrow Sy_{4A}]$

---

unscored material contributed by the dreamer, while parentheses contain interpolations
made by the scorer.

	Raw Scores	Transforms

The Free Associations

(A-15/16) which I had recently
repeated to a circle
of friends

$$E \overset{+}{\rightleftarrows} \overset{+}{Pm}_2$$
$$[Sy_{4A} \overset{+}{\equiv} E \boxdot Pm_2]$$

(A-17/18) and which I had
used as evidence in
favour of my theory

$$E \rightleftarrows Sy_{5A}$$
$$[Sy_{4A} \equiv E \boxdot Sy_{5A}]$$

(A-19) (<u>my</u> theory)

$$[E \updownarrow Sy_{5A}]$$

(A-20) that forgetting is very
often determined by an
unconscious purpose and
that it always enables
one to deduce the secret
intentions of the person
who forgets (circumlocu-
tion for: "forgetting very
often is deliberate").

$$[\updownarrow \overset{+}{\updownarrow} \overset{+}{\updownarrow}]$$

(A-21/22) A young woman was
accustomed to re-
ceiving a bouquet of
flowers from her
husband

$$E \overset{+}{\rightarrow} \overset{+}{Sp}_2$$
$$[\overset{+}{Sy}_{2D} \overset{\pm}{=} E(Pm_3) \boxdot Sp_2]$$

(A-23) (her husband)

$$[Sp_2 \updownarrow Pm_3]$$

(A-24) on her birthday

$$[\overset{+}{Sy}_{2D} \updownarrow Sy_{6A}]$$

(A-25) (<u>her</u> birthday).

$$[Sp_2 \updownarrow Sy_{6A}]$$

(A-26/27) One year this token
of his affection failed
to appear, and she
burst into tears.

$$E \rightleftarrows \underline{Sp}_2$$
$$[\overset{+}{Sy}_{2D} \equiv E(Pm_3) \boxdot Sp_2]$$

(A-28) Her husband

$$[Sp_2 \updownarrow Pm_3]$$

(A-29) came in

$$E \rightarrow Sp_2$$

(A-30) and had no idea why
she was crying

$$[Pm_3 \updownarrow \underline{Sp}_2]$$

(A-31) till she told him that

$$Sp_2 \overset{+}{\rightarrow} \underline{E}$$

	Raw Scores	Transforms

The Free Associations

(A-32) to-day was her
      birthday. $[Sp_2 \overset{+}{\updownarrow} Sy_{6A}]$

(A-33) He clasped his hand
      to his head ($E \prec E = \underline{E}$)
      and exclaimed: $\underline{E} \overset{+}{\rightarrow} Sp_2$

(A-34/35) "I'm so sorry, but
      I'd quite forgotten
      (your birthday) $[\underline{Pm_3} \overset{}{\updownarrow} Sy_{6A}]$
      (your birthday). $[Sp_2 \updownarrow Sy_{6A}]$

(A-36/38) I'll go out at once
      and fetch your
      <u>flowers</u> $E \overset{+}{\rightrightarrows} \overset{+}{Sy}_{2D}$ $E \overset{+}{\rightrightarrows} \overset{+}{Sp}_2$ (A-39)

                              $E \overset{+}{\rightrightarrows} Sp_2$

                              $[\overset{+}{Sy}_{2D} \overset{+}{\equiv} E(Pm_3) \boxdot Sp_2]$

(A-39) (your flowers)." $[Sp_2 \updownarrow \overset{+}{Sy}_{2D}]$

(A-40) But she was not to be
      consoled; for she
      recognized that her
      husband's $[\underline{Sp_2} \updownarrow Pm_3]$

(A-41) forgetfulness (of
      birthday) $[Pm_3 \overset{}{\updownarrow} Sy_{6A}]$

(A-42) (she recognized) $[Sp_2 \equiv Pm_3 \boxed{\updownarrow} Sy_{6A}]$

(A-43) was a proof that she no
      longer had the same
      place in his thoughts $[Sp_2 \overset{+}{\updownarrow} Pm_3]$

(A-44) as she had formerly.— $([Sp_2 \overset{+}{\updownarrow} Pm_3])$

(A-45) This lady, Frau L., had
      met my wife two days
      before $Sp_2 \rightrightarrows E$

(A-46) (<u>my</u> wife) $[E \updownarrow Sp_1]$

(—) [I had the dream,]

(A-47) had told her that $Sp_2 \overset{+}{\rightrightarrows} E$

(A-48) she was feeling quite
      well $[\overset{+}{Sp}_2 \overset{+}{\equiv} Sp_2 \boxdot E(Sp_1)]$

(A-49) and enquired $Sp_2 \rightrightarrows E$

(A-50) after me. $[E \equiv Sp_2 \boxdot E(Sp_1)]$

	Raw Scores	Transforms

The Free Associations

(A-51) Some years ago she had come to me — $Sp_2 \rightleftharpoons E$

(A-52/53) for treatment. — $E \rightleftharpoons Sp_2$

$[Sy_{7A} \equiv E(F_{1A}) \boxminus\!\!\rightarrow Sp_2]$

(–) [I now made a fresh start.]

(B-1) Once, [I recalled,] I really __had__ written some-thing in the nature of a __monograph__ — $E \overset{+}{\underline{\odot\!\!\rightarrow}} \overset{+}{Sy}_{1A}$

(B-2) __on a plant__, — $[Sy_{1A} \updownarrow Sy_{2A}]$

(B-3) namely a dissertation on the __coca-plant__, — $[\overset{+}{Sy}_{1A} \updownarrow Sy_{2E}]$

(B-4/5) which had drawn Karl Koller's attention to the anaesthetic properties of cocaine. — $E \rightleftharpoons \overset{+}{Sy}_{7B}$ — $E \rightleftharpoons \overset{+}{F}_1$ (B-29); $E \rightleftharpoons \overset{+}{F}_2$ (B-41); $E \rightleftharpoons \overset{+}{F}_{1D}$ (B-49)

$[Sy_{1A,2E} \equiv E(Pm_4) \boxminus\!\!\rightarrow Sy_{7B}]$

(B-6) I had myself indicated this application of the alkaloid — $\overset{+}{E} \overset{+}{\underline{\odot\!\!\rightarrow}} \overset{+}{Sy}_{7B}$ — $\overset{+}{E} \overset{+}{\underline{\odot\!\!\rightarrow}} \overset{+}{F}_1$ (B-29); $\overset{+}{E} \overset{+}{\underline{\odot\!\!\rightarrow}} \overset{+}{F}_2$ (B-41); $\overset{+}{E} \overset{+}{\underline{\odot\!\!\rightarrow}} \overset{+}{F}_{1D}$ (B-49)

(B-7) in my published paper — $[Sy_{1A,2E} \equiv E \;\boxed{\odot\!\!\rightarrow}\; | Sy_{7B}]$

(B-8) (__my__ published paper), — $[E \updownarrow Sy_{1A,2E}]$

(B-9) but I had not been thorough enough to pursue the matter further. — $\underline{E} \rightleftharpoons \overset{+}{Sy}_{7B}$ — $\underline{E} \rightleftharpoons \overset{+}{F}_1$ (B-29); $\underline{E} \rightleftharpoons \overset{+}{F}_2$ (B-41); $\underline{E} \rightleftharpoons \overset{+}{F}_{1D}$ (B-49)

(–) [This reminded me that on the morning of the day after the dream—I had not found

	Raw Scores	Transforms

The Free Associations

time to interpret it till the
evening–]

(B-10) I had thought about
cocaine in a kind of
day-dream. $[E \stackrel{\updownarrow}{-} Sy_{7B}]$

(B-11) If ever I got glaucoma
$(E \prec E = \underline{E})$, I had
thought, I should travel
to Berlin $\underline{E} \stackrel{\rightharpoonup}{=} Sy_{8A}$ $\underline{E} \stackrel{\rightharpoonup}{=} F_{1B}$ (B-14)
(B-32)

(B-12) – $*[Sy_{8A} \updownarrow Sy_{7B}]$

(B-13/16) and get myself
operated on, in-
cognito, in my
friend's (Fliess's)
house, by a surgeon $F_{1B} \stackrel{\preceq}{} \underline{E}$
$*[F_{1B} \updownarrow Sy_{8A}]$
$[Sy_{7A} \equiv F_{1B} \boxed{\prec} E]$
$[Pm_5 \equiv F_{1B} \boxed{\prec} E]$

(B-17/18) recommended by him. $Pm_5 \stackrel{+}{\rightharpoonup} E$
$[F_{1B} \equiv Pm_5 \boxed{\rightarrow} E]$

(B-19) The operating surgeon,
who would have no idea
of my identity, $[\overset{+}{F}_{1B} \stackrel{\updownarrow}{-} \underline{E}]$

(B-20/21) would boast once
again $F_{1B} \stackrel{+}{\rightharpoonup} E$
$[\overset{+}{F}_{1B} \stackrel{+}{\equiv} F_{1B} \boxed{\rightarrow} E]$

(B-22/23) of how easily such
operations could be
performed $F_{1B} \stackrel{+}{\underset{+}{\preceq}} E$
$[Sy_{7A} \stackrel{+}{\equiv} F_{1B} \boxed{\prec} E]$

(B-24/25) since the introduc-
tion of cocaine; $E \circledcirc\!\!\rightarrow \overset{+}{Sy}_{7B}$ $E \circledcirc\!\!\rightarrow \overset{+}{F}_1$ (B-29)
$E \circledcirc\!\!\rightarrow \overset{+}{F}_2$ (B-41)
$E \circledcirc\!\!\rightarrow \overset{+}{F}_{1D}$ (B-49)
$[Sy_{7B} \stackrel{+}{\equiv} F_{1B} \boxed{\prec} E]$

	Raw Scores	Transforms

The Free Associations

(B-26) and I should not give
the slightest hint $E \rightleftharpoons F_{1B}$

(B-27) that I myself had had a
share in the discovery. $\overset{+}{E} \underline{\odot\!\!\rightarrow} \overset{+}{Sy}_{7B}$ $\overset{+}{E} \underline{\odot\!\!\rightarrow} \overset{+}{F}_1$ (B-29)

                                                        $\overset{+}{E} \underline{\odot\!\!\rightarrow} \overset{+}{F}_2$ (B-41)

                                                         $\overset{+}{E} \underline{\odot\!\!\rightarrow} \overset{+}{F}_{1D}$ (B-49)

(−) [This phantasy had led on
to reflections of]

(B-28/31) how awkward it is,
when all is said and
done, for a physician
to ask for medical
treatment for himself
from his professional
colleagues. $E \rightleftharpoons \overset{+}{F}_1$

                                      $\overset{*}{}[F_1 \updownarrow Sy_{7B}]$

                                      $\overset{+}{F}_1 \rightleftharpoons E$

                                      $[Sy_{7A} \equiv F_1$

                                              $\boxminus\!\rightarrow E(F_{1A})]$

(B-32) The Berlin eye-surgeon $[Sy_{8A} \updownarrow F_{1B}]$

(B-33) would not know me, $[F_{1B} \underline{\updownarrow} E]$

(B-34/35) and I should be able
to pay his fees $E \rightleftharpoons F_{1B}$

                                      $[\overset{+}{Sy}_{9A} \equiv E \boxminus\!\rightarrow F_{1B}]$

(B-36) like anyone else. $[E \updownarrow Pm]$

(B-37) − $\overset{*}{}[Pm \underline{\updownarrow} Sy_{9A}]$

(B-38) − $\overset{*}{}[Pm \updownarrow F_{1B}]$

(−) [It was not until I had
recalled this day-dream
that I realized that the
recollection of a specific
event lay behind it.]

(B-39) Shortly after Koller's
discovery, $E \overset{+\;+}{\odot\!\!\rightarrow} Sy_{7B}$ $E \overset{+\;+}{\odot\!\!\rightarrow} F_1$ (B-29)

                                                         $E \overset{+\;+}{\odot\!\!\rightarrow} F_2$ (B-41)

                                                         $E \overset{+\;+}{\odot\!\!\rightarrow} F_{1D}$ (B-49)

(B-40) my father $[E \updownarrow F_2]$

	Raw Scores	Transforms

The Free Associations

(B-41) — $*[F_2 \updownarrow Sy_{7B}]$

(B-42) had in fact been
attacked by glaucoma; $E \overset{+}{\prec} F_2$

(B-43) my friend $[E \updownarrow Pm_6]$

(B-44) — $*[Pm_6 \updownarrow F_2]$

(B-45) Dr. Königstein, the
ophthalmic surgeon, $[Pm_6 = F_{1C}]$

(B-46/47) had operated on him; $E \overset{}{\prec} F_2$

$[Sy_{7A} \equiv E (F_{1C})$

$\boxed{\prec} F_2]$

(B-48) while Dr. Koller $[Pm_4 = F_{1D}]$

(B-49) had been in charge of
the cocaine anaesthesia $[\overset{+}{F}_{1D} \updownarrow \overset{+}{Sy}_{7B}]$

(B-50) and had commented $F_{1D} \rightrightarrows E$ $\underline{also}\ F_{1C} \rightrightarrows E$ (B-53)

(B-51/56) on the fact that this
case (F_2) had brought
together all of the three
men $[E \overset{\updownarrow}{} F_{1C}]$

$[E \updownarrow F_{1D}]$

$[F_{1C} \updownarrow F_{1D}]$

$[F_2 \equiv E \boxed{\updownarrow} F_{1C}]$

$[F_2 \equiv E \boxed{\updownarrow} F_{1D}]$

$[F_2 \equiv F_{1C} \boxed{\updownarrow} F_{1D}]$

(B-57) who had had a share in
the introduction of
cocaine. $\overset{+}{E} \underline{\circ \rightarrow} \overset{+}{Sy}_{7B}$ $\overset{+}{E} \underline{\circ \rightarrow} \overset{+}{F}_1$ (B-29)
$\overset{+}{E} \underline{\circ \rightarrow} \overset{+}{F}_2$ (B-41)
$\overset{+}{E} \underline{\circ \rightarrow} \overset{+}{F}_{1D}$ (B-49)

(—) [My thoughts then went on
to the occasion when]

(B-58) I had last been reminded
of this business of the
cocaine. $[E \overset{+}{\updownarrow} \overset{+}{Sy}_{7B}]$

(B-59) It had been a few days
earlier, when I had been
looking at a copy $E \rightrightarrows \underline{Sy}_{1A}$

	Raw Scores	Transforms

The Free Associations

(B-60) of a <u>Festschrift</u>

$[Sy_{1A} \updownarrow Sy_{1A3}]$

(B-61/62) in which grateful
pupils had celebrated
the jubilee of their
teacher

$\overset{+}{E} \overset{+}{\rightrightarrows} \overset{+}{F}_{3A}$

$[Sy_{1A,1A3} \overset{+}{\equiv} E(Pm_{7A})$
$\quad \boxed{\rightarrow} F_{3A}]$

(B-63) (<u>their</u>)

$[\overset{+}{Pm}_{7A} \updownarrow F_{3A}]$

(B-64) and laboratory director.

$[\overset{+}{F}_{3A} \updownarrow \underline{Sy}_{5B}]$

(B-65) Among the laboratory's
(director's) claims to
distinction which were
enumerated in this book

$[\overset{+}{Sy}_{1A,1A3} \updownarrow \overset{+}{F}_{3A}]$

(B-66) I had seen a mention

$[E \overset{+}{\updownarrow} Sy_{1A,1A3}]$

(B-67/68) of the fact that
Koller had made his
discovery there of the
anaesthetic properties
of cocaine.

$E \underline{\obslash} \overset{+}{Sy}_{7B}$

$E \underline{\obslash} \overset{+}{F}_1$ (B-29)
$E \underline{\obslash} \overset{+}{F}_2$ (B-41)
$E \underline{\obslash} \overset{+}{F}_{1D}$ (B-49)

$[Sy_{5B} \equiv E(Pm_4)$
$\quad \boxed{\obslash} \, Sy_{7B}]$

(−) [I then suddenly perceived
that my dream was connected
with an event of]

(B-69) the previous evening.
I had walked home

$E \overset{+}{\rightrightarrows} Sy_{10A}$

$E \overset{+}{\rightrightarrows} Pm_4$ (B-71)

(B-70) −

$*[Sy_{10A} \updownarrow Sy_{5B}]$

(B-71) −

$*[Sy_{10A} \updownarrow Pm_4]$

(B-72) −

$*[Sy_{10A} \updownarrow Sy_{7B}]$

(B-73) precisely with Dr.
Königstein

$[E \overset{+}{\updownarrow} F_{1C}]$

(B-74) and had got into
conversation with him

$E \rightrightarrows F_{1C}$

<u>also</u> $E \rightrightarrows F_{1D}$ (B-53)
<u>also</u> $E \rightrightarrows F_{3B}$ (B-80)

	Raw Scores	Transforms

The Free Associations

(B-75) about a matter which
never fails to excite
my feelings whenever
it is raised.

$$[\overset{+}{Sy}_{4B} \equiv E \boxminus\to F_{1C}]$$

(B-76) While I was talking to
him

$E \overset{+}{\to} F_{1C}$

<u>also</u> $E \overset{+}{\to} F_{1D}$ (B-53)
<u>also</u> $E \overset{+}{\to} F_{3B}$ (B-80)

(B-77) in the entrance-hall,

$$[Sy_{10A1,10A} \overset{\pm}{=} E \boxminus\to F_{1C}]$$

(B-78) Professor <u>Gärtner</u> $[F_{3B} \updownarrow Sy_2]$

(B-79) —   *$[F_{3B} \updownarrow Sy_{10A1,10A}]$

(B-80) —   *$[F_{3B} \updownarrow F_{1C}]$

(B-81) —   *$[Sy_2 \updownarrow Sy_{10A1,10A}]$

(B-82) —   *$[Sy_2 \updownarrow F_{1C}]$

(B-83) and his wife $[F_{3B} \updownarrow M]$

(B-84/85) had joined us; $F_{3B} \rightrightarrows \overset{+}{E}$

<u>also</u> $F_{1C} \rightrightarrows \overset{+}{E}$ (B-80)
<u>also</u> $M \rightrightarrows \overset{+}{E}$ (B-83)

$M \rightrightarrows \overset{+}{E}$

<u>also</u> $F_{3B} \rightrightarrows \overset{+}{E}$ (B-83)

(B-86/87) and I could not help
congratulating them
both

$E \overset{+}{\rightrightarrows} \overset{+}{F}_{3B}$

<u>also</u> $E \overset{+}{\rightrightarrows} \overset{+}{F}_{1C}$ (B-80)
<u>also</u> $E \overset{+}{\rightrightarrows} \overset{+}{M}$ (B-83)

$E \overset{+}{\rightrightarrows} \overset{+}{M}$

<u>also</u> $E \overset{+}{\rightrightarrows} \overset{+}{F}_{3B}$ (B-83)

(B-88/89) on their <u>blooming</u>
looks.

$$[\overset{+}{F}_{3B} \overset{\pm}{=} E \boxminus\to F_{3B}]$$
$$[\overset{+}{M} \overset{+}{=} E \boxminus\to M]$$

(B-90) But Professor Gärtner
was one of the authors
of the <u>Festschrift</u> I
have just mentioned,

$E \circledcirc\to \overset{+}{Sy}_{1A,1A3}$

$E \circledcirc\to \overset{+}{F}_{3A}$ (B-65)
$E \circledcirc\to \overset{+}{F}_{3B}$ (B-91)
$E \circledcirc\to \overset{+}{Sp}_2$ (B-94)

(B-91) and may well have
reminded me of it.

$$[F_{3B} \overset{+}{\updownarrow} \overset{+}{Sy}_{1A,1A3}]$$

(B-92) Moreover, the Frau L.,
whose disappointment
on her birthday

$$[Sp_2 \updownarrow Sy_{6A}]$$

	Raw Scores	Transforms

The Free Associations

(B-93) — $*[Sp_2 \updownarrow F_{3B}]$

(B-94) — $*[Sp_2 \updownarrow Sy_{1A,1A3}]$

(B-95) — $*[Sy_{6A} \updownarrow F_{3B}]$

(B-96) — $*[Sy_{6A} \updownarrow Sy_{1A,1A3}]$

(−) [I described earlier,]

(B-97/98) was mentioned—
though only, it is
true, in another con-
nection—in my con-
versation with Dr.
Königstein. $E \to F_{1C}$ also $E \to F_{1D}$ (B-53)

                                                         also $E \to F_{3B}$ (B-80)

                                   $[Sp_2 \equiv E \boxminus\!\!\rightarrow F_{1C}]$

(to X-6/8)

(−) [I will make an attempt at
interpreting the other
determinants of the
content of the dream
as well.]

(C-1) There was a dried specimen
of the plant included in the
monograph, $[\underline{Sy_{2A}} \updownarrow Sy_{1A}]$

(C-2) as though it had been a
herbarium. $[Sy_{1A} \equiv Sy_{2B}]$

(−) [This led me to a memory
from]

(C-3) my secondary school. $[E \updownarrow Sy_{11A}]$

(C-4) — $*[Sy_{11A} \updownarrow Sy_{1A}]$

(C-5) — $*[Sy_{11A} \updownarrow Sy_{2B}]$

(C-6) Our headmaster $[\overset{+}{E} \updownarrow F_{3C}]$

(C-7) — $*[\overset{+}{F}_{3C} \updownarrow \underline{Sy_{11A}}]$

(C-8/9) once called together
the boys from the
higher forms $\overset{+}{E} \rightrightarrows F_{3C}$

                                   $[F_{3C} \equiv E(+ Pm_{7B})$

                                   $\boxminus\!\!\rightarrow F_{3C}]$

	Raw Scores	Transforms

The Free Associations

(C-10/11) and handed over the
school's (his)
herbarium to them

$$F_{3C} \rightleftharpoons \overset{+}{E}$$
$$[Sy_{2B} \equiv F_{3C}$$
$$\boxed{\rightarrow} E(+ Pm_{7B})]$$

(C-12) (his) $[F_{3C} \updownarrow Sy_{2B}]$

(C-13) to be looked through $\overset{+}{E} \overset{+}{\rightleftharpoons} Sy_{2B}$ $\overset{+}{E} \overset{+}{\rightleftharpoons} F_{3C}$ (C-12)

(C-14) and cleaned. $(\overset{+}{E} \rightleftharpoons Sy_{2B})$

(C-15) Some small worms—
book-worms—had found
their way into it. $\underline{\overset{+}{E}} \prec Sy_{2B}$ $\underline{\overset{+}{E}} \prec F_{3C}$ (C-12)

(C-16/17) He does not seem to
have had much con-
fidence in my help-
fulness, $E \rightleftharpoons F_{3C}$
$$[F_{3C} \equiv E \boxed{\rightarrow} F_{3C}]$$

(C-18/19) for he handed me
only a few sheets. $F_{3C} \rightarrow E$
$$[Sy_{2\underline{B}1,2B} \equiv F_{3C}$$
$$\boxed{\rightarrow} E]$$

(C-20) These, as I could still
recall, included some
Crucifers. $[\overset{+}{Sy}_{2B1} \overset{+}{\updownarrow} \overset{+}{Sy}_{2F}]$

(C-21) I never had a
specially intimate
contact with botany. $[E \overset{+}{\updownarrow} Sy_{2,5}]$

(C-22) – $*[Sy_{2,5} \updownarrow Sy_{2B1}]$

(C-23) – $*[Sy_{2,5} \updownarrow Sy_{2F}]$

(C-24) In my preliminary
examination $[E \updownarrow \underline{Sy_{11B}}]$

(C-25) in botany $[Sy_{11B} \updownarrow Sy_{2,5}]$

(C-26/27) I was also given
a Crucifer $F_3 \rightarrow E$
$$[Sy_{2F} \overset{+}{=} F_3 \boxed{\rightarrow} E]$$

(C-28/29) to identify— $E \rightleftharpoons Sy_{2F}$
$$[Sy_{2A,4C} \equiv E$$
$$\boxed{\rightarrow} Sy_{2F}]$$

	Raw Scores	Transforms

The Free Associations

(C-30/31) and failed to do so.
$$E \rightleftharpoons Sy_{2F}$$
$$[Sy_{2A,4C} \equiv E$$
$$\boxdot Sy_{2F}]$$

(C-32/33) My prospects (in identification) would not have been too bright,
$$\underline{E} \rightleftharpoons Sy_{2F}$$
$$[Sy_{2A,4C} \equiv E$$
$$\boxdot Sy_{2F}]$$

(C-34/35) if I had not been helped out by my theoretical knowledge
$$E \overset{+}{\rightarrow} Sy_{2F}$$
$$[\overset{+}{Sy}_{5A} \overset{+}{=} E \boxdot Sy_{2F}]$$

(C-36) (<u>my</u>).
$$[E \updownarrow \overset{+}{Sy}_{5A}]$$

(C-37) I went on from the Cruciferae to the Compositae.
$$[\overset{+}{Sy}_{2F} \updownarrow \overset{+}{Sy}_{2G}]$$

(C-38) It occurred to me that artichokes were Compositae,
$$[\overset{+}{Sy}_{2G1} \updownarrow \overset{+}{Sy}_{2G}]$$

(C-39) and indeed I might fairly have called them my <u>favourite</u> <u>flowers</u>
$$[\overset{+}{Sy}_{2G1} \overset{+\,+}{\updownarrow} Sy_{2D}]$$

(C-40) (<u>my</u>).
$$[E \overset{+\,+}{\updownarrow} Sy_{2D}]$$

(C-41/42) Being more generous than I am, my wife often brought me back these favourite flowers
$$\overset{+}{Sp}_1 \overset{+}{\rightarrow} E$$
$$[\overset{+}{Sy}_{2D} \overset{+}{=} Sp_1 \boxdot E]$$

(C-43) of mine
$$[E \overset{+\,+}{\updownarrow} Sy_{2D}]$$

(C-44/45) from the market.
$$\overset{+}{\leftarrow} E, Sy_{3B}$$
$$[\overset{+}{Sy}_{2D} \overset{+}{=} \boxminus E(Sp_1),$$
$$Sy_{3B}]$$

	Raw Scores	Transforms

The Free Associations

(to X-3)

(−) [I saw the monograph
   which I had written <u>lying</u>
   <u>before</u> <u>me</u>. This again led
   me back to something.]

(D-1/2) I had had a letter from
   my friend (Fliess) in
   Berlin the day before $\quad Pm_5 \overset{+}{\geq} E$

$\qquad [Sy_{1B} \overset{+}{=} Pm_5 \boxminus\!\!\!\rightarrow E]$

(D-3) (<u>my</u> friend) $\qquad [E \updownarrow Pm_5]$

(D-4) (<u>in</u> Berlin) $\qquad [Pm_5 \updownarrow Sy_{8A}]$

(D-5/6) in which he had shown
   his power of visualization: $\overset{+}{Pm_5} \geq E$

$\qquad [Sy_{1B} \equiv Pm_5 \boxminus\!\!\!\rightarrow E]$

(D-7) "I am very much oc-
   cupied with your
   dream-book $\qquad [Pm_5 \overset{+}{\updownarrow} Sy_{1A,12A}]$

(D-8) (<u>your</u>). $\qquad [E \updownarrow Sy_{1A,12A}]$

(D-9/10) <u>I see it lying finished</u>
   <u>before me</u> $\qquad [\overset{+}{Sy}_{1A,12A} \updownarrow \underline{Pm_5}]$

$\qquad [Pm_5 \equiv Sy_{1A,12A} \boxed{\updownarrow} Pm_5]$

(D-11/12) <u>and I see myself</u>
   <u>turning over its pages.</u>" $\quad E \geq \overset{+}{Sy}_{1A4}$

$\qquad [Pm_5 \equiv E(Pm_5)$
$\qquad\qquad \boxminus\!\!\!\rightarrow Sy_{1A4,1A,12A}]$

(D-13) How much I envied him
   his gift as a seer! $\qquad E \overset{+}{-\!\!\!<} \overset{+}{Pm_5}$

(D-14) If only <u>I</u> could have
   seen it lying finished
   before me! $\qquad [\overset{+}{Sy}_{1A,12A} \updownarrow \underline{E}]$

(to X-4/5)

(−) The <u>folded</u> <u>coloured</u> <u>plate</u>.

(E-1/2) While I was a medical
   student $\qquad [E \equiv Pm_{7C}]$

$\qquad [Pm_{7C} \updownarrow Sy_7]$

(E-3) I was the constant victim
   of an impulse only to

	Raw Scores	Transforms

The Free Associations

learn things out of monographs.	$\underline{E} \overset{+}{\rightleftharpoons} \overset{+}{Sy}_{1A}$	$\underline{E} \overset{+}{\rightleftharpoons} \overset{+}{Pm}_{7C}$ (E-4)
(E-4) –	*$[Sy_{1A} \updownarrow Pm_{7C}]$	
(E-5) –	*$[Sy_{1A} \updownarrow Sy_{7}]$	
(E-6) In spite of my limited means,	$[E \overset{\updownarrow}{-} Sy_{9A}]$	
(E-7) –	*$[Sy_{9A} \updownarrow Sy_{1A}]$	
(E-8) –	*$[Sy_{9A} \updownarrow Sy_{7}]$	
(E-9/10) I succeeded in getting hold of a number of volumes of the proceedings of medical societies	$\underline{E} \overset{+}{\rightarrow} \overset{+}{Sy}_{1A,7}$ $[Sy_{9A} \overset{+}{=} E \boxdot Sy_{1A,7}]$	
(E-11) and was enthralled by their coloured plates. I was proud of my hankering for thoroughness. $(E \rightarrow \overset{+}{E} = \overset{+}{E})$	$\overset{+}{Sy}_{1A1} \overset{+}{\rightarrow} \overset{+}{E}$	
(E-12) –	*$[Sy_{1A1} \updownarrow Sy_{1A,7}]$	
(E-13) When I myself had begun to publish papers,	$\overset{+}{E} \oslash\!\!\rightarrow \overset{+}{Sy}_{1A}$	$\overset{+}{E} \oslash\!\!\rightarrow \overset{+}{Pm}_{7C}$ (E-4)
(E-14) I had been obliged to make my own drawings	$E \oslash\!\!\rightarrow \overset{+}{Sy}_{1A1}$	
(E-15) (my own)	$[E \overset{+}{\updownarrow} \overset{+}{Sy}_{1A1}]$	
(E-16) to illustrate them	$[\overset{+}{Sy}_{1A1} \updownarrow \overset{+}{Sy}_{1A}]$	
(E-17/18) that one of them had been so wretched that a friendly colleague had jeered at me over it.	$\overset{+}{Pm}_{8} \overset{+}{\prec} E$ $[\underline{Sy}_{1A1} \overset{+}{=} Pm_{8} \boxed{\prec} E]$	
(–) [There followed, I could not quite make out how, a recollection from]		

	Raw Scores	Transforms

The Free Associations

(F-1) very early youth. It had
once amused my father $[E \updownarrow F_2]$

(F-2/5) to hand over a book
with <u>coloured plates</u>—
an account of a journey
through Persia—for me $\overset{+}{F_2} \rightrightarrows \underline{E}$ also $\overset{+}{F_2} \underset{+}{\prec} \underline{E}$ (F-29)

also $\preceq F_2 , \underline{E}$ (F-36)

$[Sy_{1A} \equiv F_2 \boxdot E]$
$[Sy_{1A} \overset{+}{\updownarrow} Sy_{1A1}]$
$[Sy_{1A} \updownarrow Sy_{8B}]$

(F-6/7) and my eldest sister
to destroy. $\overset{+}{\underline{E}} \prec Sy_{1A}$ also $\overset{+}{\underline{E}} \overset{+}{\circledcirc} Sy_{1A}$ (F-8)

also $\overset{+}{\underline{E}} \overset{+}{\rightrightarrows} Sy_{1A}$ (F-29)

$[F_2 \overset{+}{\equiv} E(+Si)$
$\boxed{\prec} | Sy_{1A}]$

(F-8) Not easy to justify from
the educational point of
view! $[\overset{+}{\prec} \underline{\updownarrow} \circledcirc\rightarrow]$

(F-9) I had been five years old
at the time and my sister
not yet three; $[\underline{E} \overset{+}{\updownarrow} Si]$

(F-10) and the picture of the
two of us $([E \underline{\updownarrow} Si])$

(F-11) blissfully pulling the
book to pieces $\overset{+}{\underline{E}} \overset{+}{\prec} Sy_{1A}$ also $\overset{+}{\underline{E}} \overset{+}{\circledcirc} Sy_{1A}$ (F-8)

also $\overset{+}{\underline{E}} \overset{+}{\rightrightarrows} Sy_{1A}$ (F-29)

(F-12) —leaf by leaf, $[Sy_{1A} \overset{+}{\underline{\updownarrow}} Sy_{1A5}]$

(F-13) like an <u>artichoke</u>, I
found myself saying— $[Sy_{1A5} \underline{\updownarrow} Sy_{2G1}]$

(F-14) was almost the only
plastic memory that I
retained $[E \overset{+}{\updownarrow} Sy_{12B}]$

(F-15) — $*[Sy_{12B} \updownarrow Sy_{1A5}]$

(F-16) — $*[Sy_{12B} \updownarrow Sy_{2G1}]$

(F-17) from that period of my
life (childhood memory). $[\underline{E} \updownarrow Sy_{12B}]$

	Raw Scores	Transforms

The Free Associations

(F-18) Then, when I became a
student, $[E \equiv Pm_{7C}]$

(F-19) − $*[Pm_{7C} \updownarrow Sy_{12B}]$

(F-20) I had developed a
passion for collecting $E \overset{+}{\underset{}{\rightleftharpoons}} \overset{+}{S}y_{1A}$ also $E \overset{+}{\underset{}{\prec}} \overset{+}{S}y_{1A}$
(F-29)

also $\overset{+}{\preceq} E, \overset{+}{S}y_{1A}$
(F-36)

(F-21) and owning books, $[E \overset{+}{\underset{}{\updownarrow}} \overset{+}{S}y_{1A}]$

(F-22/23) which was analogous
to my liking for
learning $[\overset{+}{\rightarrow} \updownarrow \overset{+}{\rightarrow}]$
$[\overset{+}{\updownarrow} \updownarrow \overset{+}{\rightarrow}]$

(F-24) out of monographs: $E \overset{+}{\underset{}{\rightarrow}} \overset{+}{S}y_{1A}$ also $E \overset{+}{\underset{}{\prec}} \overset{+}{S}y_{1A}$
(F-29)

also $\overset{+}{\leftarrow} E, \overset{+}{S}y_{1A}$
(F-36)

(F-25) a favourite hobby. $[\overset{+}{S}y_{1A} \updownarrow \overset{+}{S}y_{13A}]$

(F-26) −The idea of "favourite"
had already appeared in
connection with
cyclamens $[\overset{+}{S}y_{13A} \overset{+}{\underset{}{\updownarrow}} \overset{+}{S}y_{2C}]$

(F-27) and artichokes.− $[\overset{+}{S}y_{13A} \overset{+}{\underset{}{\updownarrow}} \overset{+}{S}y_{2G1}]$

(F-28) I had become a book-
worm. $E \overset{+}{\underset{}{\rightleftharpoons}} \overset{+}{S}y_{1A}$ also $E \overset{+}{\underset{}{\prec}} \overset{+}{S}y_{1A}$
(F-29)

also $\overset{+}{\preceq} E, \overset{+}{S}y_{1A}$
(F-36)

(F-29/30) I had always, from
the time I first began
to think about myself,
referred this first
passion of mine back
to the childhood
memory I have men-
tioned (F-11). $[\overset{+}{\rightarrow} \overset{+}{\underset{}{\updownarrow}} \overset{+}{\prec}]$
$[\overset{+}{\updownarrow} \overset{+}{\underset{}{\updownarrow}} \overset{+}{\prec}]$

(F-31) Or, rather, I had

	Raw Scores	Transforms

The Free Associations

recognized that the
childhood scene (F-11) $\overset{+}{E} \overset{+}{\prec} Sy_{1A}$ <u>also</u> $\overset{+}{E} \oplus\rightarrow Sy_{1A}$ (F-8)
$\qquad\qquad\qquad\qquad\qquad\qquad\qquad\qquad\quad$ <u>also</u> $\overset{+}{E} \overset{+}{\Rightarrow} Sy_{1A}$ (F-29)

(F-32) was a "screen memory" $[Sy_{12B} \overset{+}{=} E(+Si)$
$\qquad\qquad\qquad\qquad\qquad\qquad\boxed{\prec} Sy_{1A}]$

(F-33/34) for my later
$\qquad$ bibliophile
$\qquad$ propensities[1]. $E \overset{+}{\rightarrow} \overset{+}{Sy}_{1A}$ <u>also</u> $E \overset{+}{\prec} \overset{+}{Sy}_{1A}$
$\qquad\qquad\qquad\qquad\qquad\qquad\qquad\qquad\quad$ (F-29)
$\qquad\qquad\qquad\qquad\qquad\qquad\qquad\qquad\quad$ <u>also</u> $\overset{+}{\leftarrow} E, \overset{+}{Sy}_{1A}$
$\qquad\qquad\qquad\qquad\qquad\qquad\qquad\qquad\quad$ (F-36)
$\qquad\qquad\qquad\qquad\qquad$ $[Sy_{12B} \overset{+}{=} E \boxdot\rightarrow Sy_{1A}]$

(F-35) —[1] Cf. my paper on
$\qquad$ screen memories.— $E \oplus\rightarrow Sy_{1A,1\overset{+}{2}B}$ $E \oplus\rightarrow \overset{+}{F}_4$ (F-38)
$\qquad\qquad\qquad\qquad\qquad\qquad\qquad\qquad$ <u>also</u> $E \overset{+}{\prec} \overset{+}{F}_4$ (F-8
$\qquad\qquad\qquad\qquad\qquad\qquad\qquad\qquad\quad$ <u>and</u> F-38)

(F-36) And I had early dis-
$\qquad$ covered, of course, that
$\qquad$ passions often lead to
$\qquad$ sorrow. $[\overset{+}{\rightarrow} \overset{+}{\updownarrow} \overset{+}{\leftarrow}]$

(F-37/39) When I was seventeen
$\qquad$ I had run up a largish
$\qquad$ account at the book-
$\qquad$ seller's $\underline{E} \overset{+}{\Rightarrow} F_4$ <u>also</u> $\underline{E} \overset{+}{\prec} F_4$ (F-29)
$\qquad\qquad\qquad\qquad\qquad\qquad\qquad\qquad$ <u>also</u> $\overset{+}{\leftarrow} \underline{E}, F_4$ (F-36)

$\qquad\qquad\qquad\qquad\qquad$ $*[F_4 \updownarrow Sy_{1A,12B}]$
$\qquad\qquad\qquad\qquad\qquad$ $[Sy_{9A} \overset{+}{=} E \boxdot\rightarrow F_4]$

(F-40) (the bookseller's) $[\overline{F_4} \updownarrow Sy_{1A,3A}]$
(F-41) and had nothing (no
$\qquad$ money) $[E \updownarrow \underline{Sy_{9A}}]$
(F-42) to meet it $E \Rightarrow \overline{F_4}$ <u>also</u> $E \prec F_4$ (F-29)
$\qquad\qquad\qquad\qquad\qquad\qquad\qquad\qquad$ <u>also</u> $\leftarrow E, F_4$ (F-36)

(F-43) with; $[\underline{Sy_{9A}} = E \boxdot\rightarrow F_4]$
(F-44) and my father had
$\qquad$ scarcely taken it as
$\qquad$ an excuse $F_2 \underline{\prec} \underline{E}$ <u>also</u> $F_2 \oplus\rightarrow \underline{E}$ (F-8)
$\qquad\qquad\qquad\qquad\qquad\qquad\qquad\qquad$ <u>also</u> $F_2 \Rightarrow \underline{E}$
$\qquad\qquad\qquad\qquad\qquad\qquad\qquad\qquad\quad$ (F-29)

	Raw Scores	Transforms

The Free Associations

(F-45) that my inclinations might have chosen a worse outlet.

$E \rightrightarrows \underline{Sy}_{13A}$ $E \rightrightarrows \underline{F}_{1C}$ (F-47)

also $E \prec\!\!\!- \underline{F}_{1C}$ (F-29) and (F-47)

also $\preceq E, \underline{F}_{1C}$ (F-36) and (F-47)

(—) [The recollection of this experience from the later years of my youth at once brought back to my mind]

(F-46) the conversation with my friend Dr. Königstein (B-74)

$E \rightrightarrows F_{1C}$ also $E \prec\!\!\!- F_{1C}$ (F-29)

also $\preceq E, F_{1C}$ (F-36)

(F-47) — $*[F_{1C} \updownarrow Sy_{13A}]$

(F-48) (my friend) $[E \updownarrow Pm_6]$

(F-49) (friend Dr.). $[Pm_6 = F_{1C}]$

(F-50/51) For in the course of it we had discussed

$E \rightrightarrows F_{1C}$ also $E \prec\!\!\!- F_{1C}$ (F-29)

also $\preceq E, F_{1C}$ (F-36)

$F_{1C} \rightrightarrows E$ also $F_{1C} \prec\!\!\!- E$ (F-29)

also $\preceq F_{1C}, E$ (F-36)

(F-52) the same question of my being blamed

$Pm_9 \prec\!\!\!- E$ also $Pm_9 \; \odot\!\!\rightarrow E$ (F-8)

also $Pm_9 \rightrightarrows E$ (F-29)

also $F_{1C} \prec\!\!\!- E$ (F-53)

also $F_{1C} \; \odot\!\!\rightarrow E$ (F-8) and (F-53)

also $F_{1C} \rightrightarrows E$ (F-29) and (F-53)

(F-53) — $*[Pm_9 \updownarrow F_{1C}]$

(F-54) for being too much absorbed in my favourite hobbies

$E \stackrel{+}{\to} \overset{+}{Sy}_{13A}$ $E \stackrel{+}{\to} \overset{+}{F}_{1C}$ (F-47)

	Raw Scores	Transforms
The Free Associations		
		$\underline{also}$ E $\overset{+}{\prec}$ $\overset{+}{F}_{1C}$ (F-29)
		$\underline{and}$ (F-47)
		$\underline{also}$ $\overset{+}{\leftarrow}$ E, $\overset{+}{F}_{1C}$ (F-36)
		$\underline{and}$ (F-47)
(F-55) (my favourite hobbies).	[E $\overset{+}{\updownarrow}$ $\overset{+}{Sy}_{13A}$]	E $\overset{+}{\rightarrow}$ $\overset{+}{F}_{1C}$ (F-23)
		$\underline{and}$ (F-47)
		E $\overset{+}{\prec}$ $\overset{+}{F}_{1C}$ (F-30)
		$\underline{and}$ (F-47)

The associations end on this ambiguous note, with the precise referent of "hobbies" unspecified. Were Freud our research subject or patient, rather than his own, this surely is a point where we would have pressed for clarification. One possibly relevant additional comment by Freud [1900, p. 175] is that "(O)ne of my patients, who bore the charming name of Flora, was for a time the pivot of our discussion." In context, it seems likely that Freud's treatment for, and sexual-etiological theory of, hysteria may have been the grounds on which he was "being blamed."

The Lexicon

Sy$_1$ – literary
- 1A publication
- 1A1 plate/drawing
- 1A2 title
- 1A3 dedication
- 1A4 page
- 1A5 leaf
- 1B letter

Sy$_2$ – botanical
- 2A plant
- 2B herbarium
- 2B1 sheet of herbarium
- 2C cyclamen
- 2D flowers
- 2E coca plant
- 2F crucifer
- 2G composite
- 2G1 artichoke

Sy$_3$ – commercial
- 3A shop
- 3A1 window
- 3B market

Sy$_4$ – verbal
- 4A anecdote
- 4B "matter"
- 4C name, classification

Sy$_5$ – scientific
- 5A theory
- 5B laboratory

Sy$_6$ – temporal
- 6A birthday

Sy_7 —medical Sy_8 —geographical Sy_9 —financial
  $_{7A}$ treatment $_{8A}$ Berlin $_{9A}$ money
  $_{7B}$ cocaine $_{8B}$ Persia

Sy_{10} —residential Sy_{11} —educational Sy_{12} —psychological
  $_{10A}$ Freud's home $_{11A}$ school $_{12A}$ dreams
  $_{10A1}$ entrance hall $_{11B}$ examination $_{12B}$ memory

Sy_{13} —avocational
  $_{13A}$ hobby,
         interest

Pm_1 —plant-taker F_1 —physicians
Pm_2^+ —circle of friends $_{1A}$ Freud as
Pm_3 —Herr L. $_{1B}$ Berlin eye-surgeon
Pm_4 —Koller $_{1C}$ Königstein
Pm_5 —Fliess $_{1D}$ Koller
Pm_6 —Königstein F_2 —Freud's father
Pm_7 —students F_3 —teachers
  $_{7A}$ university $_{3A}$ Stricker (teacher/director)
  $_{7B}$ childhood $_{3B}$ Gärtner
  $_{7C}$ Freud as $_{3C}$ master
Pm_8 —friendly colleague F_4 —bookseller
Pm_9 —blamer Sp_1 —Frau Freud
                                        Sp_2 —Frau L.

CHAPTER 13

From Sentence to Structure

Association-Path Analysis

Justification and Overview

As is evident from the scoring of "Botanical Monograph" and its free associations (chapter 12), SSLS generates a considerable mass of scores (sentences) for the texts to which it is applied. Its simple enumeration of textual transformations presents a confused picture for dream-interpretation psychology, and an impossible one for dream-structure or dream-process psychology. What is required is some way of organizing the separate sentences generated by SSLS's scoring so that the inner structure or logic of the text might be revealed.

Association-path analysis is one attempt at providing such organization for any collection of SSLS sentences. It traces out some logical, and hopefully some psychological, connections within the dream and free-association material. The underlying principle (logically), and assumption (psychologically), is that greater similarity implies closer connectedness.

Association-path analysis is applied to *the basic superordinate unit of SSLS, the association chain. A dream-episode, as defined by the dreamer, is an association chain.* Generally the dreamer spontaneously will label dream material in terms of somewhat disconnected "parts," "sections," "segments," and so on, thought, nonetheless, to be part of a common dream. Where the dreamer does not identify dream-episodes, but the action seems discontinuous, it is incumbent upon *guides* (the persons supervising the reporting of the dream—experimenters, therapists, etc.) that they elicit from the dreamer such perceived connectednesses and disjointednesses. We rely on dreamers for final demarcation of dream-episodes, since they alone are privy to the unfolding of the pictorial drama and their knowledge of it may be only imperfectly reflected in their verbal accounts.

A free-association chain is the parallel unit of free-association analysis. While the dreamer's comments are likely to be helpful here also, segregation of this unit ultimately relies on the analyst's judgment, rather than on that of the dreamer. Both analyst and dreamer have access to the same verbal output, but the former is likely to be more skilled at its organization for SSLS's purposes. A free-association chain begins when the dreamer states, or associates to, some sentence in the manifest-dream scoring. The chain then "leads away" from its origin. It "ends" when the dreamer returns to the same origin to recommence associating, returns to some other sentence in the manifest dream to be used as a new origin, or says he or she can associate no further.

Association-path analysis is performed both on dream scorings themselves (*association chains*) and upon the free associations stimulated by particular dream sentences (*free-association chains*). In the dream case, the *origin of the path* is the first associative sentence of the dream narrative. In the free-association case, the path's origin is the dream sentence (associative *or* interactive) to which the associations have been given. In either case, *the path leaves its origin along a route of least associative-sentence dissimilarity, and its subsequent course follows the same principle of minimal dissimilarity of succeeding from preceding associative sentences.* Thus the ordering of associative sentences in association-path analysis is logical rather than strictly chronological.

Steps on the path are limited to association sentences, since the goal of association-path analysis is to identify features of the transformational network, or "connective tissue," either within the dream itself or between the dream and its motivationally significant associations (i.e., its "basic dream thoughts" [Freud] or its "interaction sentences" [SSLS]).

Similarity is defined, in association-path analysis, in terms of *noun* elements. That is, *the first step of the path will be that associative sentence containing the greatest proportion of noun elements found in the origin of the path; the second step will be that associative sentence containing the greatest proportion of noun elements found in the first step of the path; and so forth.* [1] *Verb* similarity or form is almost totally ignored in association-path analysis.

The reason for this neglect of associative-sentence verbs lies in their very nature. Unlike their interactive-verb counterparts, associative-verb categories conceal gross intracategory variability while failing to imply significant inter-category variability. The category $\updownarrow$, for instance, defines, in one sense, vastly different phenomena: is physically proximate to, is moving together with, reminds me of, is inside of, contains the same number of letters as, and so on. Yet, in another sense, both it and the other two associative verbs, = and = ... $\square$, all define the same fact: association. SSLS's separation of associative verbs into categories rests, unlike the case for interactive verbs, not so much on conceptual differentiation as on considerations of "administrative" convenience. The Means verb, for example, allows SSLS to rewrite interactive sentences in various desirable ways (indicating role relationships, third-party interactions, etc.) without complicating the relatively simple conventions regarding permissible forms of interactive sentences themselves. The Equivalence verb also serves pragmatic functions: it permits SSLS to keep track of identity across role transformations (which is useful in path analysis) while separating out the implications of a person's different roles (i.e., since = sentences do not justify the writing of transformed interaction sentences, motivational imputations regarding one role are not automatically generalized to another role held by the same person). Thus the associative verb categories probably reveal more of the necessities of SSLS than they do of the structure of the dreamer's text (or mind). For this reason, the form of the associative verb is not considered in association-path analysis.

Procedure

We begin considering the implementation of association-path analysis by means of a simple example. Say that the stimulating dream sentence for a free-association chain is $E \prec Sy_{3A}$. Let the *association* sentences in that chain be as follows:

$$\text{Sentence} \quad 1) \quad [Sy_{3A3B} \updownarrow Sy_{3C}];$$
$$2) \quad [Sy_{3A} \updownarrow Sy_{3B}];$$
$$3) \quad [Sy_{3B} \updownarrow Sy_{4D}];$$
$$5) \quad [Sy_{3B3C} \updownarrow Pm_2];$$

[1] An element is defined as a discriminable lexical subscript, i.e., a separate entry in the lexicon. Thus Pm_{1A} contains one element, but $Sy_{1A,2A}$, a composite noun, contains two elements.

7) $[Sy_{3C} = E \Rightarrow Pm_2]$;

8) $[Sy_{3C} \updownarrow Sy_6]$;

9) $[Pm_2 \updownarrow F_2]$;

11) $[E \updownarrow F_2]$.

Then the association path will be defined as follows.

						Noun Communality %
Origin (0)	=	$E \prec Sy3A$				
Step (1)	2)	$Sy3A \updownarrow Sy3B$				100
(main (2) chain)	1)	$Sy3A$	$3B \updownarrow Sy3C$			100
(3)	5)	Sy	$3B$	$3C \updownarrow Pm2$		67
(4)	7)	Sy		$3C \Rightarrow Pm2$		67
(5)	9)			$Pm2 \updownarrow F2$		50
(side chain) (2A)	3)	Sy	$3B$		$\updownarrow Sy4D$	50
(side chain) (5B)	8)	Sy		$3C$	$\updownarrow Sy6$	50

This example illustrates several conventions of association-path analysis which supplement the general rule of noun communality. (Readers disinterested in pursuing detailed scoring conventions of the analysis might want to skip ahead to the summary of this section.)

(1) E is not considered a relevant noun element in determining the course of the path. By assumption, E is related to *all* noun elements in the path analysis—they constitute, after all, *E's* associations. Thus E is not a *discriminating* noun element, and is excluded from noun communality computations. Thus sentences 1 and 2, both of which contain the element Sy_{3A}, contain 100% (not 50%) of the relevant noun elements of the origin of the path.

(2) In case of a tie in noun communality percentage, preference is given, other considerations equal, to that sentence which introduces the smaller number of *new* noun elements to the path. That sentence clearly is less dissimilar to the preceding step of the path. Thus sentence 2 is the first step of the path above, rather than sentence 1.

(3) The sentence not selected in the case of a tie often still can be integrated into the *main path*. Where it is possible to so align it according to its noun communality percentage, this is done. Thus, sentence 1 in the example above, rejected as a first step, becomes the second step of the path since it alone contains 100% of the relevant nouns from the first step.

(4)   Where a sentence not selected in case of a tie, or with chronically inferior noun communality figures, cannot subsequently be integrated into the main path, it may be the first step on a *side chain* off the main path.[2] Thus sentence 3 is the first (and only) step of a side chain off the main chain, since it possessed inferior noun communality percentages in relation to steps (1), (2), and (3), where element Sy_{3B} served as its only basis for potential linkage to the main chain.

(5)   A side-chain sentence is said to be *joined* to the main path at the earliest sentence in the main path (including the origin) with which it has its own highest communality percentage (i.e., is most similar to the main path). Thus sentence 3 would have had a 50% communality as step (2), but only a 33% communality as steps (3) or (4), of the main path. Hence it is said to be joined to the main path at step (1); sentence 2 is the origin of its side path. It is assigned the same step number it would have had in the main path (2), but its side-chain status is indicated by an accompanying letter designation. Thus sentence 3 becomes, in the above example, step (2A).

(6)   The main path must be completed before any side chains can be initiated, and all side chains joined to the main path at step (*n*) must be completed before any side chain can be initiated from step (*n + 1*) of the main path. (Where two side chains can be initiated from the same step of the main path, priority is given to forming the side path which is connected to the main chain by earlier-introduced elements [elements toward the left-hand side of the work sheet]). It is in order of their priority, thus defined, that chains are assigned letter designations, and that they are listed on the work sheet. Thus the second side chain of the example, consisting of sentence 8, is designated by the letter B and listed below the A side chain. Sentence 8 becomes step (5B), since its highest communality with the main path is with step (4) (sentence 7), namely 50%.

(7)   In case of a tie in noun communality percentage, priority is given to that sentence containing more (including, but not limited to, the case of 1 versus 0) *character referents* (as opposed to Sy, *symbol referents*) in common with the preceding step of the path. Thus, in the example, both sentences 8 and 9 have 50% noun-communality percentages with step (4) of the main path, but only sentence 9 continues a character referent (Pm_2); it therefore becomes step (5), while sentence 8 is relegated to the position of (5B) in a side chain. The logic behind this rule is that greater associative "force" is imagined to attach to person-associations than to symbol-associations, which

---

[2] "May be" instead of "is," since sometimes it will, instead, be a step in a side chain initiated by another sentence which has greater priority in the initiation of side chains (see rule (6)).

may only stand indirectly for persons, and that persons seem less likely, because of their own intrinsic psychic "force," to be used as the indifferent stuff of symbolization than do objects, creatures, or concepts.

(8) For similar reasons as underlie convention (1) above, association-path analysis does not separately code those sentences in which E is related, by sentences of the form [E $\updownarrow$ . . .] or [. . . = E $\boxed{\updownarrow}$ . . .] to an element or to elements already contained in the path. Thus sentence 11 in our example is not a step in the main path or in any side chain, since it only relates E to an element already contained in the main path. We already *assume* E's relationship to *all* elements contained in the path, and do not differentiate E's path relationships which are implicitly based on our assumption from those which are explicitly stated in an association sentence in the text. (Were a sentence of the form [E $\updownarrow$ . . .] or [. . . = E $\boxed{\updownarrow}$ . . .] *uniquely* to link one or more path elements to other path elements or to novel elements, e.g., [E $\updownarrow$ Sy$_{1A,2B,4C}$], it would be included in the path analysis, but with the E element itself omitted.)

The following conventions are not illustrated in the example, but are employed in association-path analysis.

(9) Side chains can have their own side chains (side-side-chains?), and so on. However, all side chains to the main chain must be completed before any side chain to a side chain can be formed, and so forth. Once all side chains, and side-chains-to-side-chains, etc., have been determined, however, side-chains-to-side-chains joined to the main path at step (*n*) are considered as being prior to (are listed on the work sheet before) simple side chains to the main path at step (*n + 1*).

(10) Formation of side chains, once the main path is completed and has been entered on a preliminary work sheet, begins by considering possibilities at step (0), then moves, in order, through steps (1), (2), (3), and so on. However, not all potential side chains at step (0) will be initiated, since initiation requires not only that a sentence be linked more compellingly than any other to the main chain at step (0) (i.e., have a higher noun communality percentage, add fewer new elements to the chain, etc.) but also that its own communality with the main chain be highest at step (0). Thus a sentence with a uniquely high attachment (e.g., 50%) to the main path at step (0) (no other potential side-chain sentence is so strongly connected to the path at that point) cannot initiate a side chain there if it has a higher attachment (e.g., 75%) to some subsequent step of the main path where its own noun communality percentage is highest in relation to that path.

(11) Where conventions (2) and (7) conflict—e.g., one sentence breaks a

tie by introducing fewer new terms to the path but another uniquely continues some line of characterization, precedence is given to convention (7).

(12) Associative sentences with the verb = (role transformations) are not
entered as separate steps in the analysis but in conjunction with those other
associative-sentence steps with which they are most closely connected.

Thus, where these are the raw scores for associations to dream element
0:

0)	I was with this guy . . .	$= [E \updownarrow Pm_1]$;
1)	He used to be a friend.	$= [E \underline{\updownarrow} Pm_1]$;
2)	He had a car.	$= [Pm_1 \underline{\updownarrow} Sy_{1A}]$;
3)	We used to sit there together	$= [E \underline{\updownarrow} Pm_1]$;
4)	(car was the medium of association).	$= [Sy_{1A} \equiv E \boxed{\updownarrow} Pm_1]$;
5)	Now he's a cop,	$= [Pm_1 \overset{+}{=} F_1]$;
6)	with a police car.	$= [F_1 \updownarrow Sy_{1B}]$;

they lead to this association-path analysis:

Path *origin*: (0) E $\updownarrow$ Pm$_1$ [sentence 0)] ;

step: (1)   Pm$_1$ $\updownarrow$ Sy$_{1A}$ [sentence 2)]

                    Pm$_1$ $\boxed{\updownarrow}$ Sy$_{1A}$ [sentence 4)] ;

        (2)   [Pm$_1$ =   = F$_1$] $\updownarrow$ Sy$_{1B}$ [sentences 5)/6)] .

Note that: the role transformation—sentence 5—is entered in connection with
the most pertinent association sentence—sentence 6; that it is entered in a characteristic way, $[x = \dots = y]$, enclosing the roles involved; that it can serve
as a link in the series of nouns—without it, there would be no bond between
the elements of sentence 6 and those of sentences 2 and 4; but that the intra-
bracket composite it generates figures only as a *single* element (*which is the
newly introduced role*) in determining subsequent noun communality—a
subsequent $[F_1 \updownarrow Sy_2]$ sentence, for example, would have a 50% and not a
33% communality with step (2) in the path above; and that the new role in
a bracketed role-composite is *not* considered a new element to the path in
application of rule (2) above (although it will be so considered in structural
diagrams of the association path).

(Parenthetical entries in Means sentences preceded by a plus sign, e.g.,
Pm$_{1A}$ in $[Sy_{1A} = E (+ Pm_{1A}) \boxed{\rightarrow} F]$, are *not* treated as role equivalencies;
therefore, the above rule does not apply to them. In the example given,
Pm$_{1A}$ is a full-fledged noun element, and must be so considered in tracing the
associative path.)

Where it is impossible to apply convention (12)—i.e., where there *is* no other associative sentence employing the new role—then the = sentence itself will be scored. This would happen, for instance, if the associations above simply stopped at sentence 5. In this case the sentence is written as if it were a ↕ sentence, and subsequent communalities are figured accordingly.

The association-path analysis above also illustrates another scoring convention. Where two or more sentences contain precisely the same noun elements (whatever their associative verbs) they define only *one step* in the path (sentences 2 and 4 in the illustration). The only exception is where, in a free-association chain, both the dream stimulus (0) and a free-association sentence (1) contain the same noun elements. The dream origin of a free-association chain always is kept discrete.

(13) Where there is a tie, and convention (7) above does not apply, and the immediately preceding step includes a role transformation, priority is given to associative sentences which pursue the newly introduced role. Thus, if, for possible steps (3) in the immediately preceding path-example, we had sentences:

7) $[Pm_1 ↕ Sy_2]$;
8) $[F_1 ↕ Sy_2]$;

we could not discriminate their priority on the basis of character continuity—both continue a character "element" from the prior step. But, following the present rule, our choice would be sentence 8, which continues the new role. The logic here is that a role transformation is a sufficiently striking change of associative direction to have considerable associative "force" behind it. The present rule assumes priority over rule (2) above. Note that no special priority attaches to encoding a role-transformation statement itself in the path; the present rule refers only to the case where such a statement already has, by virtue of its other merits, been included as a step in a path, and we wonder what *next* to do.

(14) Where a tie cannot be broken, successively, either by rule (7) or by rule (13), another rule assumes precedence over rule (2). This is where the "new" element one sentence would introduce to the path at step $(n + 1)$ actually is an element already described somewhere earlier in the path—it is new, that is, only in the sense that it is not present at step (n)—while the new element another sentence would introduce to the path at step $(n + 1)$ is genuinely novel—new in relation not only to step (n), but also to the entire path so far described.

Here priority is given to the sentence which, however many "new" noun elements it adds to the prior step of the path, refers back to an older element in the path. Not unreasonably we might consider this sentence to be less dissimilar to the path already described than one which would introduce truly novel elements to it. Thus, consider this example:

Path step: $(n - 3)$ Sy2A3B;
    $(n - 2)$ Sy2A3B Pm1;
    $(n - 1)$ Pm1 Pm2;
    (n) Pm2 Pm3;
    $(n + 1)$ Pm2 Pm3 Sy4.

Imagine that the two candidates for path step $(n + 2)$ are, in their chronological order:

    a)   Sy4 Sy5
    b) Sy 3B   Sy4

Both candidates a and b have 33% communality with step $(n + 1)$, and both continue characterization to the same degree (i.e., not at all). Rule (13) does not apply, since there is no role transformation at step $(n + 1)$. But, by the present rule, the choice must be b. Sentence b breaks the tie by containing "new" element Sy_{3B}, in fact already introduced to the path at step $(n - 3)$, while the "new" element for sentence a in position $(n + 2)$ would be genuinely novel to the path as a whole, and not only in relation to path step $(n+1)$.

The principle of this rule, that earlier-introduced elements have, other things equal, priority over novel ones, also may be applied to the case in which *both* sentence candidates would introduce, at step $(n + 2)$, an element "new" in relation to step $(n + 1)$ but contained earlier in the path. Here priority is accorded the sentence whose new element was introduced *earlier* to the path. Thus, in the example above, a candidate $[Sy_4 \updownarrow Sy_{3B}]$ would receive priority over $[Sy_4 \updownarrow Pm_1]$, since Sy_{3B} was introduced to the path earlier than was Pm_1. "Earlier" is defined in terms of *position on the association-path work sheet*, i.e., main-path sentence $(n + 1)$ is *earlier* than side-path sentence (nA), since the entire main path is described before any side path is entered on that work sheet. This rule applies regardless of the number of truly novel elements either sentence might also contain.

Suppose that one potential tie-breaker sentence contains one earlier path element, while another contains two such elements. Priority would be given the latter, regardless of where the elements in question were introduced (a backward-looking noun-communality principle takes precedence over one of elemental chronicity). Suppose both potential tie-breakers contain the same number, $n > 1$, of earlier path elements. Where these elements were introduced, respectively, at lines 2 and 6 and lines 1 and 5 of the work sheet, the latter case would be accorded priority, since its elemental-priority $\overline{X}$ is less (were the $\overline{X}$'s identical, a choice could not be made on the basis of this convention).

(15) Where a tie exists with one potential next step leading from one element and another potential next step leading from another element, select the step leading from the element introduced earlier to the path. This rule takes precedence only over rules (2) and (16).

(16) Where there is a tie, and neither conventions (2), (7), (13), (14), nor (15) suffice to break it, favor attaches to the chronologically prior (i.e., earlier-numbered in the raw scoring) associative sentence. Although association-path analysis need not follow the chronology of the dreamer's text (e.g., the transposition of sentences 2 and 1 in our initial example), it generally is not greatly discrepant from a mere chronological ordering of associative sentences. This, of course, is how it should be, for the dreamer's chrono-logic in dream reporting and her or his logic in dream thinking must be assumed to have some positive correlation with one another. Thus, where "logic" fails us, we are as likely to be faithful to the structure of the dreamer's thought if we follow her or his chrono-logic as if we adopt any other alternative rule. However, the editing which undoubtedly transpires between thought organization and report organization leads us to prefer logic, where available, and to resort to chrono-logic only where, as here, logic proves insufficient.

(17) So far, various conventions have been considered for breaking ties in cases where two (or more) candidates for some position $(n + 1)$ in a path have the same noun communality percentage with step (n). No exceptions have been made, however, to the rule of noun communality itself. Now we make such an exception, the only one within the rules governing association-path analysis. Where an associative sentence with some character and some symbol continuity, or with only some character continuity, has a lower noun communality with step (n) than does an associative sentence whose noun communality percentage rests *entirely* upon symbolic elements, favor is accorded the former sentence as a candidate for step $(n + 1)$. The rationale is similar to that for convention (7), namely that character associations are assumed to have greater associative force than symbolic ones. Thus, consider the following case.

		Noun communality %
step (n): Sy 1A1B1C1D Pm2		
sentence: a) 1A1B1C1D Pf2		80
b) 1A 1D Pm2		60

Sentence b, rather than sentence a, becomes step $(n + 1)$. This is so, since, despite its higher communality value, sentence a fails to continue the character dimension.[3]

Summary and Association-Path Analyses of "Botanical Monograph"

We may summarize the major rules guiding sentence selection for path positions (i.e., the general principle of noun communality percentage, plus conventions (2), (7), (13), (14), (15), (16), and (17)) in the form of a flow chart. Figure 13-1 is such a chart. Following the chart are the association-path analyses for the "Botanical Monograph" dream and its free-associational chains (figures 13-2 to 13-7).

It should be noted that the rules proposed above for organizing dream and free-association sentences into associative paths, as well as the rules to be proposed below for making structural diagrams of these paths, are viewed as tentative ones. Specifically, more experience with them is required to establish that: (1) they generate intuitively satisfying resolutions of the data—i.e., they agree with the more compelling of the impressionistic analyses which SSLS is trying rulefully to simulate; and (2) they generate empirically valid hypotheses about the structure of the dreamer's thoughts and motives *outside* the dream context. (Intuitive Evaluation, pp. 292–99, considers the first and second criteria as they specifically apply to "Botanical Monograph" and Freud. Chapter 16 discusses the more general question of dreamer-psychology validations of SSLS's method of analyzing dream and free-associative texts.) Here, as elsewhere in part IV, what deserves stress is not so much the particular rules of SSLS at present as the fact that SSLS presents a framework in which dream analysis can be made ruleful, and in which better rules can evolve.

Structuregrams

Justification and Overview

Symbol and character terms in the "Botanical Monograph" free-association chains (figures 13-3 to 13-7) generally fall along an upper-left to lower-

---

[3] Where several sentences qualify on account of their character continuity, but not noun communality, choice is made on the basis of criteria used more generally in breaking ties, i.e., the conventions described earlier.

FIGURE 13-1

Flow Chart for Association-Path Analysis

For any two sentences (a) and (b), considered as candidates for position $(n + 1)$ in a path, where:

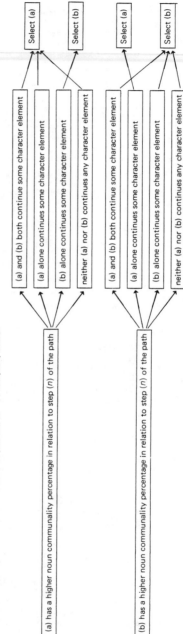

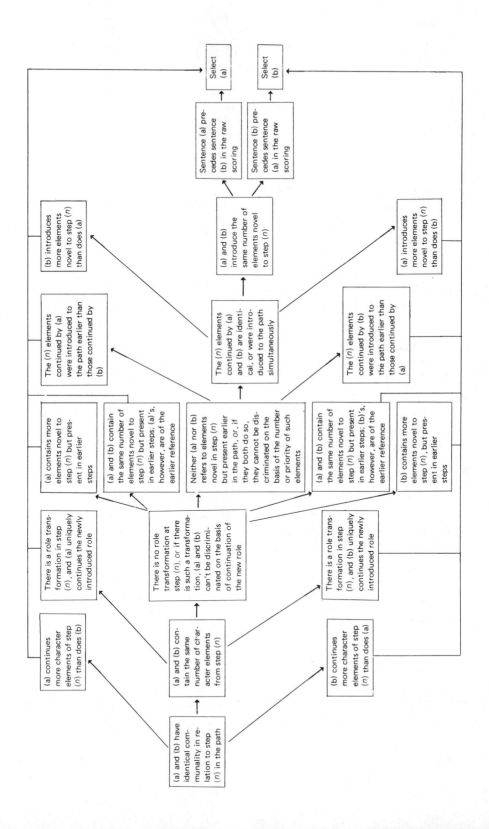

FIGURE 13-2

Association-Path Analysis for "Botanical Monograph": The Dream

Step	Sentence(s)	Symbols		Characters/Roles
(0)	X-2, X-6	1A, 2A		
(1)	X-5	1A	1A1	
(1A)	X-8	2A	2B	Pm1

right axis. This indicates that these paths do describe associative elements which are increasingly remote from the stimulating manifest-dream element. And, it should be remembered, *associative distance along these paths is being described in terms of free-associative data supplied by the dreamer,* rather than in the "standard" but arbitrary terms of some general psychological theory. These are important contributions of association-path analysis.

But association-path analysis clearly is only an intermediate step in the organization of SSLS's associative sentence scores. The linearity of the "path" concept obscures the fact that associative elements are structured more as a *network* than as a *chain*. What now is required is a reasonable set of rules according to which the reticulate connectedness of associative elements may be defined and portrayed. As we shall see, the association-path analysis itself contains all the information needed to generate network *structures* from its own *paths*. Specifically, in *structuregram analysis*, the results of the path analysis are used to identify a set of points representing SSLS associative elements and a set of lines indicating associative connections among such points.

The origin of a structuregram consists of the SSLS nouns at the origin of the dream or free-association path. Subsequent points of the structuregram describe those noun elements later introduced to the association path. Directed lines (arrows) indicate priority in the path, earlier-introduced path elements having priority ($\rightarrow$) in relation to later-introduced ones. Specifically, priority is determined by row position in the association-path analysis work sheet (i.e., the main path is prior to any side chain).

Structuregrams may be formed for: an *association chain (dream structuregram)*; a *free-association chain (free-association structuregram)*; or an association chain *plus* all of its free-association chains *(composite structuregram)*. Rules for forming structuregrams of the simple and composite variety are given on pp. 285 and 287; then, the full set of dream and free-association structuregrams for "Botanical Monograph" are given on pp. 290–92.

Structuregrams themselves are intermediate steps in SSLS's overall analytic scheme. Their points and lines are drawn so as to permit further analysis in terms of mathematical models of structure (chapters 14 and 15). But, although not the final stage of SSLS's analysis, the structuregram is a suffi-

FIGURE 13-3

Association-Path Analysis for "Botanical Monograph": Free-Association Chain A

Step	Sentence(s)	Symbols	Characters/Roles
(0)	X-1, X-2	1A, 2A	
(1)	A-2	1A 3A1	
(2)	A-3	1A 3A1, 3A	
(3)	A-4	1A 1A2	
(4)	A-6	1A 2C	
(5)	A-5	1A 1A2, 2C	
(6)	A-7	2C, 2D	Sp1
(7)	A-10, A-13	2D	Sp1
(8)	A-48, A-50		Sp1, Sp2
(9)	A-39	2D	Sp2
(10)	A-22, A-27, A-38	2D	Sp2, Pm3
(11)	A-23, A-28, A-30 A-40, A-43, A-44	2D	Sp2, Pm3
(12)	A-42	6A	Sp2, Pm3
(13)	A-25, A-32, A-35	6A	Sp2
(14)	A-53	7A	Sp2 F1A
(8A)	A-24	2D, 6A	
(9A)	A-34, A-41	6A	Pm3
(8B)	A-14	2D 4A	
(9B)	A-16	4A	
(10B)	A-18	4A, 5A	Pm2

FIGURE 13-4

Association-Path Analysis for "Botanical Monograph": Free-Association Chain B

Step	Sentence(s)	Symbols	Character/Roles
(0)	X-1, X-2	1A, 2A	
(1)	B-2	1A, 2A	
(2)	B-3	1A 2E	
(3)	B-7	1A 2E, 7B	
(4)	B-5	1A 2E, 7B	
(5)	B-48/49	7B	Pm4
(6)	B-53		[Pm4 = F1D] F1D, F1C
(7)	B-56		F1D, F1C, F2
(8)	B-55		F1D F2
(9)	B-41	7B	F2
(10)	B-44/45		[F1C =, F2, = Pm6]
(11)	B-54		F1C, F2
(12)	B-47	7A	F1C, F2
(13)	B-75	4B	F1C
(14)	B-80		F1C F3B
(15)	B-91	1A 1A3	F3B
(16)	B-88	1A3	F3B
(17)	B-78	2	F3B
(18)	B-83		F3B, M
(19)	B-93		F3B Sp2
(20)	B-94	1A 1A3	Sp2
(21)	B-98	1A	F1C Sp2
(22)	B-82	2	F1C
(23)	B-77	10A, 10A1	F1C
(24)	B-79	10A, 10A1	
(25)	B-95	6A	
(26)	B-96	1A 1A3 6A	F3B
(27)	B-60	1A 1A3	F3B
(28)	B-65	1A 1A3	F3A
(29)	B-62	1A 1A3	F3A, Pm7A

Ref	Specimen	Character codes
(30)	B-63	F3A, Pm7A
(31)	B-64	F3A
(32)	B-68	7B, 5B, Pm4
(33)	B-71	10A
(34)	B-81	2, 10A, 10A1
(35)	B-72	7B, 10A, 5B, Pm4
(36)	B-70	7B, 10A, 5B
(6A)	B-12	7B, 8A
(7A)	B-25	7B, F1B
(8A)	B-15, B-23	7A, F1B
(9A)	B-14, B-32	8A, F1B
(10A)	B-21	F1B
(11A)	B-16, B-18	F1B, Pm5
(12A)	B-35	9A, F1B
(13A)	B-38	F1B
(14A)	B-37	9A, Pm
(6B)	B-29	7B, Pm
(7B)	B-31	7A, M
(19C)	B-89	6A, Sp2, F1
(20D)	B-92	F1, F1A

FIGURE 13-5

Association-Path Analysis for "Botanical Monograph": Free-Association Chain C

Step	Sentence(s)	Symbols	Characters/Roles
(0)	X-6, X-7, X-8		Pm1
(1)	C-1	1A, 2A 2B	
(2)	C-2/5	[1A = 2B], 11A	
(3)	C-12	2B	F3C
(4)	C-11	2B	F3C, Pm7B
(5)	C-9		F3C, Pm7B
(6)	C-19	2B 2B1	F3C
(7)	C-7	11A	F3C
(8)	C-17		F3C
(2A)	C-4	1A 11A	
(2B)	C-29, C-31, C-33	2A 4C, 2F	
(3B)	C-20	2B1 2F	
(4B)	C-22	2B1 2, 5	
(5B)	C-23	2F, 2, 5	
(6B)	C-24	2, 5, 11B	
(4B1)	C-27	2F	F3
(5B1)	C-35	2F 5A	
(6B1)	C-37	2F 2G	
(7B1)	C-38	2G, 2G1	
(8B1)	C-39	2G1, 2D	
(9B1)	C-42	2D	Sp1
(10B1)	C-45	2D, 3B	Sp1

FIGURE 13-6

Association-Path Analysis for "Botanical Monograph":
Free-Association Chains D and E

Step	Sentence(s)	Symbols			Characters/Roles
Chain D					
(0)	X-3	1A			
(1)	D-8, D-14	1A, 12A			
(2)	D-7, D-9, D-10	1A, 12A			Pm5
(3)	D-12	1A, 12A, 1A4			Pm5
(4)	D-2, D-6		1B		Pm5
(5)	D-4			8A	Pm5
Chain E					
(0)	X-4, X-5	1A1, 1A			
(1)	E-16	1A1, 1A			
(2)	E-12	1A1, 1A, 7			
(3)	E-5	1A, 7			
(4)	E-10	1A, 7, 9A			
(5)	E-7	1A	9A		
(6)	E-8	7, 9A			
(7)	E-2	7			Pm7C
(8)	E-4	1A			Pm7C
(1A)	E-18	1A1			Pm8

ciently high-level organization of associative-sentence data that I will conclude this chapter with an informal evaluation of how well the methods
herein described have captured the "structure" and "meaning" of "Botanical
Monograph."

Rules for Forming Simple Structuregrams

(1) *A noun element is considered antecedent to another (i.e., a directed
line is drawn from it to the other) when it first appears in the path at some
step (n), the other element first appears in the path at some step (n + . . .),
and there is somewhere among the scores an associative sentence (association-
path work-sheet row) in which the two elements both are present.*

(2) Where two or more noun elements first appear in the path at step (n)
and immediately recur together at step (n + 1), they are considered a *composite element* and are joined with a hyphen. Using rule (1), a composite
element is considered antecedent to any noun elements subsequently sharing
a work-sheet row with it *or with any one of its individual components.*
(Where two or more noun elements appear together at the *origin*, they are
considered a composite element, even should they never recur together.)

FIGURE 13-7

Association-Path Analysis for "Botanical Monograph": Free-Association Chain F

Step	Sentence(s)	Symbols	Characters/Roles
(0)	X-4, X-5	1A1, 1A	
(1)	F-4	1A1, 1A	
(2)	F-3	1A	F2
(3)	F-7	1A	F2, Si
(4)	F-32	1A, 12B	Si
(5)	F-34	1A, 12B	
(6)	F-38	1A, 12B	F4
(7)	F-40	1A, 3A	F4
(8)	F-39, F-43	9A	F4
(1A)	F-5	1A, 8B	
(2A)	F-12	1A, 1A5	
(3A)	F-15	12B, 1A5	
(4A)	F-16	12B, 2G1	
(5A)	F-13	1A5, 2G1	
(6A)	F-27	2G1, 13A	
(7A)	F-25	1A, 13A	
(8A)	F-26	13A, 2C	
(9A)	F-47	13A	
(10A)	F-49		F1C
(11A)	F-53		F1C, Pm6, Pm9
(6B)	F-19	12B	F1C, Pm7C

(3) Structuregram terms included in an interactive sentence within the scored text under analysis are enclosed with a box: e.g., $\boxed{\text{Pm}_3}$.

(4) Structuregram terms for which the scored text under analysis contains a sentence of the form [E ⇕ . . .] or [E = . . .] are called *ego-points*, and their lexical designation is underlined: e.g., $\underline{\text{Pm}_3}$ or $\boxed{\underline{\text{Pm}_3}}$.

Rules for Forming Composite Structuregrams

In a composite structuregram, the dream structuregram is combined with its various free-association structuregrams. The result, in all but the simplest cases (of which "Botanical Monograph" is *not* one), is a rather complex array of lines and points defying immediate visual analysis. For this reason, composite structuregrams are not presented here. However, since structures not visually comprehensible can be treated mathematically (chapter 14), a few rules are given for forming such structuregrams. The rules themselves will serve to introduce the general features of composite structuregrams as well as any detailed visual illustration might.

(1) The simple free-association structuregrams generated in response to the dream structuregram are combined with it, following the same general procedures outlined above.

(2) Problems will arise where a noun element is not encoded in a similar fashion in two or more simple structuregrams being used to form the composite structuregram. Where the same noun occurs sometimes alone and sometimes in a composite noun and/or in different composite nouns, the following conventions apply:

(a) The earlier composite form is recorded for element X (e.g., an X-Y composite) even where X later appears alone. Relationships of the later X are referred to the earlier structural element X-Y. E.g., if $Sy_{2A,2B}$ appears in chain A, and Sy_{2B} in chain B, all relationships of $_{2B}$ in chain B are drawn in relation to the structural element $_{2A,2B}$. ("Early" and "late" are determined by the order: Dream, Association Chain A, Association Chain B, etc., where letters are assigned to free-association chains on the basis of their chronology in the free-association session.)

(b) Where an early-appearing noun (e.g., D) later appears in a composite noun (e.g., A-D), both forms are included in the composite structuregram, and the former becomes an antecedent ($\rightarrow$) of the latter.

(c) When an early-appearing composite noun (e.g., A-B) contains a noun (e.g., A) which later appears in a second composite noun (e.g., A-D), both

composites are included in the composite structuregram, and the former becomes an antecedent (→) of the latter.

Rules (b) and (c) may be illustrated as:

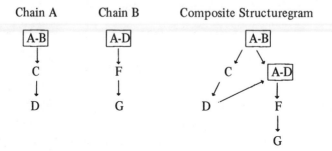

Note that the earlier-appearing joined structure A-B and separate element
D are considered antecedents of the later-appearing composite unit including
A and D.

(d) Where the association-path analysis of a later chain indicates that a
noun element had priority in that chain over another one, but where there is
a priority across chains for the other element, both forms of priority are
drawn. Thus, in the example below, where $\boxed{\text{A-B}}$ is prior to Pf in chain A, but
where an elemental component of $\boxed{\text{A-B}}$ (viz., A) appears together with Pf in
chain B such that Pf → A within that latter chain, then the composite shows
a bidirectional relationship of $\boxed{\text{A-B}}$ and Pf.

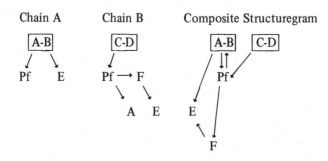

(e) Where a later (say, chain C) composite noun contains one or more
elements which appeared in different forms in earlier chains, only the earliest
such appearance is considered antecedent (→) to this later composite. For
example:

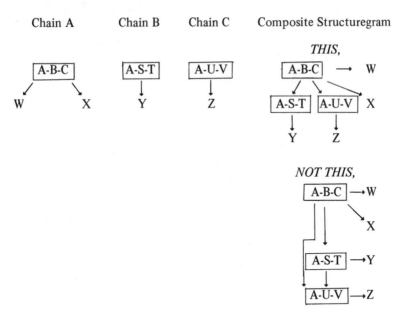

[Were *the dreamer* to explicitly associate from AST to AUV, of course, the second composite structuregram would be appropriate. This rule refers only to connections routinely assigned *by the analyst* in accord with rule (c)].

(3) For some purposes, it may be desirable to have standardization of element display within the structuregram. One solution is to follow the logic of Northway's target sociogram (1952). In a *target structuregram*, three concentric circles are drawn: elements of "deepest structure" are considered to be those referring to the family of origin (M, F, Si); elements of "intermediate depth" are those referring to peers (Pm, Pf) or mate; elements of "least deep structure" are those designated Sy or C. A vertical diagonal splits the two innermost circles, with male elements drawn to the left of the diagonal and female elements drawn to the right of the diagonal. (A more immediate solution, of course, is simply to correlate vertical structure position with row number in the association-path work sheet.)

Structuregrams of "Botanical Monograph"

Figures 13-8 to 13-14 give the dream and free-association structuregrams for the association-path analyses (figures 13-2 to 13-7) of "Botanical Monograph."

FIGURE 13-8

Structuregram for "Botanical Monograph": The Dream

FIGURE 13-9

Structuregram for "Botanical Monograph":
Free-Association Chain A

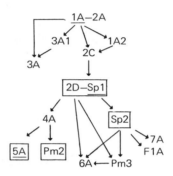

FIGURE 13-10

Structuregram for "Botanical Monograph": Free-Association Chain B

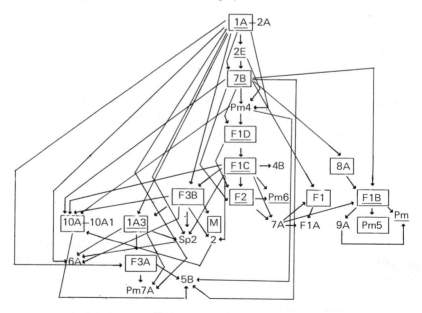

FIGURE 13-11

Structuregram for "Botanical Monograph": Free-Association Chain C

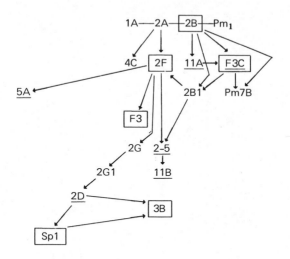

FIGURE 13-12

Structuregram for "Botanical Monograph": Free-Association Chain D

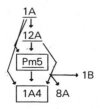

FIGURE 13-13

Structuregram for "Botanical Monograph": Free-Association Chain E

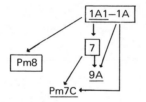

FIGURE 13-14

Structuregram for "Botanical Monograph": Free-Association Chain F

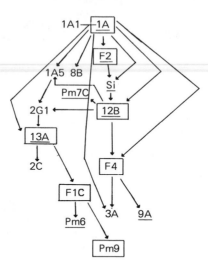

SSLS's Analysis of "Botanical Monograph": An Intuitive Evaluation

The ultimate value of SSLS's procedures for translating dream and free-association texts into sentence form (chapter 11, chapter 12, and appendix A), for organizing a subset of these sentences into paths (chapter 13, pp. 267-77), and for forming graphic structures to represent these paths (chapter 13, pp. 277-92) can be determined only through empirical research conducted with the system. To that end, chapters 14 to 17 will consider possible applications of SSLS to some of the more significant problems of dream psychology.

Meanwhile, however, there is nothing to prevent us from conducting an intuitive evaluation of the reasonableness of SSLS, as judged through the transformations it has worked on the text of "Botanical Monograph." By design, the specimen analysis has used a dream familiar to students of dreaming, and one about which much has been written by others (e.g., Fromm, 1951; Riesman, 1954; Grinstein, 1968), in addition to extensive treatment by the dreamer himself (Freud, 1900). Thus, we have certain expectations about what a decent analysis of "Botanical Monograph" should yield. These expectations have been generated by unformalized procedures whose better outcomes we wish to simulate by more lawful means. The expectations are important, actually, in two separate ways. First, they indicate a minimal set of translations we expect from any useful scoring system—if all SSLS told us from "Botanical Monograph" was that Freud disliked botany, for example, that statement, though true, wouldn't strike us as constituting a satisfactorily *complete* analysis of the text. Second, they give us the baseline against which to judge the *productivity* of the system—ideally, we would like SSLS not only to tell us some things we already "know," but also to point out some things we didn't know or fully appreciate before, but which, now having been pointed out to us, seem reasonable enough.

Let us now consider the results of the specimen analysis in this light. Judging by these results, how reasonable are the various assumptions, conventions, and rules of the content analysis itself? Of the path analysis? Of the structure formation?

It is interesting, first of all, that no symbol transformations have emerged which enable one to replace single dream terms with other single terms that convincingly explicate the dream text. Thus, the transforms which the dreamer's free associations permit of his dream sentences X-1 and X-7 only hint at possible dimensions of underlying meaning: the autobiographical and childhood sources of Freud's scholarly productivity and his alienation from colleagues and father-figures. That is, the transforms do not, in any single-minded way, enable one to "interpret" the dream satisfactorily. This outcome strikes me as being realistic. Because of their multiple associative sources, dream texts seldom should allow simple, unique symbolic resolutions.

The contribution of a dream scoring system, then, might better be evaluated in terms of its ability to reliably identify the multiple, and often conflicting, sources of dream imagery. From this perspective, it seems that SSLS has isolated many of the dream-thoughts or motives commonly ascribed to Freud from the "Botanical Monograph" text. For example:

(1) competing demands of family and work—

$$\text{(A-9)} \quad \underline{E} \rightleftharpoons Sp_1 ;$$

$$\text{(A-15)} \quad E \overset{\pm}{\rightleftharpoons} Pm_2^+ ;$$

$$\text{(A-17)} \quad E \rightleftharpoons Sy_{5A} ;$$

$$\text{(A-21)} \quad E \overset{+}{\rightarrow} Sp_2^+ ;$$

$$\text{(B-1)} \quad E \overset{+}{\underset{\odot}{\rightarrow}} \underline{Sy}_{1A}^+ ;$$

$$\text{(B-39)} \quad E \overset{+}{\underset{\odot}{\rightarrow}} Sy_{7B}^+ ;$$

$$\text{(D-11)} \quad E \rightleftharpoons Sy_{1A4}^+ ;$$

(F-24) $E \overset{+}{\to} \overset{+}{Sy}_{1A}$;

(F-54) $E \overset{+}{\to} \overset{+}{Sy}_{13A}$;

(2) ambivalence toward, and an asymmetric relationship with, his wife—

(A-9) $\underline{E} \rightleftharpoons Sp_1$;

(A-10) $[\overset{+}{Sy}_{2D} \equiv E \boxed{\to} Sp_1]$;

(C-41) $\overset{+}{Sp}_1 \overset{+}{\to} E$;

(C-42) $[\overset{+}{Sy}_{2D} \overset{\pm}{\equiv} Sp_1 \boxed{\to} E]$;

(3) temptations offered by a female-patient clientele—

(A-21) $E \overset{+}{\to} \overset{+}{Sp}_2$;

(A-31) $Sp_2 \overset{+}{\to} E$;

(A-22) $[\overset{+}{Sy}_{2D} \overset{\pm}{\equiv} E \, (Pm_3) \boxed{\to} Sp_2]$;

(A-53) $[Sy_{7A} \equiv E \, (F_{1A}) \boxed{\to} Sp_2]$;

(4) competing demands of lonely science and peer-group professionalism—

(A-15) $E \overset{\pm}{\equiv} \overset{+}{Pm}_2$;

(A-16) $[Sy_{4A} \overset{\pm}{\equiv} E \boxed{\to} Pm_2]$;

(A-17) $E \rightleftharpoons Sy_{5A}$;

(A-18) $[Sy_{4A} \equiv E \boxed{\to} Sy_{5A}]$;

(5) doubts about his ability to sustain his scholarly ambitions—

(B-9) $\underline{E} \rightleftharpoons \overset{+}{Sy}_{7B}$;

(F-28) $E \overset{\pm}{\equiv} \overset{+}{Sy}_{1A}$;

(F-28T) $E \overset{+}{\leqslant} \overset{+}{Sy}_{1A}$;

(F-28T) $\overset{\pm}{\leqslant} E, \overset{+}{Sy}_{1A}$;

(C-15) $\overset{+}{\underline{E}} \leqslant Sy_{2B}$;

(F-11) $\overset{+}{E} \overset{+}{\leqslant} Sy_{1A}$;

(C-28) $E \rightleftharpoons Sy_{2F}$;

(E-10) $[\underline{Sy}_{9A} \overset{\pm}{\equiv} E \boxed{\to} Sy_{1A,7}]$;

(E-18) $[\underline{Sy}_{1A1} \overset{\pm}{\equiv} Pm_8 \boxed{\prec} E]$;

(F-43) $[\underline{Sy}_{9A} \equiv E \boxed{\to} F_4]$;

(6) lingering conflict over the attribution of the cocaine discovery, and, in a more general vein, uncertainty over narcissistic versus communal paths to scientific discovery—

(B-8) $[E \updownarrow Sy_{1A, 2E}]$;

(B-5) $[Sy_{1A, 2E} \equiv E \, (Pm_4) \boxed{\to} Sy_{7B}]$;

(B-7) $[Sy_{1A,2E} \equiv E \boxed{\circledcirc\rightarrow} Sy_{7B}]$;

(B-68) $[Sy_{5B} \equiv E (Pm_4) \boxed{\circledcirc\rightarrow} Sy_{7B}]$;

(7) castration fantasies toward the father, and castration anxieties in regard to the father—

(B-47) $[Sy_{7A} \equiv E (F_{1C}) \boxed{\overset{}{\prec}} F_2]$;

(B-42) $E \overset{+}{\prec} F_2$;

(F-44) $F_2 \overset{}{\prec} E$;

(B-87) $E \overset{+}{\gtrless} M$;

(B-15) $[Sy_{7A} \equiv F_{1B} \boxed{\overset{}{\prec}} E]$;

(B-19) $[\overset{+}{F}_{1B} \updownarrow E]$;

(8) ambivalence toward colleagues as partaking of ambivalence to the father—

(B-45) $[Pm_6 = F_{1C}]$;

(B-43) $[E \updownarrow Pm_6]$;

(B-51) $[E \updownarrow F_{1C}]$;

(F-46) $E \rightrightarrows F_{1C}$;

(F-46T) $E \overset{}{\prec} F_{1C}$;

(F-46T) $\overset{}{\preceq} E, F_{1C}$;

(9) Freud's scholarly pursuits as the means by which he surpasses, and subdues, but is yet subdued by, the father—

(B-24) $E \circledcirc\rightarrow \overset{+}{S}y_{7B}$;

(E-9) $\underline{E} \overset{+}{\rightarrow} \overset{+}{S}y_{1A,7}$;

(B-47) $[Sy_{7A} \equiv E (F_{1C}) \boxed{\overset{}{\prec}} F_2]$;

(B-25) $[Sy_{7B} \overset{+}{\equiv} F_{1B} \boxed{\overset{}{\prec}} E]$;

(10) Fliess as the current father-surrogate, and a bivalent object of Freud's feelings—

(B-16) $[Pm_5 \equiv F_{1B} \boxed{\overset{}{\prec}} E]$;

(D-1) $Pm_5 \overset{+}{\gtrless} E$;

(D-3) $[E \updownarrow Pm_5]$;

(D-13) $E \overset{}{\prec} \overset{+}{Pm}_5$;

(11) criticisms of Freud (over his sexual theory/treatment of hysteria?)—

(B-75) $[\overset{+}{Sy}_{4B} \equiv E \boxed{\rightarrow} F_{1C}]$;

(B-98) $[Sp_2 \equiv E \boxed{\rightarrow} F_{1C}]$;

(F-52)　　$Pm_9 \preceq E$;

(F-54)　　$E \overset{+}{\rightarrow} \overset{+}{Sy}_{13}$;

and so forth.

The "Botanical Monograph" text has been so worked over that expectations of novel motive formulations are perhaps unrealistic, but SSLS does highlight a rare, and, therefore, interesting feature of the motive-packed free-association chain F, in which Freud himself found "the ultimate meaning of the dream" (1900, p. 191). This feature is the perceived interconnectedness of several modes of relationship such that, for instance, involvement ($\rightarrow$) and creation ($\circledcirc\rightarrow$) are equated with destruction ($\prec$).

Transformations of one verb to another are infrequent scores in SSLS, perhaps because the verb's meaning is so fundamental, the implied conflict so basic. Moving intimately toward something—a patient, a subject matter, a person (himself [the personal analysis]? Breuer? Fliess?)—seems, for Freud, inevitably to carry the seeds of Thanatos as well as Eros. One translation of SSLS's $\rightarrow$ verb, "penetration," carries this sense of the unity of a fundamental duality—communion/destruction. We seem to hear Freud saying, "Everything in which I invest myself or which I create, I manage to tear apart, to its (and my) detriment," a conviction he traced back to infantile fantasies of "leaf by leaf ... piecemeal dismemberment" (ibid.). Thus, in the dream, Freud's botanical investment results in an intellectual achievement—a book [$\overset{+}{Sy}_{1A}$]—at the expense of transforming live material [$\underline{Sy}_{2A}$] to inert form: the dried-out, dead botanical specimen, which perhaps has literal (the Fleischl von Marxow incident[4]) as well as symbolic (e.g., Fromm, 1951) significance for him. It is easy to imagine that Freud was content to cease associating after free-association chain F not only because he there more fully elucidated the precipitating dream-day event (the "question of my being blamed ... too much absorbed in my *favourite hobbies*") but also because he there discovered the basic "instinctual" conflicts for which he was looking.

One clear advantage of SSLS's analysis, then, is the multiplicity of motives it generates. By virtue of its exhaustive rather than intuitively selective textual analysis, SSLS both suggests the incompleteness of many earlier analyses of "Botanical Monograph" and places constraints upon selectivity in future analyses—the would-be analyst now has, laid before her or him, a large but finite set of interaction sentences to *all* of which her or his summary statements must be sensitive.

This same multiplicity of SSLS motives might, however, be viewed as a mixed blessing, or none at all. Shouldn't there be revealed one, or, at most,

---

[4]Freud in 1884 offered cocaine to his friend Fleischl as a substitute for the morphine to which he had become addicted. Freud later blamed himself for Fleischl's cocaine addiction and early death (Grinstein, 1968).

a few simple motives which underlie all of the dream text? As already discussed, probably not. Dream images derive from a complex associative network. And, are we to imagine that most or all of the numerous commentators on "Botanical Monograph," who seem to have seen different things in it, have been misled? Isn't it more likely that each has grasped at least a partial truth?

If not an ontological embarrassment, isn't this motive multiplicity a methodological one? What is one to do with all these motives? How are they to be organized or synthesized? Here SSLS has advantages yet to be demonstrated: the ease with which it can identify "conflicts" among motive structures (chapter 16) and the way in which it can formalize the interconnectedness of motive structures (their "distance" from one another, etc.; chapter 14).

With respect to the *kind* of motive structures revealed by SSLS's analysis of "Botanical Monograph," there also may be some feeling of disappointment. Is there, after all, enough *depth* to them? Wouldn't Freud's own analysis of this dream have gone "deeper"? Freud's final analysis of the dream undoubtedly delved into the infantile period and the vicissitudes of sexuality in a way that the SSLS analysis does not. And *cannot*, since any *textual* base for Freud's further motive ascriptions has been suppressed—or, perhaps, as suggested in chapter 4, the ultimate translations rest on theory, not on data at all. It clearly is unreasonable to expect SSLS, which must begin with a censored free-associative text, and only a text, to generate solutions fully commensurate with those achieved by access to the full text or by recourse to some implicit theory. We have done what *we* can with the text available. Our solutions *are* consistent with Freud's, *at that level*: both downgrade infantile factors in relation to contemporary, often work-related, ones. That is the most that can be hoped for.

This argument reminds us once again of the interrelatedness of the free-association process and the analytic resolution of the dream. As is often noted for the mathematical procedure of factor analysis, you can't get more out of an analytic system than you put into it. SSLS's scoring of the "Botanical Monograph" associations (chapter 12) indicated that there were points where Freud was purposefully vague or imprecise ("a matter which never fails to excite my feelings"; "my favourite hobbies"; etc.). The only meaningful way of resolving this kind of textual ambiguity, as already noted (chapter 11), is that the would-be user of SSLS must be sensitive, *at the time associations are generated*, to its analytic requirements. There must be pressure for clarity and fullness of expression. On hearing the free associations, the user must visualize their conformity to the requirements of SSLS's translation, path, and structural transformations. One may need to ask: "How did you get from there to there?"; "Who's that?"; "What's the connection there?" and so on. Our association generators cannot be permitted the laxity the published Freud permits himself—we must strive for the completeness and coherence the unpublished Freud undoubtedly demanded of himself. Appropriately employed, SSLS should be guiding data *collection*, as well as data *analysis*. Doesn't this imply a drastic loss of spontaneity in "free" association itself, then? Not really, for what we are asking for are clarifying probes, rather than a standardized "interview" format.

When we turn from SSLS's sentence translations to its path analyses and related structuregrams, it also appears that the "Botanical Monograph" results are intuitively satisfying. At the least, the results are not counterintuitive. They seem to follow the general logic of Freud's associative process, insofar as we can reconstruct it by sheer intuition. Thus, in the dream itself, we have as separate associative offshoots from "Botanical Monograph" its two most salient features: the colored plate and the dried specimen. The main path of free association chain A deals with Frau L.: her flowers, her forgetful husband, her treatment by Freud. Cyclamen flowers are "pivotal," in that they lead the path from symbols to characters (to Frau Freud, Frau L.'s "sister" in husbandly neglect). The major side chain deals with a parenthetical aside: "I've told this anecdote to colleagues and used it to support my theory."

Free-association chain B's main path describes the major "paternal" figures of this complex but interrelated set of recollections: Father—Koller—Königstein—Gärtner—Stricker. Cocaine is a "pivot" here, both in that it leads the main path from symbols to characters and in that it is the origin of the two most significant side chains: Berlin surgery and difficult-to-approach colleagues. The main path of chain C deals with the secondary-school recollection, with herbarium as a "pivot." The major side chain is concerned with the test over crucifers, and a side chain off that brings us to the more contemporary wife/artichoke situation. In chain D, dream-book is the "pivot," and the Fliess relationship the characterological "goal." Chain E remains fairly close to its "bookish" stimulus (Freud's obsession, as a student, with medical monographs), while a side chain introduces the jeering colleague.

Free-association chain F's main path also hews closely to "books"—the book destroyed by Freud and his sister, the bookseller, etc.—while a large side chain deals with screen memories, artichokes, and hobbies, as well as with the Königstein conversation. The side chain, in short, masses together precisely that material wherein Freud himself found the main symbolic and literal indications of the determinants of the dream as a whole.

If SSLS's organization of these data strikes the reader as being unexceptional in comparison to the results of earlier, intuitive analyses of "Botanical Monograph," it needs to be pointed out that the analysis possesses three great advantages not shared by "intuitional" methods. It is comprehensive. It is ruleful. And, it is reliable (see appendix B).

The fit of SSLS to "Botanical Monograph" may not seem compelling, since it will be imagined that SSLS's own rules have been juggled about precisely to produce that fit. This certainly was true of early versions of SSLS. The present version, however, evolved from analysis of other dream materials, and the results in both chapter 12 and this one reflect a return of SSLS to "Botanical Monograph" after a year or more's continuous revision based on these other materials. The rules now being "turned back" on "Botanical Monograph" often bear very little resemblance to those originally generated by it.

Nonetheless, the criticism is just in the sense that the ultimate proof of the pudding is whether it will be edible in other contexts. That is something which can't yet be judged. But, so far at least, SSLS does seem to meet the minimal (necessary, but not sufficient) requirement that it be faithful to its own data base. We now must turn to a consideration of those other contexts in which its final utility is to be determined.

CHAPTER 14

From Structure
to Matrix to Index

Overview

We now turn to the question of how SSLS's linguistic dream codes facilitate the study of the processes and structures of the sleeping mind. Structuregrams presented for "Botanical Monograph" (figures 13-9 to 13-14, pp. 290-92) indicate a free-association flow outward from one or more sentences in the manifest dream. For any such structuregram, S, there is a *converse*, S', containing the same points but reversing the direction of each arrow, so that distant free-associative points now are the source of a flow toward the manifest dream sentence(s). Figure 14-1, for instance, presents the structuregram S' of free-association chain A of "Botanical Monograph."

It is the structuregram S' which is of interest to dream-process psychology. It was on the basis of an intuitive understanding of such a structuregram that Freud attempted to characterize the laws of mental organization which permit the transformation of conflicting mental structures into manifest dream imagery. These laws are summarized in Freud's concept of "dreamwork," and include condensation, displacement, and a concern with pictorial representability (see chapter 4).

Freud's complete dream-process psychology, of course, includes con-

FIGURE 14-1

Structuregram S′ for Free-Association Chain A

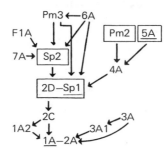

More formally,

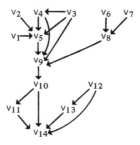

sideration not only of these dream-work transformations (the "physiology" of the sleeping mind) but also of the structures so transformed (the "anatomy" of the sleeping mind). According to Freud, the dream is explained when we can start with certain identifiable premises (conflicting mental structures) and then show, on the basis of an understanding of the intervening processes of psycho-logic which characterize the state of sleep (the "dream-work"), how these premises might have generated a certain manifest dream (see chapter 4).

Having now arrived at a more reliable and formalized conception of S′ than Freud, we also are able to suggest more reliable and formalized ways of analyzing S′ than the intuitive processes so brilliantly pursued by Freud. Noting that S′ always will consist, in essence, of a finite series of points and a finite set of directed lines linking these points, that there will be no *parallel lines* contained therein (i.e., SSLS imposes the constraint on its structuregrams that one and only one A → B line may be drawn), and that there are no *loops* contained therein (i.e., SSLS imposes the additional constraint that there can be no reflexive—e.g., A⟲—lines in its structuregrams), then we see that S′ is what mathematicians call a *digraph*. Since it is known that a powerful series of mathematical operations can be performed on digraphs to reveal structural properties of the empirical entities mapped into their points and lines, we therefore have brought our dream-process and dream-structure interests into coordination with a set of valuable mathematical tools.

Harary, Norman, and Cartwright (1965) have thoroughly described these mathematical tools and have considered their potential relevance to psychology (predominantly social psychology, where digraph points are people and digraph lines are affectional or communicative relationships between people). In order that the presentation of this monograph be self-contained, however, I now will sketch in certain basic features of digraph analysis. The presentation generally will closely follow Harary et al., although certain points of major interest to them will be omitted. In addition, many niceties of their mathematical detail will be glossed over. After the review of digraph operations themselves, we will be in a position to consider their relevance to dream-process psychology (chapter 15).

Fundamentals of Digraph Theory

Kinds of Digraphs

Four classes of digraphs, D, may be distinguished:

(1) *strong digraphs*, where every two points $(v_1 v_2)$ are mutually reachable (there is a path $v_1 \rightarrow v_2$ and a path $v_2 \rightarrow v_1$);
(2) *unilateral digraphs*, where for every two points $(v_1 v_2)$ at least one is reachable from the other (there is either a path $v_1 \rightarrow v_2$ or a path $v_2 \rightarrow v_1$ or both);
(3) *weak digraphs*, where every two points $(v_1 v_2)$ are joined by one or more lines of any directionality;
(4) *disconnected digraphs*, where none of the above conditions holds true.

These definitions require further explanation. First, however, we may illustrate the four classes of digraphs (figure 14-2) and consider their relevance to our case, S'.

It is clear that S' never can be disconnected (D4). Each element in a free-association structuregram always will "reach" the manifest-dream element it helps to explain, and hence, it will be joined with all other such elements,

FIGURE 14-2

Examples of Digraph Classes

(v_1, v_2, and v_3 are points)

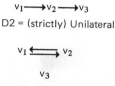

D1 = Strong

D2 = (strictly) Unilateral

D3 = (strictly) Weak

D4 = Disconnected

which will have the same property. Both the nature of the free-association process generating the data mapped into S' and the ways we have chosen to organize these data in structuregrams guarantee that this always will be the case. At the other extreme, though theoretically possible in a composite structuregram, it seems quite unlikely that S' ever will be strong (D1), i.e., that each element in the association structure will stimulate and be stimulated by every other such element. For any one free-associational chain, a strong S' simply is precluded by the rules governing structuregram formation. Thus S' must be either unilateral (D2) or weak (D3).

S' would be unilateral in cases where the associational "tree" had no "branches", i.e., where the dreamer's associations are of the form "X reminds me of Y which, in turn, reminds me of Z." The more typical case, however, would be that where, due to some combination of subject conscientiousness and experimenter direction, the dreamer's associations are of the form "X reminds me of Y; Y reminds me both of the sequence A, B, and C, and of the sequence D, E, and F." Thus our primary interest in digraph analysis will be in a D which is weak. To be more precise, since any strong or unilateral D also is weak, and since any strong D also is unilateral, our major interest will be in cases where D is *strictly weak* (conditions of weakness but not of unilaterality are met), with peripheral interest attaching to the case where it is *strictly unilateral* (conditions of unilaterality but not of strength are met).

Kinds of Connectedness

This classification of digraphs obviously rests upon consideration of the way in which points are "connected" with one another. Digraph theory formalizes the notion of connectedness, and thus amplifies the definitions of D classes given above, in the following way. A *semipath* is a collection of n points and n - 1 lines in either direction, e.g., $v_1 \to v_2 \to v_3 \leftarrow v_4$. A *di-*

rected path is a collection of n points and n – 1 lines in a common direction, e.g., $v_1 \to v_2 \to v_3 \to v_4$. All directed paths, or more simply *paths*, are semipaths, but not vice versa, so we also may distinguish semipaths which are not paths as *strict semipaths*. Therefore, S' is strictly unilateral where all points are joined by one or more paths and at least two points, v_1 and v_2, are so joined only unidirectionally, while S' is strictly weak where all such points are joined by a semipath and at least two points, v_1 and v_2, are joined only by a strict semipath. *Reachability*, in our definitions of strong and unilateral digraphs, is defined in terms of paths. Point v_2 is *reachable* from point v_1 if and only if there is some path from v_1 to v_2. *Joining*, in our definition of weak digraphs, is defined in terms of semipaths. Points v_1 and v_2 are *joined* if there is some semipath between them.

In the weak digraph D3, portrayed in figure 14-2, point pairs $v_1 v_3$ and $v_2 v_3$ are connected by a path, while point pair $v_1 v_2$ is joined only by the strict semipath: $v_1 \to v_3 \leftarrow v_2$. Point v_3 is reachable from points v_1 and v_2; points v_1 and v_2 are joined but neither is reachable from the other. Were v_1 and v_2 persons in a social network, we might say that v_1 and v_2 were joined in the sense that both could contribute input to v_3 (a communication network) or that both were attracted to v_3 (a sociometric network). For our dream case, S', we expect to find a number of cases where two associative elements are joined only in the sense that they converge upon some common third element.

An alternative terminology for describing the connectedness of points which proves useful in certain contexts is the following. For any pair of points, v_1 and v_2, we say they are:

1-connected, if they are joined by a strict semipath;

2-connected, if they are joined by either some path from v_1 to v_2 or by some path from v_2 to v_1, but not both;

3-connected, if they are joined by paths both from v_1 to v_2 and from v_2 to v_1.

Thus a strictly weak D (C = 1) is one in which all points are at least 1-connected and in which at least two points, v_1 and v_2, are only 1-connected. A strictly unilateral D (C = 2) is one in which all points are at least 2-connected and in which at least two points, v_1 and v_2, are only 2-connected. (For disconnected D's, C = 0; for strong ones, C = 3). In an S', all points will be 2-connected with the manifest dream (2-joined to it), but usually not with one another.

Kinds of Points

So far we have been concerned primarily with the characterization of D as a whole, although this has involved a more microscopic analysis of the connectedness of single pairs of points. Digraph theory also supplies several interesting ways of characterizing the points themselves.

Basic to one such characterization is the concept of an *adjacency matrix* for D: A(D). Any entry a_{ij} in the ith row and j^{th} column of A(D) will be 1 if a line exists in D which leads from the point represented by the ith row to the point represented by the jth column, and 0 if no such line exists. Thus, the A matrix for the strictly unilateral D2 of figure 14-2 would be

$$
A(D2) = \begin{array}{c|ccc}
 & v_1 & v_2 & v_3 \\
v_1 & 0 & 1 & 0 \\
v_2 & 0 & 0 & 1 \\
v_3 & 0 & 0 & 0
\end{array}
$$

while for the strictly weak D3 of the same figure it would be

$$
A(D3) = \begin{array}{c|ccc}
 & v_1 & v_2 & v_3 \\
v_1 & 0 & 0 & 1 \\
v_2 & 0 & 0 & 1 \\
v_3 & 0 & 0 & 0
\end{array}
$$

Since, by definition of D, loops are not permitted, the diagonal entries of A(D) always will be 0. A(D) proves to be a matrix of great importance in other contexts, since many other matrices can be generated from it strictly by matrix-algebra operations. Here, however, we consider some point properties which A(D) defines.

The row sum of point v_i gives its *outdegree* (od). Thus, both in A(D2) and in A(D3), $od(v_1) = 1$, $od(v_2) = 1$, and $od(v_3) = 0$. The column sum of point v_i gives its *indegree* (id). In A(D2), $id(v_1) = 0$, $id(v_2) = 1$, and $id(v_3) = 1$; while in A(D3), $id(v_1) = 0$, $id(v_2) = 0$, and $id(v_3) = 2$. Outdegree gives the number of lines in an *outbundle* from a point, while indegree gives the number of lines in an *inbundle* to a point; outdegree gives the number of points *adjacent from* a point, while indegree gives the number of points *adjacent to* a point. The sum of all row sums equals the sum of all column sums equals the number of discrete lines in D.

A point is said to be a *transmitter* when od > 0 and id $= 0$; a point is a *receiver* when od = 0 and id > 0, and a point is a *carrier* when od = id = 1 (any *other* point is called an *ordinary point*). Thus in D2, figure 14-2, v_1 is a transmitter, v_2 is a carrier, and v_3 is a receiver, while in D3, v_1 and v_2 are transmitters and v_3 is a receiver. It will be a property of S, any free-association structuregram (excepting perhaps certain composite structuregrams), that a dream element will be a transmitter point, and of S', its converse generated for purposes of studying dream formation, that a dream element will be a receiver point.

Nontrivial semipaths and nontrivial paths (i.e., those involving more than one point and zero lines) may be defined in terms of transmitter (t) points, receiver (r) points, and carrier (c) points. A nontrivial semipath exists where, in a succession of joined points, neither the first nor last is c, there is an r between any two t's, and there is a t between any two r's. This also will be a nontrivial path if and only if there is exactly one t and one r in the sequence; otherwise it will be a strict semipath. A *maximal path* in any semipath L is contained in L, but is not a subpath of any longer path in L; it will consist of one r, one t, and any number of c's ≥ 0. Any two maximal paths in L can have only one point in common, a *linking* point. Thus in D3, figure 14-2, $v_1 \rightarrow v_3$ and $v_2 \rightarrow v_3$ are maximal paths in the semipath $v_1 v_2$, and v_3 is a linking point.

Matrix Generation: Reachability

One useful property of A(D) for our purposes is that, by interchanging its rows and columns, we get A(D'). For example, consider the converse of D3:

D3'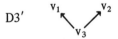

By the operation just proposed (i.e., making the nth row of A(D3) the nth column of A(D3')), the adjacency matrix A(D3'), or simply A', should be:

$$A(D3') = \begin{array}{c|ccc} & v_1 & v_2 & v_3 \\ \hline v_1 & 0 & 0 & 0 \\ v_2 & 0 & 0 & 0 \\ v_3 & 1 & 1 & 0 \end{array}$$

The result clearly agrees with our inspection of the structuregram D3'. Thus we see that there will be no difficulty in going from A(S) to A(S'), i.e., in deriving an adjacency matrix for S', the dream-formation model, from the adjacency matrix for S, the free-associational structuregram.

A' is useful in another respect, the product AA' giving for each v_{ii} entry the outdegree of v_i, and for each v_{ij} entry, the number of points to which v_i and v_j both are adjacent. The product A'A, on the other hand, gives as its v_{ii} entry the indegree of v_i, and for each v_{ij} entry the number of points from which both v_i and v_j are adjacent.

Thus the product $A(D3) \times A(D3')$ is

$$
AA' = \begin{array}{c|ccc} & v_1 & v_2 & v_3 \\ \hline v_1 & 1 & 1 & 0 \\ v_2 & 1 & 1 & 0 \\ v_3 & 0 & 0 & 0 \end{array}
$$

Referring back to D3, figure 14-2 (p. 303), we see that the outdegree of v_1 is 1 (entry v_{11}), the outdegree of v_2 is 1 (entry v_{22}) and the outdegree of v_3 (entry v_{33}) is 0. We see that v_1 and v_2 (entry $v_1 v_2$ or $v_2 v_1$) are adjacent to exactly one common point, which is, of course, v_3.

Obviously, however, neither A(D) nor A(D') by itself immediately reveals important properties of the "connectedness of points" in D; A(D) does not directly tell us, for example, for D2, figure 14-2, that, while v_3 is not adjacent from v_1, it is reachable from v_1. Another useful matrix, then, will be a *reachability matrix*, R(D). An entry r_{ij} in R will be 1 if any path leads from the point represented by the ith row to the point represented by the jth column, and 0 if no such path exists. We assume that if the two points are identical, there is reachability, hence diagonal entries always are 1's. Thus by inspection of D2, figure 14-2, we have R(D2):

$$
R(D2) = \begin{array}{c|ccc} & v_1 & v_2 & v_3 \\ \hline v_1 & 1 & 1 & 1 \\ v_2 & 0 & 1 & 1 \\ v_3 & 0 & 0 & 1 \end{array}
$$

It is important to note, however, that one need not rely on inspection to form R(D2). It can be derived mathematically from A(D2). More generally, where we have p points in D, we need to multiply A(D) by itself p − 1 times to find if there is any sequence of length n from any point v_i to v_j. If the entry of any matrix A^1 to A^{p-1} is 1, then v_j is reachable from v_i. Formally, $R = (I + A)^{p-1}\#$, where I is an identity matrix, with 1's in the

diagonal and 0's elsewhere (recall that in A, where $v_i = v_j$, we do not consider a point adjacent to itself, whereas in R, where $v_i = v_j$, we do want to
consider it reachable from itself), and # indicates that we are to use Boolean
arithmetic, in which $1 + 1 = 1$.

Performing this operation on A(D2) above, we get

$$I + A(D2) = \begin{matrix} 1 & 1 & 0 \\ 0 & 1 & 1 \\ 0 & 0 & 1 \end{matrix}$$

Matrix multiplication operations give us $(I + A(D2))^2$ #:

$$(I + A(D2))^2 \# = \begin{matrix} 1 & 1 & 1 \\ 0 & 1 & 1 \\ 0 & 0 & 1 \end{matrix}$$

With $p = 3$, $(p - 1) = 2$, hence $(I + A(D2))^2$ is identical to R(D2), as may be
verified by a comparison with the R matrix generated by inspection above.
The important point here is that R(D) for any matrix D need not be ascertained by visual inspection, which may prove difficult and fallible in the
case of complicated D's, but can be generated mathematically from A(D).

Note also that, in general, A^n # tells if there is a sequence of length n
from v_i to v_j, e.g., entries in $A(D2)^2$ # will tell us whether v_j is reachable from
v_i by way of a path consisting of two discrete lines. Since $A(D2)^2$ # is:

$$\begin{matrix} 0 & 0 & 1 \\ 0 & 0 & 0 \\ 0 & 0 & 0 \end{matrix}$$

we see that v_3 is reachable from v_1 at distance 2, and that this describes the
only reachability at this distance within D2. We also see that

$$R(D) = [I + A(D) + A(D)^2 + \cdots \cdots + A(D)^{p-1}] \#$$

That is, a $1^{i,j}$ entry in I or any $A(D)^n$ # matrix up to $n = p - 1$ means that
there will be a $1^{i,j}$ entry in R(D). If none of these matrices contains an i, j
entry of 1, then the i, j entry in R(D) will be 0.

Note, too, that the formula $R = (I + A)^{n-1}$ #, where $n \leqslant p$ will give us
a subset of the reachabilities within D which we define as the *n-reachable*

subset $R_n(v)$ of all reachabilities R of point v. Thus we can define not only reachabilities within D, but also *limited reachabilities* within D. Where v_j is reachable from v_i, but is not $\leq$ n-reachable, for instance, we might consider v_j, for our particular purposes, as essentially unreachable from v_i. We can, therefore, for any $n < p$ define a set of reachabilities which accord with our stricter standard that, to be of interest to us, points must be $\leq$ n-reachable, and we can ascertain these reachabilities purely mathematically. In a dream-formation structuregram S', for instance, we might decide that we wish to consider points associated with interaction statements in formal "conflict" with one another as generating "significant" conflict if and only if one is reachable from the other within a certain distance. We now see that such n-reachable conflicts can be identified by mathematical operations performed on A(S').

Where we are concerned with a slightly different question than considered above, that is, with the *number* of sequences of length n from v_i to v_j, entries in A^n will give those numbers. Entries in the matrix A^2, for example, indicate the number of sequences of length 2 from v_i to v_j. Thus, to take an example given by Harary et al. (1965, p. 112), where

$$
A = \begin{array}{c|cccc}
 & v_1 & v_2 & v_3 & v_4 \\
\hline
v_1 & 0 & 0 & 1 & 0 \\
v_2 & 1 & 0 & 0 & 0 \\
v_3 & 0 & 1 & 0 & 1 \\
v_4 & 1 & 0 & 1 & 0 \\
\end{array}
$$

then

$$
A^2 = \begin{array}{c|cccc}
 & v_1 & v_2 & v_3 & v_4 \\
\hline
v_1 & 0 & 1 & 0 & 1 \\
v_2 & 0 & 0 & 1 & 0 \\
v_3 & 2 & 0 & 1 & 0 \\
v_4 & 0 & 1 & 1 & 1 \\
\end{array}
$$

which states, for example, that there is one sequence of length 2 between point v_1 and v_2, that there are two sequences of length 2 between v_3 and v_1, and that there are no sequences of length 2 between v_4 and v_1. Inspection of the digraph D5, which generated A, reveals these statements to be correct.

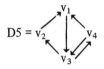

$$D5 = v_2$$

The expansion A^n gives, strictly speaking, the number of *sequences* of length n between v_i and v_j, not the number of paths between them (sequences of length *n* may include a given point more than once, while paths of length *n* always include n – 1 discrete points). A *path-matrix*, P_n, giving the number of paths between v_i and v_j, also may be obtained mathematically. From P_n, a *detour-matrix* also may be derived, giving the paths of *maximal* length between any v_i and v_j.

Further explication is needed of the notion of reachable sets. The *reachable set* R(v) of any point v is the collection of all points reachable from v. The reachable set R(S) of a set (S) of points is the collection of all points reachable from any point contained in S. The *point basis* of D is the minimum collection of D points where R(S) = V, V representing all the points v_1 – v_p within D, where no subset of S has this same property. The *antecedent set* Q(v) of any point v is the collection of all points from which v is reachable. The antecedent set Q(S) of a set (S) of points is the collection of all points from which any point in S is reachable. The *point contrabasis* of D is the minimum collection of D points where Q(S) = V, V representing all the points v_1 – v_p within D, where no subset of S has this same property. Any point v is a *source* of D if R(v) = V; any point v is a *sink* of D if Q(v) = V. If there is only one such point v, we speak of a *unique source* or a *unique sink*, and D has a point basis or point contrabasis consisting of only one point. Generally speaking, our free-association structuregram S will have a unique source, and our dream-formation structuregram S′ will have a unique sink, the point in each case representing the associated-to element of the manifest dream.

Matrix Generation: Fundamental Sets

A maximal reachable set of points within D is a *fundamental set*, while a maximal antecedent set of points within D is a *contrafundamental set*. Consider digraph D2, figure 14-2 (p. 303). The reachable set from v_2 is v_2, v_3; since the reachable set from v_1, however, is v_1, v_2, v_3, it is this latter set which is fundamental. Likewise, the antecedent set for v_2 is v_1, v_2; but since the antecedent set for v_3 is v_1, v_2, v_3, it is this latter set which is contrafundamental. A digraph has a source if and only if it has exactly one fundamental set; it has a sink if and only if it has exactly one contrafundamental set. The point v defining these sets would be, respectively, either the *origin* or the *terminus* of the set. It is clear that the associated-to elements in a dream generally will be an origin of a free-association fundamental set, but the terminus of a dream-formation contrafundamental set. In the latter case, there may be one (strictly unilateral D) or more than one (strictly weak D) fundamental set. Also in the latter case, any set of points consisting of one origin from each fundamental set will be the point basis of the digraph. One set of points of particular interest in a strictly weak D with >1 fundamental set will be those lying within the *intersection* of the two or more fundamental sets contained within D. In social-psychological models, these points might be people subject to "conflict" on account of their being subject to different channels of information or influence. Clearly the conflict concept also might apply to the dream-formation case as well, although it would be intrapsychic rather than interpersonal in nature.

The fundamental sets of D can be determined by matrix operations. One starts with the R matrix and then forms R'. This is illustrated now for D2, figure 14-2, whose reachability matrix R(D2) is repeated below:

$$
\begin{array}{c c c c}
 & v_1 & v_2 & v_3 \\
v_1 & 1 & 1 & 1 \\
R(D2) = v_2 & 0 & 1 & 1 \\
v_3 & 0 & 0 & 1 \\
\Sigma v_i & 1 & 2 & 3 \\
\end{array}
$$

Note that v_1 is a unique source of D2. The converse matrix $R(D2')$, or R', is formed following procedures already described:

$$
\begin{array}{c c c c}
 & v_1 & v_2 & v_3 \\
R(D2') = v_1 & 1 & 0 & 0 \\
v_2 & 1 & 1 & 0 \\
v_3 & 1 & 1 & 1 \\
\end{array}
$$

Note that v_3 is a unique source of D2'. An *elementwise* product $R \times R'$ then is computed:

$$
\begin{array}{c c c c c}
 & v_1 & v_2 & v_3 & \Sigma v_i \\
R \times R' = v_1 & 1 & 0 & 0 & 1 \\
v_2 & 0 & 1 & 0 & 1 \\
v_3 & 0 & 0 & 1 & 1 \\
\end{array}
$$

Where the row sum of v_i in $R \times R'$ is equivalent to a column sum of v_i in R, the element v_i is an origin of a fundamental set. Hence point v_1 is the origin of a fundamental set in D2. Furthermore, those points whose entry in the ith row of R is 1 comprise the fundamental set. Hence the fundamental set in D2 with origin v_1 includes v_1, v_2, v_3. Note that a fundamental set may contain more than one origin, as in the following digraph, D6.

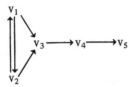

Here both v_1 and v_2 are origins of the fundamental set v_1, v_2, v_3, v_4, v_5.

Matrix Generation: Distance

Our discussion of reachability spirited in another useful concept which now needs more careful examination: distance. We see, for example, that both in $v_1 \to v_2 \to v_3 \to v_4 \to v_5 \to v_6$ and in $v_1 \to v_6$, v_6 is reachable from v_1, but v_6 is "closer" to v_1 in the second case than in the first. We define the *geodesic* of points v_1 and v_2 as the path of minimal length connecting v_1 and v_2. Thus, for the following digraph, D7, line x is the geodesic connecting v_1 to v_2.

Note that digraphs are transitive, in that if v_1 can reach v_3, and v_3 can reach v_2, then v_1 can reach v_2, and that where d = distance, $d(v_1 v_2) \leqslant d(v_1 v_3) + d(v_3 v_2)$.

A distance matrix N(D) giving all geodesic lengths between points v_i and v_j in D can be obtained from A(D) by matrix operations: (1) If the reachability from v_i to $v_j = 0$, then $d_{i,j} = \infty$; (2) the entry in N(D) for v_{ii}, from any point v to that same point v, is 0; hence diagonal entries in N(D) always are 0; (3) other entries of the N(D) matrix are filled as follows: $d_{i,j}$ is the smallest power n to which A must be raised so that $a_{ij}{}^n \# = 1$. Alternatively, of course, the distance matrix N(D) can be obtained by inspection of the digraph D. For digraph D5 (p. 310),

	v_1	v_2	v_3	v_4
v_1	0	2	1	2
$N(D5) = v_2$	1	0	2	3
v_3	2	1	0	1
v_4	1	2	1	0

Now, since a point v_k is on the geodesic between v_i and v_j if and only if $d_{ik} + d_{kj} = d_{ij}$, we then can use the row and column entries of N(D) to find the geodesics from v_i to v_j. To find the geodesics from v_3 to v_1, for example, we align the N(D) matrix row for v_3 and the matrix column for v_1 as follows:

	v_1	v_2	v_3	v_4	
from v_3	2	1	0	1	$(d_{v3,k})$
to v_1	0	1	2	1	$(d_{k,v1})$
	—	—	—	—	
	2	2	2	2	

Since, in this case, all points have $d = 2$, which corresponds to the $v_3 - v_1$ entry in N(D), all lie on the geodetic subgraph from v_3 to v_1. The points giving rise to these column sums then are arranged in order of their distance from v_3, e.g., $v_3 - v_2 - v_1$ since the corresponding distances from v_3 are 0-1-2 and $v_3 - v_4 - v_1$ since the corresponding distances from v_3 are 0-1-2. We then check D5 to see whether either or both of these paths are contained therein. Both paths are present in D, and both are geodesics from v_1 to v_3.

Descriptive Indices

We now consider some indices which combine the concepts of reachability and distance in describing properties of D. The *outnumber* of a point v, o(v), is the largest entry in v's row in the distance matrix N(D). The *innumber* of a point v, i(v), is the largest entry in v's column in the distance matrix N(D). The *associated number pair* of v is defined as o(v), i(v). For point v_1 in digraph D5 (p. 310), the *associated number pair* is 2,2. If v is a source, it may further be defined as an n-source, where n = o(v). If v is a sink, it may further be defined as an n-sink, where n = i(v).

Distance indices include: the *distance sum d_i from point v_i*, i.e., the sum of finite entries in v_i's row in N(D); the *distance sum d_j to point v_j*, i.e., the sum of finite entries in v_j's column in N(D). For digraph D5, the distance sum d_i for point v_1 is 5, while the distance sum d_j for the same point v_1 is 4. One also may compute Σd_{ij}, the *sum of all finite distances* in N(D). For D5 above, $\Sigma d_{ij} = 19$. In communication networks, Σd_i gives the cost or effort involved in transmission of a message from person v_i to all persons reachable by that person. Of more direct relevance to the dream-formation digraph S' is the notion that as Σd_i increases, so does message "distortion" for messages initiated by v_i.

Components and Other Structural Properties

A generally important middle-range concept, between that of the single point, on the one hand, and that of the total collection of points in D, on the other, is that of D's *components*. A subgraph ⟨S⟩ is defined as a subgraph of D with point set S and containing all lines from D which join these points. Subgraphs are *maximal* for a certain property, such as unilaterality, if they have it, as do no larger subgraphs of which they are part. Thus we can speak of D's *strong components* (maximal subgraphs for the property of strength), *unilateral components* (maximal subgraphs for the property of unilaterality), and *weak components* (maximal subgraphs for the property of weakness). Every point of D is contained in exactly one weak component and in exactly one strong component. It lies within at least one unilateral component. We can speak for any point v_i of components defined in reference to that point.

Since the dream case most often will deal with weak digraphs, we now apply the component concept to the weak digraph D3, figure 14-2 (p. 303). Strong components of any point v_i in D are given by entries of 1 in the v_i row of the elementwise product R × R'. For D3 we have:

$$
R = \begin{array}{c|ccc}
 & v_1 & v_2 & v_3 \\
\hline
v_1 & 1 & 0 & 1 \\
v_2 & 0 & 1 & 1 \\
v_3 & 0 & 0 & 1
\end{array}
\qquad
R' = \begin{array}{c|ccc}
 & v_1 & v_2 & v_3 \\
\hline
v_1 & 1 & 0 & 0 \\
v_2 & 0 & 1 & 0 \\
v_3 & 1 & 1 & 1
\end{array}
$$

$$
R \times R' = \begin{array}{c|ccc}
 & v_1 & v_2 & v_3 \\
\hline
v_1 & 1 & 0 & 0 \\
v_2 & 0 & 1 & 0 \\
v_3 & 0 & 0 & 1
\end{array}
$$

Thus, in the typical dream digraph, the only strong components generally will be single points, e.g., strong component v_i for point v_i. Exceptions will occur in composite structuregrams where there is mutual reachability of points: $v_1 \rightleftarrows v_2$.

If the notion of strong components generally leads to structural units of triviality, i.e., we simply return to the points of D, the notion of weak components leads to units of hopeless generality. By definition, every point in a weak D is weakly connected to every other point in that D. Weak components, given by entries of 1 in the row for element v_i in the matrix $(I + A + A')^{p-1}\#$, always will be universal within D. That is, all points of D will comprise the weak component for any point, v_i.

Unilateral components, which need not be unique for any point v_i, can be defined in reference to the matrix $(R + R')\#$. For D3,

$$(R + R')\# = \begin{array}{c|ccc} & v_1 & v_2 & v_3 \\ \hline v_1 & 1 & 0 & 1 \\ v_2 & 0 & 1 & 1 \\ v_3 & 1 & 1 & 1 \end{array}$$

All points of D3 lie on at least one nontrivial unilateral component, since there is at least one nondiagonal 1 entry in $(R + R')\#$ for each such point. The unilateral components of D3 are $\langle v_1 v_3 \rangle$ and $\langle v_2 v_3 \rangle$, corresponding to its fundamental sets.

The connectedness of all points in D may be expressed by the connectedness matrix, C(D), whose entries, 0-3, express the degrees of connectedness defined earlier. Entries v_{ij} of C(D) for any weak D are obtained by the formula: v_{ij} entry in R + v_{ij} entry in R' + 1. Thus, for D3,

$$C(D3) = \begin{array}{c|ccc} & v_1 & v_2 & v_3 \\ \hline v_1 & 3 & 1 & 2 \\ v_2 & 1 & 3 & 2 \\ v_3 & 2 & 2 & 3 \end{array}$$

The minimal entry in C(D) gives the category of the whole D. Here, as we already know, D3 is weak (C = 1). Strong components for point v_i are given by 3 entries in v_i's row. Weak components for v_i are given by nonzero entries in v_i's row.

Other structural properties may be assigned to points and lines in D. Line X is a *bridge* if it is the only *semipath* joining two points. Line X is *basic* if it is the only *path* joining two points. In any weak digraph, a line is a bridge if and only if removal of that line will generate a D for which C = 0, i.e., a disconnected D. Where C_i defines D, and C_j defines D - X, X is a bridge where it is an i, j line defined by i, 0. If line X is not basic, it is *neutral*— i.e., i = j, or, removal of the line will not affect the connectedness, C, of D. Thus some lines in any D may prove more critical to its preservation of certain structural properties than will other ones.

It can be shown that, in general, an index of the structural complexity of D based simply on the number of lines in D will not prove highly predictive of D's *connectedness* properties. Nonetheless, within a given C category, it may index other properties of D which have some useful empirical applications. Thus, if we define the *line requirement* of D $[1r(D)]$, as the minimal number of lines whose presence is required to prevent a decrease in C's index number, then the *line surplus* of D $[1s(D)]$ may be defined as the maximum number of lines in a set of lines in D, such that that set is neutral. For a strictly weak D, $1r(D) = p - 1$, where p = the number of points in D, and $1s(D)$ = actual number of lines in D minus the quantity $(p - 1)$. (The actual number of lines in $D = \Sigma a_{ij}$ in A(D).) The *line basis* of D is that minimal set of lines needed to preserve the condition that R(D) remains intact.

Two paths (or semipaths) between v_1 and v_2 are called *point-disjoint* where their only common points are v_1 and v_2. They are *line-disjoint* where they share no common line. A point v_1 is *1-between* two other points if every semipath joining these two points goes through v_1. Such a point is called a *cutpoint*. Removal of a cutpoint disconnects D, just as does removal of a bridge. Hence both concepts refer to vulnerable elements of D.

A *block*, B, of D is a maximal weak subgraph of D containing no point v such that the digraph B - v will have C = 0, i.e., will be disconnected. Every line of D is in exactly one block. Every point other than a cutpoint in D is in exactly one block. Every cutpoint in D lies in more than one block. Consider:

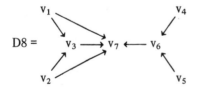

D8 itself is a maximal weak subgraph. However, it does not have the property of a block, since removal of points v_6 or v_7 will disconnect it. No weak D can itself be a block if it contains cutpoints. Knowing that v_6 and v_7 are cutpoints, we look for the > 1 blocks they define, since whenever two points of a weak D are not in a common block, there is a cutpoint on every semipath between them.

$B_1 = v_1, v_2, v_3, v_7$
$B_2 = v_6 v_7$
$B_3 = v_4 v_6$
$B_4 = v_5 v_6$

Now blocks B_2-B_4 for D8 are trivial in the sense that removal of a point v_n will result in a maximal strong subgraph which is trivial, consisting of the trivial strong component which is the remaining point. B_1, however, is of interest to us, since for any dream-formation structuregram S', it is an empirically realizable structural component whose range lies between D as a whole and v_n as a trivial microlevel component.

Cycles and Levels

A *cycle* can be defined as any path from v_1 to v_n in conjunction with a discrete line back from v_n to v_1. A *semicycle* is any semipath from v_1 to v_n in conjunction with a discrete line between v_n and v_1. Our dream-formation structuregrams most often will be *acyclic*, i.e., without any pair of mutually reachable points. D8 is such a digraph. In such cases (cf. also D3, p. 303), the adjacency matrix can be made *upper-triangular*, i.e., constructed so that all nonzero entries lie (*on*, which does not apply to the A matrix, *or*) *above* the diagonal.

$$
A(D8) = \begin{array}{c c}
 & \begin{array}{ccccccc} v_1 & v_2 & v_3 & v_4 & v_5 & v_6 & v_7 \end{array} \\
\begin{array}{c} v_1 \\ v_2 \\ v_3 \\ v_4 \\ v_5 \\ v_6 \\ v_7 \end{array} &
\begin{array}{ccccccc}
0 & 0 & 1 & 0 & 0 & 0 & 1 \\
0 & 0 & 1 & 0 & 0 & 0 & 1 \\
0 & 0 & 0 & 0 & 0 & 0 & 1 \\
0 & 0 & 0 & 0 & 0 & 1 & 0 \\
0 & 0 & 0 & 0 & 0 & 1 & 0 \\
0 & 0 & 0 & 0 & 0 & 0 & 1 \\
0 & 0 & 0 & 0 & 0 & 0 & 0
\end{array}
\end{array}
$$

In such a matrix it is possible to designate points by *level* indices, numbers from 1 to p (p = the number of points in D), in such a way that no two points have an identical level and that no point reachable from v_n has a number less than or equal to that of v_n. For instance, the subscripts assigned to points v in D8 comprise one such set of *levels* for those points. Note that this is not a unique level assignment for D8, however, since we could have interchanged the designations of points v_1 and v_2 or v_4 and v_5. More generally, assignment of levels to any points not connected by a path is arbitrary. One could, of course, eliminate this arbitrariness by employing external criteria. For a dream-formation structuregram S', for instance, chronological association sequence could be employed.

The assignment provided by the subscripts of v in D8 is an *ascending level assignment*, in which, if there is a line v_iv_j, then subscript $v_i < v_j$; alter­natively, we might have provided a *descending level assignment*, in which if there is a line v_iv_j, then subscript $v_i > v_j$. This probably makes more sense in S', since higher numbers would then denote levels more removed from its unique sink, i.e., the manifest dream element.

While unique level assignment for all *points* v is possible only in an acyclic digraph, every digraph lends itself to *quasi-level assignments* (which will, however, be trivial where $C = 3$). This is useful, for it may sometimes happen that a composite structuregram, S', has some cyclic component. Here one assigns integers to the points of D so that, in the descending case, if there is a line v_iv_j, then subscript $v_i \geq v_j$ and so that subscript $v_i = v_j$ only if the points are mutually reachable. Even where S' does not have a cyclic component, it may have a semicyclic one, e.g., $v_1 v_3 v_7$ and $v_2 v_3 v_7$ in D8.

Clearly, such semicycles do not preclude the assignment of levels to the points v_i of D. However, it is important to note that a D such as D8, which can and often does occur for single associational chains, does *not* have certain properties which some attribute to the results of free association to dream elements.

Polombo (1973), for instance, who also has suggested conceiving free-associational data in terms of structural analysis, assimilates these data to the model (for dream interpretation) of a *tree from a point*.

Dream

Presumably his dream-formation model would be that of a *tree toward a point*.

Dream

Such models assume that no semicycles exist within D, and that there is one point, in the dream-formation case, with an outdegree of 0, while all other points have an outdegree of 1. In these models, it also follows that each line is a bridge, i.e., that its removal would disconnect D.

I do not make these assumptions here, for it seems to me, on the basis of working through some actual free-association data, that the case illustrated by D8 is likely to occur fairly often. That is, we generally won't have pure "trees," but, rather, will be working with structures containing semicycles. Thus, in D8, neither line $v_1 v_3$ nor line $v_2 v_3$ is a bridge; removal of either or both of these lines leaves D's structure intact, i.e., weakly connected.

Representation of Dynamic Scores

It might be wondered if structural analysis can encode SSLS's dynamic scores, i.e., its modifiers of nouns and verbs. Although, as noted earlier (chapter 11), little provision has been made as yet for the routine analysis of SSLS's dynamic scores, it is important to note that they do lend themselves to future inclusion in a structural analysis of the general form indicated above.

There are several ways in which the dynamic content of interaction statements, i.e., verb selection, as well as the more general phenomena of dynamic modification, might someday be incorporated in a mathematical structural analysis:

(1) Signed digraphs (Harary et al., 1965, ch. 13), extensively used in "balance" models of cognition and of social-psychological phenomena, permit the characterization of lines in the digraph as carrying either positive or negative valence. One might "condense," in the structural-analytic sense (letting single points of D stand for subgraphs of D), the dream structuregram to those points with interaction statements attached to them, and then let the sign of the lines in the outbundles from those points be determined, by formula, from the nature of those interaction statements. $E \rightarrow Sp$, for instance, would imply a positive valence, i.e., a $\rightarrow$ line, while $E \prec Sp$ would imply a negative valence, i.e., a $\dashrightarrow$ line. Or, within a class of relations, $E \overset{+}{\rightarrow} Sp$ might lead to a $\rightarrow$ line, while $E \rightrightarrows Sp$ might lead to a $\dashrightarrow$ line.

(2) More generally, numerical values might be assigned to the lines of such a digraph (which would become, technically, a *network*, in which self-reflexive statements also could be allowed [Harary et al., 1965, ch. 14]). Both verb class and intensity could be employed to derive an empirical metric which best accounts for the dream data to be explained. Instead of an adjacency matrix, one then would have a *value matrix*, with each entry reflecting the determinative force v_i has on v_j, or the intrapsychic "cost" of v_i moving toward v_j, with that cost perhaps disproportionately increasing for certain contents as they move toward the network sink, i.e., the manifest

dream. Empirical work with such matrices is well established in statistical, political, and economic areas.

(3) Alternatively (or also), one might encode the modifiers of the associative sentences in the path analysis generating the structuregram S. This could be done either in valence form ($\rightarrow$ or $---\rightarrow$) or numerically. For example, the introduction, from Sy_{1A}, of Sy_{1B} might have been as follows:

That strongly reminded me of . . . = $[Sy_{1A} \overset{+}{\updownarrow} Sy_{1B}]$.

Or, it might have been something more like this:

I don't really see the connection, but next I sort of
thought of . . . = $[Sy_{1A} \updownarrow Sy_{1B}]$.

Following the model of signed digraphs, and letting $Sy_{1A} = v_1$ and $Sy_{1B} = v_2$, we might draw these lines in S, respectively, for the two cases:

$v_1 \longrightarrow v_2$;
$v_1 ---\rightarrow v_2$.

It is important to realize that the potential extensions of a structural model to dream dynamics which have been suggested here would build upon techniques already developed in other areas of application of structural analysis. That is, the tools for such extensions already are available—at least in the form of elementary models of what might be required.

Summary

For readers handicapped by an instinctive aversion to mathematical or formal symbolic translations of observations, this probably has been a difficult chapter. It has, however, a central place in the overall argument. Dream psychology badly needs a "scientific" (ruleful, reliable) way of identifying and determining the interrelatedness of those associative and motivational structures connected with, and by assumption, causally responsible for, the particular images of the manifest dream. The content-analytic aspects of SSLS move partway toward meeting this need: they identify particular structures. SSLS's association-path analysis helps to put these individual structures in a form (the dream-formation structuregram) where their interrelatedness may be studied. That form, as this chapter has demonstrated, is one which permits the application to SSLS's data transformations of a powerful and versatile set of mathematical techniques—digraph theory. It has been the aim of this chapter to suggest that power and that versatility. In some cases the relevance of the operations which I have discussed to dream data has been self-evident: the ability to characterize structural properties of associative networks and of their components, the possibility of reliably specifying interitem connectedness and distance in such networks, and so on. In other cases, relevance may have been less apparent, and, in fact, may not yet have been established. In either event, the presentation does indicate a fascinating array of possibilities for operationalizing the description and manipulation of free-associative data in dream-process psychology.

In the following chapter, I shall try to work through a few of these possibilities. In particular, I shall try to demonstrate that Freud's "dream-work" mechanisms, the "transformational" part of his dream grammar, can be operationally defined and empirically studied in terms of a digraph analysis of dream-formation structuregrams. I also hope to show that digraph analysis not only permits us to "update" Freud, but also to reopen, more generally and from a relatively atheoretical perspective, the question of the associative processes of the mind in sleep.

CHAPTER 15

From Index to Grammar: "Dream-Work"

Analysis of a Dream-Formation Digraph

To appreciate some of the potential empirical applications of digraph analysis in the study of dream processes, let us return to Figure 14-1 (p. 301), which gives structuregram S' for free-association chain A of "Botanical Monograph." First, I propose to analyze it in a purely formal manner, introducing some new terminology along the way.

We note, by inspection, that this S' is a weak digraph; all points are joined by semipaths. But, since there are certain pairs of points (e.g., $v_5 v_8$) such that neither is reachable from the other, i.e., since our "tree" has separate "branches," it is not unilateral. Thus S' is strictly weak. S' has a unique sink, v_{14}, corresponding to the dream element to be explained—"botanical monograph"—but no source. The adjacency matrix of S' is:

$$A(S') =$$

	v_1	v_2	v_3	v_4	v_5	v_6	v_7	v_8	v_9	v_{10}	v_{11}	v_{12}	v_{13}	v_{14}	od(v_i)
v_1	0	0	0	0	1	0	0	0	0	0	0	0	0	0	1
v_2	0	0	0	0	1	0	0	0	0	0	0	0	0	0	1
v_3	0	0	0	1	1	0	0	0	1	0	0	0	0	0	3
v_4	0	0	0	0	1	0	0	0	1	0	0	0	0	0	2
v_5	0	0	0	0	0	0	0	0	1	0	0	0	0	0	1
v_6	0	0	0	0	0	0	0	1	0	0	0	0	0	0	1
v_7	0	0	0	0	0	0	0	1	0	0	0	0	0	0	1
v_8	0	0	0	0	0	0	0	0	1	0	0	0	0	0	1
v_9	0	0	0	0	0	0	0	0	0	1	0	0	0	0	1
v_{10}	0	0	0	0	0	0	0	0	0	0	1	0	0	1	2
v_{11}	0	0	0	0	0	0	0	0	0	0	0	0	0	1	1
v_{12}	0	0	0	0	0	0	0	0	0	0	0	0	1	1	2
v_{13}	0	0	0	0	0	0	0	0	0	0	0	0	0	1	1
v_{14}	0	0	0	0	0	0	0	0	0	0	0	0	0	0	0
id(v_j)	0	0	0	1	4	0	0	2	4	1	1	0	1	4	$\Sigma a_{ij} = 18.$

Points v_1, v_2, v_3, v_6, v_7, and v_{12} are transmitters; v_{14} is a receiver; v_{11} and v_{13} are carriers; v_4, v_5, v_8, v_9, and v_{10} are ordinary points. In dream structuregrams S', we shall further define points with id > 1 and od $= 1$ as *condensing carriers*, and their degree of condensation will be defined by id; thus v_5 is a 4-condensing carrier, v_8 a 2-condensing carrier, and v_9 a 4-condensing carrier. Points with id $= 1$ and od > 1 are *diffusing carriers*, and their degree of diffusion will be defined by od; thus points v_4 and v_{10} are 2-diffusing carriers.

The reachability matrix of S' is:

$$R(S') =$$

	v_1	v_2	v_3	v_4	v_5	v_6	v_7	v_8	v_9	v_{10}	v_{11}	v_{12}	v_{13}	v_{14}	Σr_{vi}
v_1	1	0	0	0	1	0	0	0	1	1	1	0	0	1	6
v_2	0	1	0	0	1	0	0	0	1	1	1	0	0	1	6
v_3	0	0	1	1	1	0	0	0	1	1	1	0	0	1	7
v_4	0	0	0	1	1	0	0	0	1	1	1	0	0	1	6
v_5	0	0	0	0	1	0	0	0	1	1	1	0	0	1	5
v_6	0	0	0	0	0	1	0	1	1	1	1	0	0	1	6
v_7	0	0	0	0	0	0	1	1	1	1	1	0	0	1	6
v_8	0	0	0	0	0	0	0	1	1	1	1	0	0	1	5
v_9	0	0	0	0	0	0	0	0	1	1	1	0	0	1	4
v_{10}	0	0	0	0	0	0	0	0	0	1	1	0	0	1	3
v_{11}	0	0	0	0	0	0	0	0	0	0	1	0	0	1	2
v_{12}	0	0	0	0	0	0	0	0	0	0	0	1	1	1	3
v_{13}	0	0	0	0	0	0	0	0	0	0	0	0	1	1	2
v_{14}	0	0	0	0	0	0	0	0	0	0	0	0	0	1	1
Σr_{vj}	1	1	1	2	5	1	1	3	9	10	11	1	2	14	$\Sigma r_v = 62.$

Since Σr_{vj} for v_{14} = 14, we verify that v_{14} is a sink, and see, furthermore, that it is a unique sink for S'. Since no Σr_{vi} = 14, we verify that S' has no source. We define Σr_{vi} for any point v_i as its *cause potential* (cp) and Σr_{vj} as its *effect potential* (ep). Thus cp (v_7) = 6 and ep (v_7) = 1. A point's *causation index* (ci) is $cp(v_i)/ep(v_i)$. For v_7, ci = 6.

We next form the converse of matrix R, which will be, of course, the reachability matrix of the digraph of the original free-association structuregram which had the dream-element as source.

	v_1	v_2	v_3	v_4	v_5	v_6	v_7	v_8	v_9	v_{10}	v_{11}	v_{12}	v_{13}	v_{14}
v_1	1	0	0	0	0	0	0	0	0	0	0	0	0	0
v_2	0	1	0	0	0	0	0	0	0	0	0	0	0	0
v_3	0	0	1	0	0	0	0	0	0	0	0	0	0	0
v_4	0	0	1	1	0	0	0	0	0	0	0	0	0	0
v_5	1	1	1	1	1	0	0	0	0	0	0	0	0	0
v_6	0	0	0	0	0	1	0	0	0	0	0	0	0	0
$R' = v_7$	0	0	0	0	0	0	1	0	0	0	0	0	0	0
v_8	0	0	0	0	0	1	1	1	0	0	0	0	0	0
v_9	1	1	1	1	1	1	1	1	1	0	0	0	0	0
v_{10}	1	1	1	1	1	1	1	1	1	1	0	0	0	0
v_{11}	1	1	1	1	1	1	1	1	1	1	1	0	0	0
v_{12}	0	0	0	0	0	0	0	0	0	0	0	1	0	0
v_{13}	0	0	0	0	0	0	0	0	0	0	0	1	1	0
v_{14}	1	1	1	1	1	1	1	1	1	1	1	1	1	1.

Here, v_{14} is the unique source, and there is no sink. We use the elementwise product $R \times R'$ to determine if there are any nontrivial strong components of S', and to identify its fundamental sets. From the fact that all nontrivial R entries are above the diagonal and all nontrivial R' entries are below the diagonal, we see that the $R \times R'$ product will be a matrix containing 1 entries only in the diagonal cells. That is, S' is acyclic, without mutually reachable points or nontrivial strong components.

We determine the origins of the fundamental sets of S' by looking for points v_i such that Σv_i in $R \times R' = \Sigma v_j$ in R, i.e., where Σv_j in R = 1. These points are v_1, v_2, v_3, v_6, v_7, and v_{12}. None lies within the same fundamental set. Thus these points are the point basis of S'. The fundamental sets which the origins define are given by 1 entries in their row in R, and are as follows:

1) $v_1, v_5, v_9, v_{10}, v_{11}, v_{14}$
2) $v_2, v_5, v_9, v_{10}, v_{11}, v_{14}$
3) $v_3, v_4, v_5, v_9, v_{10}, v_{11}, v_{14}$
4) $v_6, v_8, v_9, v_{10}, v_{11}, v_{14}$
5) $v_7, v_8, v_9, v_{10}, v_{11}, v_{14}$
6) v_{12}, v_{13}, v_{14}

These sets define the unilateral components of D. We define a *trunk intersect* as any point other than the sink included in all of the fundamental sets of S'. This S' has no trunk intersects. A *branch intersect* is any point other than the sink included in > 1 fundamental set, s, but in $< \Sigma s$ fundamental sets. In this S', v_5, v_8, v_9, v_{10}, and v_{11} are branch intersects. When condensing carriers are branch intersects, they are called *branch condensers* (e.g., v_5); when they are trunk intersects, they are called *trunk condensers*.

Next, we determine the distance matrix of S':

	v_1	v_2	v_3	v_4	v_5	v_6	v_7	v_8	v_9	v_{10}	v_{11}	v_{12}	v_{13}	v_{14}	Σd_i	$o(v)$
v_1	0	∞	∞	∞	1	∞	∞	∞	2	3	4	∞	∞	4	14	4
v_2	∞	0	∞	∞	1	∞	∞	∞	2	3	4	∞	∞	4	14	4
v_3	∞	∞	0	1	1	∞	∞	∞	1	2	3	∞	∞	3	11	3
v_4	∞	∞	∞	0	1	∞	∞	∞	1	2	3	∞	∞	3	10	3
v_5	∞	∞	∞	∞	0	∞	∞	∞	1	2	3	∞	∞	3	9	3
v_6	∞	∞	∞	∞	∞	0	∞	1	2	3	4	∞	∞	4	14	4
v_7	∞	∞	∞	∞	∞	∞	0	1	2	3	4	∞	∞	4	14	4
v_8	∞	∞	∞	∞	∞	∞	∞	0	1	2	3	∞	∞	3	9	3
N(S') = v_9	∞	∞	∞	∞	∞	∞	∞	∞	0	1	2	∞	∞	2	5	2
v_{10}	∞	∞	∞	∞	∞	∞	∞	∞	∞	0	1	∞	∞	1	2	1
v_{11}	∞	∞	∞	∞	∞	∞	∞	∞	∞	∞	0	∞	∞	1	1	1
v_{12}	∞	∞	∞	∞	∞	∞	∞	∞	∞	∞	∞	0	1	1	2	1
v_{13}	∞	∞	∞	∞	∞	∞	∞	∞	∞	∞	∞	∞	0	1	1	1
v_{14}	∞	∞	∞	∞	∞	∞	∞	∞	∞	∞	∞	∞	∞	0	0	0
Σd_j	0	0	0	1	4	0	0	2	12	21	31	0	1	34		
$i(v)$	0	0	0	1	1	0	0	1	2	3	4	0	1	4		

$\Sigma d_{ij} = 106.$

We define Σd_i as element v_i's index of *cause diffusion* (cd). Thus cd $(v_4) = 10$. We define Σd_j as element v_j's index of *effect diffusion* (ed). Thus ed $(v_4) = 1$. The *diffusion index* (DI) for $S' = \Sigma d_{ij}$. Here DI $(S') = 106$. We note that v_{14} is a 4-sink of S'. Entries in the $N(S')$ column for v_{14} (the sink) give, for each v_i, its *associative distance level minimum*. Thus $adl_{min}(v_4) = 3$.

We note that S' has a line surplus. Specifically, $ls(S') = \Sigma a_{ij} - (p - 1) = 18 - 13 = 5$. We define $ls(S')$ as the index of *associative interconnection* for S' [AI(S')]. Where $AI(S') > 0$, not all lines in S' are bridges. Specifically, the following lines in our S' are not bridges:

$v_3 v_4$;
$v_4 v_5$;
$v_3 v_5$;
$v_4 v_9$;
$v_3 v_9$;
$v_5 v_9$;
$v_{10} v_{11}$;
$v_{11} v_{14}$;
$v_{10} v_{14}$;
$v_{12} v_{13}$;
$v_{13} v_{14}$;
$v_{12} v_{14}$.

The following lines in S' are not basic, i.e., are neutral, and are neither required to preserve the reachability in S' nor in the line basis of S':

$v_3 v_5$;
$v_4 v_9$;
$v_3 v_9$;
$v_{10} v_{14}$;
$v_{12} v_{14}$.

We call the neutral lines of S' *collaterals* (cl), their points of origin (here: v_3, v_4, v_{10}, v_{12}) *multideterminative points* (mp), and their points of termination *multidetermined termini* (mt). We note the relationship of the presence of these phenomena to the existence of semicycles in S'.

Cutpoints in our S' are v_5, v_8, v_9, v_{10}, and v_{14}. These cutpoints help to define the nontrivial blocks in S', namely:

v_3, v_4, v_5, v_9;
v_{10}, v_{11}, v_{14};
v_{12}, v_{13}, v_{14}.

The presence of nontrivial blocks in S' is, of course, related to the presence of collateral lines and multideterminative points.

Because $A(S')$ was upper-triangular in form, S' is acyclic, and the subscripts assigned to v in $A(S')$ are one possible set of ascending-level assignments. These particular subscripts are not unique, however (for instance, we could switch the subscripts on v_1 and v_2 for another, valid ascending-level assignment). In any event, a more useful ordering of points in the dream-formation case is the following:

$$v_1 = 5 \qquad v_8 = 4$$
$$v_2 = 5 \qquad v_9 = 3$$
$$v_3 = 6 \qquad v_{10} = 2$$
$$v_4 = 5 \qquad v_{11} = 1$$
$$v_5 = 4 \qquad v_{12} = 2$$
$$v_6 = 5 \qquad v_{13} = 1$$
$$v_7 = 5 \qquad v_{14} = 0.$$

These values are entries from the detour matrix relating points v_i to v_{14}, the sink of S'. That is, they describe the longest point-sink paths. These values are called the *associative distance level maximum* (adl_{max}) of points v_i. Thus $adl_{max}(v_8) = 4$.

Differences between adl_{max} and adl_{min} are related to the presence of blocks in S'. The following measures have a family resemblance in that all describe the richness of associative interconnection in S' over and above the minimal organization required to maintain a strictly weak S': $AI(S')$, mp $n(S')$, mt $n(S')$, nontrivial block $n(S')$, nontrivial block size within S', and $\Sigma[(adl_{max}) - (adl_{min})]$ for all points v_i in S'.

The absolute values of adl_{min} and adl_{max} may be put to another use, however. Specifically, the largest value adl_{min}, for any point v_i in S', is $ADL_{min}(S')$, or the *minimal depth* of S'; the largest value adl_{max}, for any point v_i in S', is $ADL_{max}(S')$, or the *maximal depth* of S'. For our S', $ADL_{min} = 4$ and $ADL_{max} = 6$.

Summarizing, we have developed two sets of numbers directly relating points v_i to v_{sink}, i.e., to the manifest dream, and have suggested several new indices characterizing v_i's more general position in S':

Points	adl_{min}	adl_{max}	cp	ep	ci	cd	ed
v_1	4	5	6	1	6	14	0
v_2	4	5	6	1	6	14	0
v_3	3	6	7	1	7	11	0
v_4	3	5	6	2	3	10	1
v_5	3	4	5	5	1	9	4
v_6	4	5	6	1	6	14	0
v_7	4	5	6	1	6	14	0
v_8	3	4	5	3	1.7	9	2
v_9	2	3	4	9	.4	5	12
v_{10}	1	2	3	10	.3	2	21
v_{11}	1	1	2	11	.2	1	31
v_{12}	1	2	3	1	3	2	0
v_{13}	1	1	2	2	1	1	1
v_{14}	0	0	1	14	.1	0	34.

In addition, some novel terms have been proposed for the qualitative characterization of points (condensing carriers, diffusing carriers, branch intersects,
trunk intersects, branch condensers, trunk condensers, and multideterminative points and termini) and lines (collaterals), along with some novel terms
for the quantitative description of S' itself: $DI(S')$; $AI(S')$; $ADL_{min}(S')$; and
$ADL_{max}(S')$.

Let us now see whether these tools, together with the basic techniques
and concepts of structural analysis, can facilitate the coordination of digraph
theory and Freud's conceptualization of dream-work.

Digraph Analysis and "Dream-Work"

Condensation

At one point Freud considers the possibility "that the overdetermination of the elements of dreams [i.e. condensation] is no very important dis-

covery, since it is a self-evident one" (1900, p. 307). While he ultimately rejects this possibility, there is something to be said in its favor.

The purpose of free association is to have the dreamer conjure up a structure of meaning in which a formerly cryptic dream element assumes some integral role, hence makes some sense. In fulfilling this purpose, the dream associator usually seems to work under the self-imposed, externally imposed, or task-imposed burden of generating an associative structure with some referential branching. That is, he or she offers the interpreter several discrete sets of potential clues as to the dream's meaning. When this is the case, we know that S' will be a strictly weak digraph, which in turn means that associative overdetermination, or condensation, must exist for some points in S'. It can be no other way. In this sense, that there will be condensation is preordained by the nature of the free-association process which generates the observations upon which we base our characterization of dream-work. From association to dream entails transformation from the many to the few.

However, there are at least two senses in which condensation might be said to be an empirical discovery. The first "discovery" would be this: Freud showed that an associative process generating a strictly weak digraph, S, with referential branching, generally is required to make sense of a dream. That is, this structure is a typical *task* requirement. Given this task structure, then, condensation is a necessary corollary. Freud's discovery is meaningful, since it separates the process of determining the meaning of even some of the more specialized or arcane terms in waking language systems from that of determining the meaning of almost all terms used in sleeping language systems. We may wonder, for instance, what a "lanner" is. The dictionary tells us that:

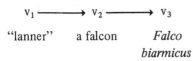

The structure of this answer is that of a strictly unilateral digraph. For most other terms found in written or spoken language systems, the answer which proves minimally satisfying to most meaning-inquirers has this form.[1]

Even for compound terms, where the waking-meaning digraph does seem to have a strictly weak form, the typical case is "condensation" on the term

---

[1] Philologists, etymologists, etc., clearly may have other requirements, and it also is true that those of obtuse character can make of any simple definition in the unilateral form a much more complex one. The typical case, however, fits this rule.

in question, but not in the referential network antecedent to that term. For example,

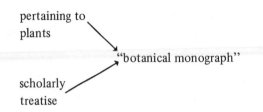

pertaining to
plants

"botanical monograph"

scholarly
treatise

The condensation in dream meaning-structures, on the other hand, not only can be on the dream term to be explicated, but also often occurs in the referential network used in the explication. We may reformulate Freud's discovery, then, as follows: To make sense of the dream, an associative process generally is required which generates a strictly weak digraph, S, with a converse digraph, S', the unique sink of which must have id > 1 and/*or* one or more other points in which must have id > 1 and od $= 1$ (i.e., must be condensing carriers), with the fulfillment of the latter requirement a typical outcome.

Now it may be objected that there is something "slippery" in the waking-sleeping comparisons just offered, for I have contrasted *denotative* meanings of terms in the waking-language system with *connotative* meanings of terms in the sleeping-language system, and it is well known that connotative meaning structures are multidimensional and more complex than those for denotative meaning (e.g., Osgood, 1952). Yet this objection gives us still another way to state Freud's discovery: The only meaning of those dream terms which we ordinarily would consider subjecting to interpretation is connotative. Thus, to impute meaning to a dream, our method must be one geared to producing structures of connotative meaning. Free association which is really free ranging, i.e., does not generate a simple unipathic structure, is such a method.

From this perspective, we may conclude that condensation's presence in the dream-work is self-evident, given the method employed. One is reminded of certain "discoveries" of group properties in sociometric structures (e.g., the existence of an ingroup of admiration) where the sociometric technique is carefully prescribed (e.g., one and only one choice must be made by each group member); these allegedly "empirical" discoveries proved to be necessary structural corollaries, given the method employed—that is, they were perfectly predictable on purely mathematical grounds (Harary et al., 1965, p. 325). Condensation in the sense of many-to-few seems to be such an "empirical discovery" in the study of dream-work. Yet that fact should not be allowed to obscure the larger finding, which is both empirical and tremendously important, that determination of dream meaning generally requires a method which has connotative meaning as its goal and condensation as a necessary dream-formation corollary.

The second sense in which Freud's condensation concept is an empirical discovery lies in Freud's characterization of condensation as the selection of those "few" which *best represent* the "many." If it is self-evident that dream-formation digraphs must contain condensation (many-to-few) in a *structural* sense, it is not at all obvious on what *semantic* bases, if any, particular free-associative elements will be selected as condensing points. Highest semantic communality with other points? Lowest semantic communality with other points? Selection without regard to semantic communality with other points? Freud's "second" discovery was that *structural condensation* was effected on the basis of *maximal semantic representation* by the condensation point (e.g., "botanical monograph") of the elements it was condensing (e.g., "cocaine," "blooming looks," "artichokes," "dream-book," etc.). Because the basis on which condensation points are selected is *not* a logical implication of structural condensation, it is not assumed in the SSLS variant of structural analysis. This means that the SSLS analysis may be used to independently test the "second discovery" I have ascribed to Freud. SSLS identifies points which condense and points which are condensed. Quite independently of its structural descriptions, SSLS labels its points semantically. Within the SSLS framework, it is an empirically answerable question as to whether Freud was correct in concluding that condensation proceeds along lines of economical semantic representation.

This last illustration indicates, I think, the role which SSLS can play more generally in the empirical study of condensation. It does not permit us to discover whether such a thing as structural condensation exists, whether Freud was "right" or "wrong" about the existence of condensation as a structural concept. He clearly was right, because structural condensation is not an empirical discovery at all, but a logical implication of the method employed. However, *that structural condensation must exist somewhere in a dream-formation digraph entails neither its more particular structural characterization nor any semantic characterization at all. Questions regarding the optional structural and semantic features of condensation may be asked, and empirically answered, in an SSLS analysis of the dream-formation digraph.*

SSLS permits, first of all, the reliable characterization of associative elements which condense. *Condensers* (or condensation points) are dream-formation digraph points with id > 1 and od ≤ 1. Points feeding directly (path of distance 1) into a condenser are called *condensees*. The line joining a condenser and a condensee is called a *condensation path*. The condensers so defined, then, can further be reliably characterized in several ways: in terms of how "condensing" they are (a point is an *n-condenser* when n-condensation paths lead to it); in terms of their condensation properties as related to their local structural properties (a condenser either is a condensing carrier or a condensing receiver); and in terms of their regional-structural property (a condenser may be a branch condenser or a trunk condenser). Thus, in "Botanical Monograph," free-association chain A, we have this set of condensers:

Point	dream element	n-condenser	carrier/receiver	branch/trunk
v_5	$\boxed{Sp_2}$	4-condenser	carrier	branch;
v_8	Sy_{4A}	2-condenser	carrier	branch;
v_9	$\boxed{Sy_{2D}\text{-}Sp_1}$	4-condenser	carrier	branch;
v_{14}	$\underline{Sy_{1A}\text{-}Sy_{2A}}$	4-condenser	receiver	trunk (sink).

Once these condensing associative elements have been identified, certain questions about condensation can be investigated with reliable empirical procedures. For example, we can ask what *structural properties* condensers have—for most dreamers, or for a given dreamer, or for a particular dream. For instance, what are the relative frequencies of 2-condensation and of $\geqslant$ 3-condensation, of condensation in carriers and in receivers, of condensation in branches and in the trunk? At what distance from the sink is condensation most likely to occur? How is condensation's magnitude (where the *n* term in n-condensation defines magnitude) related to its distance from the sink?

Furthermore, bearing in mind that each point v_i also can be characterized semantically, we also can investigate, as already has been noted in the context of Freud's representational view of structural condensation, what kinds of *content elements* get condensed, how, and where. For example, are boxed elements, i.e., those points with associated interactive sentences, especially liable to condensation, or to condensations with particular structural features? Does condensation generally occur in the direction $F \rightarrow Pm$ rather than $Pm \rightarrow F$? and so on. How often, and in what structural circumstances, does a condenser take the form of a *collective image* (perhaps we can coordinate this concept with a condenser which stands by and for [i.e., is in a box] itself—like $\boxed{Sp_2}$ in chain A of "Botanical Monograph"); a *composite image* (perhaps this is similar to a compound condenser—like $\boxed{Sy_{2D}\text{-}Sp_1}$ in chain A); or a *compromise* (neither of the above sets of conditions is present—as in the case of Sy_{4A} in chain A)?

Thus some kind of coordination can be made between theoretically important questions about the process of condensation, on the one hand, and a reliable technique for answering them through SSLS's combination of content and structural analysis, on the other. Most significantly, as noted earlier, Freud's "discovery" that condensation proceeds along lines of maximal semantic representation becomes an empirically testable hypothesis.

Displacement

Let us turn now to Freud's concept of displacement—or, following a suggestion made earlier (chapter 4)—to his still more basic concept of censorship. We have seen that Freud distinguishes "essential dream-thoughts" from an associative network created to permit the transvaluation of these basic dream-thoughts. Clearly it is the former whose value is displaced—or censored—while the latter merely provides a means to accomplish this end. I propose, in line with earlier suggestions, that Freud's distinction be coordinated with that in SSLS between motivational (interactive sentence) and associative (associative sentence) structure.

A point in an association chain which is boxed, i.e., has an associated motivational structure (interactive sentence), is called a *live point*. All other points are *inert*. Live points correspond to Freud's concept of basic dream-thoughts. *Displacement* occurs whenever two live points are joined by a path, have no live point between them, and do not have identical interactive sentences associated with them. The origin of this path is a *displacer*. Its terminus is a *displacee* (displacement point). The path itself, which, unlike a condensation path, can include more than one line, is a *displacement path*. It is the minimal path between displacer and displacement point.

In S' for chain A of "Botanical Monograph," there are several live points: v_5, v_6, v_7, and v_9. They define these displacement paths:

$v_5 v_9$;

$v_6 v_9$;

$v_7 v_9$;

$v_9 v_{14}$.

(Point v_{14} has no interaction sentence in this chain, but it does have one in the *dream* structuregram, and hence qualifies as a displacement point.) Path $v_5 v_9$ is of distance 1, hence v_5 is a 1-displacer. Points v_6, v_7, and v_9 are 2-displacers, where *n-displacement* refers to the length of the displacement path.

Displacement leads us to think of the associative structure S' as a set of pegs, on some of which motive structures are hung. In this sense, the six fundamental sets of our S' indicate several different patterns of motive representation. The following two sets are accompanied by motives at their origin:

$$v_6, v_8, v_9, v_{10}, v_{11}, v_{14} - \quad E \to Pm_2 ;$$
$$v_7, v_8, v_9, v_{10}, v_{11}, v_{14} - \quad E \to Sy_{5A} .$$

The following three sets are accompanied by motive structures within the set—at a common branch intersect—but not at the origin:

$$v_1, v_5, v_9, v_{10}, v_{11}, v_{14} ;$$
$$v_2, v_5, v_9, v_{10}, v_{11}, v_{14} ;$$
$$v_3, v_4, v_5, v_9, v_{10}, v_{11}, v_{14} - \quad E \to Sp_2 ;$$
$$Sp_2 \to E.$$

All five of these sets share the branch intersect, v_9, accompanied by the motives coded as:

$$E \to Sp_1 ;$$
$$Sp_1 \to E;$$
$$E \to Sy_{2D} .$$

Finally, the set v_{12}, v_{13}, v_{14} is accompanied by no motive structure at its origin and has no branch intersect. As noted above, however, its terminus, the terminus of all other fundamental sets as well, *is* accompanied by a motive structure in the dream episode.

Our definition of displacement is, like that of condensation, a minimal, structural one. Also as in the case of condensation, this means that the more precise structural characterization of a process, as well as its entire semantic characterization, is not assumed, but is open to independent empirical investigation. For instance, what *are* the relationships of motive structures (interactive sentences) in the dream to these S' free-associative variables: *structural properties of live points* (e.g., distance from sink, reachability and distance from one another, role as *live transmitter* [v_6 ; v_7] versus *live condensing-carrier* [v_5 , v_9] , multideterminative or not, cause-potential, causation index, cause-diffusion, etc.); *structural properties of fundamental sets containing such points* (presence/frequency of live branch versus trunk intersects; whether any pairs of sets describe lines lying in a common block, etc.); *structural properties of the structuregram itself* (depth, associative interconnection, diffusion index, etc.); *content* (noun, verb, E role as subject/object, etc.) *of interaction sentences* at live points; *"conflict" form* (e.g., E → X versus E ─< X) and *distance between conflicting structures*; and so on? While it is not clear that any easy answer will emerge to the question of how these variables relate to the dream's motivational structure, it is of tremendous significance that SSLS even permits us to ask this question in a meaningful— i.e., *potentially* answerable—way. SSLS could, in effect, make the representation of motives in dreams an empirically predictable process.[2]

As also was true of condensation, it seems clear that displacement, to Freud, was more than the minimal structural concept we have defined here. There was an additional semantic assumption, one not incorporated in SSLS but open to independent empirical analysis within its framework. The assumption was that the latent dream-thoughts (underlying motive structures) must be transformed, via displacement, which is a semantically distorting process, *"in order to prevent the generation of anxiety or other forms of distressing affect"* (Freud, 1900, p. 267). Thus we may envision a basic dream-thought "pressing" toward the sink, wanting "expression," then coming in conflict with an avoidance vector, pushing the thought away from the sink, demanding no-expression.

Following the formal outline of J. S. Brown's analysis of approach-avoidance conflict (1948), we might illustrate the following situation:

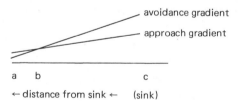

From distance a to b, the thought can be entertained in its raw form, and can move unimpeded toward direct representation in dream consciousness. At point b, however, contemplation of the anxiety or distressing affect likely to be generated by conscious recognition of the thought overtakes the movement toward expression, and there is a situation of blockage for the untransformed dream-thought. If it were to be transformed, however, into a substitute thought—if a "detour" were to be effected such that the substitute

---

[2]Bearing in mind, of course, the probability that consideration also will have to be given to dynamic codes as well as to structural ones.

thought had a lower avoidance gradient, then there could be further progress toward expression. Thus, we might illustrate the situation as follows:

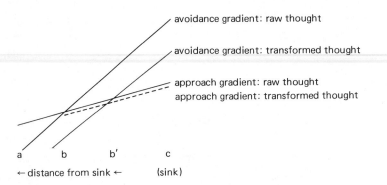

Progress now could be made to point b′ closer to the sink. By a series of such transformations, eventually we would have a transformed thought whose approach gradient would be higher than its avoidance gradient at point c, that is, which could find direct expression in the dream.

This formal analysis of approach-avoidance conflict has proved useful empirically in situations where, for example, rats run toward a goal box where they have been both fed and shocked. It has been widely extolled as a reduction of the seemingly complex phenomenon of conflict into operational terms which prove satisfying to those who demand rigorous empirical analyses of behavior. Note that its application to particular instances of behavior depends upon specification of the gradients associated with a particular behavior (motive, or behavior-intention) and ability to determine distance from the goal of that behavior (motive, or behavior-intention).

Now, note that SSLS's analysis of dream structure can, in principle, supply all the requisites for analysis of dream-formation "behaviors" according to the Brown model. Thus, we can specify (associative) distance from goal (sink), we can describe original motives (interactive sentences) and their transformations (displacees), and there is nothing to prevent us from having these motives scaled for their attractiveness-repulsiveness to the dreamer's (waking) consciousness. Thus we are in a position to determine whether Brown's conflict model (which is identical, really, to Freud's own model) fits the dream case. That is, we can determine whether the transformations of interactive-sentence material in the dream-formation structure fit the model that transformations move from more repulsive to more attractive sentence content as a function of decreasing distance from the manifest dream.

Heretofore I have called interactive-sentence structural transformations "displacements." This label cannot be construed as being theoretically neutral. The term obviously smuggles in all sorts of Freudian implications, the major one being that displacement-transformations occur *"in order to prevent the generation of anxiety or other forms of distressing affect"* (Freud, 1900, p. 267). I now am suggesting that SSLS permits a relatively direct test of this implication. Should it be sustained, we might well decide to retain the term "displacement" as a shorthand descriptor for "interaction sentence shifts along a path toward the sink." Should the implication not be borne out by the test, then we might want to coin a neologism devoid of any theoretical value to describe the same phenomenon. Either way, we have gained a more precise knowledge of what that phenomenon does and does not imply.

Thus, the SSLS model for studying dream formation is close enough to Freud's to demonstrate that Freud's dream-work mechanisms are potentially incorporable into its ruleful and reliable set of definitions and analytic operations, but it also is sufficiently atheoretical to permit independent assessment of the truth-value of some of Freud's more controversial assumptions or observations. Specifically within the motive-transformation realm of "displacement," SSLS does *not* assume that: dream elements must be distorted; dream elements must have been generated by motive structures; dream elements must reflect motivational conflicts of specified, or indeed of any, sorts. The whole question of distortion or dream censorship has been left open to independent empirical analysis.

Pictorial Representability

Freud's "considerations of pictorial representability" find no easy translation to any concepts of analysis heretofore introduced, for SSLS makes no distinction between associational elements which are purely "ideational" and those which are perceptual. However, suitability for iconic representation could, with little difficulty—at least, theoretically—be "tacked onto" its analysis. There is nothing, for example, to prevent one from scaling various symbolic and other referents for certain iconic properties, and adding these scale variables to those whose analysis has been suggested. In association chain A of "Botanical Monograph," for instance, we might find that, where Sy_{2D}, and not Sy_{4A}, proved to be an ultimate carrier for sources Pm_2 and Sy_{5A}, that choice was related not only to the fact that Sy_{2D} was more overdetermined than Sy_{4A}, but also to the fact that it is easier to picture a "flower" than it is an "anecdote."

Additional Mechanisms

We now have observed that Freud's key concepts of dream-work can be coordinated with our system of analysis. The operational definitions are not always letter-perfect translations of Freud, but in general they seem to represent a reasonable tradeoff of losses in theoretical purity for gains in empirical precision. We now might go further, however, and ask if SSLS suggests, or could suggest, any novel dream-work concepts. It would be a useful feature of the system if it not only could make Freud's concepts empirically viable, but also could introduce heretofore unrecognized concepts of equal viability and utility. The answer is that it certainly seems possible that SSLS could do this, and that there are some hints that it may already have done so.

We have, for example, already identified a process of structural *multi-determination* which is not synonymous with Freud's concept of associative overdetermination (condensation). The following diagram illustrates the contrast.

condensation on v_3 *multidetermination of* v_3
(overdetermination)

Specifically, *multidetermination* occurs when any element v_2 has >1 discrete path to any other element v_3 (postulation of this process implies, of course, the existence of semicycles within S'). A *multidetermined path* is that path between v_2 and v_3 which is not basic, i.e., which is a collateral. (From the standpoint of the multideterminative point [e.g., v_2 in the preceding illustration], the process might be thought of as one of *diffusion*; from the standpoint of the multidetermined terminus [e.g., v_3], however, it is better thought of as one of *structural multidetermination*.)

Multidetermination is like the unlabeled process Freud described (see chapter 4), but then failed to further categorize, when he noted that a single dream-thought might take, say, two different paths toward the dream, terminating at two discrete dream elements (which could, however, themselves be associatively linked *within* the dream structure, thus creating two paths from the dream-thought to at least one of the dream-elements in question). Here is a case, then, in which Freud had a valid insight but failed to formalize it. With our operational concepts of collaterals, multideterminative points, and multidetermined points, we can do so.

Another possible associative process in the dream-work is suggested by cases where elements v_1, v_2, and v_3 are joined, and only joined, on their path to the sink, by lines v_1v_2 and v_2v_3, and where v_2 is an inert point. Suppose, for example, there were no point v_{11} in the S' for chain A of "Botanical Monograph." Then the role of v_{10}, between points v_9 and v_{14}, could have nothing to do with condensation or multidetermination; since v_{10} is inert, its implication in displacement would be obscure. Point v_{10}—cyclamen—seems no more nor less pictorially representable than v_9—flowers/wife—nor v_{14}—plant/monograph. Cyclamen seems to be a purely symbolic transformation, whose function in the original free-association structuregram is to address a botanical category which has a wide range of motivational implications and whose function in the dream-formation structuregram is to particularize these motive structures so that a "fresh" day-residue impression might be found to represent them. Points v_{11} (Sy_{1A2} = book-title), v_{12} (Sy_{3A} = shop), and v_{13} (Sy_{3A1} = window of shop) in our structuregram S' all seem to share the property that, as fresh day-residue impressions, they provide a symbolic link between the significant motives of the dreamer's life and the events of his dream-day. Structurally, the day-residue may be a more "precious" material than Freud imagined. Specifically, it may be the means by which more significant dreamer associative and motivational structures are "addressed" in long-term storage, and, conversely, the means by which these structures are structurally constrained in their passage to dream experience.

Little more can be said about this process at present. However, it seems to me significant that the formalization of Freud's dream-process model already has suggested the insufficiency of *his* representational processes—viz., condensation and pictorial representability—in accounting for all the associative "work" underlying the dream. It also seems significant that, however it ultimately is characterized, the process just alluded to seems unlikely to be unique to sleep. It is, in short, the kind of process Freud was likely to have taken for granted in his search for the more esoteric, sleep-specific processes of the dreaming mind. But, upon a moment's reflection, it surely seems unlikely that the associative mechanisms specifically imposed by the conditions of sleep (i.e., *condensation*, by the simultaneous activity of a number of different thought-structures, and *pictorial representability,* by the medium in which the dream message will find surface realization) can, by themselves, explain the dream from an associative point of view. We must imagine, rather, that these mechanisms are merely superimposed upon associative mechanisms *generally* characteristic of mind. It is the great virtue of SSLS's formalization that it makes this point obvious.

It is its further virtue that it should, in principle, permit the description and study of these more general mechanisms of mind which also are required to explain the dream.

Summary

We have analyzed an SSLS dream-formation structuregram ("Botanical Monograph," free-association chain A) in terms of the general methods of mathematical structure analysis and in terms of some additional definitions and operations supplied by SSLS for the dream-formation case. This analysis has shown that Freud's key dream-work concepts can be operationally defined in terms of these analytic tools, and that they therefore now are open to serious empirical study. Furthermore, we have seen that the methods in question also permit the study of the operations of the dreaming mind from a more theoretically neutral point of view, as shown by the associative mechanisms they propose which were not formalized in Freud's dream-work concept.

PART V

APPLICATIONS/

IMPLICATIONS

OF THE MODEL

CHAPTER 16

Dream Interpretation and Clinical Dream Psychology

One of the fundamental goals underlying the construction of SSLS was to organize dream and free-associative materials so that they could be used to generate reliable and nontrivial statements about dreamers as persons. It now remains to be demonstrated how the data yielded by SSLS might be used to implement this goal.

Following the logic, if not the consistent terminology, of Freud (1900), I distinguish between the subgoals of making statements about the dreamer (*dream-interpretation* statements) and of making statements about dreaming (*dream-process* statements). When associations are being used to isolate those motivational structures which initiated the dream, one is interpreting, while when associations are being used to reconstruct the transformation of these same motivational structures during the act of dream formation, one is proposing a psychology of dream processes (see figure 16-1).

FIGURE 16-1

Dream Interpretation and Dream Formation

(a motive structure)

The act of dream interpretation   The hypothetical act of dream formation

In one important respect, a focus on dream interpretation is less demanding than one upon the dreaming process. Specifically, in a strictly interpretive frame of reference, little or no attention need be paid to the associational sequence between the manifest dream and the motivational structures assumed to have generated it. The payoff is simply that such structures have been "uncovered" and that we now are able to impute them to the dreamer in some account of her or his waking conduct.

It is evident that *both* viewpoints lead to statements about dreamers: the one, about their motives, and the other, about the way these motives are presumed to be "worked over" as dreams are dreamed. Only the interpretive frame of reference, however, might properly be designated as lying within the boundaries of what is called "person psychology," since it alone aims at a characterization of a particular dreamer, of the unique constellation of motives which has guided her or his life history and continues to work itself out in the dreamer's daily life. Validation of interpretive statements comes through matching them with observations of the dreamer's current or future waking behaviors and/or by demonstrating their utility in explaining the dreamer's life history. The process frame of reference, on the other hand, aims at a characterization of the act of dreaming which is not person-specific. We wish to describe, in general, how dreams arise out of a matrix of motives and cognitions, what regularities occur, across persons, in the transformation of motive structures to the pictorial dramas we call dreams. Validation here must be both more indirect—since we are purporting to describe a process which is not open to direct observation—and more universal—we want to know about dreaming, not merely about the dreams of any particular person.

What really is unique about SSLS is its attempt to simultaneously fulfill both the person *and* the process aims of dream psychology. As has been noted earlier, certain content-analysis systems already in existence (e.g., Hall and Van de Castle, 1966; Foulkes and Shepherd, 1971) permit the characterization of dreamer motives. While SSLS is seen as an improvement on these earlier systems in several senses (e.g., it analyzes dream and association statements exhaustively and at a more "latent" level), it isn't qualitatively different from them with respect to its general aims in the area of dream interpretation. Unlike these earlier systems, however, SSLS also aspires to permit a reliable formulation of the transformations undergone by "latent dream-thoughts" in the process of constructing a manifest dream. In this respect, it is more faithful than earlier content-analysis systems to the spirit, and major focus, of Freud's own work (see chapter 4). The next, and last, chapter considers the use of SSLS in dream-process psychology. Here I would like briefly to assess the system's potential in dream-interpretation psychology.

The Person as Symbolizer

It should be noted that I have not limited the validation of dreamer statements to matches with specific current (concurrent validity) or future (predictive validity) waking behaviors. I believe that the goals of science extend beyond those of prediction and control. To take an example discussed by Sherwood (1969, p. 13), it may seem sufficient that we have been able to describe observed contingencies between balloon explosions and balloon-fire distances, that we have been able to use the descriptions to predict successfully at what distances subsequently observed balloons will explode, and that we finally have been able, through precise manipulations of balloon-fire distances, to make balloons explode "at will."

This is, however, a rather restrictive understanding of what science is all about, one that stresses its feedback to our hands rather more than its feedback to our minds. From science we also require an understanding or explanation of all the above—as, for example, might be offered by the kinetic theory of gases. In psychology, as Sherwood makes clear, the most comprehensive form such explanation can take is the case-history narrative.

From this perspective, an important consideration in evaluating SSLS is whether its units are consistent with those units likely to be of value in case-history narratives, particularly with those units employed in clinical psychology, where narrative-histories are most likely to be formulated. Because the units of SSLS are symbolic/linguistic/propositional, I believe that they will be of particular value in the clinical context. Specifically, they can be integrated with recently evolving clinical conceptions of the person as symbolizer and of "mental illness" as symbolic dysfunction.

As Szasz has effectively demonstrated, the "illness" model of clinical problems and quasi-physical explanations of their etiology are useful neither scientifically nor clinically. In his terms, the province of psychology is not "mental illness" but "sign-using behavior" (1961, p. 51). The clinical symptom is not an energy displacement, but an intentional sign carrying a message. Szasz goes on to show that the original Breuer-Freud contribution (1895) to the study of hysterical symptoms was precisely this: that symptoms are symbolic acts. His idea of the form in which such symbolic acts might themselves be conceptualized is remarkably similar to SSLS's interactive sentence: *"the task of psychoanalysis as a science is to study and elucidate the kinds of objects people need, and the exact ways in which they need them"* (1961, p. 143). The *explanation* of such acts lies in specifying the *rules* (grammar) by which they are unconsciously generated.

Freud himself certainly vacillated on the relative value of ultimate physicalist reductions of symptom behaviors as compared to their explanation in symbolic terms. In his most lucid explanatory moments, however, he was unequivocally symbolic. For instance, in his paper on the mechanisms of paranoia (1911*b*), he imagines male paranoia as a set of defensive transformations on the proposition: "I (male) love X (male)." In a persecutory variant of paranoia, the verb is transformed: "I hate X"; in an erotomanic variant, the object is transformed: "I (male) love Y (female)"; in a jealousy variant, the subject is transformed: "Y (female) loves X (male)." (A final case is where the whole proposition is suppressed: essentially, "I don't love anybody.") This remarkable account presages the Suppes-Warren model (1975) of defense mechanisms as transformations on elementary propositions, and is, of course, fully compatible with the notion of paranoia as a symbolic dysfunction.

Edelson also has discussed the semantic distortions which are indicated by symptoms. He develops the idea that the distinctive feature of "psychotherapy" is that it treats symbolic disorders by symbolic means. He concludes that "the dominant theme in Freud's empirical work is a view of man in terms of conflicting motives as these are manifested in symbolic processes with different characteristics and aims" (1971, p. 31).

Conflict

The last quotation indicates a useful property we might expect to find in any comprehensive system of dream analysis: its ready identification and characterization of dreamer conflicts. With its many different "schools," dream psychology probably has no propositions to which universal assent would be accorded. However, the statement that dreams reflect and reveal dreamer conflicts would surely stand very high on the list of those propositions which have achieved some kind of consensual validation among dream clinicians.

The sentence-form of SSLS's motive constructs (interactive sentences) in fact does permit an efficient and comprehensive formulation of dreamer conflicts. Specifically, SSLS can be used to identify the following classes of *structural conflict.*

(1) E's interactive relationship, as grammatical subject, with a given grammatical object is described by more than one verb, e.g., $E \rightarrow X$; $E \prec X$.

(2) E's interactive relationship, as subject, to an object X is asymmetric with E's interactive relationship, as object, to the subject X, e.g., $E \rightarrow X$; $\leftarrow X, E$.

(3) Two or more interactive sentences are scored in the form $E \rightarrow \ldots$, but with different objects, e.g., $E \rightarrow Pf_1$; $E \rightarrow M$. The idea here is that affection, interest, love, and so on, are finite in quantity, and thus that each investment in one object subtracts from that available for other objects.

(4) Two or more Means sentences exist with identical interactive subjects, objects, and verbs, but with different role/means modification. A good example is contained in free-association chain A, "Botanical Monograph":

$$A\text{-}22 \;\; [\overset{+}{S}y_{2D} \overset{+}{=} E(Pm_3) \boxed{\Rightarrow} Sp_2];$$
$$A\text{-}53 \;\; [Sy_{7A} \equiv E(F_{1A}) \boxed{\Rightarrow} Sp_2].$$

Does Freud approach Frau L. as spouse with flowers, or as physician with treatment?

A role conflict is assumed to exist even when E assumes a role in one Means sentence, but no role in another such sentence (again, with the same subject, object, and verb in the interactive unit). As a variant of this role conflict, we might also define a conflict when subject and object of the interactive unit are identical but when role helps to define a different relationship (verb) between the two. For example, from "Botanical Monograph," free-association chain B:

$$B\text{-}5 \;\; [Sy_{1A,2E} \equiv E(Pm_4) \boxed{\Rightarrow} Sy_{7B}];$$
$$B\text{-}7 \;\; [Sy_{1A,2E} \equiv E \boxed{\odot\rightarrow} Sy_{7B}].$$

The paper was the means by which Koller *saw* the anaesthetic properties of cocaine, but by which Freud—as himself—*discovered* them.

(5) Another form of structural conflict may be seen in those rare, but

highly significant, sentences in which two verbs are associated with one another via the verb With. For example, from "Botanical Monograph":

F-8 $[\overset{+}{-}\!< \; \updownarrow \; \odot\!\!\rightarrow]$;

F-23 $[\overset{+}{\updownarrow} \; \updownarrow \; \overset{+}{\rightarrow}]$;

F-29 $[\overset{+}{\rightarrow} \; \overset{+}{\updownarrow} \; \overset{+}{-}\!<]$;

F-30 $[\overset{+}{\updownarrow} \; \overset{+}{\updownarrow} \; \overset{+}{-}\!<]$;

F-36 $[\overset{+}{\rightarrow} \; \overset{+}{\updownarrow} \; \overset{+}{\leftarrow}]$.

The conflict here is over the quality of relating itself, rather than consisting of a more focal conflict regarding a limited set of potential objects. This "instinctual" conflict generalizes across *all* potential objects of the verbs in question.

(It might be wondered if SSLS's third-party exclusionary rule for interactive sentences doesn't arbitrarily eliminate another type of structural conflict it would be important to capture in our analysis: namely, a conflict of the form: $E \rightarrow X$ versus $A \rightarrow X$. However, there is logic underlying the exclusionary rule here as well as elsewhere (cf. chapter 11). I may love X, while A also loves X, but this becomes a conflict for me only to the extent that it leads, for example, to $\leftarrow X$, E, in which case the conflict already is subsumed by rule (2) above.)

It may be objected that, literally following rules (1) to (5), SSLS leads us to *too many* conflicts for any particular dream. In "Botanical Monograph," for example, a very large number of conflicts can be identified by these rules. There are two basic responses to this objection. One response is like that already given in refutation of the charge that SSLS identifies too many motives, or basic dream-thoughts (chapter 13), namely, that it is rather simplistic to imagine a unitary conflict source for as extended and seemingly complex an event as a dream.

Also, it is unlikely that there could be so much disagreement among reasonable persons about the correct interpretation of certain dreams were there not the possibility that some degree of truth might attach to the efforts of each interpreter. It is to be expected, then, that a system which analyzes dreams exhaustively, rather than selectively, will produce multiple conflictual sources for any given dream.

The second line of response is to admit that the objection has some merit, and to place some constraints upon those conflicts identified by rules (1) to (5) which the interpreter routinely can map into E's waking life. One such constraint might be that the conflict identified by SSLS in any single dream would have to be confirmed by its recurrence at some specified frequency in a dream series of the same dreamer (Hall and Nordby, 1972). Alternatively, we could insist that conflicts identified in one dream or association chain of a single dream be confirmed within that chain—i.e., more than one instance must occur of each interactive sentence forming the conflicting pair of sentences—and/or that conflicts identified in one dream or association chain be confirmed within another such chain of the same dream material. Generally speaking, these conventions sound like very reasonable interpretive precautions, as well as being conveniences for a potentially over-burdened interpreter.

Another class of restraints upon all those conflicts which emerge from SSLS analysis is more interesting theoretically. Suppose we say that for any two interactive sentences which are in conflict according to rules (1) to (5) to be considered as *strongly* conflictive (i.e., we're willing to use them to form propositions about the dreamer's waking life), they must demonstrate a certain degree of "contact" with one another. "Botanical Monograph" free-association chain A, for instance, gives us five discrete sentence types of the form $E \rightarrow \ldots$, viz.:

A-9 $\underline{E} \rightleftharpoons Sp_1$;

A-15 $E \overset{+}{\underset{}{\rightleftharpoons}} \overset{+}{Pm_2}$;

A-17 $E \rightleftharpoons Sy_{5A}$;

A-21 $E \overset{+}{\underset{}{\rightarrow}} \overset{+}{Sp_2}$;

A-36 $E \overset{+}{\underset{}{\rightleftharpoons}} \overset{+}{Sy}_{2D}$.

By rule (3), any pair of these sentences might be considered to be in conflict. Inspection of the structuregram for chain A, however, indicates that $E \rightarrow Sp_1$, $E \rightarrow Sy_{2D}$, $E \rightarrow Sy_{5A}$, and $E \rightarrow Pm_2$ form one grouping of "in contact" interaction sentences, while $E \rightarrow Sp_1$, $E \rightarrow Sy_{2D}$, and $E \rightarrow Sp_2$ form another. "In contact" here means that an associative path connects the points of the associational structure which give rise to these sentences.

One might, therefore, consider $E \rightarrow Pm_2$ and $E \rightarrow Sy_{5A}$ to be in active conflict (should Freud invest his energies in his colleagues or his theories?), while $E \rightarrow Pm_2$ and $E \rightarrow Sp_2$ would not be considered as strongly conflictive (investments in colleagues versus patients). The logic underlying such a convention might be that people can successfully manage potential conflicts by the defense of isolation, and that those conflicts likely to emerge as active determinants of waking behavior (i.e., likely to be of interpretive interest) are precisely those which cannot be walled-off from one another in dream consciousness.

The argument up to this point has been of a rather broad nature. "In contact" has been defined in a rather simple way, and degrees of contact have not been distinguished. But, as we already know (chapter 14), structural analysis permits much more precise statements about the connectedness of, and the distances separating, any two points in SSLS structuregrams. For any given structuregram, perfectly reliable and highly specific criteria can be developed for points in the structuregram, such that interpretive rules of the following sort could be formed:

> Interactive sentences A and B are considered to indicate significant intrapsychic conflict if and only if the points of the association structure to which they are coordinate lie within distance *n* of one another along a path in that structure, and if they meet one of the general criteria [rules (1)–(5)] for intersentence conflict.

The particular form in which such a rule might be stated, of course, would rely upon empirical criteria, i.e., it would be a generalization from previous observations of dream structure properties in relation to extra-dream person properties. It might prove to be true, for instance, that interactive sentences attached to *ego-points* (chapter 13) in a structuregram would have more predictive value than those attached to other points.

SSLS's scored sentences also permit, of course, the determination of *dynamic conflicts*. Thus ambivalence toward Sp_2 (wife? female patients? women?) might be assumed from these two "Botanical Monograph" sentences:

A-21 $E \overset{+}{\underset{}{\to}} \overset{+}{Sp_2}$;
A-26 $E \gtrless \underline{Sp_2}$.

Or, in a more complex case, structural symmetry might be accompanied by dynamic asymmetry, e.g.:

A-9 $\underline{E} \gtrless Sp_1$;
A-10 $[\overset{+}{Sy_{2D}} \equiv E \boxed{\rightarrow} Sp_1]$;
C-41 $\overset{+}{Sp_1} \overset{+}{\to} E$;
C-42 $[\overset{+}{Sy_{2D}} \overset{+}{=} Sp_1 \boxed{\rightarrow} E]$.

Freud's disinterest in approaching his wife through a particular symbolic means is "in conflict" with his wife's strong interest in approaching Freud in the same manner.

Summary

Both at a theoretical and at an operational level, then, an SSLS dream analysis has specific features that could contribute to its usefulness in the clinical domain. Several other such features already have been noted (the rulefulness by which person-propositions may be formulated; the nonselectivity and exhaustiveness of SSLS's analysis; the ruleful segregation of motive-relevant [interactive] and -irrelevant [associative] material in dream and free-associative protocols; the verifiability of propositions cast interpersonally, rather than intrapsychically; and so on).

Another set of investigative possibilities can only be alluded to here, although they probably are much more interesting from the point of view of clinical research and theory than the practical applications heretofore stressed. Insofar as SSLS permits reliable identification of thought and language mechanisms, it can be used to characterize these mechanisms in a variety of psychopathological states, both in sleep and in wakefulness. If these states involve different kinds of symbolic dysfunction, then SSLS can identify specific dimensions symbolically discriminating them from one another as well as from nonpathological states.

SSLS also can be used to systematically address the question of parallels in dream and schizophrenic "language." Is it true, for example, that the normal subject's sleep-onset stage of ego destructuralization (see chapter 5) is "schizophrenic" in quality, while her or his REM sleep is not? SSLS also might be a valuable method in the characterization of momentarily altered states of waking consciousness in "normal" subjects (Tart, 1969, 1975). Is it true that dreams are like waking thought in their linguistic properties, while many "other" altered states of consciousness are not? What are the dimensions of similarity and difference in particular cases?

Freud's free-association technique could be a most valuable tool in investigating "states of consciousness" or "mental operations" in *any* case where the person's "inputs" are from storage rather than from external reality. Formalization of Freud's technique might supply the missing step in making it appealing to research workers in other areas of psychology where reliable characterization of mental structures and mental operations is a primary concern. It is pleasant to contemplate that Freud's other major interest—psychopathology—someday too may be incorporated within the mainstream of cognitive psychology, and that altered states of consciousness might be rescued from the hands of those with more enthusiasm for subject matter than aptness of conceptualization or capability of method.

CHAPTER 17

Dream Processes and Experimental Dream Psychology

As indicated in chapter 5, a major motive guiding the development of a reliable system for coding and organizing free-associative data was the perception that the associationless sleep-and-dream approach of the past twenty years has not contributed much to our understanding of dream meanings or dream processes. I now will indicate how SSLS, which includes rules for coding and organizing free associations, presents new possibilities for more meaningful empirical studies of dream processes. Basic to all of these possibilities is SSLS's ability to identify structures of the sleeping mind and some transformational processes operating upon them (see chapters 4 and 15). Following the presentation of a small sample of programmatic suggestions regarding some of the specific problems researchable via SSLS, I will close with a brief defense of the underlying model that we can study how the mind works in sleep through the analysis of dream reports and their free associations.

Research Possibilities

The Uniqueness of Dreams

Dreams are puzzling because they seem unlike the products of waking associative processes. But the product dissimilarity need not imply a fundamental process dissimilarity. In fact, an unresolved, but very basic, question in dream psychology concerns the extent to which the processes of dream formation can be unique to sleep (cf. chapters 4 and 15). Clearly there are different kinds of waking thought, as well as different kinds of sleeping thought, so that the problem is more complex than often has been imagined. Recent empirical work (Foulkes and Fleisher, 1975), for example, suggests much overlap between dreams and thought contents periodically sampled in relaxed wakefulness.

Where subjects' sleeping- and waking-thought samples are obtained similarly, are associated to similarly, and are analyzed by SSLS's content and structural analyses, we should be able to determine in a relatively precise way the extent to which given associative mechanisms operate in the generation of both dreams and labeled forms of waking thought. We can substitute a deep-to-surface empirical analysis for the armchair observation and surface-level comparison which previously have been used to answer the question at issue.

Structurally, we also would be able to test the oft-repeated allegation that free association to any mental content (e.g., a phone number) ultimately leads to the same result as free association to dreams. Is there anything about dream reports, as free-associative stimuli, which makes them more likely to generate deep motive structures in free-associative responses?

Dream-Work in Different Stages of Sleep

Psychophysiological research (as discussed in chapter 5) suggests the necessity of several structural models for sleep, not just one. It now is known that sleep onset, non-REM sleep, and REM sleep produce somewhat distinctive psychological content.

However, research has rarely gone beyond superficial description of dreams characterizing different physiological states to a careful characterization of the quality or level of mental organization modal to these states. Associations are not collected. There is no attempt to trace out the ways in which underlying concerns are reflected in manifest dream content nor to characterize the mechanisms involved even for any one of these states, much less on a comparative basis across stages. [Foulkes and Vogel, 1974, p. 12]

Heretofore there was no efficient tool with which to undertake comparative studies of dream-work in different psychophysiological states; now there is. SSLS was developed precisely for this purpose. It can be applied to any appropriate set of dream and associational materials collected across the several psychophysiological states of sleep.

Home Dreams and Laboratory Dreams

Another important issue for laboratory dream research has been the extent to which laboratory-collected dreams differ from home-collected dreams. Domhoff has characterized laboratory dreams as "dull" and as having little putative value in studying "unconscious fantasies and symbolism" (1969, p. 215). Several systematic comparisons of home and laboratory dreams in which dream-sampling factors have been held constant have, on the other hand, suggested few significant differences between dreams collected in the laboratory and those collected at home (Weisz and Foulkes, 1970; Foulkes and Shepherd, 1972b). Yet the feeling seems to persist among many workers in the dream area that laboratory-collected dreams somehow are more trivial products of a less rich process than are home-collected dreams. Since product comparisons seem not to have convinced anybody, it is appropriate to suggest process comparisons. SSLS's content and structural analyses will permit such comparisons, and perhaps allow some conclusions to be drawn about the relative richness of the underlying thought processes in the two settings.

Structural Similarities in Sleep Mentation

A more basic topic for which recent dream research has achieved no very satisfactory resolution is that of the interrelatedness of the mental activity occurring within the night for a given subject (e.g., Trosman, Rechtschaffen, Offenkrantz, and Wolpert, 1960; Rechtschaffen, Vogel, and Shaikun, 1963). Analytic techniques in such studies have dwelt on manifest content similarities from REM period to REM period or from non-REM period to REM period; private meanings have been considered only unsystematically, and structural relationships have not received much attention at all. It would, therefore, be of great interest to use SSLS in investigating such questions as: specific contents aside, what are the structural relationships among the dreams of a night, e.g., are *dream structuregrams* for dreams of the same night more similar than their manifest contents might indicate? when one considers the hypothetical generative structures and processes underlying the dreams of a night—i.e., *dream-formation structuregrams*—are these generative structures more similar than their ultimate products might indicate? is there, as Gerald Vogel has suggested to me, a tendency for structural similarity *across* nights of REM-period dreams with the same ordinal position within each night?

Individual Differences

Individual differences also might be approached from a structural point of view. Even where different generators (live digraph points) and results (dream elements) are involved, is there a reliable tendency for a given person to use the same mix of transformational processes over time in an idiosyncratic way? Do the initiating structures persist over time in a manner not immediately discernible in the manifest dream?

Epistemological Questions

Validation of Dream-Process Statements

Students of dreaming forever are reminding their readers, and themselves, that the datum of dream analysis is a dream report, not a dream. A dream is an *experience*, which no third party can observe, and for which there can be no interobserver reliability. Thus any dream discourse involves processes of inference as much as of observation.

The situation seems to become much more acute when we purport not only to be describing what has been dreamed—something to which at least one member of the species can bear direct testimony—but also to be characterizing the formative matrix from which the dream experience emerged—which, to our knowledge, no one ever has observed or could observe. Thus we need to give some consideration now as to how, if at all, one possibly could validate what we have been calling a dream-process statement. How do we know that our reconstruction describes how the dream "really" was dreamed?

The obvious answer, of course, is that we have no way of "knowing" that. There is no other, more direct observation of dream causation to which we may refer dream-process statements generated by the free-association/explanation model. There is no way of establishing that these statements *describe* how dreams "really" happen.

This, however, is how it always is in cognitive psychology. We do not observe mental operations directly. We assess the situation or context in which an output is generated and we describe the output. The rest always is reconstruction—of the rules which most efficiently relate known inputs to observed outputs. The only novelty of Freud's model, or of the dream case, is that we cannot so easily assess situational or contextual inputs to the process as we can in wakefulness, where these inputs can be observable, manipulable stimuli. The dreamer's "inputs" are internal. But, in his free-association method, Freud has given us both a reliable and a plausible way of reconstructing the associative context from which the dream emerged.

Freud's dream-process statements, then, or those generated by his free-association/explanation model more generally, are not meant to be descriptive. He realized that "observation" of dream formation was out of the question.[1] What he was trying to do when he introduced the concepts of dream formation and dream-work was to fulfill the most basic mission he set for himself—the scientific *explanation* of dream phenomena. Dream-process statements are to be evaluated, then, not for their accuracy as description, but for their adequacy as explanation.

Explanatory Value

For Freud, and for anyone using his free-association/explanation model, a dream is explained when we can specify an introductory set of premises—dream-thoughts—and an intermediate set of premises—dream-work mechanisms transforming those dream-thoughts—such that the manifest dream is a comprehensible outcome. The criteria we must use in evaluating these premises, then, are the formal and empirical criteria used in the judgment of explanations (e.g., Sherwood, 1969). The explanatory statements must be consistent, on the one hand, with what we know about the requirements of explanation and, on the other, with what we know about dreams. From them, we should be able to deduce dream phenomena, with both power and efficiency.

I see nothing inherently unsatisfactory in the general form of Freud's model of dream explanation, or with any SSLS variant thereof. Freud begins with operationally defined antecedent events from a relevant domain. Plausibly, I think, he focuses on certain motive structures, which, on the basis of waking

[1] Modern psychophysiological research techniques, particularly those employing "microscopic" correlation of dream quality with discrete phasic physiological indicators in sleep (e.g., Molinari and Foulkes, 1969; Pivik, 1970; Pessah and Roffwarg, 1972; Watson, 1972; Foulkes and Pope, 1973) have teased us with the possibility that we might get some physiological indices of fluctuations in ongoing dream processes so that these processes could, as it were, be "read from outside." That is still a possibility, but it is one which apparently eludes our present technology and/or imagination. Even when and if such indices emerge, moreover, they may give us more of a grasp on dream development than on dream formation. There are several suggestions in *The Interpretation of Dreams* that Freud felt that dream formation was quite unconscious—i.e., in principle unobservable (see Foulkes, 1964).

observations, seem relatively likely to assume a dominant role in the organization of thought in psychophysiological states characterized by external stimulus occlusion. The intermediate steps of the explanation—the dream-process statements themselves—can, as we have seen, in principle be defined in terms of reliable observations in the relevant domain. They also can be checked for consistency with other observations we can make in that domain (cf., Freud, 1900, chs. I, V). In Freud's case, there is the additional factor that his dream-work mechanisms may have utility in other domains, such as symptom formation in neurosis and slips of speech (Freud, 1917*a*). Taken together, the introductory premises regarding basic dream-thoughts and the intermediate ones specifying dream-work transformations define what could be a coherent and fairly parsimonious explanatory framework. It certainly is superior to any other, since there has been no other serious attempt at dream explanation (as opposed, for instance, to REM-state explanation).

Once the scoring system makes its particular substantive entries in Freud's general explanation model, moreover, there are additional empirical checkpoints. First, we can, through a form of construct validation, determine how much sense it makes to say that the dreamer "has" the motive structures ascribed to her or him as interactive sentences. This is simply the process of validating an interpretation (see chapter 16).

But this last step is not sufficient for validating the explanation. Even if interpretations seem justified, we still do not know whether the motives in question, coupled with subsequently imputed dream-work processes, have much explanatory value in the dream context. The second empirical checkpoint, then, must be the determination of the model's explanatory power and subsumptive range. How well is any particular aspect of a dream explained by this model? How much of a dream is explained by it? To how many other dreams does it apply? It should be clear that formalization of Freud's model into a scoring system and a system of structural analysis provides a means by which dream explanations can be judged. That is, not only does such formalization permit rigorous definitions of terms used in explanations, it also allows empirical study of the explanatory power and efficiency of various alternative terms which might be so defined.

Now this brings up an important objection to the general model. Since we must assume that free association is a determined process in an organized system, doesn't it follow, trivially, that the products of that lawful associative process can be turned around and used to explain, lawfully, the stimulating dream element? The fact of *some* empirical fit may, in this sense, be pre-ordained. But it is neither trivial nor self-evident to inquire what particular translations have to be made of free associations in order to generate what particular explanatory premises in terms of which dreams can be explained powerfully and economically.

Further, we may compare premises generated by free association with those generated in other ways. Even if Freud's tactic of using X to stimulate Y and then turning Y around to become a hypothetical generator of X may preordain some sort of empirical fit in a dream-formation model, it does not indicate whether a set of Y's generated in one specifiable way will prove superior to a set of Y's generated in some other way. Freud wants to maintain something more than the hypothesis that dreams can be assigned meanings and can be inserted within the stream of waking psychic activity. This hypothesis had long since been employed, albeit unsystematically, by others. Freud wants to demonstrate that the technique of free association, since it simulates some of the conditions of sleep—for example, relative freedom from boundedness to external stimulation and from considerations of waking logic—yields peculiarly powerful and subsumptive explanations of dreams. Thus, once again, it is not trivial to determine those particular entries in a general $X \rightarrow Y \rightarrow X$ model which yield a best fit of all potential fits in the final "prediction" of X.

A related objection to the model is that it is circular, in the sense that we seem to need to know X in order to know the Y which explains X. Basic dream-thoughts are not determined in, but they *are* determined after the occurrence of, the dream to be explained. The antecedent events are not *specified* antecedently. In what sense, then, can the explanation be "causal"? How can it ever be predictive?

I am reminded of what I take, as a rank layman, to be the situation in meteorology. Good reasons generally can be found, *ex post facto*, for the weather having turned out the way it did. It depends on today's outcome how we select and order yesterday's variables in framing these good reasons. True prediction in meteorology is less conspicuously successful than this sort of after-the-fact rationalization. I think the analogy is applicable to dream psychology in several respects.

First, it *has* been a genuine scientific accomplishment to develop a moderately efficient framework in which we can understand current weather conditions as a function of antecedent variables in the same domain and of intervening processes claiming a certain degree of lawfulness. It has, for most of us, removed weather from the extra-scientific sphere of the supernatural or of blind chance. Freud aspired to do the same sort of thing for dreams, and, I think, in this he was largely successful.

Second, the formalization of a scientific model of *ex post facto* explanation is likely to give us a better "handle" on the more ambitious goal of true prediction. Formalization forces us to be more precise in conceptualization and more operational in definition of dependent and independent variables. Its successes and its failures indicate which variables bear more intense watching. Thus it leads naturally toward attempts to transcend the limits of postdiction. This, we may imagine, will be the case in dream psychology, where *there is nothing in principle to limit us to dreams as the empirical base for the ascription of regnant motive states to the dreamer. And, should dream-work mechanisms prove to have some generality across occasions, it might be possible, in test cases, to dispense with* ex post facto *observations altogether.* This might not give us very *good* explanations, but could demonstrate a modicum of predictive value to those for whom such a demonstration is critical or in those situations where it becomes a practical requirement.

Third, the analogy suggests a range in which prediction might soon become possible, and a range in which its immediate achievement seems implausible. For instance, just as it is improbable that anyone now can, or soon will be able to, predict with high certainty all those variables whose confluence will constitute tomorrow's 2 P.M. weather in any particular locale marked by climatological variability, so too it is improbable that dream forecasting ever will enable us to predict the precise form of any particular manifest dream on any given REM-period awakening. But it does not seem so impossible that we might, particularly, as in the weather case, over the short run, be able to use extra-dream variables to predict some of the structural forms of variation in thought during sleep. Some limited predictive success already has been noted in studies of influencing dreams (chapter 5). More may be expected when we know not only external stimuli but also the hypothetical properties of the sleeping mind which reconstructs and transforms these stimuli. While particular associative paths and particular symbolic outcomes no doubt will remain relatively insusceptible to predictive analysis, it is not out of the question that we might have some predictive success with, for example, the coded structuring of dream interactions.

Thus, if we use meteorology as a cautionary guide, our immediate predictive aspirations may be relatively modest, but prediction is a possible consequence of the *ex post facto* free-association/explanation model. It may seem strange that prediction poses such acute problems in the study of sleeping thought. The "noise" introduced by the external world is, after all, rather minimal in sleep. But what our case may indicate is merely that whatever predictive successes waking psychology has enjoyed have rested largely on finding or manipulating patterns in that noise. They are achievements of social ecology, more than of personology. When we consider sleep, where the interiorization rather than the external form of social reality matters, we see how little we really know of persons. Since Freud, that has been the frustration, but also the challenge, of dream psychology.

APPENDICES

APPENDIX A

Supplemental Scoring Rules for SSLS

The rules given below supplement category definitions and scoring rules presented in chapter 11. Thus, one cannot enter the book at this point to determine all scoring operations of SSLS's content analysis. Furthermore, intelligent application of SSLS demands an understanding of its rationale and orienting assumptions, as discussed in chapter 11.

Structural Analysis

What Is Scored

Because both the intent and the underlying conceptual framework of SSLS differ from those of traditional grammar, it is not expected that there will be a perfect, or even close, correspondence between ordinary grammatical structures or constituents and those of an SSLS analysis. Thus, in general, there is not a 1 : 1 relationship between textual sentences and SSLS sentences, or between textual verbs and SSLS verbs, or between textual nouns and SSLS nouns. SSLS is concerned with abstracting from a text specified kinds of relational structures which can and do appear in a variety of grammatical guises.

Verbs. SSLS's verb is defined by a grammatical verb in the text plus any grammatical modifiers needed to establish the form of a subject-object relationship in terms of SSLS's verb categories. Thus, in

I moved toward X

"moved" is the grammatical verb, "toward" is a preposition, and "X" is the object of the prepositional phrase. To SSLS, however, "moved toward" defines a relationship between "I" and "X," and thus is the textual constituent corresponding to an SSLS verb.

SSLS's broader definition of verb also is required in cases where English grammar *objectifies action or relationship.* Thus, in

I gave help to X

"help" is a noun, the direct object, while "X" is an indirect object. SSLS defines only one species of object, here corresponding to X. Thus, the text is translated as

I (ego)/helped (moved toward)/X (object).

"Giving help" defines the nature of the E-X relationship (cf., "giving hell"), and "help," rather than describing any "thing," describes an activity of a particular sort—that is, it corresponds to an SSLS verb. Thus, SSLS converts "action nouns" and "relationship nouns" (e.g., "they had a good *relationship*") to their true verb status.

In certain intermediate cases, *a noun in the text defines both the verb and a Means-sentence noun.* For example, in

I gave poison to Pm_1

"poison" both defines the verb $-\!\!\prec$ and is the specific, palpable instrument by which the $-\!\!\prec$ relationship is accomplished. Hence, SSLS scores the textual statement as

1) $E -\!\!\prec Pm_1$;
2) $[Sy_{1A} = E \boxed{-\!\!\prec} Pm_1]$.

Or, where an action-noun is adjectivally modified so as to give it a more palpable instrumental reference, the same effect can be achieved. For example,

I gave medical help to Pm_1

is scored as

1) $E \rightarrow Pm_1$;
2) $[Sy_{1A} = E \boxdot Pm_1]$;

where Sy_{1A} = medicine, or medical substances, or medical "procedures"— the last translation making this a most marginal case of nounlike instrumentality. A more clear-cut case is

I gave financial help to Pm_1

where "money" is an obvious palpable means by which the $\rightarrow$ interaction is sustained.

One grammatical sentence in the text may lead to several SSLS sentences because the textual sentence contains *multiple and coordinate subjects, verbs, or objects*. Thus

I both liked and disliked Jack, Jill, and the old woman

leads to 6 SSLS sentences:

1) $E \rightarrow Pm_1$;   2) $E \prec Pm_1$;
3) $E \rightarrow Pf_1$;   4) $E \prec Pf_1$;
5) $E \rightarrow M_1$;   6) $E \prec M_1$;

(where we assume Jack and Jill are contemporaries of the dreamer).

Where some *additional interconnectedness of parallel initiators or recipients of the same interactive sentence is explicit*, one or more associative sentences also should be written. For example,

We [i.e., he and I] walked to school together

would be scored

1) $\overset{+}{E} \rightarrow Sy_{1A}$;
2) $[E \, ⍾ \, Pm_1]$.

Here it is the "together" which justifies the second sentence. A phrase such as "all three of us together" might have justified three additional associative sentences, namely E with A, E with B, and A with B. However, *without such explicit additional linking terms, an interactive "we"* (or "we all", or "us both") *is translated as $\overset{+}{E}$, and neither separate interactive nor separate associative sentences are written explicating its composition.* Thus,

> We were walking to school

is scored simply as

$$\overset{+}{E} \rightarrow Sy_{1A}.$$

(Where explicit additional linkages are *partial* [e.g., "I did X with my brother and sister"], only those partial linkages are scored [E with brother and E with sister, but not brother with sister; that is, the sentence seems to mean "I, with my brother, and I, with my sister, did X"].)

Associative sentence linkages, on the other hand, are routinely scored, whatever the textual wording, whenever verb and object or subject and verb are identical for parallel *associative* relationships. If, for example, in asserting that "we were in the car," the dreamer seems to be referring to herself, to her mother, and to her father, then the appropriate scoring would be

$$[E \updownarrow Sy_{1A}];$$
$$[M \updownarrow Sy_{1A}];$$
$$[F \updownarrow Sy_{1A}].$$

In such cases, the paired associative sentences are scored *as a block*, with ordering within the block correlated with order of character introduction in the text, and the whole block preceding any "tie-in" sentences which might be required by rule (5), p. 383. In effect, *there is no associative $\overset{+}{E}$ which stands for "we"* (or "they"). Separate associative sentences must be written indicating, insofar as it is ascertainable, the composition of the "we."

A parallel kind of sentence blocking occurs whenever *an interactive "they"* requires, because of its diverse age/sex composition and the independence of relationships otherwise scored for its separate elements, separate interactive sentences. For example, if a female dreams of two peers, one male and one female, hitting a female friend, then, instead of

$$\overset{+}{E} \prec Pf_1$$
(they) (hit) (friend)

the appropriate scoring would be

$$Pm_1 \prec E$$
(he) (hit) (friend)

and

$$E \prec Pf_1$$
(she) (hit) (friend)

scored as a block. (Tie-in sentences following a block always would be written according to the order of sentences within that block.)

Sometimes *multiple subjects, verbs, or objects are textually described in superordinate/subordinate terms*, rather than coordinately. Here SSLS follows the sense of the text, and places the superordinate term in an interactive sentence, and the subordinate one in an associative sentence. For example,

Along with all the guys, I walked to school

is scored, for a male dreamer, as:

1) $[E \updownarrow \overset{+}{P}m_1]$ [1];
2) $E \to Sy_{1A}$.

In the verb case, we might have the textual statement,

I lovingly hit my husband

which would be scored as

1) $E \prec Sp_1$;
2) $[\overset{+}{\to} \updownarrow \prec]$.

(It may be wondered why "lovingly" is not considered a *dynamic modifier* of "hit." The reason is that love and hate are considered as qualitatively different forms of relationship, while modifiers encode factors augmenting or attenuating any single form of relationship. Thus, adverbial forms of $\circledcirc\to$, $\to$, and $\prec$ are scored as described here. However, withdrawal

[1]The dynamic scores in this and subsequent examples are explained later, pp. 405–18.

[←] *would* be considered an attenuative modifier of $\odot\rightarrow$, $\rightarrow$, and $\prec$, and, in its adverbial form [e.g., "neglectfully"], would be scored as such, rather than in a separate associative sentence. Thus,

> I neglectfully loved the man

is scored as

> $E \rightleftharpoons Pm_1$.)

At times, *the distinction between coordinate and superordinate/subordinate construction is blurred.* For example,

> 1) I walked to school;
> 2) All the guys did, too.

Or,

> 1) I was making love to my husband;
> 2) I did it violently.

In cases such as these, where there is an explicit or implicit repetition of the subject, verb, and object in a grammatically complete second sentence, two interactive sentences would be scored, even though the second textual sentence seems merely to qualify the first. Thus:

> 1) $E \rightarrow Sy_{1A}$;
> 2) $\overset{+}{E} \rightarrow Sy_{1A}$;

and

> 1) $E \overset{+}{\rightarrow} Sp_1$;
> 2) $E \overset{+}{\prec} Sp_1$.

(In the former case, there is an additional applicable convention, that governing successive repetition of the same interactive sentence—see pp. 416–18.)

Where, *in describing an activity encoded by a single verb, the dreamer repeats the textual units justifying the verb and the non-E noun element,* the interactive structure is to be scored twice. For example,

> They went home, went home . . . ,

is scored as

1) $\overset{+}{\text{E}} \rightarrow \text{Sy}_{1A}$;
2) $\overset{+}{\text{E}} \rightarrow \text{Sy}_{1A}$.

The repetition of a single textual unit (responsible for the subject *or* verb *or* object score) *or of E-verb units* results in dynamic augmentation of elements in a single sentence structure (see pp. 405–18). Thus:

1) I, I went home $= \overset{+}{\text{E}} \rightarrow \text{Sy}_{1A}$;
2) I went, went home $= \text{E} \overset{+}{\rightarrow} \text{Sy}_{1A}$;
3) I went home, home $= \text{E} \rightarrow \overset{+}{\text{Sy}}_{1A}$;
4) The man, he went home $= \overset{+}{\text{E}} \rightarrow \text{Sy}_{1A}$;
5) I was, I was home $= [\overset{+}{\text{E}} \updownarrow \text{Sy}_{1A}]$.

Note that pronominal, as well as literal, repetition is scored as dynamic augmentation for nouns.

We have seen that an adverb ("lovingly") can be scored as an SSLS verb; the same is true of *an adjective.* For example,

A generally loving mother sometimes hits her child.

Here, two interactive sentences would be scored, since two alternating relationships are asserted:

1) The mother generally loves her child;
2) The mother sometimes hits her child.

(Where, however, the implication seems to be simultaneity of action, as in

The loving mother hit her child

then the adjectival modifier is used, as in the case of

I lovingly hit my husband

to code a separate association statement $[\overset{+}{\rightarrow} \updownarrow \prec]$. Superordinate/subordinate status clearly is present in the dreamer's description.[2])

---

[2] It will be noted how often the scoring of the preceding instances depends upon the precise wording of the material being analyzed. For this reason it is absolutely essential that SSLS be applied to the dreamer's own account of her or his dreams and associations (as it has been tape-recorded or written out), rather than to some summarization of these materials by others.

Sometimes the text will contain *grammatical verbs which serve a function of adjectival modification* rather than one of relationship assertion. For example,

1) The woman *was* pretty = $\overset{+}{P}f$;
2) The bucket *was* rusty = $\underline{Sy}_{1A}$.

In neither example does the grammatical verb relate the SSLS noun to another SSLS noun, nor divide the original noun into discriminable components. *No novel structural relationship is asserted*, and none is scored. The "being" verb in these cases merely aids in the global characterization of the one noun's suitability for some relationship. The dynamic score is added to the SSLS sentence which codes that relationship. For example,

1) The woman was pretty.
2) I liked her. $= E \rightarrow \overset{+}{P}f_1$.

(Where there is no such other sentence, i.e., where an entire dream report consists of a sentence such as "The woman was pretty," a *defective* sentence—see Dynamic Analysis, pp. 238-42—must be scored.) It is interesting that neuropsychological data suggest a discrimination of sentences such as

The woman *was* pretty.

from sentences such as

The bucket *was* above the well.

Luria (1973) indicates that damage to the "tertiary" zones of the parietal cortex spares understanding of sentences such as the former, while rendering incomprehensible sentences such as the latter, sentences which *do* propose SSLS structural relationships.

In summary, although there is bound to be a correlation between textual verbs and the sentences they define, and SSLS verbs and the sentences *they* define, it will be an inexact one. The question in the analyst's mind should be one not of the *sentences* in the text but of the *relationships* these sentences assert. For any given textual sentence, there may be zero, one, or more than one such relationship, hence zero, one, or more than one SSLS sentence to be scored.

Nouns. SSLS's noun terms are defined by grammatical nouns in the text plus any grammatical modifiers required to place the referent in an appropriate SSLS noun category. Thus, in the sentence

The *old* lady moved toward me

or in the sentence

The lady, *who was old*, moved toward me

the italicized noun modifiers are used to place the character in the appropriate SSLS noun category, viz., M. Such "noun modifiers" are considered parts of SSLS's noun classification, rather than as SSLS dynamic modifiers.

A major problem in regard to noun scoring is that *SSLS considers some textual nouns to be "nonstructural," hence ineligible for separate SSLS coding.* For example, in the following sentence,

I was painting the picture in bad *weather*:
    cold *wind*, *rain*, and *sleet*,

the underlined terms describe conditions adverse to the consummation of the painting project; hence, they are negative dynamic modifiers of the verb "to paint":

$$E \xrightarrow{\ominus} Sy_{1A}$$

(I create, in adverse conditions, a picture). Or, if in describing a picnic, the subject rhapsodizes:

The *sky* was clear. The *grass* was green. The
trees were lush. There were *birds* . . .

the intent seems to be not one of elaborating structural relationships integral to the dream narrative but simply one of saying "conditions were perfect" for the picnickers' "approach" to their food:

$$\overset{+}{E} \overset{+}{\rightarrow} Sy_{1A}.$$

More generally, *climatic or other setting/background descriptions of nouns without direct characterological involvement in the dream narrative* are considered dynamic modifiers, rather than coded as SSLS nouns.

Specifically,

    1) It was a sunny day;
    2) The sun was shining;

would not lead to the formation of a "celestial" noun class, with a "sun" entry therein. Rather, an adjacent interactive verb would be dynamically modified, generally positively. However,

    The sun shone on me

does bring the sun into "interaction" with a character, that is, there is an assertion of the relationship,

    Sun/moves toward/me

and sun would be entered in the dream lexicon as an SSLS noun. The key in discriminating structural from dynamic uses of climatic, setting, and so on, features is noting whether the textual noun is associated with, or interacts with, another SSLS noun in a complete subject-verb-object unit.

As already has been noted (Lexical Classes, pp. 225–29), *the general bias of SSLS is to restrict noun codes to concrete ("poison") objects or personages* as opposed to those more abstract ("harm") concepts which actually are covert verb forms. Nonetheless, *abstract concepts (e.g., "science") may be scored as SSLS nouns* where: (1) they do not seem to be covert descriptions of activity (the focus is on the "knowledge," rather than the "knowing"); (2) there is no more concrete realization of the concept in the dream context (there is no possible alternative scoring of "test-tubes," "laboratories," etc.); and (3) the concept enters into clear-cut structural relationships with other SSLS nouns ("science reminds me of Dr. Brown," "Dr. Brown was thinking of science," etc.).

Thus, as in verb scoring, so too in noun scoring: it is the structural nature of the text, from SSLS's unique perspective, rather than its conventional grammatical analysis, which indicates how textual material is to be translated into the SSLS format.

Excluded Material. In *dream protocols,* the following material is not scored:

(1) *Waking reactions, or free associations, to the dream.* For example,

    That sure was a crazy thing to dream.

> I guess the reason I dreamed that was I took a bus yesterday to Chey-
> enne, and the driver was rude.

Such material can, of course, be scored as dream associations. The point is
that it should be excluded from the scoring of the dream-as-dream.

(2) *Dream- or report-process statements.* For example,

> The dream was hazy, you know, kind of ill-formed; the imagery never
> was terribly clear. It was "spacey."
> I'm having great difficulty remembering just what happened next, let's
> see—oh hell, I can't remember.
> Do you want me to say some more about that? I remember lots of the
> details . . .

This material characterizes the process of dreaming the dream, or of reporting it, rather than any substantive content.

(3) *Statements of differentiation or exclusion.* For example,

> In real life my pet is a collie, not a boxer.
> I wasn't in the dream.
> There was no one else there but me.
> I couldn't see any setting.

The first statement is essentially an association to the dream-element "boxer"
to the effect that "my dog is a collie." The remaining statements don't tell
us what was in the dream, but, rather, what was not in the dream. (*Statements of exclusion can, in certain instances, be used to justify the scoring of
a negative dynamic modifier.* Here the statement contrasts a dream setting/
characterization with that *almost invariably* expected for a setting/character-
ization of its class; for example,

> The field was totally barren of any vegetation = $\underline{Sy}_{1A}$.

This convention should be used sparingly, however: a folks-less home ["My
parents weren't there"], for instance, is not sufficiently unusual to merit
a negative modification of "home.")

*In scoring dream protocols, material first advanced, then retracted, is
considered a valid part of the dream account.* For example, in

> No, I'm wrong, it wasn't my father, it was my friend Bill

both father and Bill are scored as characters and as parties to the relationship in question. As Freud (1900) long ago indicated, the retraction or revision of early-reported dream details may serve to disguise what really happened in the dream, rather than serving to make the dream report more accurate.

In *free associations* to the dream, the following material is not scored:

(1) *Association-process statements.* For example,

> I didn't associate to the dream when I woke up—I had to hurry off to work. I didn't get a chance to think about it again till evening. Anyway, the first thing I thought about then was that . . .
>
> I'm having difficulty coming up with any associations to that . . . hmm, just drawing a blank . . . .
>
> Somehow, I'm not just sure what the connection is, but this last thought led on to a recollection of . . .

(2) *The dream-element associated to.* For example,

> I dreamed about a bush. . . . Let's see, that reminds me of . . .

(However, *when the dream element is "repeated" in altered form*, such that its SSLS scoring would now be different from that assigned it in the dream scoring, the new characterization of the dream material *is* scored among the free-associations. A good example of this is found in "Botanical Monograph":

> [Dream] . . . a dried specimen of the plant as though it *had been taken from* a herbarium;
>
> [Association] . . . a dried specimen of the plant . . . as though it *had been a* herbarium.

Compare the scoring in chapter 12 of these statements: [X-7/8] and [C-2].)

In scoring free associations, obviously no substantive material ever is excluded on account of its irrelevance. For example, in

> I dreamed about a bush . . . . hmm . . . Oh, say, by the way, did you ever get tickets to that concert, Dr. X?

everything is scored.

By convention, in writing out the dreamer's text, *excluded material con-*

tributed by the dreamer is put in brackets, while interpolations by the analyst are put in parentheses. Thus:

> [I can't remember what followed next
> but I seem to remember that]
> The guy asked (us) $= Pm_1 \rightleftharpoons \overset{+}{E}$
> if he was wearing clothes $= [Pm_1 \overset{+}{\updownarrow} Sy_{1A}]$.

Units of Analysis: Verbs and Verb-Defined Sentences

Sentences. Each SSLS sentence contains a subject, a verb, and an object. Superficially, *the Means sentence* is an exception to this rule, since it generally contains at least 3 nouns along with 2 verbs; for example:

$$[Sy \quad = \quad E \quad \boxed{\rightarrow} \quad Pf]$$
noun verb noun verb noun.

However, the interaction unit here is considered an *object*:

$$(Sy) \quad (=) (E \boxed{\rightarrow} Pf)$$
subject verb object.

That is, the Means sentence may be considered to relate a noun to an interaction unit, and will be scored whenever a noun modifies such a unit, whether instrumentality in the narrow sense is present or not. For example,

Home was where we met $= [Sy_{1A} = E \boxed{\updownarrow} Pf_1]$;

or

"Home modified the fact of our association."

The verb position in an SSLS sentence always is filled by one, and only one, verb code. Subject/object positions can, however, be filled by nouns or verbs. For example,

1) $[Pf_1 \updownarrow Pf_2]$ = the women, together;
2) $[\overset{+}{\rightarrow} \updownarrow \overset{+}{\prec}]$ = loving reminds me of hating.

However, verbs can fill subject/object roles only in *With* sentences. One never would score, for instance,

→ → —<.

The most general form of SSLS sentences is, of course:

noun, verb, noun.

Interactive sentences always contain one and only one SSLS category in each of the three structural positions of their sentence frame. As we have seen, separate sentences must be written for interaction statements with multiple subjects, verbs, or objects. *Associative sentences also can contain but one "functional" verb, subject, and object.* However, as we have just seen, the word "functional" covers some fudging for Means sentences, in which the "object" is, in fact, a three-code interaction unit. There is, as we shall soon see, still more fudging than this: *the Means interaction unit can, uniquely within SSLS, contain multiple subjects or objects (in parentheses)*, while retaining the overt status of possessing a single subject and a single object. Moreover, as we also shall see later, there are cases in which subjects and/or objects in *any* SSLS sentence can consist of multiple Sy *lexical* codes.

The basic decision to be made about any textually asserted relationship is, of course, whether it is interactive or associative. *SSLS recommends the adoption of a perceptual frame of reference in determining whether a relationship is associative or interactive and in determining the particular verb category to be scored.* That is, one should try to "picture" the referents of the textual assertion. Is there relative movement? If so, who/what is moving in reference to what fixed point of reference? Thus, when a dreamer says, "I was playing pool": (1) it would not be scored with the verb ↕ *—Ego* (associated) *With game* or *game-paraphernalia*—because the game is an *activity*, and the essence of the game is *relative movement*; (2) it would not be scored as *Ego Moving Toward Game* (metaphorically) or *game-paraphernalia* (literally), because in our most representative picturing of a pool game, the player retains approximately the same relative position to cue (in hand) and table (close by); (3) it *would* be scored *Ego* (as ball) *Moving Toward pocket(s)*, because this is the activity which defines the game of pool: ("played on a pool table with a cue ball and 15 other balls that are driven into the pockets" [*The Random House Dictionary, College Edition*, p. 1031]). In using a perceptual frame of reference the scorer is, of course, attempting to recreate the medium in which dreams typically occur.

As the preceding example also illustrates, *it can be very helpful to use an ordinary dictionary in resolving difficult scoring decisions.* We have been surprised at how often our implicit beliefs about the defining properties of noun or relationship terms are *not* supported by dictionary entries. Besides correcting individual-scorer errors in denotative meaning, of course, the use of a standard dictionary also should increase inter-scorer reliability.

Interactive Verbs. The basic unit of interaction or motivational analysis is the *interactive sentence* (any sentence in which the verb is coded →, ←, ─<, or ☺→). The following conventions supplement the earlier discussion (pp. 200–7) of the four interactive verbs.

(1) *Moving Toward*

(a) includes: friendly or helpful overtures to others; playful activity with others; affectionate or sexual activity with, or interest in, another, etc.

(b) includes: physical movement to, or nonhostile penetration of, objects, persons, or symbols; where no hostile intent is expressed or implied, the presumption is that *any* physical movement toward an X fits this category.

(c) includes: "mental movement" to objects, persons, or symbols, i.e.: expressions of attraction toward X; observational or attentive interest in X; increasing involvement with X; "pursuit" of X (e.g., money, material goods); "wanting" X; acting so as to confirm or support the status of X, etc.

(d) includes: vocal, gestural, etc. "movement" to others; where no hostile intent is expressed or implied, the presumption is that any speech, expressive gesture, etc., directed to another fits this category.

(2) *Moving From*

(a) includes: withdrawal or escape from others; active seeking of solitude; flight or withdrawal responses to hostile attacks, etc.

(b) includes: *actively described* cessations or inhibitions of other interactive activity. For example,

I stopped hitting Pm_1,

would be scored:

1) $E \dashv\!< Pm_1$ = I hit;
2) $\leftarrow E, Pm_1$ = I stopped.

A contrast is drawn between situations such as the one described above, in which an active verb of a dissociative sort qualifies another interactive verb, and those situations in which the other interactive verb simply is negated; for example,

I didn't hit Pm_1 ,

or,

I failed to hit Pm_1 ,

both of which would be scored:

$$E \preceq X,$$

that is, dynamically.

(c) includes: *actively described* "mental leave-takings" from objects, persons, or symbols. For example,

I put her out of mind = $\leftarrow E, Pf_1$.

A contrast is drawn between situations such as this one and ones in which the mental dissociation is more passive. For example,

I couldn't remember (*or* forgot) her = $[E \updownarrow Pf_1]$,

that is, "I couldn't think of her," a dynamic negation of the associative verb coding thought processes.

(d) includes: *actively described* vocal or gestural withdrawals from others. For example,

1) I refused to speak to her = $\leftarrow E, Pf_1$;
2) I turned my back on her = $\leftarrow E, Pf_1$.

A contrast is drawn between situations such as these and situations in which vocal, gestural, etc., approaches simply are negated. For example,

1) I didn't speak to her = $E \rightleftharpoons Pf_1$;
2) I didn't look at her = $E \rightleftharpoons Pf_1$.

(3) *Moving Against*

(a) includes: any physical, verbal, gestural, etc., movement *toward* objects, persons, or symbols mediated by an explicit or implicit *hostile intent*, including "teasing," "gossiping about," etc., where the intent is cast in a socialized form, and "punishing," where the act is justified on educational, etc., grounds.

(b) includes: any physical, verbal, gestural, etc., movement *from* objects, persons, or symbols where the *intent or effect* is to injure or deprive them, rather than to achieve relief, solitude, etc., for the self.

(c) includes: any *actively described* interference with, or frustration of, another's pursuit of some goal. For example,

1) He wanted the money = $E \rightarrow Sy_{1A}$;
2) I got in his way = $E \prec Pm_1$.

(d) includes: stealing; by convention, the stolen entity is scored as the means by which such aggression is consummated. For example,

1) He stole the car = $Pm_1 \prec E$
2) (via car) = $[Sy_{1A} = Pm_1 \boxed{\prec} E]$.

(e) includes: verbal denials of requests. For example,

1) I wanted ice cream = $E \rightarrow Sy_{1A}$;
2) Mother said no = $M \prec E$.

(f) includes: socialized competition with others (e.g., sports) in which the focus is on gaining a competitive advantage over another, rather than on individual achievement or friendly social interaction. Thus,

1) I beat him = $\overset{+}{E} \overset{+}{\prec} \underline{Pm_1}$;
2) We won = $\overset{+}{E} \overset{+}{\prec} \overset{+}{\underline{Pm_1}}$.

(g) includes: hunting. For example,

I hunted antelope = $E \prec \overset{+}{Sy_{1A}}$;

(but not fishing [cf. Gottschalk, Winget, and Gleser's similar discrimination (1969)] , thus:

I went fishing = $E \rightarrow \overset{+}{Sy_{1A}}$).

(h) includes: any physical, verbal, gestural, etc., activity toward objects, persons, or symbols where the *effect* is the loss of status, integrity, etc., of those entities, however "socialized" the justification may be for the activity. Thus,

1) I cut the melon = $E \prec Sy_{1A}$;
2) (with a knife) = $[Sy_{2A} = E \boxed{\prec} Sy_{1A}]$;

or

I took the radio apart = $E \prec Sy_{1A}$.

(i) includes: accidents, illnesses, deaths, or other apparently unmediated misfortunes occurring to dream characters—these always are considered E-initiated. Thus,

The old man died = $E \prec F$;

("killed," "shot," etc., is taken to imply agentic mediation, and would be treated somewhat differently, for example:

1) Someone shot the old man = $E \prec F$;
2) (gun as means, "shooter" as agent) = $[Sy_{1A} = E(Pm_1) \boxed{\prec} F]$).

(4) *Creating*

(a) One major problem in scoring this verb category is in differentiating helpful or supportive acts which are $\rightarrow$ from those which are $\circledcirc\!\!\rightarrow$. Generally, where, say, E "helps" X, and the help returns X to some momentarily disrupted status quo or is help which does not directly promote X's achievement of some new and better *internal state*, then one scores $E \rightarrow X$. For example,

1) (The animal had a broken leg) I fixed it;
2) (She had a flat tire) I helped her;
3) (He was depressed) I cheered him up;
4) (They were broke) I lent them money;
5) My data supported my theory.

But, where E helps X, and the help directly promotes the internal development of X, i.e., foments a "separation" process, as discussed in chapter 11, resulting in the creation of some newer, more fully developed X, then one scores $E \circledcirc\!\!\rightarrow X$. For example,

1) I gave the animal new confidence;
2) I taught her how to cope;

3) I gave him new goals;
4) I gave them a new way of looking at the situation;
5) My data suggested a new hypothesis.

(b) Specifically in child-care, $E \rightarrow C$ when one supports the child as it is, but $E \oslash\rightarrow C$ when one helps it to become something it wasn't. For example,

1) (My child cried) I comforted it = $E \rightarrow \overset{+}{C}$;
2) (My child was bored) I showed her/him how to cope with boredom = $E \oslash\rightarrow C$.

"Nurture," in the sense of maintenance (via food, protection, emotional stabilization), is scored $\rightarrow$; in the sense of promoting growth or maturation (via education, insight, emotional growth), it is scored $\oslash\rightarrow$.

(c) Another problem in scoring $\oslash\rightarrow$ is in differentiating active "discovery" from passive "realization." Typically, the object of discovery is an SSLS noun (Columbus discovered America), while that of realization is an SSLS interaction or association (I discovered my partner was stealing me blind). Thus:

Freud discovered the anaesthetic properties of cocaine = $E \oslash\rightarrow S\overset{+}{y}_{1A}$
(Freud/discovered/[useful] cocaine);

while

I discovered my partner was cheating me = $Pm \overset{}{\prec} E$
(Partner/cheats[I realize]/me).

The realization, or awareness, in the latter case is scored as negative dynamic modification—a softening of the bald declaration that "Partner cheats me"—see Rules for Scoring Dynamic Descriptors, pp. 407–16.

The Associative Verb "With." The basic unit of associative analysis is the *association sentence* (any sentence in which the verb is coded $\updownarrow$, =, or = ... $\square$). Associative sentences include two special cases (=, or an identity relationship, and = ... $\square$, the relationship of an SSLS noun to an interaction unit rather than simply to another SSLS noun). The most typical, and general, case, however, is the verb $\updownarrow$. Textual situations calling for its use include the following:

(1) *A physical relationship, falling short of identity, and lacking inter-*

active (relative movement) properties, is asserted between two SSLS nouns (or verbs). For example,

1) She was next to him = $[Pf_1 \updownarrow Pm_1]$;
2) She looked like her mother = $[Pf_1 \updownarrow M_1]$.

(2) *A mental association is asserted between two SSLS nouns (or verbs).* For example,

1) She reminds me of mother = $[Pf_1 \updownarrow M]$;
2) Loving and hating are connected, to my mind = $[\overset{+}{\rightarrow} \updownarrow \overset{+}{\prec}]$.

"Mental" includes *passive-perceptual* acts (seeing, hearing), but not *active-perceptual* acts (looking, listening), which are scored $\rightarrow$. For example,

1) I heard the bell = $[E \updownarrow Sy_{1A}]$;
2) I listened to the bell = $E \rightarrow Sy_{1A}$.

(3) *A relationship of simple ownership or possession is described.* For example,

1)   My car = $[E \updownarrow Sy_{1A}]$;
2) I had a car = $[E \updownarrow Sy_{1A}]$.

Where "possession" has a more sexual or aggressive evaluative connotation, however, $\rightarrow$ or $\prec$ may be scored, together with an appropriate set of dynamic descriptors. For example,

I owned him (in the sense that weak *he* was powerless before strong
   me) = $\overset{+}{E} \prec \underline{Pm_1}$.

An *exception* to the use of $\updownarrow$ to code possession is made where a place (Jill's house) or institution (Reverend Smith's church) is so thoroughly identified with a person (Jill, Reverend Smith) that it may be considered a roundabout way of designating the person. Here the place or institution "possessed" is omitted from the SSLS lexicon altogether. For example,

1) I went to Jill's house = $E \rightarrow \underline{Pf_1}$;
2) Where there's a TV = $[Pf_1 \updownarrow Sy_{1A}]$;

or

1) Reverend Smith's church was out to get me = $\underline{F_1}$ —< E.

The assumption here is that the geographical/institutional references are ways of expressing the distant quality of the alter in an interpersonal relationship—hence, the negative dynamic scores for the characters. Thus the scorer should be sensitive to the possibilities that: castle, White House, etc., = F; hospital = F or M (doctor); school = F or M (teacher, principal); and so on. The place or institution may simply be a mask for a person. However, this only can be determined by context. In other instances, the place or institution may play a role other than that of a simple alter-ego for a character identified with it. Then possessive scoring via ↕ is appropriate.

(4) *A part-whole relationship is asserted between a component and the whole of a previously coded SSLS noun.* For example,

One of the frames of the film . . . = $[Sy_{1A} \updownarrow \overset{+}{Sy}_{1A1}]$
(film had frames).

(Note that parts of a whole are coded as lexical subclass entries within the lexical class designation assigned the whole.) The text need not *explicitly* assert part-whole relationships for this convention to be followed. In the following example:

1) I liked the film = $E \rightarrow Sy_{1A}$;
2) One of the frames . . . = $[Sy_{1A} \updownarrow S\overset{+}{y}_{1A1}]$;

it is merely implicit that "frames" means "film frames."

There is a distinction to be made between characterization of objects by way of describing their components and characterization of objects by way of describing their global properties. The former asserts a *structural associative relationship*; the latter asserts a *modification* (see Dynamic Analysis, pp. 405–18) of the original object. For example,

1) The bucket had a hole in it = $[Sy_{1A} \updownarrow Sy_{1A1}]$;
2) The bucket was rusty = $\underline{Sy_{1A1}}$.

(5) *A noun is introduced in a textual statement which SSLS will translate as an interactive sentence (i.e., it will be the subject or object of that sentence), but it has not appeared in a prior SSLS associative sentence.* In

such cases, an associative sentence will be written to incorporate the noun in the network of associative sentences, even though there is no specific textual equivalent for this sentence. For example,

1) I looked at the *plant* $(Sy_{1A}) = E \rightarrow Sy_{1A}$;
2) There was a yellow *flower* (Sy_{1A1}) on it $= [Sy_{1A} \updownarrow Sy_{1A1}]$;
3) I love yellow *dresses* $(Sy_{2A}) = E \rightarrow S\overset{+}{y}_{2A}$;
4) $-$ $\qquad\qquad\qquad = [Sy_{2A} \updownarrow Sy_{1A1}]$.

The logic here is that the dreamer/associator has omitted a step in revealing her or his associative processes (yellow flower *to* yellow dress), and that we must fill in this step to preserve the integrity of SSLS's association-path analysis (see chapter 13). *It is a rule of SSLS's associative analyses that each noun appearing in a dream episode or associative chain consisting of more than a single interactive sentence must be coded in an associative sentence.* Thus where the entire dream (or the first two sentences of a longer dream narrative) consists of

1) I went to school $\quad = E \rightarrow Sy_{1A}$;
2) and hit the teacher $= E \prec F_1$;

we need to write

3) $-$ $\qquad\qquad = [F_1 \updownarrow Sy_{1A}]$.

This rule is implemented in one of two ways. Preference is given to *logical connectedness.* For example,

1) I had a film $\qquad\quad = [E \updownarrow Sy_{1A}]$;
2) I smudged one frame $= E \prec Sy_{1A1}$;
3) $-$ $\qquad\qquad\quad = [Sy_{1A1} \updownarrow Sy_{1A}]$.

Where there is no apparent logical connection of the newly appearing interactive subject/object with any earlier-appearing noun, chrono-logic is used. For example,

1) I looked at the plant $\;= E \rightarrow Sy_{1A}$;
2) There was a bug on it $= [Sy_{1A} \updownarrow Sy_{2A}]$;
3) I like folk music $\quad\; = E \rightarrow Sy_{3A}$;

4) —$\qquad\qquad$ = $[Sy_{3A} \updownarrow Sy_{1A}]$;

5) —$\qquad\qquad$ = $[Sy_{3A} \updownarrow Sy_{2A}]$.

No more of a logical connection links "folk music" to Sy_{1A} than to Sy_{2A}, or vice versa. In such a case, the newly introduced interactive term is associated, in as many sentences as are required, with all non-E nouns appearing in the immediately prior sentence, if it is associative, or, in a single sentence, with the non-E term of the immediately prior sentence, if it is interactive. The assumption being made here is that some part of the previous scored sentence has "sparked off" the "out-of-the-blue" element of the interactive sentence, but that, as above, one or more intervening step of the associative process has been omitted in the overt account. The goal of our "filling-in" such steps, of course, is to insure that an ordering of associative sentences can be formed, on the basis of overlapping elements, such that each interactive noun element can be located on an associative path issuing from the start of the dream episode or from the dream sentence stimulating the free associations (see chapter 13).

The same goal requires that *an associative sentence containing entirely novel noun elements must be linked to the associative path by writing one or more With sentences linking its nouns to previously appearing noun elements*. Once again, the basis of the additional sentence(s) may be logical or chronological. For example, in:

1) I looked at the sofa;$\qquad$ = $E \rightarrow Sy_{1A}$;

2) There was a bug on it;$\qquad$ = $[Sy_{2A} \updownarrow Sy_{1A}]$;

3) There was spray on the shelf$\quad$ = $[Sy_{3A} \updownarrow Sy_{1B}]$;

4) (bug–spray)$\qquad\qquad$ = $[Sy_{3A} \updownarrow Sy_{2A}]$;

5) So I sprayed him$\qquad\quad$ = $E \prec Sy_{2A}$;

6) —$\qquad\qquad$ = $[Sy_{3A} = E \boxed{\prec} Sy_{2A}]$;

the connection in sentence 4 is "logical," and, once any one element of the out-of-the-blue associative sentence has been so related back to the prior associative-sentence network, no more sentences need be written. However, in:

1) I looked at the sofa;$\quad$ = $E \rightarrow Sy_{1A}$;

2) There was a bug on it;$\,$ = $[Sy_{2A} \updownarrow Sy_{1A}]$;

3) A glass in the sink$\qquad$ = $[Sy_{3A} \updownarrow Sy_{1B}]$;

4) —$\qquad\qquad$ = $[Sy_{3A} \updownarrow Sy_{2A}]$;

5) —$\qquad\qquad$ = $[Sy_{3A} \updownarrow Sy_{1A}]$;

6) – $= [Sy_{1B} \updownarrow Sy_{2A}]$;
7) – $= [Sy_{1B} \updownarrow Sy_{1A}]$;

the connection is purely chronological, and, in such cases, each noun term of the out-of-the-blue associative sentence must be related, in a separate With sentence, to each non-E noun term of the prior scored sentence.

When the "logical" connection of an out-of-the-blue *associative* sentence is of the part-whole variety, one can, for economy's sake, code the relationship directly in the out-of-the-blue sentence. This means the sentence in question no longer is disconnected from the associative path and that no further sentences need be written. For example,

1) The horse had a saddle $= [Sy_{1A} \updownarrow Sy_{2A}]$
2) A ribbon on the tail $= [Sy_{2B} \updownarrow Sy_{1A1,1A}]$
                          (ribbon/With/tail of horse).

However, this compounding of object or subject terms to conform to the associative path is permissible *only* for part-whole relationships, and *only* within the noun class Sy. (Grammatical Constraints on SSLS Sentence Formation, pp. 394–98, indicates the only other instance in which SSLS objects or subjects can consist of multiple lexical codes.)

The one case in which a With sentence need not be written to join an interactive or associative sentence containing novel elements to the prior associative path is where such conformity will be achieved by the Means sentence accompanying that latter sentence. For example, in:

1) Jim's horse $= [Pm_1 \updownarrow Sy_{1A}]$;
2) was in the field $= [Sy_{1A} \updownarrow Sy_{2A}]$;
3) He went to it $= E \rightarrow Sy_{1A}$;
4) and rode to town $= E \rightarrow Sy_{2B}$;
5) – $= [Sy_{1A} = E(Pm_1) \boxminus\!\!\rightarrow Sy_{2B}]$;

a With sentence is not written following sentence 4, which introduces the novel element Sy_{2B} (town), since the accompanying Means sentence (via horse) links town back to the earlier appearing elements, Pm_1 and Sy_{1A}. However, where the Means sentence will not produce conformity to prior associative elements, but will, in fact, introduce *more* novel elements, a With sentence will be written joining the novel element of the original interactive or associative sentence to the prior associative path and will be inserted before the Means sentence. For example,

1) Jim's horse $\qquad = [Pm_1 \updownarrow Sy_{1A}];$
2) was in the field $\qquad = [Sy_{1A} \updownarrow Sy_{2A}];$
3) He went to it $\qquad = E \rightarrow Sy_{1A};$
4) Meanwhile, Smith (Pm_3)
   introduced Jones (Pm_1)
   to Brown (Pm_2) $\qquad = [Pm_1 \updownarrow Pm_2];$
5) $-$ $\qquad = [Pm_1 \updownarrow Sy_{1A}];$
6) $-$ $\qquad = [Pm_2 \updownarrow Sy_{1A}];$
7) (Smith introduced) $\qquad = [Pm_3 = Pm_1 \;\boxed{\updownarrow}\; Pm_2].$

(6) *Conceptual relationships are asserted which already have been anticipated by SSLS.* That is, despite the fact SSLS already has coded "old man" as "Father," when there is an association that:

"Old man" reminds me of Dad $= [F_1 \updownarrow F_2].$

Note that lexical subscripts preserve the separate identities of the two Father-class figures. No associative sentence ever is written, however, of the form: $[X_1 \updownarrow X_1]$. Since there are no permissible lexical subclasses for E, there thus can be no $[E \updownarrow E]$ sentences. "Redundant" sentences of the form $[Noun_x \updownarrow Noun_x]$ are the basis of dynamic modification; they do not receive separate structural scores. For example,

1) Father hit me $= \overset{+}{F} \prec E;$
2) He was thinking of himself ($[F \updownarrow F]$ = selfish father, which, in context, is $\overset{+}{F}$).

(Redundant $\updownarrow$ sentences *are* permitted for $[Verb \updownarrow Verb]$, however, see chapter 12, p. 262, sentence F-22).

The Associative Verbs: "Equivalence" and "Means."

(1) *Equivalence*
   Equivalence sentences are scored when a character changes identity during a dream. For example,

My father turned into a snake $= [F = Sy_{1A}].$

Equivalence sentences are scored for assertions of identity relationships. For example,

The car was a truck = $[Sy_{1A} = Sy_{1B}]$.

But,

The car was like a truck = $[Sy_{1A} \Updownarrow Sy_{1B}]$.

Equivalence sentences are scored for role assumptions or role behaviors. For example,

1) He became a doctor   = $[Pm_1 = F_1]$;
2) My friend, the doctor = $[Pm_1 = F_1]$.

However, where E assumes a role, not in the text, but only in the SSLS scoring (because of the proscription of third-party sentences), or where a new identity is implicit in behavior, rather than explicitly described, new identities are coded, where possible, in a Means sentence qualifying an interaction. Otherwise, no identity transformation is scored at all. For example, for a female dreamer,

The wife hit the husband with a stick
  (Pf_1) (Sp_1) (Sy_{1A})

is scored:

1) $E \prec Sp_1$;
2) $[Sy_{1A} = E(Pf_1)\boxed{\prec}Sp_1]$.

Or,

I gave her some pills
  (E) (Pf_1) (Sy^+_{1A})

is scored:

1) $E \rightarrow Pf_1$;
2) $[Sy^+_{1A} = E(M_1)\boxed{\rightarrow} Pf_1]$;

i.e., pills were the means through which I, as physician-healer, helped her. However:

1) The wife hit the husband $= E \rightarrowtail Sp_1$;
2) I stroked her $\quad\quad = E \rightarrow Pf_1$;

and no identity-entries (e.g., for $E = Pf_1$ in sentence 1) are coded, since no Means sentences need be scored.

(2) *Means*

Means sentences are scored for assertions of responsibility for actions or relationships. If a character, object, etc., is responsible for, or otherwise causally implicated in, the occurrence of some associative or interactive relationship, it is the Means through which the relationship was effected. For example,

1) He introduced my wife to me $= [Pm_1 = E \boxed{\updownarrow} Sp_1]$;
2) He made me miss the pop-fly $= [Pm_1 \overset{\pm}{=} \boxminus Sy_{1A}, E]$.

The concept of responsibility is generalized to include private, cognitive activity ascribed to characters other than Ego. Thus, if a person "imagines" an action or relationship, then he or she is considered responsible for it. For example,

1) He imagined that I might come home $= E \gtrdot Sy_{1A}$;
2) — $\quad\quad\quad\quad\quad\quad = [Pm_1 \equiv E \boxminus Sy_{1A}]$;

and

1) She thought that he and I were related $= [Pm_1 \updownarrow E]$;
2) — $\quad\quad\quad\quad\quad\quad\quad = [Pf_1 \equiv Pm_1 \boxed{\updownarrow} E]$.

The sentences can be translated:

1) I/hypothetically (negative modifier) move to/home;
2) Pm_1 "mentally" (negative modifier) responsible for above relation;

and

1) He/hypothetically (negative modifier) associated with/me;
2) Pf_1 "mentally" (negative modifier) responsible for above relation.

Note that events or relationships mentally conjured up are scored negatively dynamically, and that the mental mediation (i.e., the Means verb =) itself also is so scored.

Responsibility includes, still further, Ego's own "active" constructive/ imaginative cognition regarding others' relationships to one another or to Ego as object. For instance, ego would be scored as a means where the dreamer "plans," "pretends," "imagines," "dreams," "compares," "contrasts," "wishes for," "decides that," "wants," etc., an X-Y (or X-E, but *not* E-X) relationship. Thus:

1) I pretended that X hit Y = $E \underset{\sim}{<} Y$;
$$= [E \equiv E(X)\boxed{<}\,Y]\,;$$

and

2) I pretended that X hit me = $X \underset{\sim}{<} E$;
$$= [E \equiv X\boxed{<}\,E]\,;$$

but

3) I pretended that I hit X = $E \underset{\sim}{<} X$.

Included in the class of "active" cognitive words also are "see," "hear," etc.; excluded are "think," "know," "believe," "suppose," etc.

Responsibility for a relationship is not coded via the Means sentence when the cognitive activity of another character is "public," i.e., verbal, nor when E is the character passively thinking about any relationship. Thus:

1) He told them (that) = $E \overset{+}{\to} \overset{+}{P}m_1$;
2) I might come home = $E \rightrightarrows Sy_{1A}$;

and

1) I thought that I might come home = $E \rightrightarrows Sy_{1A}$.

In the former case the telling is considered an interactive act, and is scored as such; in the latter case the passive thought-mediation is considered a form of ego-distancing from the Ego-initiated action in question, and contributes to the negative modification of the verb coding that relationship. The rationale for the former scoring convention is that overtly reporting a relationship need not imply a direct causal responsibility for it (i.e., the messenger should not be shot because the message is unsatisfactory). The rationale for the latter scoring convention is that it is not informative that E is responsible for her or his own actions or for thinking about others' relationships—by assumption, E is responsible, unless otherwise indicated, for all of her or his own actions and for all the thoughts of the dream. The only novel quality of these thought-mediated assertions is that of "distancing," and it is that quality which is scored by the rule given.

Means sentences are scored for assertions of instrumentality, location, or context, when these assertions describe nouns qualifying a particular action or relationship. Thus:

1) I knifed him $= E \overset{+}{-\!\!\!<} Pm_1$;
2) (knife as instrument) $= [Sy_{1A} \overset{+}{=} E \boxed{-\!\!\!<} Pm_1]$;

and

1) We met $= [E \updownarrow Pf_1]$;
2) at home $= [Sy_{1A} = E \boxed{\updownarrow} Pf_1]$.

In the instance of:

1) I shot him $= E -\!\!\!< Pm_1$;
2) (X as instrument) $= [Sy_{1A} = E \boxed{-\!\!\!<} Pm_1]$;

there may be a question as to what constitutes the means—the gun? the trigger? the bullet? all of these? In shooting at a pool ball, is the cue the means, or is it the cue ball which we hit with the cue and which in turn hits the ball at which we "aim"? Or is it both of these? SSLS's preference in such cases is to score as means that *one global instrument most proximate to the actor who initiates the interaction,* i.e., the gun and the cue, in the above chain-of-events sequences of instrumental mediation.

"Assertions of instrumentality . . . or context" is generalized to include the content of certain verbal interactions. Specifically, where a *topic,* rather than a *proposition,* is noted as the substance of a verbal act, then that topic, if it lends itself to description as an SSLS noun, is coded as a Means modifier of the verbal interaction. Thus:

1) I talked to him $= E \rightarrow Pm_1$;
2) about Italy $= [Sy_{1A} = E \boxed{\rightarrow} Pm_1]$.

That is, I approached him by-means-of Italy. But, when the verbal communication is propositional in form, no Means sentence is scored. For example,

1) I told him $\qquad\qquad$ = $E \overset{+}{\to} Pm_1$;
2) that I'm going to Italy = $E \rightrightarrows Sy_{1A}$;

or

1) I mentioned (to him) $\;$ = $E \to Pm_1$;
2) that Alto is in Georgia = $[Sy_{1A1} \updownarrow Sy_{1A}]$.

There are texts in which the precise content of verbal communication will be ambiguous. For example, "I told her about it"—does "it" refer to a previous "topic" or to an earlier-described proposition or set of propositions? Obviously, the scorer must employ contextual evidence in attempting to resolve the ambiguity. However, *in general, SSLS prefers propositional referents to topical ones for ambiguous designations of conversation contents.* "It," we assume, more likely is a lazily-stated reference to earlier relationships than a simple pronominal substitution for an earlier-mentioned topic. Thus:

1) Rustlers were after my cattle $\qquad$ = $\overset{+}{Pm_1} \prec E$;
2) (cattle as means) $\qquad$ = $[\overset{+}{Sy}_{1A} = Pm_1 \boxed{\prec} E]$;
3) (my cattle) $\qquad$ = $[E \updownarrow \overset{+}{Sy}_{1A}]$;
4) I went to the sheriff $\qquad$ = $E \to F_1$;
5) – $\qquad$ = $[F_1 \updownarrow Sy_{1A}]$;
6) and told him $\qquad$ = $E \overset{+}{\to} F_1$;
7) about it (i.e., that rustlers were after my cattle) $\qquad$ = $\overset{+}{Pm_1} \prec E$;
8) (cattle as means) $\qquad$ = $[\overset{+}{Sy}_{1A} = Pm_1 \boxed{\prec} E]$;
9) (my cattle) $\qquad$ = $[E \updownarrow \overset{+}{Sy}_{1A}]$.

This scoring is considered preferable to an alternate sentence 7 of the form:

$$= [\overset{+}{Sy}_{1A} = E \boxed{\to} F_1] ;$$

or

$$= [\overset{+}{Pm_1} = E \boxed{\to} F_1] ;$$

since we imagine that, when I reached the sheriff, I did not say "cattle" or "men," but rather "Rustlers are after my cattle." That is, the 3-sentence propositional scoring must more faithfully reflect what was said than could any 1-sentence topical scoring. Thus, it generally is considered preferable to repeat an earlier set of scored relationships, the set being sufficiently large to reflect the complete "message," rather than to arbitrarily select a single topical referent from this set as the translation of vague descriptions of conversation content. (The *ideal* way of coping with such descriptions, of course, is to have the dreamer clarify them during her or his original account: e.g., Guide: "About what?")

The *conventions employed in writing Means sentences* already have been illustrated, but will be briefly reviewed now. The sentence, as an associative sentence, always is bracketed. The verb of the object-unit is boxed. Dynamic signs in the object-unit neither are repeated nor added: only the means noun (to the left of the = verb) and the means verb (=) are subject to dynamic modification. Role equivalencies are entered parenthetically in the object-unit. For example,

1) I became a teacher $\quad\quad\quad\quad = [E = F_1]$;
2) I hit the kindergartener $\quad\quad = E \prec C_1$;
3) with a ruler $\quad\quad\quad\quad\quad\quad = [Sy_{1A} = E (F_1) \boxed{\prec} C_1]$.

Whether roles are encoded for the first time in a Means sentence, or whether they have been coded previously, they always are scored, where appropriate, in Means sentences. Where E has been inserted by SSLS's ego-identification rules in an ostensible third-party interaction, the role E is filling always is entered parenthetically in an accompanying Means sentence. For example,

1) The woman hit the child $\quad\quad = E \prec C$;
2) with a ruler $\quad\quad\quad\quad\quad\quad = [Sy_{1A} = E (Pf_1) \boxed{\prec} C]$.

That is, E, inserted by SSLS's rules in the role of Pf_1, hit the child by means of a ruler.

In Means sentences, one codes in the object-unit persons associated with E in an interactive sequence, even though the codes in question are not E-roles or identities. Thus:

1) Tom and I went to the store
$\quad$ (Pm_1) $\quad$ (E) $\quad\quad\quad\quad\quad$ $(Sy_{1A}) = \overset{+}{E} \rightarrow Sy_{1A}$;
2) The storekeeper beat us
$\quad\quad\quad\quad$ (F_1) $\quad\quad\quad\quad\quad\quad\quad = F_1 \prec \overset{+}{E}$;
3) with a broom
$\quad\quad\quad\quad$ (Sy_{2A}) $\quad\quad\quad\quad\quad\quad = [Sy_{2A} = F_1 \boxed{\prec} E (+ Pm_1)]$.

The rationale here is that the parenthetical addition of Pm_1, with the "and" (+) notation, does in fact help to define the *role-context* of the interaction, even if E never has been literally identified with Pm_1. The result is that the Means sentence still further permits the restoration of significant features of interactive sequences which are lost in the more restrictive scoring of interaction sentences themselves.

Grammatical Constraints on SSLS Sentence Formation

Simple Sentences. SSLS's sentences (with the Means-sentence exceptions noted above) must be simple; that is, they are to contain one subject, one relational term, and one object. (Thus, as noted earlier [pp. 363–75], compound textual sentences often require the writing of several SSLS sentences). More precisely, we now may say that *only one exemplar from the class defined by categories F, M, Si, Sp, Pm, Pf, and C may appear in any given interactive sentence* (the other, obligatory noun being E) and that *no more than two exemplars from the class defined by categories F, M, Si, Sp, Pm, Pf, C, and E may appear in any given associative sentence* (with the further restriction that the two may not share both noun category and lexical subscript).

Category Sy is conspicuous by its absence from the "classes" defined above. While the same principle—only one entity as subject and only one entity as object per SSLS sentence—applies to category Sy, *an Sy exemplar can contain multiple lexical subscripts providing that, in combination, these subscripts refer to one composite entity*. For example,

botanical monograph = $Sy_{1A, 2A}$

could be such an entity and could serve either as subject or object in an interactive sentence (with E in the other role) or in an associative sentence (in relationship with some other "entity" from the class defined by categories F, M, Si, Sp, Pm, Pf, C, E, and Sy). We might even consider

botanical monograph dream = $Sy_{1A, 2A, 3A}$

as such an entity, e.g., "Freud, mulling over his botanical monograph dream," = $[F_1 ⇕ Sy_{1A, 2A, 3A}]$. No other category than Sy may enter into such composites, however. For example,

"Freud's botanical monograph dream" (as in, "*I* was thinking of Freud's botanical monograph dream") is impermissible (not $[E ⇕ F_1, Sy_{1A, 2A, 3A}]$, but $[E ⇕ Sy_{1A, 2A, 3A}]$, and $[F_1 ⇕ Sy_{1A, 2A, 3A}]$).

The assumption in permitting Sy composites is that Sy combinations may function as permanently fused unities. But, in borderline cases, the logic of the text should be followed in determining whether to fuse Sy lexical subscripts. Specifically, where the global composition of an entity is described in the form *an a-b*, fusion might be considered. For example,

a gingerbread house = $Sy_{1A, 2A}$;

while, where it is described in the form, *an a, made of b*, that is,

a house,
it was made of gingerbread = $[Sy_{1A} \updownarrow Sy_{2A}]$;

fusion seems less desirable. Other signs pointing to fusion are: (1) if the entity recurs, it is described as *an a-b*, not simply now as a *b* ("the house"); (2) if the entity recurs, however it is described, it is clear, from context, that both a and b still are implied. For example,

1) I wrote a dream-book = $E \circledcirc\!\!\rightarrow Sy_{1A,2A}$;
2) It was about Freud $\quad = [Sy_{1A, 2A} \updownarrow F_1]$;
$\qquad\qquad\qquad\qquad \neq [Sy_{1A} \updownarrow F_1]$;

where the name "Freud" indicates that "dream" still is implied by "it," i.e., that a subclass of books, rather than books-in-general, is meant; and (3) the elements of the composite do not recur (hence there is no particular advantage in discriminating them) or if some elements recur, they do not lead in *different* associative directions (e.g., for an $Sy_{1A, 2A, 3A}$ composite, $Sy_{2A, 3A}$ recurs, rather than Sy_{2A} in one context and Sy_{3A} in another).

In general, there is *a preference that interactive-sentence Sy entries be as "compact" as possible, referring only to as many symbolic classes as are absolutely required to indicate the specific focus of action, while associative-sentence Sy entries may be expanded if they help economically to incorporate a new Sy subscript into the association path.* Thus, imagine that "illustrations" (Sy_{1A1}) is a new entry, while "book" already has been scored in an associative sentence. Contrast these two ways in which Sy_{1A1} is introduced, and the scoring:

1) I was looking at the illustrations = $E \to \overset{+}{Sy}_{1A1}$;
2) – $\qquad\qquad\qquad\qquad = [Sy_{1A1} \updownarrow Sy_{1A}]$;

and not

    1) I was looking at the illustrations $= E \rightarrow Sy_{1}\overset{+}{A}_{1,\,1A}$;

however,

        1) The author annoyed me $= Pm_1 \prec \underline{E}$;

        2) with those lousy illustrations $= [Sy_{1\overset{+}{A}1,\,1A} = Pm_1 \boxed{\prec} E]$.

Once, in the latter instance, Sy_{1A1} has been assimilated to the association path, it no longer is necessary to reiterate the fusion $(Sy_{1A1,\,1A})$ if the placement of illustrations in the book seems largely to be forgotten and, for instance, there merely is a discussion of the technical inadequacy of the illustrations as art.

    Subject-Object Agreement. Subject and object in any SSLS sentence must "agree" in the sense that, if one is a noun, the other must be a noun, and that, if one is a verb, the other must be a verb. No SSLS sentence relates a noun to a verb. Sometimes, however, the text will seem to demand such scores, for example: "I loved the hitting," "The loving made me sick," and so on. In dealing with textual assertions of this form, SSLS's bias is to convert the subject/object verb to noun form, so that one ends up with a noun, verb, noun (NVN) sentence, which is the only permissible form for an interactive sentence and the most typical form for an associative sentence. Specific rules are as follows:

    (1) Where V_1 in a NV_1V_2 or V_2V_1N assertion will be coded $\rightarrow$, $\prec$, or $\odot\rightarrow$, V_2 is to be scored as the *subject* of the last prior SSLS sentence in which V_2 served as a verb. For example,

        1) Father hit brother $= F \prec E$;

        2a) I loved the hitting $= E \overset{+}{\rightarrow} F$;

        2b) The hitting bothered me $= F \prec \underline{E}$.

If that *subject* is coded identically as N in the current assertion, no new sentence is written, but an appropriate dynamic modifier is added to V_2 in the last prior sentence in which it is a verb. For example,

        1) I hit brother $= E \prec Si_1$;

        2a) I loved the hitting $=$ (no new sentence; $\overset{+}{\prec}$ above);

        2b) The hitting bothered me $=$ (no new sentence; $\underline{\prec}$ above).

(2) Where V_1 in a NV_1V_2 or V_2V_1N assertion will be coded $\leftarrow$, V_2 will be scored as the *object* of the last prior SSLS sentence containing V_2 as verb. For example,

     1) He loved her $= E \overset{+}{\rightarrow} Pf_1$;
     2a) He stopped the loving $= \leftarrow E, Pf_1$;
     2b) The love left him $= \leftarrow Pf_1, E.$

If that object is coded identically as N in the current assertion, no new sentence is written, but a negative dynamic modifier is added to that object in the prior sentence. For example,

     1) She loved me $= Pf_1 \overset{+}{\rightarrow} E;$
     2a) I stopped the loving $=$ (no new score; $\underline{E}$ above);
     2b) The love left me $=$ (no new score; $\underline{E}$ above).

(3) Where V_1 in a NV_1V_2 or V_2V_1N assertion will be coded $\updownarrow$, V_2 will be translated, in as many separate SSLS sentences as are otherwise permissible, as all nouns appearing in the last prior sentence containing V_2 as verb. For example,

     1) Father hit me $= F \prec E;$
     2) I thought of the hitting $= [E \updownarrow F];$
        (but not the impermissible $[E \updownarrow E]);$

and

     1) They were close friends $= [Pf_1 \overset{+}{\updownarrow} Pf_2];$
     2) I thought of their relationship $= [E \updownarrow Pf_1];$
     3) – $= [E \updownarrow Pf_2].$

(4) Occasionally there is justification for construing a possible verb in relationship with a noun as itself being a noun, an action-medium—i.e., means, rather than an action per se. Thus, in the following scoring,

     1) He told me the rumors $= Pm_1 \overset{+}{\rightarrow} E;$
     2) (via rumors) $= [S\overset{+}{y}_{1A} \overset{+}{=} Pm_1 \boxdot E];$
     3) That (the rumors) made me mad $= S\overset{+}{y}_{1A} \overset{+}{\prec} E;$

it is assumed that it is the *content* of the rumors, rather than their *telling*, which is disturbing. That assumption needs, of course, to be justified in context, and if it cannot be so justified, the scoring would have to be:

1) He told me the rumors $= Pm_1 \overset{+}{\to} E;$

2) (via rumors) $= [S\overset{+}{y}_{1A} \overset{+}{=} Pm_1 \boxed{\to} E] \, ;$

3) That (the telling) made me mad $= Pm_1 \overset{+}{-\!\!\!<} E.$

Location of E in Third-Party Interactions. Rules for inserting E in ostensible third-party interactions are discussed at length in chapter 11 (pp. 207-15). As noted there, *priority always is accorded to associative/contextual data supplied by the dreamer. This rule now is to be understood as including contextual data generated by SSLS's own conventions.* Thus, in "X hit Y," "Y hit X back," the appropriate scoring would be of the form: $E -\!\!\!< Y$ and $Y -\!\!\!< E$. That is, the general active-voice principle does not apply to the second sentence. Since the conventions of SSLS have forced us to identify E with X in the first sentence, this identification, just like a dreamer-generated $[E \updownarrow X]$, is assumed to give a context in which E must persistently (until contrary data are generated by the dreamer or the operations of the scoring system) be identified with X. In a text in which E's "identification figure" fluctuates over time, it always is the dreamer's, or the scoring system's, most recent identification which is followed in scoring any particular sentence.

Noun Categories

(1) *M, F, Si*

As noted in chapter 11 (p. 216, *n.* 14), *M and F characters are defined in relation to (specifically, as being a generation older than) the dreamer's current age rather than in relation to the age of other dream characters, even the characters with whom SSLS may identify E.* In cases where the age gap is of marginal generational size, the bias is to score M or F, rather than Pf or Pm. The decision as to scoring M or F, once generational criteria are satisfied, obviously is based on the character's sex. Where "parent" is not further qualified (which seems unlikely, if the dream interrogator or free-association guide is alert), score P (parent). But, where the dreamer/associator merely is unsure as to which sex older person is involved (e.g., "It could have been my aunt or my uncle. I'm just not sure.") score *both* M and F for all pertinent relationships.

In cases in which the text refers to parents (e.g., "my parents"), and they are not separately mentioned, score first the sentence(s) for the parent of like sex as the dreamer. Where parents are separately designated (e.g., "Mom and Dad"), follow the subject ordering so indicated.

For authority figures of unspecified sex (e.g., "my doctor"), and where sex is implied neither by a role (e.g., priest) nor by context, score the figures in question as being of like sex as E.

Siblings can be identified by sex (Si-m, Si-f) where this seems significant. SSLS does not routinely code sibling sex, on the ground that the sibling relationship as such (e.g., the fact that, as a sibling, any Si competes for M's love) generally may be more important than particular sibling characteristics. *Since, unlike M, F, Sp, or C, the Si category is scored only for true relations,* [E ↕ Si] *is not scored for "my brother" or "my sister."* From the fact of the Si code we already know that to be the case. Interpretively, this means that a degree of ego-identification is assumed for one's "own" parents, spouse, and offspring which is not *routinely* assumed for one's own siblings.

(2) *Sp, Pf, Pm*

Mate/spouse is scored for any dreamer-generation, opposite-sex party to a marriage or other exclusive cohabitory sexual relationship. "Steady" boy-friends or girl friends not lived with, multiple cohabitory partners, or homo-sexual mates/"spouses" are scored simply as peers (Pm, Pf).

Cousins are scored as peers (Pm, Pf).

"Friends," "other kids at school," "people who work with me," and so on, *are assumed, unless there is explicit contrary information, to be of the same sex as the dreamer.* The rationale here is that the dreamer seems, by her or his choice of words, to be describing peer relationships lacking any hetero-sexual component. "Mixed" groups, acting entirely as a unit, are scored $\overset{+}{Pm}$ for male dreamers and $\overset{+}{Pf}$ for female dreamers, even if only one group member is of like sex as E.

Persons of unspecified sex introduced in the context of an ostensibly all-male or all-female third-party dream scenario are considered to be of the same sex as the previously mentioned characters, rather than as the dreamer, should these criteria conflict.

In passive textual constructions, a subject is supplied whose age or sex are congruent with those of E (or of the character with whom E is identified) *when E* (or someone with whom E is identified) *is the recipient of an action of unknown origin.* For example, for a male dreamer,

1) I was shot = Pm_1 ⤙ E;
2) —   = [Sy_{1A} = Pm_1 ⤙ E];

that is, the "shooter" is a male peer. Or, where a female dreamer has been identified with Pf_2,

$$Pf_2 \text{ was knocked down} = Pf_3 \prec E;$$

that is, the "knocker-down" Pf_3 is a female peer.

(3) *C*

As noted in chapter 11, (p. 216, *n.* 14), *C characters are defined in relation to (specifically, as being a generation younger than) the dreamer's current age, rather than in relation to the age of other dream characters, even the characters with whom SSLS may identify E.* (In cases where the age gap is of marginal generational size, the bias is to score Pf or Pm, rather than C.) This is the rationale for scoring cousins as peers, rather than as C (e.g., "my uncle's boy"). As also noted previously, however, *when the dreamer age-regresses (is a child), her or his youthful contemporaries are scored as peers rather than as C*—i.e., the ego reference point shifts downward as does ego's represented age. The same principle holds true if it is not that E regresses, but that he or she is identified with children in SSLS's interactive sentences. Thus *the treatment of age-advanced (M, F) and age-regressed E characters is not parallel.*

Lexical Classes Within Noun Categories

Composites and their components must be discriminated where a component alone enters into textual relationships. For example, in:

1) I wrote a car-book = $E \oslash \rightarrow Sy_{1A, 2A}$;
2) I like cars   = $E \rightarrow S\overset{+}{y}_{2A}$;
                         $\neq E \rightarrow Sy_{1A, 2A}$;

the second sentence refers to a component of the composite-object of the first, rather than to the entire entity, and is scored accordingly.

Lexical subscripts are assigned in order of their referents' introduction to the scored text. That is, if a character appears in the raw text but is identified with E in an interaction sentence so that he or she is not scored directly, a lexical subclass is not formed immediately. For example, for a male dreamer, in the sequence:

1) The man hit the woman = $E \prec Pf_1$;
2) She walked away   = $\leftarrow Pf_1, E$;
3) He chased her   = $E \prec Pf_1$;
4) He had a pistol   = $[Pm_1 \updownarrow Sy_{1A}]$;

Pm_1 is assigned his subscript at sentence 4, where he is a *scored* character, rather than at sentence 1, where he is a *textual* character.

Commas between lexical subscripts set off the separate components fused in an Sy composite. Thus:

$$Sy_{1A,2A} = \text{a fusion of } Sy_{1A} \text{ and } Sy_{2A};$$

and

$$Sy_{1A1A,2A} = \text{a fusion of } Sy_{1A1A} \text{ and } Sy_{2A}.$$

Body parts are not coded as character-category lexical subclasses. Thus, the following lexicon is impermissible:

Pm_1—John
$_{1A}$—John's nose

Nose would be scored, rather, as an Sy entry. Thus,

1) I thought of John's nose $= [E \; ⇕ \; Sy_{1A}]$;
$\qquad\qquad\qquad\qquad\quad = [Pm_1 \; ⇕ \; Sy_{1A}]$;
2) I hit John in the nose $\quad = E \prec Pm_1$;
$\qquad\qquad\qquad\qquad\quad = [Sy_{1A} = E \;\boxed{\prec}\; Pm_1]$.

Where the same character is referred to by more than one name, assign different lexical subscripts to its several manifestations. For example,

Pm_1 = Jack- or John-named person;
$_{1A}$ = Jack;
$_{1B}$ = John.

More generally, of course, *separate entries in a given lexical class or subclass are assumed to share the defining property of the class or subclass, but also to differ among themselves.* For example,

Sy_3 = fruit;
$_{3A}$ = apple;
$_{3B}$ = orange;
$_{3B1}$ = orange peel;
$_{3B2}$ = orange seed;

and so on. (See the lexicon for "Botanical Monograph," chapter 12, pp. 265-66). *Where the text refers only to a generic category, the letter subscript may be omitted.* For example,

I like fruit $E \rightarrow Sy_1$.

But,

I like apples $E \rightarrow S\overset{+}{y}_{1A}$;

where the lexical class is Sy_1, fruit. Even when a class contains only one entry (e.g., apples), the subscript is to be written $_{1A}$, rather than $_1$, unless that entry clearly is generic in quality (e.g., fruit).

"People" (as in "people would think that") is scored simply $\overset{+}{P}m$ or $\overset{+}{P}f$, depending on the dreamer's sex. Even minimal specification of qualifying characteristics, however (e.g., "some people"), justifies lexical subscripts.

Transforms

The situations in which transforms are generated, and the rules for generating them, have been discussed in some detail in chapter 11 (pp. 229-35). It should be stressed that the current rules governing transforms are viewed as provisional ones, subject to modification on the basis of further empirical analyses. Some of the details of these rules (e.g., the ban on two-stage translations) may well prove unduly restrictive in the determination of symbol meanings. SSLS's major contribution to reliably and reasonably determining symbol meanings is the provision of *a framework in which rules may evolve*, rather than its particular rules.

One major question raised by the current rules is why Equivalence sentences do not give rise to transforms. If an *association* of A with B can lead to rewriting A as B, why cannot an *identity* of A and B? In reply, we may discriminate two cases: (1) the Equivalence sentence includes E; (2) the Equivalence sentence does not include E. Regarding the first case, SSLS's rules *already provide* that each interactive sentence should include E, and an Equivalence relationship is a contextual element which would be used in determining E's role in such a sentence. (The same consideration, of course, also applies to [E ⌀ . . .] *associative* sentences.) Regarding the second case, it is felt that identity or role changes during the course of a dream generally are statements of *differentiation,* rather than of *association.* In the case of a literal identity change, we have a most striking violation of the fundamental laws of everyday reality: what used to be A now is a totally different entity, B. We need, I think, to honor the radical nature of this dreamer-produced transformation. Thus, "equivalence" denotations notwithstanding, the = verb does *not* indicate object equivalencies but, paradoxically, radical alterations in the objects of the dreamer's regard. The Equivalence sentence, then, is viewed as "associative" only in this sense: it tells us that A no longer is to be construed in an A context, but rather in a B context. It is a "dissociative" kind of associative assertion.

As indicated in chapter 11 (p. 231, *n.* 20), transforms can be *dynamic* as well as *structural*. Although the details of dynamic scoring—how verbs or nouns originally get pluses or minuses—have not yet been considered, it is appropriate here to discuss several conventions governing their transformation.

(1) *The sign of the associative verb in the With sentence never is transferred to the interactive verb in the transform.* This is because the strength of the associative bond in the With sentence is viewed as a fundamentally different sort of thing than the strength of the motive structure in an interactive sentence. In fact, *dynamic transformations involve only one term of the With sentence: the term substituting for another term.*

(2) Consider the following transformation model for *nouns*:

Text	Raw Scores	Transforms
—	1) A/interactive verb/B	A/interactive verb/C
—	2) [B/↕/C]	

(where we presume that B and C are such that a structural transform is obligatory, e.g., B = Sy and C = Pf). *Signs attaching to C in sentence 2 are added to those originally attaching to B in sentence 1 in characterizing C in the transform.* Thus:

Text	Raw Scores	Transforms
—	1) $A \rightarrow \overset{+}{B}$	$A \rightarrow \overset{+}{\underline{C}}$
—	2) [B ↕ $\underline{C}$].	

However, these additions are subject to a general constraint of dynamic scoring that no lexical entry can carry more than one plus and minus score in any single sentence.

(3) Consider the following transformation model for *verbs*:

Text	Raw Scores	Transforms
—	1) A/interactive verb$_1$/B	*also* A/interactive verb$_2$/B
—	2) [interactive verb$_1$ ↕ interactive verb$_2$].	

Where the interactive verbs in sentence 2 are unmodified, or both are *"universally" modified* (e.g., $[\overset{+}{\odot}\rightarrow \updownarrow \overset{+}{\rightrightarrows}]$), *the transform verb will carry only the signs of the interactive verb in sentence 1*. More generally: *the signs of the verb in sentence 1 always carry over to the verb of the transform*. Where the With sentence contains modification only of the verb being replaced in the transform (interactive verb$_1$), no dynamic score from that sentence is added to the transform. Where the With sentence contains modification only of the verb being inserted in the transform (interactive verb$_2$), this modification is added to the transform (if it is not already there). Where the With sentence contains partial, but parallel, dynamic modification, for example,

$[\odot\rightarrow \updownarrow \rightarrow]$;
$[\overset{+}{\odot}\rightarrow \updownarrow \overset{+}{\rightarrow}]$;

no dynamic score from this sentence is added to the transform. Where the With sentence contains partial, but nonparallel, dynamic modification of its subject and object, for example,

$[\odot\rightarrow \updownarrow \overset{+}{\rightarrow}]$;
$[\overset{+}{\odot}\rightarrow \updownarrow \rightarrow]$;

the sign of interactive verb$_2$ (here, →) will be carried over to the transform. Summarizing these cases, *the modification of interactive verb$_2$ is carried over to the transform, unless its modification is parallel to that of interactive verb$_1$ in the With sentence*. (The rules in this section also apply to cases where the With sentence is of the form: $[\updownarrow \updownarrow\rightarrow]$, i.e., where verb$_1$ is the associative verb, With; see chapter 11, p. 231, *n.* 20.)

(4) One form of dynamic modification is permitted which does not require the generation of a separate transform. Consider the case of two *consecutive* sentences of the following form:

1) A/interactive verb/B;
2) [B $\updownarrow$ C].

Where C does not justify writing a transform—for example, suppose it is from class Sy—any sign attaching to it or to B in the second associative sentence may be added to B in the first, interactive sentence. Hence,

1) I went to the store = $E \rightarrow S\overset{+}{y}_{1A}$;
2) It was like a big auditorium = $[Sy_{1A} \updownarrow S\overset{+}{y}_{2A}]$.

The sentences must be scored consecutively for this rule to apply.

One additional rule is specified for structural transformations, namely: *where With sentences exist justifying a two-step (noun and verb) translation, all possible one-step and two-step transforms are written.* For example, where the original score is $E \rightarrow Pm_{1A}$, and where With sentences within the same association chain state that $[Pm_{1A} \updownarrow F_{2A}]$ and $[\rightarrow \updownarrow \prec]$, then the transform column of the analyst's work sheet would include these entries:

also $E \rightarrow F_{2A}$;
also $E \prec Pm_{1A}$;
also $E \prec F_{2A}$.

Dynamic Analysis

Three Types of Textual Modifiers

SSLS discriminates three classes of textual modifiers: (1) *class definers*, words or phrases which are used in defining SSLS verb or noun classes; (2) *dynamic descriptors*, terms which are used by SSLS to characterize the "strength" of motivational (interactive sentence) or associational (associative sentence) structures; and (3) *empty descriptors*, a residual class of textual modifiers of unknown structural or dynamic function. In addition to these intrasentence modifiers, SSLS also makes provision for the scoring of modification through intersentence relationships (e.g., rule (4), p. 404; see also Repetition and Alternation, pp. 416-18).

The concept of *class definer*, although not the term itself, has been introduced (pp. 364-72) with the observation that terms not grammatically considered nouns and verbs are so classified by SSLS. For example, in

The old lady struck *up a friendship with the old* man;

the italicized material is required to assign proper SSLS noun and verb classes:

"the old"   makes "lady" = M;
"up a friendship with" makes "struck" = →;
"the old"   makes "man" = F (but, for a male dreamer,
                   coded here as E).

Thus some textual material which, from a grammatical point of view, is modification, is used by SSLS in defining its own basic structural elements of *subject*, *verb*, and *object*.

The logic underlying the *dynamic descriptor* class has been sketched out in chapter 11. Further scoring conventions for such descriptors will be given in the immediately succeeding section. These are the only modifiers coded as such by SSLS. A *plus* or *minus* scoring format has been adopted since dynamic scores are thought to reflect the "activation" or "inhibition" of motive and associational structures. At a more operational level, however, dynamic descriptors code two somewhat different kinds of "meanings" (Edelson, 1975, pp. 88–89): "emotive" meanings (one's *attitudes* toward a proposition or its components) and "conative" meanings (the *incitive or behavior-driving power* of a proposition). It remains to be seen whether SSLS's attempt to fuse these two types of meaning under one rubric will prove to be satisfying, either conceptually or empirically.

Empty descriptors comprise a residual class of textual modifiers for which SSLS is unable to recommend any structural or dynamic scores. As we shall see, SSLS does rely on Osgood, Suci, and Tannenbaum's analysis of connotative meaning (1957) to extend its own range in dealing with textual descriptors. However, not even their technique yields intuitively satisfying resolutions of questions such as how "green" is to be coded in a description of an automobile. Does a car's greenness make it a good or bad car, a strong or weak car, an active or a passive car? It is difficult to say. Accordingly, SSLS provides no rules for scoring the modifier "green," or, more generally, for scoring many color descriptors. (An exception, of course, is when a color has, for example, thermal [active-passive] properties [e.g., "red" as "red-hot"].)

Despite much speculation as to the importance of color in dreams, there is little agreement on *how* it is important, i.e., what rules to follow in translating color statements. There also is little or no evidence to indicate that color designations reliably code information about dreamer personality. Thus, failure to code color probably is only a minimal drawback in SSLS's attempt to encode dreamer structure and dynamics.

It is hoped that SSLS's other omissions in coding modifiers (its other "empty" modifiers) are equally insignificant. If not, then rules must be devised to supplement current scoring procedures so as to encode those important classes of textual modifiers which are overlooked or ignored in the present version of SSLS. Most of the modifiers ("descriptive elements") encoded in Hall and Van de Castle's content-analysis system (1966) *are* encoded, in some form or other, in SSLS. In contrast to those authors' system, however, SSLS not only codes descriptors, but attempts to organize them in a psychologically meaningful way. It also provides a framework in which the scoring of descriptors is integrated with the scoring of the terms they describe.

One possibility, of course, is that some "empty" modifiers serve a structural, rather than a dynamic, role. In the yellow-flower/yellow-dress example given above (p. 384), this seems to be the case. Here the color term may be viewed not as a dynamic modifier but as a structural link between two Sy lexical classes—the basis, that is, for the added associative sentence $[\text{Sy}_{2A} \updownarrow \text{Sy}_{1A1}]$. "Yellow" may be *dynamically empty*, but, *structurally*, here it is *full*. Thus, an alternative conceptualization of this "empty" class might focus on its structural value, rather than on its lack of dynamic value: might "empty descriptors" better be called "*structural descriptors*"?

Rules for Scoring Dynamic Descriptors

Dynamic Modification of Verbs. Where textual words or phrases are used to modify an SSLS interactive verb by describing the strength of, force behind, or success of the activity encoded in that verb, an appropriate dynamic descriptor is scored for the verb. For example,

1) I touched her lightly $\qquad = E \rightrightarrows Pf_1$;
2) I touched her firmly and long $\quad = E \overset{+}{\rightarrow} Pf_1$;
3) I quite successfully put him down $= E \overset{+}{\longleftarrow} Pm_1$;
4) I hesitantly moved away from him $= \underset{\leftarrow}{\leftarrow} E, Pm_1$;
5) I moved like hell (from him) $\qquad = \overset{+}{\leftarrow} E, Pm_1$.

Certain textual interactive verbs themselves carry a meaning of ineffectuality or weakness versus effectuality or strength in consummating or sustaining an interactive relationship. SSLS translates such verbs as an SSLS verb plus the appropriate modifier. For example,

fled $\quad = \overset{+}{\leftarrow}$;
killed $= \overset{+}{\longleftarrow}$;
raped $= \overset{+}{\longleftarrow}$ (*plus:* $[\overset{+}{\rightarrow} \updownarrow \overset{+}{\longleftarrow}]$) ;
nicked $= \underline{\longleftarrow}$.

Note that this convention further erodes the similarity of textual structures and SSLS structures (cf. pp. 363-72). What is merely a verb in the text is, for SSLS, in effect, a verb *and* an adverb.

An attempt should be made to discriminate verbs whose extra connotation properties refer to the action or relationship itself (e.g., "slam") from those whose extra connotative properties refer to the subject of the relationship (e.g., "charm") or to the object of the relationship (e.g., "frustrate"). Thus,

1) I slam the man $= E \overset{+}{\longrightarrow} Pm_1$;

2) I charm the man $= \overset{+}{E} \rightarrow Pm_1$;

3) I frustrate the man $= E \longrightarrow \underline{Pm_1}$.

"Slam" seems to refer to an extra property of the action, "charm" to one of the initiator, and "frustrate" to one of the recipient. There are mixed cases, of course; "smash," for example, seems to relate both to the force of the action and to the consequence for the recipient. Thus,

1) I smash the man $= E \overset{+}{\longrightarrow} \underline{Pm_1}$.

By convention, the following translations are made of textual assertions of verbal interaction: ask $= \rightrightarrows$; *tell* $= \overset{+}{\rightarrow}$; *command* $= \longrightarrow$. When these verbs introduce *propositions*, they are followed by those propositions. For example,

1) I asked her $= E \rightrightarrows Pf_1$;

2) if she were coming home $= Pf_1 \rightrightarrows E$.

When these verbs do not introduce propositions, but *topics*, they are followed by topical Means sentences. For example,

1) I asked her $= E \rightrightarrows Pf$;

2) about home $(Sy_{1A}) = [Sy_{1A} \equiv E \boxed{\rightarrow} Pf_1]$.

(Note that *a Means verb always carries at least all signs of its interactive verb*: $\rightrightarrows$, $\equiv$, but it can carry its own sign as well, if only the Means relationship is qualified or if it is qualified in a different direction than is the interactive verb.) When these verbs introduce neither propositions nor topics, they can be followed by Means sentences in which the Means nouns stand for *distinctive verbal modes*. For example,

1) I asked her $= E \rightrightarrows Pf$;

2) a question $(Sy_{1A}) = [\underline{Sy_{1A}} \equiv E \boxed{\rightarrow} Pf_1]$.

Note here that the dynamic minus is carried over to the verbal mode, as well as to the Means verb (thus: "command" $= S\overset{+}{y}_{1A}$). When the content of a verbal interaction is used to define the verb category itself, no additional dynamic or structural score is required. Thus, to disagree = $-\!\!\!\prec$; to confirm = $\rightarrow$; and so on, rather than attacks-via-disagreements or approaches-via-confirmations. The "means" already has been subsumed by the choice of the verb in such cases.

Where textual words or phrases are used to modify an SSLS associative verb by describing the strength of the associative bond, an appropriate dynamic descriptor is scored for the verb. For example,

1) He was my best friend   = $[E \overset{+}{\updownarrow} Pm_1]$;
2) I could hardly remember her = $[E \underline{\updownarrow} Pf_1]$.

The dreamer's attitude toward an SSLS proposition also is indicated by the tense and mood of the textual account of the encoded relationship. In scoring relationships *structurally*, mood or tense is ignored. "I might have hit him" leads to the same structure as "I hit him." The qualifications conveyed by different textual verb forms are encoded *dynamically*. For example,

1) I could have created a theory = $E \circledcirc\!\!\rightarrow Sy_{1A}$;
2) I will go home   = $E \rightrightarrows Sy_{1A}$;
3) I had gone home   = $E \rightrightarrows Sy_{1A}$.

Specifically, *any verb form other than present, simple past, or past progressive* (I come, I came, I was coming) *is considered a psychic distancing of E from the structure he or she is describing; the verb of that structure is, accordingly, assigned a negative dynamic score.* (The two past tenses indicated above are excluded from this rule since the dream report is a historical account. *Passive* formulations are not, per se, scored negatively, since this must be a report rather than a dream phenomenon.)

"Psychic distancing" also is considered to be the basis of much of the self-ascribed "passive" cognition in dream reports or free associations (see The Associative Verbs, pp. 387–94, for an account of how to score alter-ascribed, or self-ascribed "active," cognition). *Accordingly, when such cognitions qualify an interactive or associative verb, they are scored as negative dynamic modifiers of it.* For example,

1) I was thinking about going home   = $E \rightrightarrows Sy_{1A}$;
2) I was wondering if I should go home = $E \rightrightarrows Sy_{1A}$;
3) I was hoping I would see her   = $[E \underline{\updownarrow} Pf_1]$;
4) I dreamed that I went home   = $E \rightrightarrows Sy_{1A}$.

Adverbial time descriptors also can be used for "psychic distancing," and, when so used, are scored as negative dynamic modifiers of their verb. For example,

He was a friend long ago = $[E \underline{\updownarrow} Pm_1]$.

But, when time descriptors focus on the *immediacy* or *definiteness* of a relationship, they contribute positive dynamic modification to their verb. For example,

Right then, I was walking away from her = $\overset{+}{\leftarrow} E, Pf_1$.

(Adverbial terms indicating a sequence of action in the dreamer's report [*"First . . . then . . . then, still later"*] are encoded by SSLS *only as the sequence in which described relationships are scored.* Such "chronology-of-reporting" terms do not have any dynamic attenuating or enhancing effect on the relationships whose sequence they describe.)[3]

It already has been noted (pp. 370–72) that *climatic and setting descriptors can, in certain circumstances, be scored as dynamic modifiers of relationship terms,* i.e., verbs. Most often, however, "settings"—if at all concrete—are scored structurally. For example, according to rules already described:

1) I walked to work = $E \rightarrow Sy_{1A}$;
2) He was at home = $[Pm_1 \updownarrow Sy_{1A}]$;
3) We were to meet = $[E \updownarrow Pf_1]$;
   in New York = $[Sy_{1A} = E \boxed{\updownarrow} Pf_1]$.

---

[3] There is some question as to whether the attenuating dynamic factors characterized as "psychic distancing" could represent true dream-work processes, or whether they might reflect secondary revision, i.e., distortion occurring after the dream experience has transpired. In the telling of the dream, certain events may be assigned more distant, uncertain, or cognitive statuses than is compatible with the here-and-now, perceptual "language" of the dream (cf. Freud's "considerations of representability" [1900]). The most that can be said here is that we must deal with dream reports, not dream experiences (Rechtschaffen, 1967). We may try to maximize the concordance of the two by collecting reports as soon as possible after the presumed experience being reported and by careful instruction and training of the reporters. In such circumstances (e.g., Foulkes and Pope, 1973; Bosinelli, Cicogna, and Molinari, 1974), it does appear that the language of the REM dream is more varied than is allowed by certain classical accounts (Freud, 1900), permitting waking thoughtlike mentation and qualification as well as concrete sensory imagery. Nonetheless, if the attenuating factors considered here are postdream processes, it is well to note that SSLS structural scoring is less influenced by such "secondary revision" than is SSLS dynamic scoring. Which, of course, makes good sense, since constructs at the former level are considered relatively invariant, while those at the latter level are supposed to be relatively unstable.

By convention, inhibition-overcome textual statements are scored as a simultaneous ± code for the verb in question. Thus,

I couldn't help but like him = $E \overset{+}{\underset{-}{\geq}} Pm_1$.

Dynamic Modification of Character Nouns. Where textual words or phrases modify an interactive relationship by altering the suitability of the sentence subject/object to engage in or sustain a consummated $\odot\!\!\rightarrow$, $\rightarrow$, $\prec$, *or* $\leftarrow$ *relationship, an appropriate dynamic descriptor is scored for that noun.* For example,

1) I felt sick as I tried to escape $\qquad = \overset{+}{\underset{-}{\leq}} \underline{E}, Pm_1$;
2) I was horny—I kissed her $\qquad = \overset{+}{E} \overset{+}{\rightarrow} Pf_1$;
3) I kissed him, but he was cold and distant $\quad = E \overset{+}{\rightarrow} \underline{Pm_1}$;
4) I felt the old adrenalin flowing, so I hit him $= \overset{+}{E} \prec Pm_1$.

Where textual words or phrases modify an associative relationship by altering the value of the sentence subject/object in that particular relationship, an appropriate dynamic descriptor is scored for that noun. For example,

1) I had this magical lamp $\quad = [E \updownarrow \overset{+}{Sy}_{1A}]$;
2) He was a miserable friend $= [E \updownarrow \underline{Pm_1}]$.

The *relative* nature of these value judgments needs to be stressed: a strong-willed friend is, literally, a *plus* in a dream in which the dreamer is helplessly searching for guidance but, literally, a *minus* in a dream in which autonomy is the dreamer's quest. A bouquet of flowers is a fine gift for a friend, but a lousy weapon with which to pummel a thief.

An SSLS noun is dynamically attenuated if the dreamer hesitates to definitively characterize the person, object, etc., which is its referent. For example,

I don't know who it was—it could have been my mother who
yelled at me = $\underline{M} \overset{+}{\prec} E$.

Statements of feeling are translated into dynamic descriptors. For example,

1) We were fighting, I was boiling mad = $\overset{+}{E} \prec Pm$;
2) (*we were*) $\qquad\qquad\qquad\quad = Pm \overset{+}{\prec} E$.

In this example, the interactive sentence(s) to which the feeling statement is relevant is clear. Occasionally, feeling statements appear "out of context," e.g., "I was happy—I don't know why." In such cases, ascribe the feeling to that same subject/object in the most recently scored sentence in which he/she/it appears. If the free-floating feeling appears in the initial textual sentence, obviously the direction in which this rule is applied must be reversed. *In determining the form of the dynamic score (plus/minus) one needs to consider whether the feeling at issue enhances or detracts from the suitability of a subject/object to consummate or sustain an interactive relationship or whether it enhances or detracts from the value of a subject/object in an associative relationship.*

Feelings are scored only when *specifically ascribed* to a subject/object. One does *not* infer from a verb such as "hitting" that anger is present. The feeling must be independently described. "Hitting" only indicates the form of the relational structure; it does not describe the subjective states of those so related.

Plurality of any noun class is translated as a positive dynamic descriptor. For example,

$$
\begin{aligned}
\text{a woman} \quad &= Pf_1 ; \\
\text{a group of women} &= \overset{+}{Pf_1} .
\end{aligned}
$$

Where a lexical entry is defined by its plurality, and hence can only be plural in any of its scorings, then the positive dynamic modifier always attaches to it (except in the object-term of Means sentences, where no descriptors ever are coded). For example, if the lexicon indicates that:

$\overset{+}{Pm_1}$ = a vaguely defined "they";

then Pm_1 always must be scored $\overset{+}{Pm_1}$. However, where the lexical entry is:

Pm_1 = colleague;

and "colleagues" and "colleague" both appear in the text, then:

$$
\begin{aligned}
Pm_{1A} &= \text{"colleague"}; \\
\overset{+}{Pm_1} &= \text{"colleagues"};
\end{aligned}
$$

in subsequently scored SSLS sentences. *Nondefining characteristics of persons or objects dictating dynamic modification are not routinely repeated;*

their reappearance as a dynamic score must be justified by their reappearance in the text. For example,

1) I had a big car   = $[E \updownarrow S\overset{+}{y}_{1A}]$;
2) It was in a garage   = $[Sy_{1A} \updownarrow Sy_{2A}]$;
3) I went to Steamboat = $E \rightarrow Sy_{3A}$;
4) in this big car   = $[\overset{+}{Sy}_{1A} = E \boxdot Sy_{3A}]$.

Where relative positions are described in explicit or implicit superior-inferior terminology, code the superior noun + and the inferior noun –. For example,

1) She was below me   = $[\underline{Pf_1} \updownarrow \overset{+}{E}]$;
2) The cup on the table   = $[\overset{+}{Sy}_{1A} \updownarrow \underline{Sy_{2A}}]$;
3) I put the cup on the table = $\overset{+}{E} \rightarrow \underline{Sy_{2A}}$;
4) –   = $[E = \overline{E}(Sy_{1A}) \boxdot Sy_{2A}]$.

Particularizing or demonstrative modifiers of an SSLS noun are coded +. For example,

a table, the table = Sy_{1A} ; this table, that table = $\overset{+}{Sy}_{1A}$;
a man, the man = Pm_{1A} ; a certain man, a particular man = $\overset{+}{Pm}_{1A}$.

Dynamic Modification of Symbolic Nouns. The major problem in assigning dynamic descriptors to *symbolic* nouns is that it is not as easy as it is for *character* nouns to determine whether or how textual descriptors affect the value/suitability of symbolic subjects/objects in associative/interactive sentences. If one is "moving toward" a flower, book, or town, for instance, what increases the suitability of that object for a "consummated" relationship with ego?

Fortunately, the work of Osgood and associates (Osgood, Suci, and Tannenbaum, 1957; Osgood, May, and Miron, 1975) offers guidelines for scoring the connotative meaning of symbolic objects or concepts. It appears, from Osgood's work, conducted over several decades and in a variety of cultural settings, that there are a few universal dimensions in terms of which affective value may be characterized, specifically: *good-bad* (e.g., positive-negative, complete-incomplete, beautiful-ugly); *strong-weak* (e.g., hard-soft, heavy-light, masculine-feminine, spacious-constricted, large-small); and *active-passive* (excitable-calm, hot-cold, complex-simple, interesting-boring). SSLS's suggestions for applying the Osgood et al. dimensions to the scoring of *Sy*

FIGURE A-1

Guidelines for Scoring Sy Descriptors in Interactive Relationships

	Relationships			
	Creating, female dreamer; Moving Toward, male dreamer	Creating, male dreamer; Moving Toward, female dreamer	Moving From	Moving Against
Sy Dimensions				
Good-bad				
	Good = +	Good = +	Good = +	Good = +
	Bad = –	Bad = –	Bad = –	Bad = –
Strong-weak				
	Strong = –	Strong = +	Strong = +	Strong = +
	Weak = +	Weak = –	Weak = –	Weak = –
Active-passive				
	Active = +	Active = +	Active = +	Active = +
	Passive = –	Passive = –	Passive = –	Passive = –

subjects/objects in interactive sentences are given in figure A-1. (The figure also could be used for *character* subjects/objects, although given the rules already described, such use generally would be redundant. The figure can be referred to in determining Sy's value as an exemplar of its own class in a With sentence. In a *Means sentence*, Sy value is judged relative to the interaction modified [e.g., as noted above, a flower is a nice gift but a lousy weapon]).

The figure's assignment of weights (*plus* or *minus*) to descriptors which seem to "load" predominantly on any one of the three meaning dimensions is, in most cases, relatively noncontroversial. Good and active are *plus* and bad and passive are *minus*, whatever the circumstances (interactive relationship); strong generally is *plus*; weak generally is *minus*. However, exceptions have been made to the dominant direction of scoring for the latter dimension.

Following Freud (1900), SSLS tends to interpret *Moving Toward* relationships with symbolic subjects/objects in sexual terms. This does not necessarily commit SSLS to the hypothesis that such relationships in their contemporary forms have overt sexual components, but only to the proposition that they use a symbolic vocabulary full of historically rich sexual referents (Thass-Thienemann, 1973*a*, *b*). Evidence for the stronger position is present, of course, and to some it may seem compelling. Freud and others have interpreted symbols sexually, often with the result of parsimonious, even elegant, explanations (interpretations) of complex manifest dreams. Others have been less impressed than Freud by the necessity of making sexual interpretations of *all* dreams, but have noted that when manifest content does become richly symbolic (i.e., transcends familiar subject/object categories), sexual interpretations often seem to fit the contextual use of the symbols rather well (e.g., Foulkes, 1967, 1971). Once again, however, whether or not one accepts the stronger position, SSLS commits the user only to the weaker proposition that Moving Toward relationships often use a "sexualized vocabulary"—often enough, that is, to permit us to consider sexuality as the prototype for such relationships when we assign weights to descriptors.

In line with this proposition, SSLS distinguishes the weights to be assigned strong-weak Sy terms for male dreamers and those to be assigned strong-weak Sy terms for female dreamers. Recall that E must be the other term in Moving Toward sentences using Sy; thus, we are characterizing a symbol which E plays "opposite." For the male, then, strong is *minus*, and weak is *plus*; for the female, strong is *plus*, and weak is *minus*. This convention follows from the proposition above that sexual relations provide the prototype of Moving Toward behavior and from Osgood et al.'s (1957) demonstration that "strong" is a "masculine" term and "weak" a "feminine" one. Thus a male related to a "weak" object, i.e., a "feminine" one, is in a *favorable* Moving-Toward relationship. Thus:

(Male dreamer) I felt the soft walls $\quad\quad\quad\quad = E \rightarrow \overset{+}{Sy}_{1A1}$;
(Female dreamer) I felt the stick: it was soft and rubbery $= E \rightarrow \underline{Sy}_{1A}$.

In *Creating* relationships, on the other hand, the symbol is, or was, a part of E, so now the scoring must follow a rule of sex-role similarity, rather than complementarity. For the male, strong is *plus*, and weak is *minus*; for the female, weak is *plus*, and strong is *minus*.

Some lexical entries in the Sy class, like some verb terms, may be considered to have inherent dynamic value. This value should be assigned each time there is textual justification for scoring the noun in question. For example,

skunk = $\underline{Sy}_{1A}$;
louse = $\underline{Sy}_{1A}$.

The logic here is that the textual noun really is an SSLS noun *plus* an SSLS "adjective," i.e., a dynamic modifier.

For category Sy composites, dynamic codes can apply either to a lexical component or to the whole composite. For example,

A thick car book = $Sy^{+}_{1A, 2A}$
(a thick book about a car);

but

A worn leather valise = $\underline{Sy}_{1A,2A}$
(presumably both the leather and the valise are worn).

Note the different style of recording a dynamic descriptor in these two cases: over/under a particular lexical subscript versus over/under "Sy" itself. (For character nouns, dynamic signs go over/under category labels, rather than subscripts.)

General Scoring Rules. Only a single dynamic plus or minus may be attached to any entry in an SSLS sentence. Thus,

1) The man walked to the ugly town = $E \rightarrow \underline{Sy}_{1A}$;
2) The man walked to this ugly, miserable, stinky, lousy, rotten
   little dump of a town $= E \rightarrow \underline{Sy}_{1A}$.

However, both a plus and a minus may be attached to any entry in an SSLS sentence. (Dynamic signs may be scored for any SSLS term except the object-term [the repeated interactive unit] of Means sentences.)

Repetition and Alternation

Two textual effects very much like the phenomena of dynamic modification discussed above are those of *repetition* and *alternation*. The repetition of any SSLS sentence seems to imply an enhanced "force" behind the structure in question, while alternations where subject and object remain constant but verbs shift in a toward/away, against/away, or creating/away direction seem to imply an attenuation of the force behind the first verb structure. *Sentence-repetition* effects are, in fact, scored within the framework of SSLS's *dynamic* analysis. *Alternation*, however, is, at present, scored structurally, although it is not clear that this is the better way to handle it.

Repetition of SSLS sentences is considered dynamic in quality when the sentences are consecutive. For example,

1) I touched it . . . $= E \rightarrow Sy_{1A}$;
2) I touched it . . . $= E \rightarrow Sy_{1A}$;
3) I touched it . . . reluctantly $= E \rightleftharpoons Sy_{1A}$.

By convention, such a sequence would be scored in the following manner:

1) $E \overset{+}{\rightleftharpoons} Sy_{1A}$;
2) $(E \rightarrow Sy_{1A})$;
3) $(E \rightleftharpoons Sy_{1A})$.

A simple succession of sentences in which the same subject, verb, and object are scored is indicated once in its regular form, with a *plus* sign over the verb reflecting the repetition effect, and with any other signs it or the other sentences of the succession carry. The repeated sentences themselves are indicated only parenthetically. For some purposes, the analyst may wish to consider the repeated sentences as independently valid structures; for other purposes, they might be considered only as bases of dynamic modification. The parenthetical rule permits both uses: parentheses designate sentences to be included, or excluded, as the analyst's procedure specifies.

The repetition rule applies only to successive sentences coded in the "Raw Scores" column of the analyst's work sheet. Otherwise, repetitions are coded in the usual way—as independent structures. (However, when a non-consecutive repetition uses the word "again," that repetitive modifier is coded as *plus*. For example,

1) I went to the hills $\quad= E \rightarrow \overset{+}{S}y_{1A}$;
2) Road had ice $\quad= [Sy_{2A} \updownarrow Sy_{3A}]$;
3) When I went again ... $= E \overset{+}{\rightarrow} \overset{+}{S}y_{1A}$.)

Alternation may be illustrated as follows:

1) I touched her $\quad= E \rightarrow Pf_1$;
2) Then I drew back $= \leftarrow E, Pf_1$.

Note that both grammatical sentences are reasonably complete (the SSLS object of the second clearly is implied as being identical to the object of the first). In an alternate one-sentence construction, for example,

I made a false-start movement at touching her,

the scoring would have been

$= E \rightleftharpoons Pf_1$,

that is, the start/stop sequence is scored dynamically as a tentative (minus) movement toward. It does not seem totally satisfactory that two such similar "meanings" get different SSLS codes. However, for the time being, at least, that is how it is.

The major difficulty with this situation is that if Freud (1900) is correct regarding "considerations of representability" in dreams—namely that the perceptions of sleep must use concrete, action-oriented means of expression, then the two similar statements above probably are *different descriptions* of *one and the same dream event.* However, the integrity of the ← verb category is at stake; if this verb is, so often, to be coded dynamically, in what sense is it still a valid *structural* concept? The unresolved theoretical issue on which resolution of this dilemma hinges is precisely that: is ← a structure just like →? Is it true that deep investments exist not only in being near or creating "objects," but also in escaping them? Or, are movements-away dynamic attenuations of basic motives, all of which presuppose contact with others?

Summary

The rules given in this appendix and in chapter 11 are meant to standardize scoring and to eliminate idiosyncratic judgments in treating dream and free-association data. Even more elaborate scoring rules have evolved as we have continued to use SSLS. For example, as will be mentioned in appendix B, we have developed an extensive verb dictionary, giving standard structural and dynamic SSLS equivalents for textual verbs. However, it is obvious that no set of rules could hope to encompass all cases. SSLS's rules fall far short of that goal. Private judgments are required. However, when such judgments are done within the framework of a ruleful system, they probably will be less than totally arbitrary. That is, a system of rules not only dictates how to treat a specified range of cases, it also generates a strong "set" for dealing with cases outside that range.

It is not, of course, always *rules*—or the lack thereof—which are at fault in cases of difficult scoring decisions. Sometimes it is the *data* themselves. One of the assumptions made by any set of scoring rules is that data have been well-collected—that they are sufficient to answer questions the investigator has posed, that they are unambiguous, and so on. Carefully supervised dream reporting and carefully guided free associating probably mean as much to the ultimate utility of this, or any comparable, scoring system as increasingly intricate sets of rules or scoring conventions.

APPENDIX B

Reliability of the Content Analysis

David Foulkes, Stephen F. Butler, and Patricia L. Maykuth

In studies at our laboratory in which SSLS has been applied to dreams and free associations, the standard procedure has been to have two independent scorings of the pertinent textual material. The independent scorings then are reconciled in order to arrive at a final scoring which can be used, for example, in path analysis and structuregram formation, and in subsequent characterizations of dream-work processes. The latter applications are unequivocal, in the sense that they are entirely guided by rules and free of the vagaries of human judgment. Of course, one can make mistakes in performing these applications, but those mistakes are of the same order as the mistakes one can commit in solving algebraic equations or in performing a statistical test. The best check against such mistakes, as in algebraic or statistical operations, is an independent verification of the original computations.

At the base of this edifice of data reduction, however, lies the reconciled scoring, which is, in turn, based on judgments of two or more scorers. That reconciliation of independent scorings is, in our experience, relatively easily achieved is not a sufficient argument for the rulefulness of the original scorings. It is possible, for example, that irrational processes of social influence, rather than reliance on rules, govern the reconciliation. It is necessary, therefore, to demonstrate that scoring reliability can be independently achieved by judges before their reconciliation efforts begin. Some data are presented below to document this possibility. It is important to emphasize that these data indicate only that such scoring reliability *can* be achieved, not that the system, as such, is "reliable." Reliability must be contextually defined: in relation to a certain set of materials, scored by a certain set of judges, with certain experience and/or training in using the system.

The judges whose reliability is reported below have not always found it as easy to agree with one another as the data presented here might suggest. We are, at present, simply unsure as to how much training and effort might be involved before other judges could achieve comparable reliability. We hope, however, that future judges will be as patient as we have been in familiarizing ourselves with SSLS and in applying it to a variety of materials. That SSLS is difficult has not deterred us; we hope it will not deter others. It is, of course, one of the principles underlying the development of SSLS that dream psychology—indeed, human psychology in general—needs more subtle and refined ways of dealing with the individual event, the individual observation. It never was imagined by us that such detailedness of analysis of any single event would be as easy to learn or employ as are most of the analytic techniques of today's human psychology. If, as B. F. Skinner seems to believe, the choice for today's psychologist is to generalize weakly (statistically) across large groups of organisms or to understand one organism thoroughly, our preference is for the latter alternative. We also are reminded of Freud's observation, toward the conclusion of one of the most exhaustive analyses ever conducted of any single person's behavior, thoughts, and dreams:

> In order to derive fresh generalizations from what has thus been established . . . it would be essential to have at one's disposal numerous cases as thoroughly and deeply analysed as the present one. But they are not easily to be had, and each one of them requires years of labour. So that advances in these spheres of knowledge must necessarily be slow. There is no doubt a great temptation to content oneself with "scratching" the mental surface of a number of people and of replacing what is left undone by speculation. . . . Practical requirements may also be adduced in favour of this procedure; but no substitute can satisfy the requirements of science. [Freud, 1918, pp. 105-6]

We have found two devices useful in improving the reliability of our scoring. It has seemed to us that certain ambiguities inhere in the materials to which SSLS is likely to be applied—certainly to materials collected, as most of ours have been, before there was any notion as to how they would be analyzed. It is unfair, we think, that the scoring system not only be asked to reduce unambiguous statements to its concepts but also be asked to decide what ambiguous statements mean. To whom or what, for example, does some stray "they" or "it" in the text refer? Before independent scoring commences, then, we get together and sift through the report for such semantic ambiguity, and reach what seems to us to be some reasonable consensus as to what the report is asserting. Once we agree on that, we separately score the report.

We also have developed a verb dictionary, whose current typescript length is over 100 pages. In this dictionary are found SSLS equivalents of the more commonly appearing verbs in English texts. It is on the basis of the use of this dictionary that all scorers achieved considerable consensus on their verb scoring. As the reliability results indicate, recourse to this dictionary has practically eliminated substantive disagreement on verb scoring. (Copies of this dictionary will be made available, at cost, to those with a serious interest in using SSLS.)

In many respects, SSLS reminds us of Bales' system of Interaction Process Analysis (1951). In both cases, a stream of verbal behavior is supplied, using both rules and judgment, with a categorical analysis. The results of this analysis, in both cases, are subject to subsequent data reduction of a relatively unequivocal sort (Bales' group and individual profiles, who-to-whom matrices, phase analyses, etc.). More importantly, in the present context, both face multiple problems of reliability in the case of their initial categorical judgments. (1) Is there reliability of unitizing the verbal behavior? Do judges identify the same behavioral units as requiring discrete categorization? (2) Is there reliability as to the nature of an interaction or relationship—as to its "verb" form? (3) Is there reliability as to the subject and object of the relationship? These forms of reliability are, of course, interdependent: to the extent that separate units have not been defined in common, it is difficult to imagine that judges would agree very well on unit content.

In the case of this small-scale demonstration of the potential reliability of SSLS, we have chosen to report reliabilities separately for: *unitizing* (judges agree or do not agree as to whether a text unit justifies scoring a sentence or *n*-sized group of sentences); *interactive versus associative relationship assignment* in those cases of unitizing agreement; discrete *verb assignment* ($\circledcirc\!\!\rightarrow$, $\rightarrow$, $\leftarrow$, $\prec$, $\updownarrow$, $=$, $=$ ... $\square$) in the same cases; and discrete *subject/object assignment* in the same cases.

In calculating *unit agreement*, we simply have asked how many of the sentences scored by a first judge also have been scored in response to the same textual component by a second judge in a judge pair. For *associative/ interactive agreement*, we report the percentage of those common-unit sentences which contain the same SSLS verb superclass. For *verb agreement*, we report the percentage of common-unit sentences which contain the same discrete SSLS verb code. For *subject/object agreement*, we report the percentage of *associative* sentences (except for Means sentences) which contain the same two lexical *referents* in any order (since order is irrelevant in ↕ and = sentences), even where lexical *subscripts* may differ (since lexical subscripts also are arbitrary, with an identical pattern of referent relationships recoverable from a variety of subscript assignments), combined with the percentage of *interactive* sentences which contain identical lexical referents as subject *and* as object and with the percentage of *means* sentences which contain identical lexical referents as means, and as subject, boxed verb, and object. As a *lexical summary measure*, it then is indicated what percentage of common-unit sentences are identical in *all* pertinent lexical entries: subject/verb/object for interactive sentences; means/subject/verb/ object for Means sentences; and verb and two related terms for ↕ and = sentences.

Although dynamic scores are not, at present, employed in most of the anticipated data reductions of SSLS scorings, reliability also is reported for them: (1) the number of common-unit verbs to which *identical* dynamic scores (including non-scores) are assigned over the total number of such verbs; (2) the number of common-unit sentence nouns ($n = 2$ for all sentences except Means sentences, where $n = 3$) to which identical dynamic scores (including non-scores) are assigned over the total number of such nouns.

There is nothing special about the ways we have chosen here to report reliability. A variety of other options clearly are available. We encourage others to experiment with them. For example, it may prove useful to compare individual judges with the final, reconciled scoring, rather than with one another. It is, for instance, unfair to a given judge to consider her or him unreliable if she/he gets a "correct" score which the other judge missed— correctness, with a small c, being defined by the reconciliation consensus.

The results of this reliability demonstration are presented in two parts. First, we present the complete scoring by three judges of two dream reports. These dream reports were selected in advance to be presented here in their entirety (because they were dreams from our own laboratory). Then, summary statistics are presented for the entire protocol of eight dreams (these two, plus six taken from other sources) which we had agreed would constitute the corpus for this demonstration.

In the two scored reports, bracketed textual entries indicate material defined by a prescoring consensus. Summary statistics, as described above, were calculated separately for each dream.

Dream 1

Male Dreamer

	Judge A	Judge B	Judge C
I have had an accident			
And am eating parts of myself (of myself)	$\underline{E} \prec S\dot{y}_1$ $[E \Updownarrow S\dot{y}_1]$	$\underline{E} \prec S\dot{y}_1$ $[E \Updownarrow S\dot{y}_1]$	$\underline{E} \prec S\dot{y}_1$ $[E \Updownarrow S\dot{y}_1]$
I eat my right hand (my)	$E \prec Sy_{1A}$ $[Sy_{1A} \Updownarrow Sy_1]$ $[E \Updownarrow Sy_{1A}]$	$E \prec Sy_{1A}$ $[Sy_{1A} \Updownarrow Sy_1]$ $[E \Updownarrow Sy_{1A}]$	$E \prec S\dot{y}_{1A}$ $[Sy_1 \Updownarrow Sy_{1A}]$ $[E \Updownarrow S\dot{y}_{1A}]$
And I see the flesh pulled off of the bone [of the right hand]	$\leftarrow E, Sy_{1A1}$ $[Sy_{1A1} \Updownarrow Sy_{1A}]$ $[Pm_1 \overset{+}{=} \boxdot E\,(Sy_{1A2}),\,Sy_{1A1}]$ $[E \overset{+}{=} \boxdot E\,(Sy_{1A2}),\,Sy_{1A1}]$	$\leftarrow E, Sy_{1B}$ $[Sy_{1B} \Updownarrow Sy_{1A}]$ $[E \overset{+}{=} \boxdot E\,(Sy_{1C}),\,Sy_{1B}]$ $([E = \boxdot E\,(Sy_{1C}),\,Sy_{1B}])$	$\leftarrow E, Sy_{1A2}$ $[Sy_{1A2} \Updownarrow Sy_{1A}]$ $[E \overset{+}{=} \boxdot E\,(Sy_{1A1}),\,Sy_{1A2}]$ $([E = \boxdot E\,(Sy_{1A1}),\,Sy_{1A2}])$
My eyes must go next	$^I[E \overset{+}{\Updownarrow} S\dot{y}_{1B}]$ $[Sy_{1B} \Updownarrow Sy_{1A2}]$ $[E \overset{+}{=} \boxdot E\,(Sy_{1A2}),\,Sy_{1A1}]$ $^1\overset{+}{=} S\dot{y}_{1B}, E$	$[E \Updownarrow S\dot{y}_{1D}]$ $[Sy_{1D} \Updownarrow Sy_{1C}]$ $[Sy_{1D} \Updownarrow Sy_{1B}]$ $\overset{+}{=} S\dot{y}_{1D}, E$	$[E \Updownarrow S\dot{y}_{1B}]$ $[Sy_{1B} \Updownarrow Sy_{1A1}]$ $[Sy_{1B} \Updownarrow Sy_{1A2}]$ $\leftarrow S\dot{y}_{1B}, \underline{E}$ $[E = \boxdot Sy_{1B}, E]$
Though I still have them at the moment	$([E \overset{+}{\Updownarrow} S\dot{y}_{1B}])$	$[E \overset{+}{\Updownarrow} S\dot{y}_{1D}]$	$[E \overset{+}{\Updownarrow} S\dot{y}_{1B}]$
I think: everything that I consider	$[E \overset{+}{\Updownarrow} S\dot{y}_2]$ $[S\dot{y}_2 \overset{+}{\Updownarrow} S\dot{y}_{1B}]$	$[E \overset{+}{\Updownarrow} S\dot{y}_2]$	—
Important to me	$[E \overset{+}{\Updownarrow} S\dot{y}_2]$	$[Sy_2 \Updownarrow Sy_{1D}]$	$[Sy_2 \Updownarrow Sy_{1B}]$
Is to be taken from me	$\overset{+}{=} S\dot{y}_2, E$ $[Pm_1 \overset{+}{=} \boxminus Sy_2, E]$	$\overset{+}{=} S\dot{y}_2, E$ $[Pm_1 \overset{+}{=} \boxminus Sy_2, E]$	— $\overset{+}{=} S\dot{y}_2, E$ $[Pm_1 \overset{+}{=} \boxminus Sy_2, E]$
Now something about Catholic priests runs through my mind	$[E \overset{+}{\Updownarrow} \underline{F}_1]$ $[F_1 \Updownarrow Pm_1]$ $[F_1 \Updownarrow Sy_2]$	$[E \overset{+}{\Updownarrow} \underline{F}_1]$ $[F_1 \Updownarrow Pm_1]$ $[F_1 \Updownarrow Sy_2]$	$[E \overset{+}{\Updownarrow} \underline{F}_1]$ $[F_1 \Updownarrow Pm_1]$ $[F_1 \Updownarrow Sy_2]$
Concerning the[ir] eating of the sacrament [bread, symbolizing Christ's body]	$\underline{E} \prec Sy_{3A}$ $[Sy_{3A} \Updownarrow F_1]$ $[Sy_{3A} \Updownarrow Sy_2]$ $[Sy_{3A} = F_2]$	$\underline{E} \prec Sy_{3A}$ $[Sy_{3A} \Updownarrow F_1]$ $[Sy_{3A} \Updownarrow Sy_2]$ $[Sy_{3A} = F_2]$	$\underline{E} \prec Sy_{3A}$ $[Sy_{3A} \Updownarrow F_1]$ $[Sy_{3A} \Updownarrow Sy_2]$ $[Sy_{3A} = F_2]$

Dream 1 (Continued)

	Judge A	Judge B	Judge C
And how they do not know what it is they do [in eating sacrament]	E ⊂ Sy3A [Sy3A ⊜ F₂]	E ⊂ Sy3A [Sy3A ⊜ F₂]	E ⊂ Sy3A [Sy3A ⊜ F₂]
They do not understand the nature of the rite [that the bread symbolizes Christ's body]	([Sy3A ≡ F₂]) [F₁ ≡ Sy3A ≡ F₂]	([Sy3A ≡ F₂]) [F₁ ≡ Sy3A ⊜ F₂]	([Sy3A ≡ F₂]) [F₁ ≡ Sy3A ⊜ F₂]

Sy lexicon: A
Sy₁ – body part
  1A – hand
    1A1 – bone
    1A2 – flesh
  1B – eye
Sy₂ – "everything"
Sy₃ – religious
  3A – sacrament

Sy lexicon: B
Sy₁ – body part
  1A – hand
  1B – bone
  1C – flesh
  1D – eye
Sy₂ – "everything"
Sy₃ – religious
  3A – sacrament

Sy lexicon: C
Sy₁ – body part
  1A – hand
    1A1 – flesh
    1A2 – bone
  1B – eye
Sy₂ – "everything"
Sy₃ – religious
  3A – sacrament

[1] Order of these two sentences reversed on original score sheet

RELIABILITY

Judge Pair

	A-B	A-C	B-C
Unitizing:	29/30 = 97% (98%*)	28/30 = 93% (95%*)	28/29 = 97% (97%*)
Associative/			
Interactive: I-I	n = 7	n = 7	n = 7
A-A	22	21	21
A-I	0	0	0
I-A	0 = 100%	0 = 100%	0 = 100%
Lexical Content: verb	n = 29 = 100%	n = 28 = 100%	n = 28 = 100%
sub/obj	28 = 97%	27 = 96%	28 = 100%
all terms	28 = 97%	27 = 96%	28 = 100%
Dynamic Scores: verb	22/29 = 76%	22/28 = 79%	26/28 = 93%
sub/obj	52/62 = 84%	48/60 = 80%	56/60 = 93%

*Percentage of sentences scored by both judges which were scored in common.

Dream 2
Male Dreamer

	Judge A	Judge B	Judge C
It's night and appropriately dark			
I'm lying in bed	$[\overset{+}{E} \rightleftharpoons Sy_{1A}]$	$[\overset{+}{E} \mathbin{\overset{+}{\updownarrow}} Sy_{1A}]$	$[\overset{+}{E} \mathbin{\overset{+}{\updownarrow}} Sy_{1A}]$
Next to Irma	$[E \updownarrow Pf_1]$	$[E \updownarrow Pf_1]$	$[E \updownarrow Pf_1]$
	$[Pf_1 \updownarrow Sy_{1A}]$	$[Pf_1 \updownarrow Sy_{1A}]$	$[Pf_1 \updownarrow Sy_{1A}]$
I hear sounds [people]	$[E \updownarrow P\overset{+}{m}_1]$	$[E \updownarrow P\overset{+}{m}_1]$	$[E \updownarrow P\overset{+}{m}_1]$
	$[P\overset{+}{m}_1 \updownarrow Pf_1]$	$[Pm_1 \updownarrow Pf_1]$	$[Pm_1 \updownarrow Pf_1]$
	$[P\overset{+}{m}_1 \updownarrow Sy_{1A}]$	$[Pm_1 \updownarrow Sy_{1A}]$	$[Pm_1 \updownarrow Sy_{1A}]$
In the next room	$[P\overset{+}{m}_1 \updownarrow Sy_{2A}]$	$[P\overset{+}{m}_1 \updownarrow Sy_{2A}]$	$[P\overset{+}{m}_1 \updownarrow Sy_{2A}]$
Which would suggest that several people are entering [that room]	$\overset{+}{E} \rightleftharpoons Sy_{2A}$	$\overset{+}{E} \rightleftharpoons Sy_{2A}$	$P\overset{+}{m}_1 \rightleftharpoons E$
Through the window	$[Sy_{2A1} = E(Pm_1) \boxed{\uparrow} Sy_{2A}]$	$[Sy_{2A1} = E(Pm_1) \boxed{\uparrow} Sy_{2A}]$	$[Sy_{2A1} = Pm_1 \boxed{\uparrow} E(Sy_{2A})]$
I try to move,	$\underline{\overset{+}{E} \rightleftharpoons Sy_{3A}}$	$\underline{\overset{+}{E} \rightleftharpoons Sy_{3A}}$	$\underline{E \rightleftharpoons Sy_3}$
to get some kind	$[Sy_{3A} \updownarrow Sy_{2A1}]$	$[Sy_{3A} \updownarrow Sy_{2A1}]$	$[Sy_3 \updownarrow Sy_{2A1}]$
of object	$[Sy_{3A} \updownarrow P\overset{+}{m}_1]$	$[Sy_{3A} \updownarrow Pm_1]$	$[Sy_3 \updownarrow Pm_1]$
	$[Sy_{3A} \updownarrow Sy_{2A}]$	$[Sy_{3A} \updownarrow Sy_{2A}]$	$[Sy_3 \updownarrow Sy_{2A}]$
Which will serve as a weapon	$[Sy_{3A} = Sy_{4A}]$	$[Sy_{3A} = Sy_{4A}]$	$[Sy_3 = Sy_{3A}]$
And find that I'm unable to [get weapon]	$E \rightleftharpoons Sy_{4A}$	$E \rightleftharpoons Sy_{4A}$	$E \rightleftharpoons Sy_{3A}$
The people— all men— enter the room [bedroom]	$\overset{+}{E} \rightarrow Sy_{2B}$	$\overset{+}{E} \rightarrow Sy_{2B}$	$\overset{+}{E} \rightarrow Sy_{2B}$
	$[Sy_{2B} \updownarrow Sy_{4A}]$	$[Sy_{2B} \updownarrow Sy_{4A}]$	—
They're talking [to me], but the words are muffled, absolutely unintelligible	$P\overset{+}{m}_1 \rightleftharpoons E$	$P\overset{+}{m}_1 \rightleftharpoons E$	$P\overset{+}{m}_1 \rightleftharpoons E$

Dream 2 (Continued)

	Judge A	Judge B	Judge C
I try to curse			
at them	$E \preceq P^+\hat{m}_1$	$E \preceq P^+\hat{m}_1$	$E \preceq P^+\hat{m}_1$
Or ask them	$E \rightrightarrows P^+\hat{m}_1$	$E \rightrightarrows P^+\hat{m}_1$	$E \rightrightarrows P^+\hat{m}_1$
What they're			
doing [why they're			
disturbing me]	$P^+\hat{m}_1 \curlyvee E$	$P^+\hat{m}_1 \curlyvee E$	$P^+\hat{m}_1 \curlyvee E$
I am unable to			
speak [to them]	$E \rightrightarrows P^+\hat{m}_1$	$E \rightrightarrows P^+\hat{m}_1$	$E \rightrightarrows P^+\hat{m}_1$
They pay no			
attention to me	$P^+\hat{m}_1 \rightrightarrows E$	$P^+\hat{m}_1 \rightrightarrows E$	$P^+\hat{m}_1 \rightrightarrows E$
They begin to disrobe	$\Leftarrow S\hat{y}^+_{5A} \cdot E$	$\Leftarrow S\hat{y}^+_{5A}, E$	$\Leftarrow E, P\hat{m}_1$
[themselves]]	$[P^+\hat{m}_1 \equiv \leftarrow S y_{5A}, E(Pm_1)]$	$[P^+\hat{m}_1 \equiv \leftarrow S y_{5A}, E(Pm_1)]$	$[P^+\hat{m}_1 \equiv \leftarrow E(S y_4), P^+\hat{m}_1]$
And attack Irma	$E \overset{+}{\preceq} Pf_1$	$E \overset{+}{\preceq} Pf_1$	$E \overset{+}{\preceq} Pf_1$
sexually	$[\curlyvee \Leftrightarrow \rightarrow]$	$[\curlyvee \Leftrightarrow \rightarrow]$	$[\curlyvee \Leftrightarrow \rightarrow]$
I am unable to see	$[E \Leftrightarrow Sy_{6A}]$	$[E \Leftrightarrow Sy_{6A}]$	$[E \Leftrightarrow Sy_{5A}]$
her face	$[Sy_{6A} \Leftrightarrow Pf_1]$	$[Sy_{6A} \Leftrightarrow Pf_1]$	$[Sy_{5A} \Leftrightarrow Pf_1]$
	$([Sy_{6A} \Leftrightarrow Pf_1])$	—	—
Or their faces	$[E \underline{\Leftrightarrow} S\hat{y}^+_{6A}]$	$[E \Leftrightarrow S\hat{y}^+_{6A}]$	$[E \Leftrightarrow S\hat{y}^+_{5A}]$
	$[P^+\hat{m}_1 \Leftrightarrow S\hat{y}^+_{6A}]$	$[S\hat{y}^+_{6A} \Leftrightarrow P^+\hat{m}_1]$	$[P^+\hat{m}_1 \Leftrightarrow S\hat{y}^+_{5A}]$
I am livid and attempting			
to scream [at them],	$\overset{+}{E} \preceq P^+\hat{m}_1$	$\overset{+}{E} \preceq P^+\hat{m}_1$	$\overset{+}{E} \preceq P^+\hat{m}_1$
Swear [at them],	$(\overset{+}{E} \preceq P^+\hat{m}_1)$	$(E \preceq P^+\hat{m}_1)$	$(E \preceq P^+\hat{m}_1)$
Anything which will make them	$(\overset{+}{E} \preceq P^+\hat{m}_1)$	$E \preceq P^+\hat{m}_1$	$E \preceq P^+\hat{m}_1$
stop [prevent their rape	$E \overset{+}{\rightarrow} Pf_1$	$\overset{+}{E} \overset{+}{\rightarrow} Pf_1$	$\overset{+}{E} \overset{+}{\rightarrow} Pf_1$
of Irma]	$[\curlyvee \underline{\Leftrightarrow} \rightarrow]$	$[\curlyvee \underline{\Leftrightarrow} \rightarrow]$	$[\curlyvee \underline{\Leftrightarrow} \rightarrow]$
	$[E \underline{\equiv} E(Pm_1)\;\boxed{\curlyvee}\;Pf_1]$	$[E \underline{\equiv} E(Pm_1)\;\boxed{\curlyvee}\;Pf_1]$	$[E \equiv E(Pm_1)\;\boxed{\curlyvee}\;Pf_1]$
Again, I'm unable			
to speak [to them]	$E \rightrightarrows P^+\hat{m}_1$	$E \rightrightarrows P^+\hat{m}_1$	$E \rightrightarrows P^+\hat{m}_1$

	Judge A	Judge B	Judge C
	Sy lexicon: A and B		Sy lexicon: C
	Sy1—furniture		Sy1—furniture
	1A—bed		1A—bed
	Sy2—rooms		Sy2—rooms
	2A—next room		2A—next room
	2B—bedroom		2B—bedroom
	Sy3—objects		Sy3—objects
	3A—(unspecified)		3A—weapon
	Sy4—weapons		Sy4—men's apparel
	4A—(unspecified)		
	Sy5—apparel +5A—men's clothes		Sy5—body parts
	Sy6—body parts		5A—face
	6A—face		

RELIABILITY

		Judge Pair	
	A-B	A-C	B-C
Unitizing:	38/39 = 97% (99%*)	37/39 = 95% (97%*)	37/38 = 97% (99%*)
Associative/ Interactive:			
I-I	n = 17	n = 17	n = 17
A-A	21	20	20
A-I	0	0	0
I-A	0 = 100%	0 = 100%	0 = 100%
Lexical Content: verb	n = 38 = 100%	n = 37 = 100%	n = 37 = 100%
sub/obj	38 = 100%	33 = 89%	33 = 89%
all terms	38 = 100%	33 = 89%	33 = 89%
Dynamic Scores: verb	35/38 = 92%	32/37 = 86%	33/37 = 89%
sub/obj	71/79 = 90%	67/77 = 87%	75/77 = 97%

*percentage of sentences by both judges which were scored in common

For the total sample of eight dreams, we observed the following rates of interjudge agreement, where the denominator is sentences/terms scored and the numerator is sentences/terms scored identically.

	Judge Pair		
	A-B	A-C	B-C
Unitizing:	250/257 = 97%	246/257 = 96%	255/264 = 97%
Associative/ Interactive:	246/250 = 98%	241/246 = 98%	254/255 = 99.6%
Lexical Content:			
Verb	241/250 = 96%	236/246 = 96%	250/255 = 98%
Noun	220/250 = 88%	208/246 = 85%	231/255 = 91%
All terms	219/250 = 88%	206/246 = 84%	230/255 = 90%

The basic result is that SSLS structural scoring was, for these judges, quite reliable, even for overall lexical content (sentences which were, as a unit, scored identically, with subscript-deviant but referent-identical nouns considered as matches).

The reliability of dynamic scoring for these same eight dreams was as follows:

	Judge Pair		
	A-B	A-C	B-C
Verb	208/250 = 83%	205/246 = 83%	242/255 = 95%
Noun	463/544 = 85%	448/538 = 83%	533/557 = 96%

References

The *date* assigned to a book or article in textual citations is that of the year of first publication, where ascertainable. Where two dates are indicated below, *page references* in the text are from the more recent edition. The references below do not include sources cited only within quotations from other sources.

Allport, G. W. 1954. The historical background of modern social psychology. In G. Lindzey, ed. *Handbook of social psychology*. Cambridge, Mass.: Addison-Wesley. Pp. 3–56.

Anderson, J. R., and Bower, G. H. 1973. *Human associative memory*. Washington, D.C.: V. H. Winston.

Arieti, S. 1974. *Interpretation of schizophrenia*, 2d ed. New York: Basic Books.

Aserinsky, E., and Kleitman, N. 1953. Regularly occurring periods of eye motility, and concomitant phenomena, during sleep. *Science* 118:273–74.

Bales, R. F. 1951. *Interaction process analysis*. Cambridge, Mass.: Addison-Wesley.

Bartlett, F. C. 1932. *Remembering*. Cambridge, Eng.: Cambridge Univer. Press.

Benedetti, G. 1975. Function of dreams in mental economy. In P. Levin and W. P. Koella, eds. *Sleep 1974*. Basel: S. Karger. Pp. 124–27.

Berger, R. J. 1961. Tonus of extrinsic laryngeal muscles during sleep and dreaming. *Science* 134:840.

———. 1963. Experimental modification of dream content by meaningful verbal stimuli. *British Journal of Psychiatry* 109:722–40.

———. 1969. Oculomotor control: a possible function of REM sleep. *Psychological Review* 76:144–64.

Berlucchi, G. 1965. Callosal activity in unrestrained, unanesthetized cats. *Archives Italiennes de Biologie* 103:623–34.

Berne, E. 1972. *What do you say after hello?* New York: Grove Press.

Bizzi, E., and Brooks, D. C. 1963. Functional connections between pontine reticular formation and lateral geniculate nucleus during deep sleep. *Archives Italiennes de Biologie* 101:666–80.

Blanck, G., and Blanck, R. 1974. *Ego psychology: theory and practice*. New York: Columbia Univer. Press.

Bleuler, E. 1950 (orig. 1911). *Dementia praecox or the group of schizophrenias*. New York: International Universities Press.

Bloom, L. M. 1970. *Language development: form and function in emerging grammars.* Cambridge, Mass.: M.I.T. Press.

Boden, M. A. 1974. Freudian mechanisms of defence: a programming perspective. In R. Wollheim, ed. *Freud.* Garden City, N.Y.: Anchor. Pp. 242-70.

Bogen, J. E. 1969. The other side of the brain: an appositional mind. *Bulletin of the Los Angeles Neurological Societies* 34:135-62.

Bosinelli, M., Bagnaresi, G., Molinari, S., and Salzarulo, P. 1968. Caratteristiche dell' attività psicofisiologica durante il sonno: un contributo alle tecniche di valutazione. *Rivista Sperimentale di Freniatria* 92:128-50.

Bosinelli, M., Cicogna, P., and Molinari, S. 1974. The tonic-phasic model and the feeling of self-participation in different stages of sleep. *Giornale Italiano di Psicologia* 1:35-65.

Bower, T. G. R. 1974. *Development in infancy.* San Francisco: W. H. Freeman.

Breger, L. 1969. Children's dreams and personality development. In J. Fisher and L. Breger, eds. *The meaning of dreams: recent insights from the laboratory.* Sacramento: California Dept. of Mental Hygiene. Pp. 64-100.

Breuer, J., and Freud, S. n.d. (orig. 1895). *Studies in hysteria.* Boston: Beacon Press.

Brown, J. S. 1948. Gradients of approach and avoidance responses and their relation to level of motivation. *Journal of Comparative and Physiological Psychology* 41:450-65.

Brown, R. 1976. The new paradigm of reference. Presented to Psychology and Biology of Language and Thought: A Symposium in Memory of Eric H. Lenneberg, Ithaca, N.Y.

Brown, R., and Herrnstein, R. J. 1975. *Psychology.* Boston: Little, Brown.

Brown, R. and Lenneberg, E. H. 1954. A study in language and cognition. *Journal of Abnormal and Social Psychology* 49:454-62.

Bruner, J. S. 1966. On cognitive growth: I; II. In J. S. Bruner, R. R. Olver, and P. M. Greenfield, eds. *Studies in cognitive growth.* New York: John Wiley. Pp. 1-67.

Chomsky, N. 1957. *Syntactic structures.* The Hague: Mouton.

———. 1959. A review of *Verbal behavior,* by B. F. Skinner. *Language* 35:26-58.

———. 1965. *Aspects of the theory of syntax.* Cambridge, Mass.: M.I.T. Press.

———. 1972. *Language and mind* (enlarged ed.). New York: Harcourt Brace Jovanovich.

Colby, B. N. 1975. Culture grammars. *Science* 187:913-19.

Colby, K. M. 1975. *Artificial paranoia: a computer simulation of paranoid processes.* New York: Pergamon.

Colby, K. M., and Gilbert, J. P. 1964. Programming a computer model of neurosis. *Journal of Mathematical Psychology* 1:405-17.

Cuny, H. 1965 (orig. 1962). *Ivan Pavlov: the man and his theories.* New York: Paul S. Eriksson.

Dement, W. 1955. Dream recall and eye movements during sleep in schizophrenics and normals. *Journal of Nervous and Mental Disease* 122:263-69.

———. 1960. The effect of dream deprivation. *Science* 131:1705–7.

Domhoff, B. 1969. Home dreams versus laboratory dreams: home dreams are better. In M. Kramer, ed. *Dream psychology and the new biology of dreaming.* Springfield, Ill.: C. C Thomas. Pp. 199–217.

Dostoevsky, F. 1956 (orig. 1866). *Crime and punishment.* New York: Random House.

Edelson, M. 1971. *The idea of a mental illness.* New Haven: Yale Univer. Press.

———. 1972. Language and dreams: *The interpretation of dreams* revisited. *The Psychoanalytic Study of the Child* 27:203–82.

———. 1975. *Language and interpretation in psychoanalysis.* New Haven: Yale Univer. Press.

Ellenberger, H. F. 1970. *The discovery of the unconscious.* New York: Basic Books.

Erdelyi, M. H. 1970. Recovery of unavailable perceptual input. *Cognitive Psychology* 1:99–113.

Erikson, E. H. 1954. The dream specimen of psychoanalysis. *Journal of the American Psychoanalytic Association* 2:5–56.

———. 1963. *Childhood and society*, 2d ed. New York: W. W. Norton.

Farrell, B. 1969. *Pat and Roald.* New York: Random House.

Fillmore, C. J. 1968. The case for case. In E. Bach and R. T. Harms, eds. *Universals in linguistic theory.* New York: Holt, Rinehart, & Winston. Pp. 1–88.

Fingarette, H. 1974 (orig. 1969). Self-deception and the "splitting of the ego." In R. Wollheim, ed. *Freud.* Garden City, N.Y.: Anchor. Pp. 80–96.

Fisher, C., Byrne, J., Edwards, A., and Kahn, E. 1970. A psychophysiological study of nightmares. *Journal of the American Psychoanalytic Association* 18:747–82.

Flavell, J. H. 1963. *The developmental psychology of Jean Piaget.* Princeton, N.J.: D. Van Nostrand.

Foulkes, D. 1962. Dream reports from different stages of sleep. *Journal of Abnormal and Social Psychology* 65:14–25.

———. 1964. Theories of dream formation and recent studies of sleep consciousness. *Psychological Bulletin* 62:236–47.

———. 1966. *The psychology of sleep.* New York: Charles Scribner's Sons.

———. 1967. Dreams of the male child: four case studies. *Journal of Child Psychology and Psychiatry* 8:81–97.

———. 1970. Personality and dreams. In E. Hartmann, ed. *Sleep and dreaming.* Boston: Little, Brown. Pp. 147–53.

———. 1971. Longitudinal studies of dreams in children. *Science and Psychoanalysis.* 19:48–71.

———. 1973. What do we know about dreams—and how did we learn it? Presented to Association for the Psychophysiological Study of Sleep (APSS), San Diego.

———. 1977. *Children's dreams: year 5 of a longitudinal sleep-laboratory study.* Atlanta: author (mimeo).

Foulkes, D., and Fleisher, S. 1975. Mental activity in relaxed wakefulness. *Journal of Abnormal Psychology* 84:66–75.

Foulkes, D., and Griffin, M. L. 1976. An experimental study of "creative dreaming." Presented to APSS, Cincinnati.

Foulkes, D., Larson, J. D., Swanson, E. M., and Rardin, M. 1969. Two studies of childhood dreaming. *American Journal of Orthopsychiatry* 39:627–43.

Foulkes, D., Pivik, T., Ahrens, J. B., and Swanson, E. M. 1968. Effects of "dream deprivation" on dream-content: an attempted cross-night replication. *Journal of Abnormal Psychology* 73:403–15.

Foulkes, D., Pivik, T., Steadman, H. S., Spear, P. S., and Symonds, J. D. 1967. Dreams of the male child: an EEG study. *Journal of Abnormal Psychology* 72:457–67.

Foulkes, D., and Pope, R. 1973. PVE and SCE in stage REM: a modest confirmation and an extension. *Perceptual and Motor Skills* 37:107–18.

Foulkes, D., and Shepherd, J. 1971. *Manual for a scoring system for children's dreams.* Laramie: author.

———. 1972a. *Children's dreams at ages 3–4 and 9–10: a sleep-laboratory study.* Laramie: author.

———. 1972b. *Children's laboratory dreams: four methodological studies.* Laramie: author.

Foulkes, D., Shepherd, J., and Scott, E. A. 1974. *Children's dreams: year 3 of a longitudinal sleep-laboratory study.* Laramie: author.

Foulkes, D., Spear, P. S., and Symonds, J. D. 1966. Individual differences in mental activity at sleep onset. *Journal of Abnormal Psychology* 71:280–86.

Foulkes, D., and Vogel, G. 1965. Mental activity at sleep onset. *Journal of Abnormal Psychology* 70:231–43.

———. 1974. The current status of laboratory dream research. *Psychiatric Annals* 4(7):7–27.

Frederiksen, C. H. 1975. Representing logical and semantic structure of knowledge acquired from discourse. *Cognitive Psychology* 7:371–458.

Freemon, F. R. 1972. *Sleep research: a critical review.* Springfield, Ill.: C. C Thomas.

Freud, S. 1962 (orig. 1899). Screen memories. In *The standard edition of the complete psychological works of Sigmund Freud* (hereafter: *S.E.*), Vol III. London: The Hogarth Press. Pp. 303–22.

———. 1955 (orig. 1900). *The interpretation of dreams.* New York: Basic Books.

———. 1955 (orig. 1909). Notes upon a case of obsessional neurosis. In *S.E.*, Vol X. Pp. 155–249.

———. 1957 (orig. 1910). The antithetical meaning of primal words. In *S.E.*, Vol XI. Pp. 155–61.

———. 1958 (orig. 1911a). The handling of dream-interpretation in psycho-analysis. In *S.E.*, Vol XII. Pp. 91–96.

———. 1958 (orig. 1911b). Psycho-analytic notes on an autobiographical account of a case of paranoia (dementia paranoides). In *S.E.*, Vol XII. Pp. 9–82.

———. 1957 (orig. 1915). The unconscious. In *S.E.*, Vol XIV. Pp. 166–204.

———. 1961–63 (orig. 1917*a*). Introductory lectures on psycho-analysis. In *S.E.*, Vol XV–XVI.

———. 1957 (orig. 1917*b*). A metapsychological supplement to the theory of dreams. In *S.E.*, Vol XIV. Pp. 222–35.

———. 1955 (orig. 1918). From the history of an infantile neurosis. In *S.E.*, Vol XVII. Pp. 7–122.

———. 1961 (orig. 1923*a*). The ego and the id. In *S.E.*, Vol XIX. Pp. 12–59.

———. 1961 (orig. 1923*b*). Remarks on the theory and practice of dream-interpretation. In *S.E.*, Vol XIX. Pp. 109–121.

———. 1961 (orig. 1925*a*). A note upon the "mystic writing-pad." In *S.E.*, Vol XIX. Pp. 227–32.

———. 1961 (orig. 1925*b*). Some additional notes on dream-interpretation as a whole. In *S.E.*, Vol XIX. Pp. 127–38.

———. 1961 (orig. 1931). Female sexuality. In *S.E.*, Vol XXI. Pp. 225–43.

———. 1954. *The origins of psycho-analysis. Letters to Wilhelm Fliess, drafts and notes: 1887–1902.* New York: Basic Books.

Fromm, E. 1957 (orig. 1951). *The forgotten language.* New York: Grove Press.

Galton, F. 1883. *Inquiries into human faculty and its development.* New York: Macmillan.

Gardiner, M., ed. 1971. *The wolf-man.* New York: Basic Books.

Gardner, H. 1974 (orig. 1972). *The quest for mind.* New York: Vintage.

Garfield, P. L. 1974. *Creative dreaming.* New York: Simon & Schuster.

Garrett, M. F., Bever, T. G., and Fodor, J. A. 1966. The active use of grammar in speech perception. *Perception and Psychophysics* 1:30–32.

Gass, W. The scientific psychology of Sigmund Freud. *New York Review of Books* May 1, 1975:24–29.

Goffman, E. 1959 (orig. 1956). *The presentation of self in everyday life.* Garden City, N.Y.: Anchor.

Goodenough, D. R., Shapiro, A., Holden, M., and Steinschriber, L. 1959. A comparison of "dreamers" and "nondreamers": eye movements, electroencephalograms, and the recall of dreams. *Journal of Abnormal and Social Psychology* 59:295–302.

Gottschalk, L. A., Winget, C. N., and Gleser, G. C. 1969. *Manual of instructions for using the Gottschalk-Gleser content analysis scales: anxiety, hostility, and social alienation-personal disorganization.* Berkeley: Univer. California Press.

Gray, R. 1962. Introduction. In R. Gray, ed. *Kafka: a collection of critical essays.* Englewood Cliffs, N.J.: Prentice-Hall. Pp. 1–11.

Green, C. E. 1968. *Lucid dreams.* London: Hamish Hamilton.

Greene, J. 1972. *Psycholinguistics: Chomsky and psychology.* Baltimore: Penguin.

Griffin, M. L. 1973. Storage systems in short-term memory. Senior thesis, Department of Psychology, Boston University.

Grinstein, A. 1968. *On Sigmund Freud's dreams.* Detroit: Wayne State Univer. Press.

Gutheil, E. A. 1960 (orig. 1951). *The handbook of dream analysis.* New York: Grove Press.

Haber, R. N., and Erdelyi, M. H. 1967. Emergence and recovery of initially unavailable perceptual material. *Journal of Verbal Learning and Verbal Behavior* 6:618–28.

Hadfield, J. A. 1954. *Dreams and nightmares.* Baltimore: Penguin.

Hall, C. S. 1953*a*. A cognitive theory of dreams. *Journal of General Psychology* 49:273–82.

———. 1953*b*. A cognitive theory of dream symbols. *Journal of General Psychology* 48:169–86.

———. 1959 (orig. 1953*c*). *The meaning of dreams.* New York: Dell.

———. n.d. Are all dreams wish-fulfillment? mimeo.

Hall, C. S., and Nordby, V. J. 1972. *The individual and his dreams.* New York: New American Library.

Hall, C. S., and Van de Castle, R. L. 1966. *The content analysis of dreams.* New York: Appleton-Century-Crofts.

Hallam, F. M., and Weed, S. C. 1896. A study of dream consciousness. *American Journal of Psychology* 7:405–11.

Halliday, M. A. K. 1967. Notes on transitivity and theme in English: II. *Journal of Linguistics* 3:199–244.

Harary, F., Norman, R. Z., and Cartwright, D. 1965. *Structural models: an introduction to the theory of directed graphs.* New York: John Wiley.

Hartmann, E. 1967. *The biology of dreaming.* Springfield, Ill.: C. C Thomas.

———. 1973. *The functions of sleep.* New Haven: Yale Univer. Press.

Hartmann, H. 1958 (orig. 1939). *Ego psychology and the problem of adaptation.* New York: International Universities Press.

Hauri, P., Sawyer, J., and Rechtschaffen, A. 1967. Dimensions of dreaming: a factored scale for rating dream reports. *Journal of Abnormal Psychology* 72:16–22.

Heller, E. 1974. *Franz Kafka.* New York: Viking Press.

Hilgard, E. R. 1970 (orig. 1962). The scientific status of psychoanalysis. In S. G. M. Lee and M. Herbert, eds. *Freud and psychology.* Baltimore: Penguin. Pp. 29–49.

———. 1966. Is revision to come from inside or outside psychoanalysis? *International Journal of Psychiatry* 2:549–50.

Holt, R. R. 1967. The development of the primary process: a structural view. *Psychological Issues* 5(2–3):345–83.

Horney, K. 1945. *Our inner conflicts.* New York: W. W. Norton.

Humphrey, M. E., and Zangwill, O. L. 1951. Cessation of dreaming after brain injury. *Journal of Neurology, Neurosurgery, and Psychiatry* 14:322–25.

Jacobson, A., Kales, A., Lehmann, D., and Hoedemaker, F. S. 1964. Muscle tonus in human subjects during sleep and dreaming. *Experimental Neurology* 10:418–24.

Jacobson, A., Kales, A., Lehmann, D., and Zweizig, J. R. 1965. Somnambulism: all-night electroencephalographic studies. *Science* 148:975–77.

Jakobson, R. 1973. Toward a linguistic classification of aphasic impairments. In H. Goodglass and S. Blumstein, eds. *Psycholinguistics and aphasia.* Baltimore: Johns Hopkins Press. Pp. 29–47.

Johnson, D. M. 1955. *The psychology of thought and judgment.* New York: Harper & Brothers.

Jones, R. M. 1970. *The new psychology of dreaming.* New York: Grune & Stratton.

Jung, C. G. 1974 (orig. 1948). General aspects of dream psychology. In C. G. Jung, *Dreams.* Princeton, N.J.: Princeton Univer. Press. Pp. 23–66.

Kahn, R. L., and Cannell, C. F. 1957. *The dynamics of interviewing.* New York: John Wiley.

Kales, A., ed. 1969. *Sleep: physiology and pathology.* Philadelphia: Lippincott.

Kardiner, A., Karush, A., and Ovesey, L. 1966 (orig. 1959). A methodological study of Freudian theory. *International Journal of Psychiatry* 2:489–544.

Kent, G. H., and Rosanoff, A. J. 1910. A study of association in insanity. *American Journal of Insanity* 67:37–96, 317–90.

Kimball, J. P. 1973. *The formal theory of grammar.* Englewood Cliffs, N.J.: Prentice-Hall.

Klatzky, R. L. 1975. *Human memory: structures and processes.* San Francisco: W. H. Freeman.

Lacan, J. 1966 (orig. 1957). The insistence of the letter in the unconscious. *Yale French Studies* 36–37:112–47.

———. 1968 (orig. 1966). The function of language in psychoanalysis. In J. Lacan, *The language of the self: the function of language in psychoanalysis.* Baltimore: Johns Hopkins Press. Pp. 1–87.

Laffal, J. 1973. *A concept dictionary of English.* Essex, Conn.: Gallery Press.

Lashley, K. S. 1929. *Brain mechanisms and intelligence.* Chicago: Univer. Chicago Press.

———. 1930. Basic neural mechanisms in behavior. *Psychological Review* 37:1–24.

———. 1951. The problem of serial order in behavior. In L. A. Jeffress, ed. *Cerebral mechanisms in behavior.* New York: John Wiley. Pp. 112–36.

Laurendeau, M., and Pinard, A. 1970. *The development of the concept of space in the child.* New York: International Universities Press.

Leach, E. 1970. *Claude Lévi-Strauss.* New York: Viking Press.

Leeper, R. W., and Madison, P. 1959. *Toward understanding human personalities.* New York: Appleton-Century-Crofts.

Leiber, J. 1975. *Noam Chomsky: a philosophic overview.* New York: St. Martin's Press.

Leontiev, A. A. 1975. The heuristic principle in the perception, emergence, and assimilation of speech. In E. H. Lenneberg and E. Lenneberg, eds. *Foundations of language development: a multidisciplinary approach,* Vol I. Paris: UNESCO Press. Pp. 43–58.

Lévi-Strauss, C. 1973 (orig. 1955). *Tristes tropiques.* London: Jonathan Cape.

————. 1963 (orig. 1958). *Structural anthropology*. New York: Basic Books.

Levy, L. H. 1963. *Psychological interpretation*. New York: Holt, Rinehart, & Winston.

Lilly, J. C. 1973 (orig. 1972*a*). *The center of the cyclone*. New York: Bantam.

————. 1974 (orig. 1972*b*). *Programming and metaprogramming in the human biocomputer*. New York: Bantam.

Locke, S. 1976. Motor programming and language behavior. Presented to Psychology and Biology of Language and Thought: A Symposium in Memory of Eric H. Lenneberg, Ithaca, N.Y.

Loevinger, J. 1966. Three principles for a psychoanalytic psychology. *Journal of Abnormal Psychology* 71:432–43.

————. 1969. A review of *The logic of explanation in psychoanalysis*, by M. Sherwood. *Science* 166:1389–90.

Loevinger, J., and Wessler, R. 1970. *Measuring ego development*, Vol I. San Francisco: Jossey-Bass.

Loevinger, J., Wessler, R., and Redmore, C. 1970. *Measuring ego development*, Vol II. San Francisco: Jossey-Bass.

Luk, C. 1970 (orig. 1960*a*). *Ch'an and Zen teaching, first series*. Berkeley: Shambala.

————. 1971 (orig. 1960*b*). *Ch'an and Zen teaching, second series*. Berkeley: Shambala.

————. 1973 (orig. 1962). *Ch'an and Zen teaching, third series*. Berkeley: Shambala.

Luria, A. R. 1972. *The man with a shattered world: the history of a brain wound*. New York: Basic Books.

————. 1973. *The working brain: an introduction to neuropsychology*. New York: Basic Books.

————. 1974–75. Scientific perspectives and philosophical dead ends in modern linguistics. *Cognition* 3/4:377–85.

Lyons, J. 1970. *Noam Chomsky*. New York: Viking Press.

McCarley, R. 1976. Mind-body isomorphism and dream theory. Presented to APSS, Cincinnati.

MacCorquodale, K. 1970. On Chomsky's review of Skinner's *Verbal behavior*. *Journal of the Experimental Analysis of Behavior* 13:83–99.

MacCorquodale, K., and Meehl, P. E. 1948. On a distinction between hypothetical constructs and intervening variables. *Psychological Review* 55:95–107.

McGuigan, F. J., and Schoonover, R. A., eds. 1973. *The psychophysiology of thinking*. New York: Academic Press.

McGuire, W., ed. 1974. *The Freud/Jung letters*. Princeton, N.J.: Princeton Univer. Press.

McNeill, D. 1970. The development of language. In P. H. Mussen, ed. *Carmichael's manual of child psychology*, 3rd ed. Vol I. New York: John Wiley. Pp. 1061–161.

Marmor, G. S. 1975. Development of kinetic images: when does the child first represent movement in mental images? *Cognitive Psychology* 7:548–59.

Marshall, J. C. 1974. Freud's psychology of language. In R. Wollheim, ed. *Freud*. Garden City, N.Y.: Anchor. Pp. 349–65.

Mead, M. 1949. *Male and female: a study of the sexes in a changing world*. New York: William Morrow.

Miel, J. 1966. Jacques Lacan and the structure of the unconscious. *Yale French Studies* 36–37:104–11.

Miller, G. A. 1976. Pastness. Presented to Psychology and Biology of Language and Thought: A Symposium in Memory of Eric H. Lenneberg, Ithaca, N.Y.

Miller, G. A., Galanter, E., and Pribram, K. H. 1960. *Plans and the structure of behavior*. New York: Henry Holt.

Molinari, S., and Foulkes, D. 1969. Tonic and phasic events during sleep: psychological correlates and implications. *Perceptual and Motor Skills* 29:343–68.

Monroe, L. J., Rechtschaffen, A., Foulkes, D., and Jensen, J. 1965. The discriminability of REM and NREM reports. *Journal of Personality and Social Psychology* 2:456–60.

Morris, D. 1969 (orig. 1967). *The naked ape*. New York: Dell.

Moss, C. S. 1972. *Recovery with aphasia: the aftermath of my stroke*. Urbana: Univer. Illinois Press.

Murray, E. J. 1965. *Sleep, dreams, and arousal*. New York: Appleton-Century-Crofts.

Neisser, U. 1964. Cognitive and dynamic theories in psychology. Presented to the Academy of Psychoanalysis, Montreal.

——. 1967. *Cognitive psychology*. New York: Appleton-Century-Crofts.

——. 1968. The processes of vision. *Scientific American* 219: No. 3, 204–14.

——. 1975. Images as perceptual anticipations. Presented to American Association for the Advancement of Science, New York.

Norman, D. A. 1976. *Memory and attention*, 2nd ed. New York: John Wiley.

Northway, M. L. 1952. *A primer of sociometry*. Toronto: Univer. Toronto Press.

Ornstein, R. E. 1972. *The psychology of consciousness*. San Francisco: W. H. Freeman.

Osgood, C. E. 1952. The nature and measurement of meaning. *Psychological Bulletin* 49:197–237.

Osgood, C. E., May, W. H., and Miron, M. S. 1975. *Cross-cultural universals of affective meaning*. Urbana: Univer. Illinois Press.

Osgood, C. E., Suci, G. J., and Tannenbaum, P. H. 1957. *The measurement of meaning*. Urbana: Univer. Illinois Press.

Palmer, F. 1971. *Grammar*. Baltimore: Penguin.

Pavlov, I. P. 1941 (orig. 1932*a*). Reply of a physiologist to psychologists. In I. P. Pavlov, *Lectures on conditioned reflexes*. New York: International Publishers. Pp. 117–45.

————. 1941 (orig. 1932*b*). An attempt to understand the symptoms of hysteria physiologically. In I. P. Pavlov, *Lectures on conditioned reflexes.* New York: International Publishers. Pp. 102–16.

Penfield, W. 1958. *The excitable cortex in conscious man.* Springfield, Ill.: C. C Thomas.

Perls, F. 1971 (orig. 1969). *Gestalt therapy verbatim.* New York: Bantam.

Pessah, M. A., and Roffwarg, H. P. 1972. Spontaneous middle ear muscle activity in man: a rapid eye movement sleep phenomenon. *Science* 178:773–76.

Phillips, J. L. 1975. *The origins of intellect: Piaget's theory,* 2d ed. San Francisco: W. H. Freeman.

Piaget, J. 1960 (orig. 1947). *The psychology of intelligence.* Paterson, N.J.: Littlefield, Adams.

————. 1962 (orig. 1951). *Play, dreams and imitation in childhood.* New York: W. W. Norton.

————. 1969 (orig. 1963). Language and intellectual operations. In H. G. Furth, ed. *Piaget and knowledge: theoretical foundations.* Englewood Cliffs, N.J.: Prentice-Hall. Pp. 121–30.

Piaget, J., and Inhelder, B. 1971 (orig. 1966). *Mental imagery in the child.* New York: Basic Books.

Pivik, R. T. 1970. Mental activity and phasic events during sleep. Unpublished Ph.D. dissertation, Stanford Univer.

Pivik, R. T., and Foulkes, D. 1968. NREM mentation: relation to personality, orientation time, and time of night. *Journal of Consulting and Clinical Psychology* 32:144–51.

Polombo, S. R. 1973. The associative memory tree. *Psychoanalysis and Contemporary Science* 2:205–19.

Posner, M. I. 1973. *Cognition: an introduction.* Glenview, Ill.: Scott, Foresman.

Pylyshyn, Z. W. 1973. What the mind's eye tells the mind's brain: a critique of mental imagery. *Psychological Bulletin* 80:1–24.

Ramsey, G. V. 1953. Studies of dreaming. *Psychological Bulletin* 50: 432–55.

Random House Dictionary of the English Language, College Edition. 1969. New York: Random House.

Rapaport, D., ed. 1951. *Organization and pathology of thought.* New York: Columbia Univer. Press.

————. 1960. The structure of psychoanalytic theory: a systematizing attempt. *Psychological Issues* 2, No. 2.

Rechtschaffen, A. 1967. Dream reports and dream experiences. *Experimental Neurology* Suppl. 4:4–15.

————. 1973. The psychophysiology of mental activity during sleep. In F. J. McGuigan and R. A. Schoonover, eds. *The psychophysiology of thinking.* New York: Academic Press. Pp. 153–205.

————. 1975. Scientific method in the study of altered states of consciousness with illustrations from sleep and dream research. In *Altered states of consciousness: current views and research problems.* Washington, D.C.: Drug Abuse Council. Pp. 135–91.

Rechtschaffen, A., and Foulkes, D. 1965. Effect of visual stimuli on dream content. *Perceptual and Motor Skills* 20:1149–60.

Rechtschaffen, A., and Kales, A., eds. 1968. *A manual of standardized terminology, techniques and scoring system for sleep stages of human subjects.* Washington, D.C.: Public Health Service.

Rechtschaffen, A., Verdone, P., and Wheaton, J. 1963. Reports of mental activity during sleep. *Canadian Psychiatric Association Journal* 8: 409--14.

Rechtschaffen, A., Vogel, G., and Shaikun, G. 1963. Interrelatedness of mental activity during sleep. *Archives of General Psychiatry* 9:536–47.

Reid, L. S. 1974. Toward a grammar of the image. *Psychological Bulletin* 81:319–34.

Reps, P. n.d. (orig. 1934). *Zen flesh, Zen bones.* Garden City, N.Y.: Anchor.

Riesman, D. 1955 (orig. 1954). The themes of work and play in the structure of Freud's thought. In D. Riesman, *Individualism reconsidered.* Garden City, N.Y.: Anchor. Pp. 174–205.

Rossi, E. L. 1972. *Dreams and the growth of personality.* New York: Pergamon.

Salmon, W. C. 1974 (orig. 1959). Psychoanalytic theory and evidence. In R. Wollheim, ed. *Freud.* Garden City, N.Y.: Anchor. Pp. 271–84.

Sanders, G. A. 1974. Introduction. In D. Cohen, ed. *Explaining linguistic phenomena.* Washington, D.C.: Hemisphere. Pp. 1–20.

Sartre, J.-P. 1974 (orig. 1956). *Mauvaise foi* and the unconscious. In R. Wollheim, ed. *Freud.* Garden City, N.Y.: Anchor. Pp. 70–79.

Schafer, R. 1968. *Aspects of internalization.* New York: International Universities Press.

——. 1973. Action: its place in psychoanalytic interpretation and theory. *Annual of Psychoanalysis* 1:159–96.

——. 1975. Psychoanalysis without psychodynamics. *International Journal of Psychoanalysis* 56:41–55.

——. 1976. *A new language for psychoanalysis.* New Haven: Yale Univer. Press.

Schur, M. 1966. Some additional "day residues" of "the specimen dream of psychoanalysis." In R. M. Loewenstein, L. M. Newman, M. Schur, and A. J. Solnit, eds. *Psychoanalysis–a general psychology.* New York: International Universities Press. Pp. 45–85.

Schwartz, B. A., and Lefebvre, A. 1973. Contacts veille/P.M.O. II. les P.M.O. morcelées. *Revue d'Electroencephalographie et de Neurophysiologie Clinique* 3:165–76.

Sherwood, M. 1969. *The logic of explanation in psychoanalysis.* New York: Academic Press.

Skinner, B. F. 1957. *Verbal behavior.* New York: Appleton-Century-Crofts.

Slobin, D. I. 1971. *Psycholinguistics.* Glenview, Ill.: Scott, Foresman.

Snyder, F. 1970. The phenomenology of dreaming. In L. Madow and L. H. Snow, eds. *The psychodynamic implications of the physiological studies on dreams.* Springfield, Ill.: C. C Thomas. Pp. 124–51.

Sokolov, A. N. 1975 (orig. 1972). *Inner speech and thought.* New York: Plenum.

Sperling, G. 1960. The information available in brief visual presentations. *Psychological Monographs* 74, No. 11.

Sperry, R. W. 1968. Hemisphere deconnection and unity in conscious awareness. *American Psychologist* 23:723–33.

Stern, A. 1973 (orig. 1922). Some personal psychoanalytical experiences with Professor Freud. In H. M. Ruitenbeek, ed. *Freud as we knew him.* Detroit: Wayne State Univer. Press. Pp. 50–57.

Suppes, P., and Warren, H. 1975. On the generation and classification of defence mechanisms. *International Journal of Psychoanalysis* 56:405–14.

Szasz, T. S. n.d. (orig. 1961). *The myth of mental illness.* New York: Delta.

Tart, C. T. 1975. *States of consciousness.* New York: E. P. Dutton.

Tart, C. T., ed. 1969. *Altered states of consciousness.* New York: John Wiley.

Tesler, L., Enea, H., and Colby, K. M. 1968. A directed graph representation for computer simulation of belief systems. *Mathematical Biosciences* 2:19–40.

Thass-Thienemann, T. 1973a. *The interpretation of language, volume I: understanding the symbolic meaning of language.* New York: Jason Aronson.

———. 1973b. *The interpretation of language, volume II: understanding the unconscious meaning of language.* New York: Jason Aronson.

Tolman, E. C. 1938. The determiners of behavior at a choice-point. *Psychological Review* 45:1–41.

Trosman, H., Rechtschaffen, A., Offenkrantz, W., and Wolpert, E. 1960. Studies in psychophysiology of dreams. IV. Relations among dreams in sequence. *Archives of General Psychiatry* 3:602–7.

Trupin, E. W. 1976. Correlates of ego-level and agency-communion in stage REM dreams of 11–13 year old children. *Journal of Child Psychology and Psychiatry* 17:169–80.

Tulving, E. 1972. Episodic and semantic memory. In E. Tulving and W. Donaldson, eds. *Organization of memory.* New York: Academic Press. Pp. 381–403.

Vinacke, W. E. 1952. *The psychology of thinking.* New York: McGraw-Hill.

Vogel, G. W. 1973. Discussion of paper by David Foulkes. Presented to APSS, San Diego.

———. 1975. A review of REM sleep deprivation. *Archives of General Psychiatry* 32:749–61.

Vogel, G. W., Barrowclough, B., and Giesler, D. D. 1972. Limited discriminability of REM and sleep onset reports and its psychiatric implications. *Archives of General Psychiatry* 26:449–55.

Vogel, G. W., Foulkes, D., and Trosman, H. 1966. Ego functions and dreaming during sleep onset. *Archives of General Psychiatry* 14:238–48.

Vogel, G. W., Thurmond, A., Gibbons, P., Sloan, K., Boyd, M., and Walker, M. 1975. REM sleep reduction effects on depression syndromes. *Archives of General Psychiatry* 32:765–77.

Vygotsky, L. S. 1962 (orig. 1934). *Thought and language.* Cambridge, Mass.: M.I.T. Press.

Watson, J. B. 1959 (orig. 1930). *Behaviorism*, rev. ed. Chicago: Univer. Chicago Press.

Watson, R. 1972. Mental correlates of periorbital PIPs during REM sleep. Presented to APSS, Lake Minnewaska, N.Y.

Weisz, R., and Foulkes, D. 1970. Home and laboratory dreams collected under uniform sampling conditions. *Psychophysiology* 6:588–96.

Wilden, A. 1968. Lacan and the discourse of the other. In J. Lacan, *The language of the self: the function of language in psychoanalysis.* Baltimore: Johns Hopkins Press. Pp. 157–311.

Williams, M. 1970. *Brain damage and the mind.* Baltimore: Penguin.

Wittgenstein, L. 1974 (orig. 1966). Conversations on Freud. In R. Wollheim, ed. *Freud.* Garden City, N.Y.: Anchor. Pp. 1–10.

Wolff, P. H. 1960. The developmental psychologies of Jean Piaget and psychoanalysis. *Psychological Issues* 2, No. 1.

———. 1967. Cognitive considerations for a psychoanalytic theory of language acquisition. *Psychological Issues* 5, No. 2–3:300–43.

Wolpert, E. A., and Trosman, H. 1958. Studies in psychophysiology of dreams. I. Experimental evocation of sequential dream episodes. *Archives of Neurology and Psychiatry* 79:603–6.

Wood, M. Rules of the game. *New York Review of Books,* March 4, 1976, 31–34.

Name Index

Subject Index